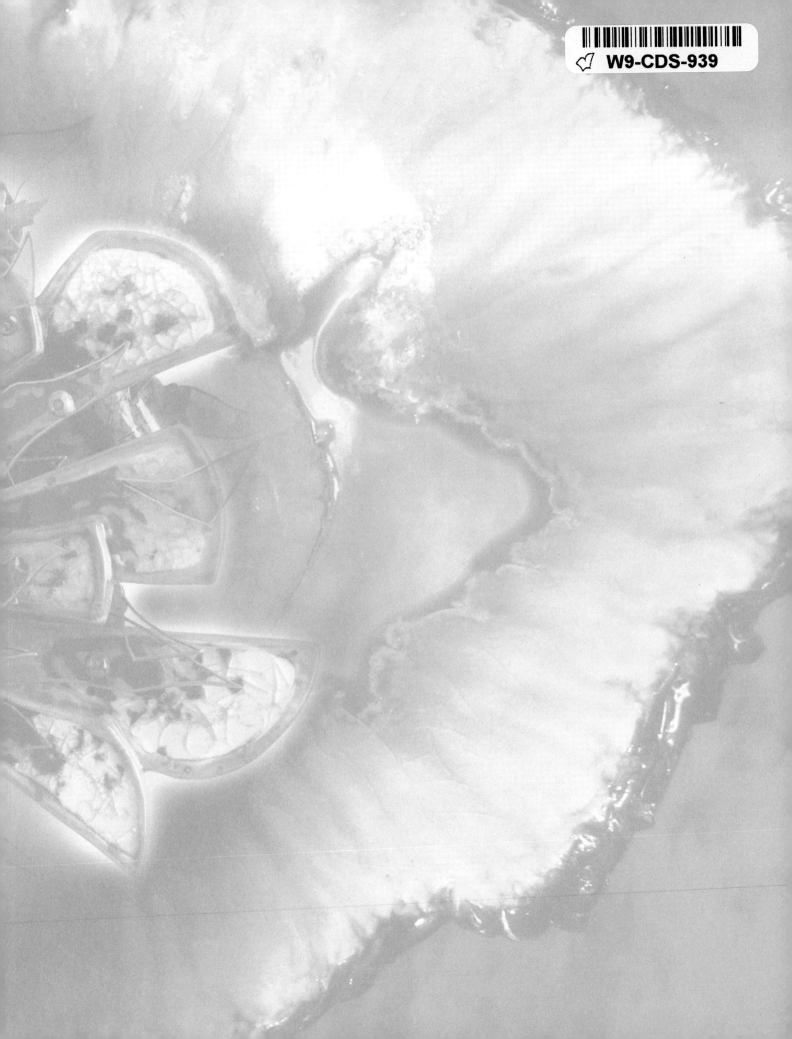

COLLECTOR'S ENCYCLOPEDIA OF

DEPRESSION GLASS

PHOTO LEGENDS INCLUDED

EIGHTEENTH EDITION

America's #1 Bestselling Glass Book!

GENE & CATHY FLORENCE

COLLECTOR BOOKS
A Division of Schroeder Publishing Co., Inc.

PRICING

All prices in this book are retail prices for mint condition glassware. This book is intended to be only a guide to prices as there are a few regional price differences that cannot reasonably be dealt with herein. You may expect dealers to pay from 50% to 60% less than the prices quoted. Glass that is in less than mint condition, i.e., chipped, cracked, scratched, repaired, or poorly moulded, will bring only a small percentage of the price of glass that is in mint condition — if wanted at all.

Prices have become reasonably well established due to national advertising by dealers, the Depression glass shows held from coast to coast, and the Internet. I have my own web page operated for books and glass (www.geneflorence.com). However, there are still some regional differences in prices due partly to glass being more available in some areas than in others. Companies distributed certain pieces in some areas that they did not in others. Generally speaking, prices are about the same among dealers from coast to coast.

Prices tend to increase on rare items; and they have increased as a whole due to more people becoming aware of the worth of Depression glass.

One of the important aspects of this book is the attempt to illustrate as well as realistically price those items that are in demand. All items listed are priced. The desire is to give you the best factual guide to collectible patterns of Depression glass available.

MEASUREMENTS

To illustrate why there are discrepancies in measurements, I offer the following sample from just two years of Hocking's catalog references:

Year	Item	Ounces	Item	Ounces	Item	Ounces
1935	Pitcher	37, 58, 80	Flat Tumbler	5, 9, 13½	Footed Tumbler	10, 13
1935	Pitcher	37, 60, 80	Flat Tumbler	5, 9, 10, 15	Footed Tumbler	10, 13
1936	Pitcher	37, 65, 90	Flat Tumbler	5, 9, 13½	Footed Tumbler	10, 15
1936	Pitcher	37, 60, 90	Flat Tumbler	5, 9, 13½	Footed Tumbler	10, 15

All measurements in this book are exact as to some manufacturer's listing or to actual measurement. You may expect variance of up to ½" or 1 – 5 ounces. This may be due to mould variations or reworking worn moulds or changes by the manufacturer as well as rounding off measurements for catalog listings.

On the front cover — Top left: Glades candle, top middle: Old English cheese compote, bottom left: No. 610 pitcher, bottom right: Cherry Blossom slag two-handled bowl, middle: Decorated Fruit Petalware tumbler, middle right: Reeded, Whirlspool jar.

On the back cover: Diana cream soup, White Band assorted pieces.

The two pieces of pottery shown on the endsheets were made by Beth Summers
using glass made from melted Depression glass from Gene Florence.

Cover design by Beth Summers
Book design by Allan Ramsey
Cover photography by Charles R. Lynch

Collector Books
P.O. Box 3009
Paducah, KY 42002-3009
www.collectorbooks.com

Gene and Cathy Florence

P.O. Box 22186
Lexington, KY 40522

or

P.O. Box 64
Astatula, FL 34705

Copyright © 2008 by Gene and Cathy Florence

Searching for a Publisher?

We are always looking for people knowledgeable within their fields. If you feel that there is a real need for a book on your collectible subject and have a large comprehensive collection, contact us.

The current values in this book should be used only as a guide. They are not intended to set prices, which vary from one section of the country to another. Auction prices as well as dealer prices vary greatly and are affected by condition as well as demand. Neither the authors nor the publisher assumes responsibility for any losses that might be incurred as a result of consulting this guide.

Proudly printed and bound in the
United States of America

CONTENTS

Acknowledgments 4
Preface 5
Adam 6
"Adams Rib" 8
"Addie" 9
Amelia 10
American Pioneer 11
American Sweetheart 13
Ardith 16
"Artura" 17
Aunt Polly 18
Aurora 20
"Avocado" 21
Beaded Block 22
"Berlin" 24
Block Optic 25
"Bowknot" 28
Cameo 29
Cherryberry 33
Cherry Blossom 34
Chinex Classic 37
Circle 39
Cloverleaf 40
Colonial 42
Colonial Fluted 44
Columbia 45
Coronation 46
Crackle 48
Cremax 49
"Crow's Foot" 50
Cube 52
"Cupid" 54
Daisy and Button w/Narcissus 56
Della Robbia 57
Diamond Quilted 59
Diana 61
Dogwood 63
Doric 65
Doric and Pansy 67
"Ellipse" 69
English Hobnail 70
Fancy Colonial 73
Fire-King Dinnerware "Philbe" 74
Floral 76
Floral and Diamond Band 79
Florentine No. 1 80
Florentine No. 2 82
Flower Garden with Butterflies 84
"Flute & Cane" 86
Fortune 87
Frances 88
Fruits 89
Gem 90
Georgian 91
Glades 93
Gothic Garden 94
Grape 95
Hex Optic 96

Hobnail 97
Homespun 98
Indiana Custard 99
Indiana Silver 100
Iris 101
Jubilee 103
Laced Edge 105
Lake Como 107
Largo 108
Laurel 109
Lincoln Inn 111
Line #555 113
"Little Jewel" 114
"Lois" 115
Lorain 116
Lotus 118
Lucy 121
Madrid 122
Manhattan 124
Maya 126
Mayfair, Federal 127
Mayfair 128
Miss America 131
Modernistic 133
Moderntone 134
Monticello 136
Moondrops 137
Mt. Pleasant 139
Mt. Vernon 140
New Century 141
Newport (Hazel-Atlas) 143
Newport (New Martinsville) 145
"Nora Bird," See
    "Peacock & Wild Rose"
Normandie 146
No. 610, "Pyramid" 147
No. 612, "Horseshoe" 149
No. 616, "Vernon" 150
No. 618, "Pineapple & Floral" 151
Old Cafe 152
Old Colony "Lace Edge" 153
Old English 156
Olive 158
"Orchid" 159
Ovide 161
Oyster and Pearl 162
"Parrot," Sylvan 164
"Party Line" 166
Patrician 167
"Patrick" 168
"Peacock Reverse" 169
"Peacock & Wild Rose,"
    "Nora Bird" 170
"Pebbled Rim" 172
"Penny Line" 173
Petalware 174
Pillar Optic 177
Primo 179

Princess 180
Queen Mary 182
Radiance 183
Raindrops 185
Reeded 186
"Ribbon" 188
Ring 189
Rock Crystal 190
"Romanesque" 194
Rose Cameo 195
Rose Point Band 196
Rosemary 197
Roulette 198
"Round Robin" 199
Roxana 200
Royal Lace 201
Royal Ruby 203
"S" Pattern, "Stippled Rose Band" . 204
Sandwich 205
Sharon 206
"Ships" 208
Sierra 210
Spiral 211
Springtime 212
Square 213
Starlight 214
Strawberry 215
"Sunburst" 216
Sunflower 217
Sunshine 218
Swanky Swigs 219
Swirl 221
Tea Room 223
Thistle 226
"Top Notch" 227
Tulip 228
Twisted Optic 230
"U.S. Scroll" 231
"U.S. Swirl" 232
"Victory" 233
Vitrock 235
Waterford 236
Whiteband 238
Windsor 239
"Woolworth" 241
Reproduction "Adam" 242
Reproduction "Avocado" 242
Reproduction "Cameo" 242
Reproduction "Cherry Blossom" ... 244
Reproduction "Floral" 246
Reproduction "Florentine No. 1" ... 246
Reproduction "Florentine No. 2" ... 246
Reproduction "Iris" 247
Reproduction "Madrid" 248
Reproduction "Mayfair" 249
Reproduction "Miss America" 251
Reproduction "Royal Lace" 252
Reproduction "Sharon" 252

ACKNOWLEDGMENTS

We want to thank everyone for their knowledge shared with us over the years. That includes dealers, collectors, and readers who have imparted information to us through writing, e-mailing, calling, and talking to us at shows throughout the country. Thanks for making known those newly found pieces for documentation and sending pictures of your discoveries. E-mail has made pictures more convenient for us to keep records of what you are finding. Thanks for letting us know of Internet auctions with unusual or unlisted items. Thank you for the promotional 1930s coupons that you've shown or sent us copies which advertise products from seeds to farm equipment with Depression glass as "inducements." Thank you also for your particular and superior knowledge regarding glassware you collect and what you are finding and can't find in the areas where you live. Long-time collectors of a specific pattern typically know more than we do about that one pattern. All this has certainly been beneficial to us and, we trust, to collectors as a whole. All our shared efforts have immeasurably added to the ever-increasing information relevant to Depression glass.

We have appreciated the shows that Depression glass clubs and show promoters have invited us to participate in over the years. Shows have added an invaluable amount of data about glass. However, we have eliminated many we've been honored to be a part of in the past as some serious health problems for both of us are requiring restrictions. Without Cathy, these 107 books on collectibles would not have been realized. She has worked diligently finding glass to picture as well as being our chief editor, critic, proofreader, and most recently, research assistant. She is the entire staff of unpacking, packing, sorting, and labeling the glass. It all became too much stress for her, and a stroke was one of the results. Few people comprehend our unbelievably hectic agendas and the many "hats" worn. Writing more books and traveling less, doesn't seem to be the answer either; so we are pulling back from life as we've known it for years. It's hard to do, but changes are ever present and sometimes necessary. Even the book industry itself is evolving. After 36 years, we have a rather smooth system at Collector Books geared for future endeavors; however, it is becoming too stressful to handle all the projects at the level we demand of ourselves. Being your own boss does have drawbacks if you are both type A personalities and insist on perfection. Aging eyes are making 16 hour days staring at a computer monitor a trial and both our doctors are saying it's time to slow our speeding lives to a more manageable pace — whatever that means.

Individual thanks regarding this book need to go to Dick and Pat Spencer and Dan and Geri Tucker. The cover and endsheets were designed by Beth Summers whose creative items on the inside covers were made from pieces of our glass broken in Gene's wreck in 2002. Talk about recycling glass in a wonderful way! Furthermore, there have also been bits and pieces of insight herein coming from readers outside the United States. Those encompass Australia, Canada, New Zealand, the Philippines, and England. We always enjoy hearing about "discoveries" from other countries.

There's a massive amount of work that must be undertaken by many workers before these books come to you with their plethora of current data. Photographs were pleasingly completed by Charles R. Lynch of Kentucky, and Dan Tucker of Ohio. Charley has become the resident digital expert which is saving hours of photography time in our sessions. Finally, no more waiting for film to be loaded or for Polaroids to develop before we take the final shot. In a 10-day session, it was amazing how much time was used for just those two functions for hundreds of setups. We now drop glass off as we find it and don't have to wait months to plan a photo session.

Glass arranging, unpacking, sorting, carting, and repacking was completed by Dick and Pat Spencer and Cathy Florence. Members of the Collector Books' shipping team simplified loading and unloading vans. Thanks for the expertise of the editorial department at Collector Books, and especially Amy Sullivan who helped us with mock-ups, photo finding, and arranging of this book. The layout was carried out by Allan Ramsey.

If you write us, please enclose a SASE (self-addressed, stamped envelope) that is large enough to return your photos if you wish them back. Writing books from January through May, finding and cataloging glass the rest of the year, attending shows and visiting markets, malls, and shops leaves inadequate time for answering the stacks of letters that arrive in our box. E-mails that can be answered even while traveling, still speedily are. If those questions have to be researched, they are usually filed to be answered when time permits — which seems never at times. We wish to thank the thoughtful people who send postcards with the possible answers to their questions for us to check off the correct response. Those are fast.

We want to make clear that our capabilities, such as they are, lie in knowledge of the patterns presented in our books. We will gladly help you any way we can with those. We honestly do not know the names, manufacturers, line numbers, and worth of every single piece of Depression glassware made nor do we have the time to research them for you. We now have four *Florence's Glassware Pattern Identification Guides* on the market that contain almost 2,000 patterns identified for you by names, dates, colors, companies, and how many pieces were made if known. They should save you searching in over 300 books on your own. No, we don't provide lists or prices for those patterns. We're trying to document those "wonder who made this" type pieces you see at markets but never in major books. Please know these words are not so much sour grapes as self-preservation. We're receiving a wave of questions about bottles, violins, porcelain, pottery, metallic objects, furniture, and clocks that we have as much knowledge of as you do.

Please don't send an envelope full of pictures asking us to identify each piece with a price and information as to where you can sell it. We don't mind a question or two, but 30 or 40 is just out of the realm of possibility. We would hate to come to the place where we would discourage your writing us at all!

As we go to press with this eighteenth edition, thank you once again, our readers, for keeping this America's #1 bestselling book on glass. We advise you to inform your friends about Depression glass. Point them to, or gift them, a book. There are only a few of us, relatively speaking, who appreciate this glass's inherent, as well as pecuniary, value. We receive letters regularly from people who have just learned about Depression glass — or who just discovered they basically gave away some family treasure at a sale. Delight yourself! Attend a Depression glass show. Collecting is sometimes frustrating, but mostly fun!

Information for this book comes from almost 40 years of research, buying and selling experiences, via consultation with fellow dealers and collectors throughout the country, and over 1,750,000 miles of traveling the country, hunting and locating glassware. We must admit that some of the most interesting (and surprising) information has come straight from readers, sharing catalogs, magazines, photographs of glass, and the glass, itself. Information for this book continues to increase and is very possibly inexhaustible.

As we continually learn about this beautiful, old Depression era glassware, we try to educate readers with the information we've assembled and in such a way that readers who have been made aware of it before, are not completely bored. It is a gargantuan task. For those who don't know, these books have been rewritten every two years to include all the latest facts, finds, prices, and changes noticed in the market; there are always some, and in this book more than normal.

Depression glass as defined by this book is the colored glassware made primarily during the Depression era (1928 – 1940) in colors of amber, blue, black, crystal, green, pink, red, yellow, and white. There are other colors and some crystal glass made before, as well as after, this time period; but essentially, the glass within this book was manufactured from the late 1920s through 1940. Further, this publication is predominantly related to the inexpensively made dinnerware turned out by machine in bulk and sold through smaller stores or given away as promotional or premium items for other products. Depression glass was often packaged in cereal boxes and flour sacks or given as incentive gifts for buying tickets at the local movie theaters or products from gasoline stations and grocery stores. Merchandise was offered with magazine subscriptions, for buying (or selling) certain amounts of seeds, or in return for amounts of coupons garnered with butter or soap purchases.

We have run out of space for adding more patterns. If we have to add more pages, this book is going to increase in price, something we have tried diligently not to do through these many years of full-color production. (Have you noticed that nearly all new books rolling off the presses have only a few pages of color clustered in the center of the book, and then miles of black and white photos and/or history filling page after page, and are always more costly than this one?)

Collectors have also sought later made patterns encompassing the time from 1940 to the 1960s, which has led to a companion book, entitled *Collectible Glassware from the 40s, 50s, 60s...*, now in its ninth edition. If your pattern is no longer found within this Depression book, you should seek it there.

Significant changes in collecting Depression glass have transpired since our first book was published in 1972. Prices overall have increased; seemingly, plentiful patterns have been gathered into countless collections throughout the world and removed from the marketplace. Collectors, now, rather than accumulating complete sets of dishes are blending a rainbow set (many colors) of one, or more, patterns. Glass is being marketed daily on the Internet, which has had a greater influence on the collectibles market than anyone could imagine. In Depression glass collecting the impact of the Internet has exposed great quantities of some patterns as well as colors previously unknown. This has been both a blessing and a curse to our market. A blessing because so many more people have been made aware of our glass and collectors have been able to fill their sets with previously missing items. A curse because so much has been unearthed that our market cannot absorb it as quickly as it is appearing. That oversupply has stifled some prices; and many basic items in major patterns are selling lower than they have in years. Now would be the time to buy; but unless more new collectors start to do that, we may not have seen the end of price adjustments.

In this book, we are addressing this decreased pricing that is becoming more and more apparent. Remember, we don't make up these prices; rather we record or acknowledge what is happening in the market. We seriously study prices and over the years of our writing, we have noticed some trends evolving regarding book prices. If a collector writes a book about items he collects, the items shown are usually magnificent, but prices tend to be inflated to make their own collection more valuable. If a dealer writes a book on items that they specialize in, there is a tendency to over evaluate common items and under value rare ones. Also, "authors" who price their books by Internet auction results cover only a small percentage of items and create large discrepancies in others, neither being a good indicator of what is really happening in the marketplace. The reason for that may be that in any auction, items that at least two people want may go for a higher price than even a rare or hard to find item does when only one bidder sees it. In other words, we don't feel auction pricing is a solid indicator of overall markets. That being said, if items are being listed for half or less than book prices and not receiving bids, then book prices are overstating today's worth. We attend shows around the country and are in and out of malls and shops wherever we find them. We're always studying prices and we have tried to value items for what they are actually selling and not with "hoped-for" prices. We often "spot" items in malls we visit three or four times a year. If the item is gone at the second viewing, the price was at a sellable range. If its there at fourth or fifth viewing, its overpriced. If the price sticker is so faded, it can't be read or the glass is so dusty, you make prints when you pick it up, those are important indications, also. We also get other dealers input in pricing, as they are more aware of what they can get for a piece they've sold repeatedly. Another flaw inherent in over pricing true market values is that it often has the scurrilous effect of depressing prices for the items being promoted. We've seen it happen in baseball cards, Jim Beam bottles, and Beanie Babies, and in some areas of our collecting glass world with high blown priced books being churned out helter-skelter. This was recently exhibited by several books on Hocking's wares in particular. When people get seriously "burned" on pricing, word spreads like wildfire, and this turns potential collectors off altogether. Everybody loses in that scenario — collectors, dealers, promoters, and the interested public. Some downturn in market prices lies with ill-informed pricing, be it by authors or dealers. All woes cannot be blamed on the Internet. Frankly, if you were fearing you'd "lost out" on being able to collect Depression glass, this is a banner time to buy it, possibly the best since the 1970s when buying was so frenetic.

ADAM, Jeannette Glass Company, 1932 – 1934

Colors: pink, green, crystal, some yellow, and Delphite blue (See Reproduction Section.)

When you actually study the intricacy of Depression glass designs, you can see echoes of the time in which it appeared. This is especially true in Jeannette's Adam pattern. The scrolled ferns and leaves in the center motif harken to past Art Nouveau influences, and yet the regulated lines, squared, round, triangular and cone shapes bespeak the Deco era as well. We had an artist write to say she was halfway through reading the book before something we said caused her to study the sheer artistry and history manifested and then she started over at the front appreciating the glass with new eyes!

There were varied items made during its brief three year distribution. When our first book was written in 1972, Adam was being seen at every flea market or show. Now, you are lucky to encounter a few pieces even at Depression glass shows which were just starting when we first began writing. Today, unless you are lucky and find someone who is downsizing and selling their collection, you will find that it will take a while to complete a set piece by piece – even with the Internet. Don't let that discourage you from trying however, as it can still be done. One lady told us recently that she'd just bought the final piece needed for an 8-place setting and it had taken her six years.

Adam continues to be one of the most hunted patterns in Depression glass. Pink is easier to find, but there are collectors who want harder-to-find items such as candy dishes, candles, iced teas and vases. All those pieces in green, except the vase, are also hard to find. The green butter dish is rarely observed. Count yourself lucky if you own one.

The lid pictured in Row 2 of the pink photo fits both the candy and sugar pictured in the top row. That makes those lids doubly hard to find, though you wouldn't know that by our photo!

New collectors continue to write us worried about Adam reproductions. Only the pink butter was reproduced and a description of how to distinguish that reproduction, as well as those in other patterns, is shown in the back of this book. You can only use the butter dish information to distinguish that one piece of old from new. Information for that reproduced butter does not apply to any other piece of Adam. Prices on pink butters dipped temporarily when the reproductions first appeared, but they are back to as normal now as can be expected 25 plus years later. Green butters were never reproduced.

Pink Adam pitchers come with both square and round bases. The square has the motif on the base while the round has only concentric rings. These round-footed pitchers are usually very light in color and can also be found in crystal. Round bottoms are much rarer than their counterparts, but do not fetch prices related to their rarity due to lack of demand by collectors. There are at least four other pieces found in crystal, i.e. ashtray, coaster, divided relish, and grill plate, but few collectors care at present even though they are truly rare. If there are not enough pieces discovered to collect a set, collectors often pass on gathering the few other pieces available.

Every round Adam plate or saucer you stumble upon is rare whether pink or yellow. Few pieces have turned up in yellow, but we once owned 4 cups, saucers and salad plates in the early 1970s.

Inner rim damage is frequently found on all bowls, having been used and stacked in cabinets for over 70 years. If you see a description that says "irr," it means "inner rim roughness." You do not want to pay mint prices for damaged merchandise; so check out the inside rims when buying.

There is a rare pink butter dish top that exhibits both the Adam motif (outside) and the Sierra (inside) mould design. One top contains two designs. You can see this butter in earlier editions of this book or in our "Treasures of Very Rare Depression Glass." The first rare lid discovered was found for $6.00 as a regular Adam butter, but sold for an eyebrow-raising $250.00 back in 1974. Today, that would be a bargain. There is also a rare, seldom seen lamp made from a frosted sherbet with a bulb attached to a metal cap. Very few own these.

		Pink	Green				Pink	Green
8 ▸	Ashtray, 4½"	24.00	24.00	3 ▸	**Cup	18.00	16.00
12 ▸	Bowl, 4¾", dessert	20.00	20.00		Lamp	495.00	495.00
11 ▸	Bowl, 5¾", cereal	60.00	50.00		Pitcher, 8", 32 ounce	35.00	45.00
13 ▸	Bowl, 7¾"	26.00	28.00		Pitcher, 32 ounce, round base	75.00	
	Bowl, 9", no cover	50.00	50.00	10 ▸	Plate, 6", sherbet	7.50	10.00
	Bowl cover, 9"	20.00	45.00	9 ▸	‡Plate, 7¾", square salad	16.00	15.00
	Bowl, 9", covered	60.00	85.00	16 ▸	Plate, 9", square dinner	30.00	30.00
14 ▸	Bowl, 10", oval	35.00	40.00	21 ▸	Plate, 9", grill	25.00	22.00
	Butter dish bottom	28.00	60.00	2 ▸	Platter, 11¾"	25.00	25.00
	Butter dish top	72.00	330.00	22 ▸	Relish dish, 8", divided	18.00	22.00
	Butter dish & cover	100.00	350.00	24 ▸	Salt & pepper, 4", footed	60.00	95.00
23 ▸	Butter dish combination with Sierra pattern	1,600.00		4 ▸	‡‡Saucer, 6", square	5.00	5.00
				19 ▸	Sherbet, 3"	28.00	35.00
17 ▸	Cake plate, 10", footed	28.00	30.00	5 ▸	Sugar	20.00	20.00
25 ▸	*Candlesticks, 4", pair	100.00	115.00	6 ▸	Sugar/candy cover	22.00	40.00
26 ▸	Candy jar & cover, 2½"	115.00	125.00	18 ▸	Tumbler, 4½"	28.00	28.00
1 ▸	Coaster, 3¼"	16.00	15.00	20 ▸	Tumbler, 5½", iced tea	65.00	68.00
7 ▸	Creamer	22.00	25.00	15 ▸	Vase, 7½"	450.00	125.00

* Delphite $225.00   ** Yellow $100.00   ‡ Round pink $60.00; yellow $100.00   ‡‡ Round pink $75.00; yellow $85.00

"ADAMS RIB," Line #900, Diamond Glassware Co., c. 1925

Colors: amber, blue, green, pink; some marigold; milk and crystal w/marigold iridescence, vaseline; and colors decorated w/gold, silver, white enamel, florals; and flashed colors of blue and orange w/black trim

"Adam's Rib" is one Diamond Glassware pattern that is gaining the attention of collectors and dealers alike. Actually, it only takes a few collectors asking for a pattern to get the dealers motivated into searching for it. It doesn't hurt that the blue is particularly striking when scattered among other glassware on display. The #900 line was one of Diamond's most circulated wares. As we searched for pieces of "Adams Rib" for our book, most of the items we obtained were found in antique malls or shops. Few pieces were displayed at shows, but in the last few years that has changed. More is being exhibited and sold at shows. Collectors appear to like the mixture of colors as well as those tall candlesticks. We keep adding pieces to our listing, but we doubt that the record below is complete. You may find additional items and we would very much appreciate a notice of such.

Most of the pieces cited below were shown in a 1928 Sears catalog that advertised six orange and black "ribbed" pieces for $1.32. Indications are that orange was a really big color craze in the country during that time. If you could find enough of these, it might make an impressive pattern for a Halloween theme show display. Many Depression glass shows feature wonderful displays of glass from members' collections. Sometimes these displays alone are worth the price of admission!

A pedestal candy that closely resembles "Adam's Rib" was made by Fenton. The knob of the Diamond Company's candy has a tiny protrusion on the top, whereas the one made by Fenton does not.

Some of the flat-bottomed bowls were originally offered on a black, three-toed pedestal base. Black bases were in fashion at the time. The marigold pieces are valued by carnival glass collectors; so, you may have competition for those. You might find an iridized blue or green pitcher that some lucky collectors are hoping for mugs to accompany. Keep your eye out should either of those colored mugs surface for they would be a find.

Though Diamond had been a fixture in the glassmaking business, it became one of those unfortunate factories that was leveled by fire in the early 30s.

		Non-iridescent	Iridescent
	Base, black, pedestal, 3 toe (for flat bowls)	15.00	
	Bowl, vegetable, flared (belled) rim	55.00	
	Bowl, flat, rolled edge	35.00	
	Bowl, 8", 3-footed, salad	40.00	
	Bowl, 10½" console, pedestal foot	45.00	150.00
5 ▸	Candy, 3-footed bonbon w/lid	40.00	
	Candy, oval, flat	55.00	
	Candy, footed jar and cover	45.00	
	Candle, blown	30.00	50.00
	Candle, tall, 9"	35.00	50.00
	Cigarette holder, footed	25.00	
7 ▸	Compote, cheese, non-ribbed	20.00	
9 ▸	Comport, flared	25.00	
8 ▸	Comport, small, rimmed	30.00	
	Comport, 6½" tall	35.00	60.00
2 ▸	Comport, large fruit	50.00	90.00
3 ▸	Cup	15.00	

		Non-iridescent	Iridescent
	Creamer	20.00	40.00
	Mayonnaise, 6", w/ladle	40.00	
	Mug (or lemonade)	30.00	75.00
11 ▸	Pitcher, lemonade, applied handle w/lid	175.00	350.00
	Plate, dessert	8.00	
1 ▸	Plate, lunch, 8"	14.00	
10 ▸	Plate, cracker, w/center rim	25.00	
4 ▸	Saucer	4.00	
	Sandwich, center flat top handle		40.00
6 ▸	Sandwich, center ½ hex handle	25.00	45.00
	Shakers, pr.	60.00	
	Sherbet, flat rim	15.00	
	Sugar, open	20.00	40.00
	Tray, oval sugar/creamer (8½ x 6¼")	17.00	30.00
	Vase, fan	40.00	60.00
	Vase, 8½", footed, flair rim	65.00	90.00
	Vase, 9¾"	85.00	130.00

"ADDIE," "TWELVE POINT," Line #34, New Martinsville Glass Mfg. Co., c. 1930

Colors: amber, amethyst, black, crystal, cobalt, green, jade green satin, pink, red, yellow; and w/Lotus Glass Co. silver decoration

"Addie" can be found in amber. We have had several e-mails with pictures confirming it. Thanks to those readers who sent the pictures we requested. The name we've heard this pattern called in the marketplace is "Twelve Point," simply because it has that many points. We found that over 20 years ago author William Heacock had inaugurated the name in acknowledgment of Addie Miller, a pioneer author for New Martinsville Glass Company wares. The company only gave it a line number (#34) as was the norm for distinguishing patterns at the time, but we will continue the name tribute.

You will discover that the Lions/heraldry design shown in our *Elegant Glassware of the Depression Era* is etched on this Line #34 as well as another New Martinsville pattern, Moondrops Line #37. This begs the question, is it a Lotus decoration?

"Addie" attracts more admirers to its cobalt blue or red color when we display it for sale at shows. Once collectors are shown the jade green satin, it may capture major attention. Regrettably, there is a shortage of that color today. Everything similar to jadite colored ware has been snatched up in the last few years. New Martinsville's jade green was marketed with black, an arresting color combination maintaining the bi- or tri-colored glassware creations of that period.

		Black, Cobalt, Jade, Red	All other colors
	Bowl, large flare rim, vegetable	40.00	30.00
8 ▸	Candlestick, 3½"	25.00	18.00
13 ▸	Cheese comport, 2½ x 5¾"	20.00	12.00
	Cream soup	25.00	15.00
6 ▸	Creamer, footed	15.00	8.00
9 ▸	Cup, demi	15.00	
4 ▸	Cup, footed	9.00	5.00
	Mayonnaise, 5"	30.00	15.00
7 ▸	Plate, 8", lunch	12.50	8.00
	Plate, 9½", dinner	20.00	12.00
	Plate, 10½", cracker	30.00	20.00
11 ▸	Sandwich, center handle	35.00	25.00
3 ▸	Sandwich tray, 2-handle	30.00	20.00
5 ▸	Saucer	2.00	1.00
10 ▸	Saucer, demi	5.00	
1 ▸	Sherbet, footed	15.00	8.00
2 ▸	Sugar, open, footed	15.00	8.00
	Tumbler, footed, 6 oz., juice	15.00	8.00
12 ▸	Tumbler, footed, 9 oz., water	18.00	12.00

AMELIA, "STAR MEDALLION," "BOXED STAR," Line #671, Imperial Glass Company, c. 1920s

Colors: amber, blue, Clambroth, crystal, green, pink, Rubigold iridescent, Smoke; Azalea, Turquoise, and Verde, 1960s; pink carnival, 1980s

Production began on Imperial's Line # 671, Amelia, in the 1920s, but not all pieces were made in all colors at any one time of manufacture. As we travel, we most often see the milk or hotel pitcher and sugar in either crystal or Rubigold (Imperial's name for their marigold carnival color). We see substantial price ranges on the pitcher, especially the Rubigold. People see a carnival colored ware and dollar signs pop in their heads. The Rubigold fluctuates in shades from deep marigold to a very light color as depicted in Row 2 of our photo.

Imperial made an iridized pink carnival color in the late 1970s and you will often spot an Amelia crimped rim compote in that color. These regularly turn up in malls and flea markets and are not as old as many seem to believe. Imperial also made several pieces of Beaded Block in pink carnival which is being accepted by collectors of that pattern. Just realize it was made in the 1970s and not the 1930s.

Rubigold Amelia custard cups and nut bowls are difficult to find. In reality, only the pitcher is regularly detected in this carnival color.

We are not discovering colored Amelia very easily — even the 1960s colors, which seems to signify a shortage in the market at present. That could mean owners are keeping it or Imperial did not produce mass quantities of colored Amelia in the first place.

		Clam-broth	Rubi-gold	Smoke	All other colors
	Butter w/cover, round				40.00
13 ▶	Bowl, 5", lily				15.00
	Bowl, 5½", square	25.00	30.00	45.00	15.00
	Bowl, 5½", deep nut, ftd.		35.00		20.00
11 ▶	Bowl, 6", round nappy	20.00	25.00	40.00	15.00
8 ▶	Bowl, 6", 2-hdld. jelly				15.00
	Bowl, 6¼", oval preserve				25.00
	Bowl, 7", oval				25.00
7 ▶	Bowl, 7½", berry, flare (belled) rim			25.00	
6 ▶	Bowl, 8", round berry				35.00
	Candlestick				25.00
	Cup, custard		20.00		10.00
	Compote, straight rim				20.00
	Compote, crimped rim (late)	30.00	30.00		12.00

		Clam-broth	Rubi-gold	Smoke	All other colors
10 ▶	Creamer				20.00
	Celery, 2-handle				30.00
	Celery vase, footed	70.00	80.00	135.00	35.00
1 ▶	Goblet, cocktail				15.00
2 ▶	Goblet, wine		45.00	75.00	20.00
	Pitcher, milk or hotel	33.00	40.00	80.00	25.00
	Plate, 6½", dessert		35.00		12.00
3 ▶	Plate, 9½", lunch	30.00	40.00	60.00	25.00
9 ▶	Sherbet				10.00
	Spoon holder (open sugar)				20.00
12 ▶	Sugar w/cover				30.00
4 ▶	Tumbler, 4"		30.00	40.00	20.00
5 ▶	Tumbler, 4½", lemonade, flare rim	25.00	35.00	35.00	

AMERICAN PIONEER, Liberty Works, 1931 – 1934
Colors: pink, green, amber, and crystal

American Pioneer pattern has fiercely loyal fans but also suffers from a lack of new collectors. This is understandable when you consider the dearth of supply. This means prices are slowly declining for common pieces, and only slightly increasing for the scarce items. Notice that the American Pioneer pattern does require those plain banded, horizontal ribbed areas in order to be American Pioneer. Various companies made similar hobnailed designs, but without the bands.

Candy jar lids are one and the same even though the two candies are shaped differently. One looks like a typical footed candy, the other is taller and has the silhouette of a footed vase. Additionally, there are two styles of cups, one being a tad more flared than the other. One has a 4" diameter and is 2½" tall; the other has a 3⅜" diameter and is 2⅜" tall. These inconsistencies are very insignificant and may well be due to mould wear differences; but collectors have observed them enough to say the flared rim cup is the more commonly found.

Vegetable bowl covers are rarely seen; although we have observed two sizes (8¾" and 9¼"), there are reports of a third size, but no confirmation has been forthcoming. We found out there were two sizes when we bought a lid only to find it would not fit the bottom we owned. That is an example of how our 39 years of experience with Depression glass will help you avoid some mistakes. We've been there and done that.

A few amber pieces exist and both sizes of covered urns have surfaced in that color. Amber cocktails have been discovered in two sizes; none have been unearthed thus far in other colors. Under liners for the hard to acquire urns (pitchers) are the regular 6" and 8" plates. However, a 6" pink plate is rarely found. Candlesticks, which are handled, are in demand by collectors of candles, but do not materialize as often as they once did. Dresser sets are sought pieces in American Pioneer and a crystal one finally surfaced. Powder jar and cologne collectors compete with those of American Pioneer to add these dresser items to their collections.

It's exhilarating to know that 70 years later, and with thousands of people collecting Depression glass, heretofore unknown items and colors are still emerging! This is what makes collecting exciting. There is the real possibility that any collector can find something rare in the next shop, market, attic, or basement.

Liberty Works was initially titled a cut glassworks. That was a part of its name. We've been long harangued by devotees of American Pioneer that this is "better glass" than your run of the mill Depression era wares and should be treated as such and placed in our *Elegant Glassware of the Depression* Era book. Possibly, it should be, but we inherited its acceptance as Depression glass when we started writing in 1972. Unfortunately, this is another glass facility that encountered fire damage in 1931 and could not recover financially from this blow. Fire seemed to be an ever-present problem of glassware manufacturing facilities back then.

11

American Pioneer

		Crystal, Pink	Green
	*Bowl, 5", handled	25.00	25.00
	Bowl, 8¾", covered	110.00	150.00
11 ▸	Bowl, 9", handled	30.00	35.00
16 ▸	Bowl, 9¼", covered	125.00	165.00
	Bowl, 10¾", console	50.00	60.00
	Candlesticks, 6½", pair	110.00	135.00
	Candy jar and cover, 1 pound	85.00	110.00
4 ▸	Candy jar and cover, 1½ pound	90.00	135.00
	Cheese and cracker set (indented platter and comport)	55.00	65.00
	Coaster, 3½"	35.00	35.00
2 ▸	Creamer, 2¾"	18.00	20.00
8 ▸	*Creamer, 3½"	18.00	20.00
14 ▸	*Cup	10.00	10.00
	Dresser set (2 colognes, powder jar, indented 7½" tray)	495.00	495.00
	Goblet, 3³⁄₁₆", 3 oz., cocktail (amber)	30.00	
	Goblet, 3¹⁵⁄₁₆", 3½ oz., cocktail (amber)	30.00	
	Goblet, 4", 3 oz., wine	30.00	45.00
	Goblet, 6", 8 oz., water	40.00	50.00
	Ice bucket, 6"	45.00	45.00
13 ▸	Lamp, 1¾", w/metal pole, 9½"		65.00
	Lamp, 5½", round, ball shape, amber	150.00	175.00
	Lamp, 8½", tall	140.00	180.00
5 ▸	Mayonnaise, 4¼"	45.00	60.00
6 ▸	Mayonnaise plate	12.00	12.00
	Pilsner, 5¾", 11 ounce	150.00	150.00
1 ▸	**Pitcher, 5", covered urn	175.00	225.00
3 ▸	‡Pitcher, 7", covered urn	195.00	250.00
	Plate, 6"	10.00	12.00
	*Plate, 6", handled	10.00	12.00
19 ▸	*Plate, 8"	10.00	10.00
9 ▸	*Plate, 11½", handled	30.00	40.00
15 ▸	*Saucer	4.00	4.00
	Sherbet, 3½"	16.00	20.00
17 ▸	Sherbet, 4¾"	40.00	45.00
12 ▸	Sugar, 2¾"	18.00	20.00
7 ▸	*Sugar, 3½"	18.00	20.00
	Tumbler, 5 ounce, juice	30.00	35.00
	Tumbler, 4", 8 ounce	35.00	45.00
	Tumbler, 5", 12 ounce	40.00	50.00
10 ▸	Vase, 7", 4 styles	125.00	150.00
	Vase, 9", round		250.00
18 ▸	Whiskey, 2¼", 2 ounce	30.00	65.00

* Amber — double the price of pink unless noted.
** Amber $300.00
‡ Amber $350.00

AMERICAN SWEETHEART, MacBeth-Evans Glass Company, 1930 – 1936
Colors: pink, Monax, ruby, and cobalt; some Cremax and color-trimmed Monax

American Sweetheart was liberally manufactured during its seven-year run and was resilient as is illustrated by the multitude of pieces remaining today. Prices on commonly seen luncheon pieces (cups, saucers, sugars, creamers, and plates) have weakened. The Internet has uncovered a copious amount of some patterns that was previously unknown. American Sweetheart is one example. On the other hand, there are still pieces that are not turning up in sufficient quantities; so those items are holding fairly steady in price. These rarely found items include the seldom seen Monax sugar lid (with two different styles of knobs), and the large (18", triple wide, flat rim) or small console bowls that appear in Monax; the larger console was also produced in red and blue and are notably impressive when on the table.

Both pink and Monax (white with translucent edges) shakers are seldom found, but the price has slipped somewhat due to collectors unwillingness to pay the prices being asked. You will find plates in Monax that come with and without a center motif. Plates vary slightly in size due to the number of years this pattern was made. Moulds wore out and were reworked. There may be a $\frac{1}{16}$" or even an $\frac{1}{8}$" size discrepancy. We had stacks of American Sweetheart plates in our shop. Often collectors endeavored to find six or eight plates to match precisely, and sometimes could not accomplish that feat.

Dealers often think that everybody knows about Depression glass by now, but they do not. We still hear stories from those who gave it away, sold it for pennies at a garage sale, or simply threw away their aunt or grandmother's dishes because they had no clue they were valuable. Books are cheap compared to tossing out hundreds of dollars.

Monax pieces were often trimmed in colors. Gold trimmed is the least desirable, but also the most plentiful trim. If the gold is a distraction, you can remove it carefully with an art gum eraser. Some Monax pieces are found with colored edgings of yellow, green, pink, and smoky/black, any of which is extremely collectible. That smoke trim, as it is known to collectors, is pictured on the bottom of page 15. It is the most coveted by collectors. A four-piece set was advertised in a 1934 catalog for $3.00.

Even though this dinnerware is somewhat fragile looking, it was extraordinarily long lasting. A Louisville Tin & Stove Company catalog, dated 1937, offered a 32-piece set of Monax American Sweetheart for $2.75 as well as a 42-piece set (including a two-piece sugar) for $4.15. Remember, an average wage in the 1930s ran from 20 cents to a dollar a day. These sets cost three to 20 days work for an average worker; so most people only owned the pieces that were giveaways or premiums for buying necessities. These were everyday dishes, so it's a wonder so many survived until now.

Pitchers and water tumblers are found only in pink, but there are analogous shaped pitchers having no design that were marketed with plain, Dogwood shaped tumblers. These pitchers are not American Sweetheart, though some people do buy them to go with their sets. If it does not have the pattern, it is not considered to be American Sweetheart, nor is it Dogwood without the Dogwood silk screen flowers. These plain pitchers usually sell in the $40.00 range – but not quickly.

Ruby, cobalt, and Monax were used for tidbit servers (plates drilled in center connected with a metal rod), 15" sandwich plates, and the 18" console bowl. There is no listing of a pink tidbit ever being made, but all you need to make a tidbit is the plates, hardware, and a drill with a proper bit.

Sherbets are found in two sizes, with the smaller 3¾" harder to find. Peg bottom sherbets are found in metal holders — but only in crystal.

Cremax (beige color) items were made in the mid-30s, presumably to compete with the china trade. It probably didn't work well since it is rarely seen today.

American Sweetheart

	Ruby	Cobalt	Cremax	Smoke & other trims
Bowl, 6", cereal			12.00	45.00
Bowl, 9", round berry			40.00	250.00
Bowl, 9½", soup				165.00
Bowl, 18", console	1,100.00	1,250.00		
Creamer, footed	150.00	200.00		90.00
Cup	100.00	125.00		90.00
Lamp shade			495.00	
Lamp (floor with brass base)			795.00	
Plate, 6", bread and butter				18.00
Plate, 8", salad	100.00	120.00		25.00
Plate, 9", luncheon				40.00
Plate, 9¾", dinner				80.00
Plate, 12", salver	150.00	250.00		100.00
Plate, 15½", server	325.00	425.00		
Platter, 13", oval				195.00
Saucer	18.00	24.00		14.00
Sherbet, 4¼", footed (design inside or outside)				90.00
Sugar, open footed	150.00	200.00		110.00
Tidbit, 2 tier, 8" & 12"	250.00	335.00		
Tidbit, 3 tier, 8", 12" & 15½"	625.00	750.00		

			Pink	Monax
23 ▸	Bowl, 3¾", flat berry		60.00	
21 ▸	Bowl, 4½", cream soup		75.00	90.00
1 ▸	Bowl, 6", cereal		15.00	16.00
20 ▸	Bowl, 9", round berry		40.00	50.00
2 ▸	Bowl, 9½", flat soup		60.00	70.00
13 ▸	Bowl, 11", oval vegetable		55.00	65.00
	Bowl, 18", console			395.00
10 ▸	Creamer, footed		12.00	9.00
11 ▸	Cup		15.00	7.00
	Lamp shade			495.00
8 ▸	Plate, 6" or 6½", bread & butter		5.00	5.00
18 ▸	Plate, 8", salad		12.00	7.00
	Plate, 9", luncheon			12.00
17 ▸	Plate, 9¾", dinner		26.00	18.00
25 ▸	Plate, 10¼", dinner			25.00
	Plate, 11", chop plate			18.00
24 ▸	Plate, 12", salver		20.00	18.00
	Plate, 15½", server			165.00
5 ▸	Platter, 13", oval		50.00	60.00
6 ▸	Pitcher, 7½", 60 ounce		1,050.00	
19 ▸	Pitcher, 8", 80 ounce		795.00	
7 ▸	Salt and pepper, footed		550.00	450.00
12 ▸	Saucer		4.00	2.00
3 ▸	Sherbet, 3¾", footed		22.00	
22 ▸	Sherbet, 4¼", footed (design inside or outside)		16.00	16.00
	Sherbet in metal holder (crystal only)		3.00	
9 ▸	Sugar, open, footed		12.00	7.00
	*Sugar lid			450.00
	Tidbit, 2 tier, 8" & 12"		60.00	60.00
	Tidbit, 3 tier, 8", 12" & 15½"			325.00
16 ▸	Tumbler, 3½", 5 ounce		80.00	
15 ▸	Tumbler, 4¼", 9 ounce		60.00	
14 ▸	Tumbler, 4¾", 10 ounce		110.00	

* Three styles of knobs

ARDITH, Paden City Glass Company, c. 1920s

Colors: amber, black, crystal, cobalt, green, pink, ruby, yellow

Ardith's floral motif can be found on several Paden City mould blanks. It occurs on the squared (#412) and round (#890) Crow's Foot blanks; the squared, cropped cornered #411 Mrs. B line; the #211 four Spire line; the #210 Stacked paneled line; the #215 Glades line; and the #555 "Teardrop and Bead" line. You could possibly find Ardith on other blanks. The problem is finding any Ardith and then worrying about which mould line you have.

We seem to turn up more yellow in our travels in the South, but have not seen a yellow piece in the northern areas we haunt.

Don't be mislead into thinking this is easily found, even though this flowered motif seems to have been a prevalent etching if you go by number of blanks on which it occurs. The few pieces we see are usually unidentified by the seller, but priced highly in case it might be "good." Many sellers use that theory, and do not understand why their glass does not sell quickly. You need to research what you have or price it based upon what you paid for it and move on down the road to find another treasure. The profit from "sold" items might pay for something you want for yourself.

We are pricing all colors and lines together. Red, black, and cobalt blue will bring 20% – 25% more than the listed price and crystal at least 50% less.

		* All Colors
	Bowl, 5⅝", 2 hdld.	40.00
	Bowl, 9", ped., ftd., sq.	100.00
	Bowl, 9½", sq. ped., ftd.	100.00
	Bowl, 10", rolled edge console	70.00
	Bowl, 10", sq.	70.00
	Bowl, 10", 2 hdld.	90.00
	Bowl, 10½", sq.	65.00
	Bowl, 12", sq.	70.00
	Bowl, 12½", 4-toed console	75.00
	Candle, 4", rolled edge	100.00
	Candle, 4⅝", sq. flattened top	35.00
	Candle, 5¼", keyhole	35.00
	Candle, 6", "wings"	50.00
	Candle, 6", center circle	50.00
	Candy, w/lid, 2-part	100.00
	Candy, w/lid, 3-part	100.00
	Candy, w/lid, 8", ftd.	150.00
	Cake stand, 9¼", ped., ftd.	75.00
	Compote, 6½" high, sq.	55.00
4 ▶	Creamer, flat	35.00
	Creamer, ftd.	40.00

* Crystal 50% less

		* All Colors
7 ▶	Cup	50.00
	Cheese & cracker, 10¼" plate; 5" sq. stand	110.00
2 ▶	Ice bucket w/ball	95.00
	Ice bucket w/lid	175.00
	Mayonnaise, w/ladle & liner plate	60.00
	Pitcher, 7¼"	210.00
	Plate, 5⅞"	12.00
3 ▶	Plate, 8⅜", sq.	30.00
8 ▶	Saucer	15.00
9 ▶	Sugar, flat	40.00
	Sugar, ftd.	45.00
	Tray, 7½", 2 hdld.	50.00
	Tray, 9", cupped center hdld.	90.00
1 ▶	Tray, 10" sq., center handle	70.00
	Tray, 10¼", sq., center handle	70.00
	Tumbler, 3 oz.	45.00
	Vase, 3", high	185.00
	Vase, 4¼", ivy/rose, ftd.	75.00
	Vase, 5½", elliptical	150.00
	Vase, 7½", bulbous bottom	135.00
	Vase, 8½", horizontal ribbed	150.00

"ARTURA," Pattern #608, Indiana Glass Company, c. 1930s
Colors: crystal and w/color decoration, green, pink

"Artura" was simply a numbered line at Indiana. Glass companies regularly used line numbers to identify patterns. Few used names and it was only when collectors starting seeking the different patterns most of those names came into play. People tend to want to identify their patterns by a name and not a number. It is amazing how some Depression patterns gained favor with collectors once an actual name became known.

According to one serious collector, tumblers "are not available." Well, we now own two and they are both damaged, so "Artura" must have been well used.

"Artura" is a noticeably small pattern which was advertised in 15-, 21-, and 27-piece sets to utilize for breakfast, luncheon, or bridge settings. Its distinctive feature is a double rib which occurs at each of the nine points in its design. It is an unusual, nine-sided glassware. Moulds are usually found with even numbered sides and most popular then were four, eight, and ten.

"Artura" has the Deco linear look, which is softened by "question mark" curving handles. It repeatedly sits unrecognized, but we see more of it in Midwestern antique malls than other places we travel. Cups often lack saucers which themselves are hard to spot when seen alone.

A sherbet has surfaced with a linear type etching. We believe we have seen a plate to match it.

Some collectors are attracted to the crystal decorated pieces. Note the ships decorated server in our photo with its ornate handle. There is a small luncheon set of crystal decorated with black and yellow highlights that is rather intriguing. Notice also the crystal accented by a black handled cup and center on plate and saucer.

		Green, Pink, Crystal Decorated
6 ▶	Cup	7.00
3 ▶	Creamer	12.00
4 ▶	Plate, 7½", salad	6.00
7 ▶	Saucer	2.00
	Sherbet	10.00
1 ▶	Sugar, open	12.00
5 ▶	Tray, sandwich w/ornate center handle	35.00
	Tray, sugar and sugar	15.00
2 ▶	Tumbler, ftd.	25.00

AUNT POLLY, U.S. Glass Company, Late 1920s
Colors: blue, green, and iridescent

Collecting Aunt Polly creates problems for perfectionists since most pieces have rough mould seams. Many of U.S. Glass Company's patterns from this era suffer from that malady. It is distracting, but there is no way to change the way it was manufactured; so if it bothers you, you need to find another pattern to collect.

There are no cups or saucers. Additionally, there are distinctly diverse hues of green and blue found. Scrutinize the color disparities shown in the photos. This would not be much of a problem if more Aunt Polly were available from which to choose. Nevertheless, passionate collectors accept these foibles as normal distinctions, or part of the "character" of the pattern.

The green, two-handled, covered candy (lid interchangeable with sugar) pictured in the top row has never been discovered in blue although it has been found in iridescent. The blue, open candy (footed, double handled) pictured in the top row is missing from many Aunt Polly collections as are the oval vegetable, sugar lid, shakers, and butter dish. The butter bottom is interchangeable with other U.S. Glass patterns of the time, specifically Floral and Diamond, Strawberry, Cherryberry, and U.S. Swirl; but since those patterns were not made in blue, the blue Aunt Polly butter bottoms will always be in short supply.

Some creamers are found with a more prominent lip than others. These were made by hand with a wooden paddle while the glass was still hot, and since quality control was not high on the agenda for this cheaper glassware, variations are everywhere.

Note the ruffled vase to the right. This vase was created from the regular vase mold. It may have been experimental or a worker's lunch break whimsy.

		Iridescent	Green, Blue				Iridescent	Green, Blue
11 ▶	Bowl, 4¾", berry	6.00	13.00		14 ▶	Creamer	30.00	50.00
3 ▶	Bowl, 4¾", 2" high	14.00			1 ▶	Pitcher, 8", 48 ounce		210.00
18 ▶	Bowl, 5½", one handle	15.00	22.00		8 ▶	Plate, 6", sherbet	6.00	10.00
17 ▶	Bowl, 7¼", oval, handled, pickle	15.00	30.00		4 ▶	Plate, 8", luncheon		17.00
12 ▶	Bowl, 7⅞", large berry	20.00	40.00		10 ▶	Salt and pepper, pr.		225.00
9 ▶	Bowl, 8⅜", oval	75.00	150.00		7 ▶	Sherbet	9.00	9.00
13 ▶	Butter dish and cover	200.00	200.00		15 ▶	Sugar	20.00	30.00
	Butter dish bottom	80.00	100.00		16 ▶	Sugar/candy cover	50.00	145.00
	Butter dish top	120.00	100.00		2 ▶	Tumbler, 3⅝", 8 ounce		26.00
19 ▶	Candy, cover, 2-handled	70.00			6 ▶	Vase, 6½", footed	30.00	55.00
5 ▶	Candy, footed, 2-handled	25.00	50.00					

19

AURORA, Hazel-Atlas Glass Company, Late 1930s
Colors: cobalt blue, pink, green, and crystal

Aurora's small bowls (4½") have finally saturated market demand. Again, the Internet has exposed more than previously known. Once the seeming lack of small, deep bowls in cobalt made the price jump; but now that has been adjusted. You don't have to be an Internet geek to learn that some glassware in your attic or garage may be more valuable than you imagined as you see it selling on an Internet auction. Instead of giving it to charity or selling it at an estate sale, millions have learned how to auction it on the Internet and reap the rewards. This has changed the whole marketplace for collectibles including Depression glass. Now, the middle man or "picker" for dealers is being eliminated; and items go directly from owner to buyer (dealer or collector depending upon who bids the highest).

Aurora in a cobalt blue setting can be acquired for a smaller fortune than any other. Here, in Florida, many windows exhibit cobalt glassware as an adornment. Cobalt glassware absorbs heat; so be careful about putting it in direct sunlight. We've heard several stories about pieces of glass "just blowing up." Of course that also happens at shows when coats, purses, or bags drag by a booth of glass. "Did you see that? That glass just jumped on the floor! I didn't touch it!" Suicide prone glass is the thorn in the side of glass dealers.

Pink Aurora pieces bring a price comparable to the blue as a result of their shortage. The deep bowl, creamer, and tumbler have so far never been found in pink. Canadian collectors indicate that pink and green are more readily found there than in the States. Green and crystal cereal bowls, cups, and saucers have turned up, but few collectors seek them.

We have several collector reports that creamers were given away as premiums for buying a breakfast cereal in the late 1930s. By the way, while we were doing research for *The Hazel-Atlas Glass Identification and Value Guide*, we noticed that a Hazel-Atlas catalog from the 50s shows that deep bowl in crystal listed as a "utility" bowl. So, if you can't find it in cobalt, you might try the latest glass fashion and mix in a crystal one. However, the only one of those we have seen so far was in that catalog.

		Cobalt, Pink
1 ▶	Bowl, 4½", deep	50.00
2 ▶	*Bowl, 5⅜", cereal	11.00
3 ▶	Creamer, 4½"	25.00
6 ▶	**Cup	14.00
	Plate, 6½"	9.00
5 ▶	‡ Saucer	3.00
4 ▶	Tumbler, 4¾", 10 ounce	24.00

* Green $8.00 or crystal $5.00
** Green $8.00
‡ Green $2.50

"AVOCADO," "SWEET PEAR," No. 601, Indiana Glass Company, 1923 – 1933

Colors: pink, green, crystal; white, 1950s; yellow mist, burnt honey, and water sets in myriad frosted and transparent colors for Tiara Home Products, 1974 – 1998 (See Reproduction Section.)

"Avocado" was the name given to Indiana's #601 line by early Depression glass authors. It was initially called "Sweet Pear" by authors of pattern glass books and that is more apropos as those fruits look like pears and not avocados.

Unfortunately, there isn't enough of the older green and pink "Avocado" emerging these days for new collectors to become mesmerized. Prices were steady for several years, but of late, these have been faltering on all but pitchers and tumblers which are seldom offered for sale. Newer collectors often seek less expensive patterns to start their collecting and "Avocado" is not an inexpensive pattern. We have purchased two collections in recent years, but selling them took a while until we were willing to wholesale pieces to other dealers.

The once-in-a-blue-moon sightings of pitcher and tumblers have stymied all but the most ardent and wealthy collectors. Be aware that Indiana reproductions of these two items abound in pink, but the pink repro is frequently an orange tinted pink. Original pink pitchers are usually very light in hue. Be sure to check out the Reproduction Section in the back depicting the various "Avocado" items and colors produced by Indiana for the Tiara Home Products line during their 1970 – 1998 life span. You don't want to be caught paying exorbitant prices for more recent wares. The yellow items you find are Tiara.

We now price items we can document in crystal "Avocado." Crystal prices have taken a bigger hit as fewer collectors want to spend the time necessary to gather a set since it is so rarely found. A few pieces of white were made in the 1950s, but only bowls, pitchers, and tumblers are seen regularly. We know frosted pitcher and tumbler sets were made since 1970s for Tiara, as well as numerous other transparent and frosted colors not originally produced.

		Crystal	Pink	Green			Crystal	Pink	Green
	Bowl, 5¼", 2-handled	10.00	27.00	30.00	15 ▸	*Pitcher, 64 ounce	350.00	1,000.00	1,500.00
7 ▸	Bowl, 6", footed relish	9.00	25.00	27.00	13 ▸	‡Plate, 6⅜", sherbet	5.00	12.00	14.00
10 ▸	Bowl, 7", 1-handle preserve	8.00	25.00	25.00	12 ▸	**Plate, 8¼", luncheon	7.00	15.00	18.00
1 ▸	Bowl, 7½", salad	13.00	45.00	65.00	8 ▸	Plate, 10¼", 2-handled, cake	14.00	40.00	60.00
6 ▸	Bowl, 8", 2-handled, oval	12.00	25.00	30.00	5 ▸	Saucer, 6⅜"		15.00	15.00
14 ▸	Bowl, 9½", 3¼", deep	25.00	140.00	165.00	11 ▸	‡Sherbet		45.00	55.00
2 ▸	‡Creamer, footed	12.00	25.00	25.00	3 ▸	‡Sugar, footed	12.00	25.00	25.00
4 ▸	Cup, footed, 2 styles		25.00	25.00	9 ▸	*Tumbler	25.00	200.00	300.00

*   Caution on pink. The orange-pink is new. White: Pitcher $300.00; Tumbler $35.00.
**   Apple design $15.00. Amber has been newly made.
‡   Remade in dark shade of green.

BEADED BLOCK, #710, Imperial Glass Company, 1927 – 1930s; Late 1970s – Early 1980s
Colors: pink, green, crystal, ice blue, Canary, iridescent, amber, red, opalescent colors, and milk white

We need to point out that to true enthusiasts of this pattern there is a difference between plain Beaded Block and the frosted, stippled pieces that they are careful to distinguish as "Frosted Block."

Beaded Block plates are typically found on square shapes; round plates are in shorter supply. Evidently, the 8¾" – 9" round "plates" were altered into bowls and even round bowls are scarce in collecting circles. There are size variances in this pattern as seen in the round plate which varies a ¼". All sizes shown here were acquired from our actually measuring the pieces and not those cataloged by Imperial. The two-handled jelly (Imperial terminology) was designated a cream soup by most glass companies and varies from 4¾" to 5". Be sure to read the section on measurements. We have found early company catalog size listings were mostly rough estimates rather than precise calculations.

The red lily bowl remains one of the rarer Beaded Block items and was made during that 1930s thirst for red. They appear to have been distributed around Vandalia, Ohio. However, prices for that red bowl have really taken a hit over the last few years as more have turned up than there are collectors for them. Present collectors settle for one and there are no other pieces being found in red to encourage more people to focus on that color.

Beaded Block pitchers are not as scarce as once thought; crystal and green can be found without much searching. Pink and white pitchers are a different matter as few of these have turned up over the years, causing demand to actually slacken. We have found that some things can be so obscure as to decrease demand. Beaded Block had slight recognition until the Internet auctions came along. New devotees were impressed with Beaded Block's color and style. They embraced it and prices went soaring. That too, has subsided somewhat since supply has out gunned the demand.

Six inch vases offered as Beaded Block often are not. The true vase has a scalloped top as shown in the top row. There is a 6" vase/parfait with a straight top and no beading that was called a footed jelly by Imperial. These are normally found in pink or green. Level rimmed jellies were premium items sold at grocery stores with a spice product such as dry mustard or pepper inside. Ones with labels and tops say "Frank Tea & Spice Co., Cin., O." Just realize they are "go-with" pieces and not truly Beaded Block pattern.

Neophyte dealers and sellers on the Internet usually misidentify this as older glassware than it is. It was sold at Woolworth's. We have also seen at least one source crediting the 1930s Sea Foam decoration (white edges) to about 40 years before that production by Imperial.

Imperial remade pink and iridized pink (pink carnival) in the late 1970s into the early 1980s. These pieces are clearly marked IG on the bottom. Visiting the factory in 1981, we learned that the white was made in the early 1950s and the IG mark (for Imperial Glass) was first used around 1951. Few marked pieces of Beaded Block are found, but they include the covered pear. This two-part candy in the shape of a large pear dates from the mid-50s. Pears have also been found in yellow, green, pink, and amber. Still, this item is desired by Beaded Block collectors.

		*Crystal, Pink, Green, Amber	Opalescent colors			*Crystal, Pink, Green, Amber	Opalescent colors
3 ▸	Bowl, 4⅞" – 5", 2-handled jelly	15.00	35.00		Bowl, 7½", round, plain edge	25.00	45.00
12 ▸	**Bowl, 4½", round, lily	18.00	40.00		Bowl, 8¼", celery	35.00	50.00
5 ▸	Bowl, 5½", square	18.00	35.00	6 ▸	Candy, pear shaped	395.00	
17 ▸	Bowl, 5½", 1-handle	15.00	30.00	1 ▸	Creamer	15.00	40.00
8 ▸	Bowl, 6", deep, round	22.00	35.00		‡Pitcher, 5¼", pint jug	65.00	
11 ▸	Bowl, 6¼", round, flared	22.00	35.00	15 ▸	Plate, 7¾", square	18.00	35.00
	Bowl, 6½", round	22.00	35.00	16 ▸	Plate, 8¾", round	25.00	40.00
4 ▸	Bowl, 6½", 2-handled pickle	25.00	50.00	13 ▸	Stemmed jelly, 4½"	25.00	45.00
10 ▸	Bowl, 6¾", round, unflared	22.00	35.00		Stemmed jelly, 4½", flared top	25.00	45.00
9 ▸	Bowl, 7¼", round, flared	25.00	45.00	2 ▸	Sugar	15.00	40.00
7 ▸	Bowl, 7½", round, fluted edges	25.00	45.00	14 ▸	Vase, 6", bouquet	20.00	50.00

*All pieces 25% to 40% lower   ** Red $495.00   ‡ White $195.00, pink $175.00, crystal $85.00

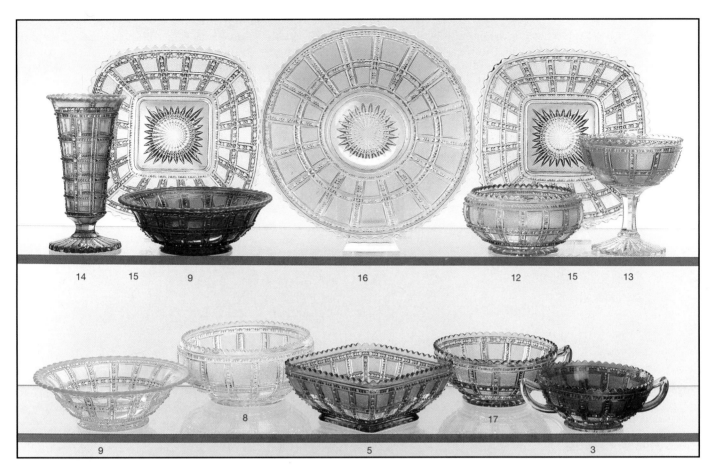

14   15   9   16   12   15   13

9   8   5   17   3

1   2   2   1   2   1

3   3   4   3   3

5   2   1   6   7

8   9   10   11   8

"BERLIN," "REEDED WAFFLE," Line #124, Westmoreland Specialty Company, c. 1924

Colors: blue, crystal, green, pink; ruby, c. 1980s

Westmoreland's Line #124 has been called "Berlin" or "Reeded Waffle" due to its resemblance to an older pattern glass design predominantly produced in the 1870s. That older ware is usually found with colored stains of ruby or amber. Westmoreland made at least 15 pieces of this #124 pattern in pink, green, blue, and crystal during the time normally associated with Depression glass. Even though hand produced, rather than machine moulded, as was most Depression glass, it was offered at five and dime stores. Hence the less than copious amounts of items found today.

There have been problems telling the difference between this pattern and one known as "Plaid" or "Open Plaid," which is comparable at first glance. However, "Plaid" has a distinct basketweave design and was only produced in crystal.

Supposedly, Westmoreland remade a #124 line ruby colored pitcher during the 1980s. We have not found one offered for sale to show you. Pattern glass books convey that the older "Berlin" design produced tumblers, wines, cracker jars, cruets, cups, butter dishes, etc. As a result, various items appear in this design, but were often other glass companies' (Adams, Bryce, and U.S, Glass) products.

		*Crystal			*Crystal
7 ▸	Basket	27.50	2 ▸	Creamer	15.00
	Bowl, bonbon, 1 handle	15.00	6 ▸	Mayonnaise	25.00
	Bowl, 6½", round	12.00	4 ▸	Pitcher	55.00
1 ▸	Bowl, square	17.00	5 ▸	Plate, 7"	10.00
8 ▸	Bowl, 2-handle cream soup	17.00		Plate, 9", lunch	15.00
11 ▸	Bowl, 7", round	20.00	3 ▸	Sugar	15.00
9 ▸	Bowl, 7½", round	20.00		Tray, 2- handle, celery	30.00
	Bowl, oval, pickle	20.00	10 ▸	Vase, footed	35.00

*Double price of crystal for colors.

24

BLOCK OPTIC, "BLOCK," Hocking Glass Company, 1929 – 1933

Colors: green, pink, yellow, crystal, and some amber, blue, and clambroth green

Green Block Optic can be assembled with a large number of stems and tumblers. However, gathering pink is more demanding due to its inadequate production. Not all pieces were made in pink. Very few items were made in crystal and yellow; so collecting those is a task. However, small sets can be put together with time and work.

Around the 1928 – 1932 period, glass companies started to make bi-colored wares, either by decorating that way, or by actually fusing two (or three) colors. Hocking's effort gave us a more Deco look by their firing black over the stems and foot of regular green sherbets and goblets. Note the high sherbet pictured with other stems as an example. A few collectors now seek those scarce Deco pieces.

New collectors should be aware that Block Optic has five variations of sugars and creamers, due to their variety of handles, their being footed or flat, or their having rayed or non-rayed bottoms. Our individual pictures should help you differentiate styles.

Block stems are difficult to find now. Many people liked their shape and capacity whether they collected much glass or not. Both yellow and green fluoresce in black light, a display technique being used more and more often. Do not fall for the tale that this guarantees glass to be old, however; it simply means there's uranium oxide among the mix, something still being used to produce glassware by some factories today.

Both sizes of water goblets hold nine ounces and are now used more for wine than water. Today's wine enthusiasts use goblets that hold more than the older wines which only held 2 – 3 ounces.

Hocking's Block Optic pattern rates highly with collectors, primarily for its availability due to length of production. Also, its simplicity of design and variety of colors are appreciated as well as its history of being reasonably priced. There are a few pricey items, but, in general, most collectors can afford to accumulate this pattern. Many beginners started with Block and went on to collect other patterns when time and money permitted.

Some Block was satinized or frosted, a decorating technique of that era. Items were dipped in camphoric acid which gave them a softer look and feel. Some have an aversion to satinized glass. Every time we unpacked glassware in our Grannie Bear shop, mother would use paper or cloth to pick up those pieces that were frosted. In the very early days of collecting, no one wanted anything to do with the satinized wares unless they were hand painted with flowers, birds, or other colorful decorations. However, that, too, is changing. We've now had customers asking if we have any satinized pieces.

Block Optic

	Green	Yellow	Pink
Bowl, 4¼" diam., 1⅜" tall	8.00		11.00
Bowl, 4½" diam., 1½" tall	25.00		40.00
Bowl, 5¼", cereal	12.00		25.00
Bowl, 7¼", salad	125.00		135.00
Bowl, 8½", large berry	35.00		30.00
*Bowl, 11¾", rolled-edge console	60.00		60.00
**Butter dish and cover, 3" x 5"	50.00		
Butter dish bottom	30.00		
Butter dish top	20.00		
‡Candlesticks, 1¾", pr.	100.00		65.00
12 ▶ Candy jar & cover, 2¼" tall	55.00	75.00	55.00
Candy jar & cover, 6¼" tall	60.00		175.00
Comport, 5⅜" wide, mayonnaise	60.00		60.00
Creamer, 3 styles: cone shaped, round, rayed-foot & flat (5 kinds)	11.00	12.00	12.00
14 ▶ Cup, four styles	6.00	7.00	8.00
Goblet, 3½", short wine	525.00		525.00
Goblet, 4", cocktail	35.00		35.00
4 ▶ Goblet, 4½", wine	40.00		40.00
Goblet, 5¾", 9 ounce	25.00		28.00
5 ▶ Goblet, 7¼", 9 ounce, thin		25.00	
Ice bucket	40.00		95.00
Ice tub or butter tub, open	55.00		110.00
Mug	35.00		
1 ▶ Pitcher, 6", 36 ounce, juice			450.00
2 ▶ Pitcher, 7⅝", 54 ounce, bulbous	90.00		400.00
3 ▶ Pitcher, 8½", 54 ounce	55.00		50.00
9 ▶ Pitcher, 8", 80 ounce	90.00		150.00
8 ▶ Plate, 6", sherbet	2.00	2.00	2.00

	Green	Yellow	Pink
7 ▶ Plate, 8", luncheon	6.00	7.00	7.00
Plate, 9", dinner	22.00	45.00	35.00
6 ▶ Plate, 9", grill	150.00	125.00	
Plate, 10¼", sandwich	22.00		22.00
Plate, 12¾"	35.00		
Salt and pepper, footed, pair	40.00	80.00	75.00
Salt and pepper, squatty, pair	100.00		
Sandwich server, center handle	60.00		60.00
Saucer, 5¾", with cup ring	8.00		7.00
15 ▶ Saucer, 6⅛", with cup ring	8.00		7.00
Sherbet, non-stemmed (cone)	3.00		
Sherbet, 3¼", 5½ ounce	5.00	9.00	6.00
13 ▶ Sherbet, 4¾", 6 ounce	15.00	18.00	15.00
11 ▶ Sugar, 3 styles: as creamer	11.00	12.00	12.50
Tumbler, 3 ounce, 2⅝"	25.00		30.00
Tumbler, 5 ounce, 3½", flat	22.00		25.00
Tumbler, 9½ ounce, 3¹³⁄₁₆", flat	12.00		15.00
Tumbler, 10 or 11 oz., 5", flat	16.00		15.00
Tumbler, 12 ounce, 4⅞", flat	25.00		22.00
Tumbler, 15 ounce, 5¼", flat	45.00		45.00
Tumbler, 3 ounce, 3¼", footed	30.00		30.00
Tumbler, 9 ounce, footed	18.00	27.50	17.00
Tumbler, 6", 10 ounce, footed	35.00		38.00
Tumble-up night set	75.00		
Tumbler, 3" only	60.00		
Bottle only	15.00		
Vase, 5¾", blown	365.00		
Whiskey, 1⅝", 1 ounce	45.00		45.00
10 ▶ Whiskey, 2¼", 2 ounce	30.00		30.00

* Amber $45.00
** Green clambroth $250.00, blue $500.00, crystal $150.00
‡ Amber $50.00

Tumblers, left to right: 15 ounce, 5¼"; 12 ounce, 4⅞"; 9½ ounce, 3¹³⁄₁₆"; 5 ounce, 3½"; 3 ounce, 2⅝"; 2 ounce, 2¼"; 1 ounce, 1⅝".

Bowls: 4½", 5¼", 7¼".

Left, heavy moulded sherbet; right, thin blown sherbet.

Left to right: 9 ounce, 7¼" goblet; 6 ounce, 4¾" sherbet; 9 ounce, 5¾" water; 3 ounce, 3½" short wine; 3½ ounce, 4½" wine; 3 ounce, 4" cocktail.

Cups, bottom row, left to right: rounded plain handle; mug; angled handle. Top row: rounded fancy handle; cone-shaped; pointed handle.

Creamers and sugars, left to right: rounded plain handle; cone-shaped pointed handle; flat; cone-shaped plain handle; round fancy handle.

It has been our experience that "Bowknot" pieces sell well, when we can find them! Depression glass novices should know that many dealers do not carry smaller patterns such as "Bowknot" to glass shows because they take up the same precious space as more expensive items or patterns having numerous collectors. Space is at a premium in a show booth and increasing expenses (gas, food, motel, and booth rent) curtail profits before the first customer arrives. As a consequence, smaller patterns are often left behind, and you will have to ask if the dealers have any pieces in inventory that they did not bring.

Normally, "Bowknot" was heavily used, so it is necessary to check pieces for inner rim roughness (irr), particularly on the bowls and sherbets. Cereal bowls and tumblers are on many collectors' wish lists. There are two styles of tumblers, a footed and a flat version. The flat tumbler seems to be rarer than the footed one and is missing from our photo.

No saucer has turned up for the cup, but that is not too surprising. It was a practice back then to produce custard cups alone. People don't drink custard much these days, but judging from the pages of these found in older company catalogs, it seems to have been a very popular beverage back then, equivalent to our ice cream consumption today.

5 ▸	Bowl, 4½", berry	20.00
	Bowl, 5½", cereal	25.00
2 ▸	Cup	8.00
3 ▸	Plate, 6¾", salad	10.00
4 ▸	Sherbet, low footed	18.00
	Tumbler, 5", 10 ounce	22.00
1 ▸	Tumbler, 5", 10 ounce, footed	18.00

CAMEO, "BALLERINA," or "DANCING GIRL," Hocking Glass Company, 1930 – 1934
Colors: green, yellow, pink, and crystal w/platinum rim (See Reproduction Section.)

We receive numerous letters and e-mails about rare, unidentified pieces of Cameo being found. Just last week, we had an e-mail from someone who had inherited a collection with numerous small pieces that were not listed in our book. Had he read the copy instead of just the prices, he would have seen that we mention that miniature pieces have been made as children's pieces and called "Jennifer" sets by the Mosser Glass Company in Cambridge, Ohio. All miniature pieces with the Cameo design have been made in the last 20 years. These were never made originally by Hocking. The so-called undiscovered pieces such as salt dips or miniature bowls are also items from this children's set production. We've now seen the miniature comport peddled as a rare item and as a salt dip. If you see a small piece that looks like a smaller version of a normally found Cameo item, it is likely new! See the Reproduction Section (page 242) regarding these "Jennifer" sets. We have noticed that these have sometimes fetched laughable sums from the unaware on Internet auctions.

While we are discussing what isn't Cameo, be sure to look at Springtime (page 212) for the pattern (now collectible) from which Cameo was apparently derived. Monongah's glass was plate etched, made in crystal, and usually was gold trimmed. Hocking took the plate etchings and converted them into their moulds when they absorbed that plant into their growing concern.

We should remind you of the imported, weakly patterned shakers that appeared a few years ago in pink, and a darker green and cobalt blue color that were never made originally. Don't buy these bogus items, and if no one buys them, maybe they will stop producing them. We borrowed the one in the reproduction section (page 242) so we would not add to the coffers of the makers.

The centered-handled sandwich server and short, 3½" wines (both pictured) are the rarest pieces found in Cameo. A few pink wines are being found but lately no more green ones. A yellow, 15 ounce, flat Cameo tumbler is pictured beside the 11 ounce tumbler to illustrate the differences in their sizes. A dozen of these unusual 15 oz. tumblers were found and quickly were absorbed into collections. Cameo yellow butter dishes and milk pitchers are rare. However, yellow cups, saucer/sherbet plates, footed waters, dinner and grill plates abound and go begging unless priced inexpensively. They can be bought almost as cheaply as new dishes, so if yellow appeals to you, now would be a great time to snatch some.

That rare Cameo saucer has an indented "sunken" 1¾" diameter cup ring. Hocking typically made a smooth center, dual-purpose saucer/sherbet plate for their patterns that will accommodate the foot of a sherbet. No recessed ring, yellow Cameo saucers have ever been confirmed even though we get a dozen or so letters a year from people not comprehending what an indented recess is. It's like a 1¾" hole or pond in the smooth surface of the piece that the foot of the cup fits exactly.

Collecting a large set of green Cameo can be accomplished without spending a fortune if you do not purchase the rarer pieces and settle on only one or two sizes of stems or tumblers.

Two styles of grill ("t" shape dividers) plates exist. One has tab handles and one does not. Both styles are common in yellow. However, the green grill with the tab or closed handles is harder to find. Today's collectors do not seem to care as much about this as we older collectors did. The 10½" rare, rimmed dinner or flat cake plate is a heavy edged (no tabs) grill plate sans dividers. The one pictured has an optic center. Regular dinner plates have a large center as opposed to the small centered sandwich plate, though people use both as dinners since they are similarly priced.

Cameo designed dark green bottles are marked on the bottom "Whitehouse Vinegar." These were sold with a cork. The water bottle stopper does not have the Cameo design, and is still harder to find than the bottom.

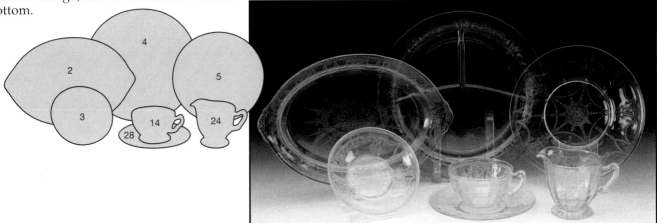

29

Cameo

	Green	Yellow	Pink	Crystal w/ plat.
Bowl, 4¼", sauce				8.00
Bowl, 4¾", cream soup	175.00			
3 ▸ Bowl, 5½", cereal	35.00	35.00	130.00	8.00
26 ▸ Bowl, 7¼", salad	65.00			
23 ▸ Bowl, 8¼", large berry	40.00		150.00	
Bowl, 9", rimmed soup	75.00		200.00	
21 ▸ Bowl, 10", oval vegetable	35.00	45.00		
Bowl, 11", 3-legged console	85.00	110.00	75.00	
27 ▸ Butter dish and cover	200.00	1,350.00		
Butter dish bottom	135.00	450.00		
Butter dish top	65.00	900.00		
29 ▸ Cake plate, 10", 3 legs	20.00			
Cake plate, 10½", flat	100.00		150.00	
13 ▸ Candlesticks, 4", pair	110.00			
12 ▸ Candy jar, 4", low, and cover	80.00	100.00	595.00	
Candy jar, 6½", tall, and cover	195.00			
Cocktail shaker (metal lid) appears in crystal only			795.00	
Comport, 5⅜" wide, mayonnaise	38.00		225.00	
1 ▸ Cookie jar and cover	60.00			
24 ▸ Creamer, 3¼"	18.00	16.00		
Creamer, 4¼"	28.00		125.00	
14 ▸ Cup, 2 styles	12.00	8.00	85.00	5.50
6 ▸ Decanter, 10", with stopper	165.00			300.00
Decanter, 10", with stopper, frosted (stopper represents ⅓ value of decanter)	35.00			
30 ▸ Domino tray, 7", with 3" indentation	200.00			
Domino tray, 7", with no indentation			275.00	175.00
43 ▸ Goblet, 3½", wine	750.00		400.00	
10 ▸ Goblet, 4", wine	72.00		200.00	
11 ▸ Goblet, 6", water	62.00		165.00	
42 ▸ Ice bowl or open butter, 3" tall x 5½" wide	200.00		750.00	395.00
Jam jar, 2", and cover	240.00		175.00	
Pitcher, 5¾", 20 ounce, syrup or milk	295.00	2,000.00		

	Green	Yellow	Pink	Crystal w/ plat.
Pitcher, 6", 36 oz., juice	70.00			
18 ▸ Pitcher, 8½", 56 oz., water	60.00		1,500.00	500.00
28 ▸ Plate, 6", sherbet	3.00	2.00	90.00	2.00
Plate, 7", salad				3.50
5 ▸ Plate, 8", luncheon	10.00	8.00	30.00	4.00
22 ▸ Plate, 8½", square	40.00	250.00		
35 ▸ Plate, 9½", dinner	20.00	8.00	85.00	
Plate, 10", sandwich	20.00		55.00	
47 ▸ **Plate, 10½", rimmed, dinner	100.00		195.00	
4 ▸ Plate, 10½", grill	12.00	10.00	50.00	
20 ▸ Plate, 10½", grill with closed handles	60.00	6.00		
48 ▸ Plate, 10½", with closed handles	18.00	14.00		
2 ▸ Platter, 12", closed handles	28.00	40.00		
Relish, 7½", footed, 3 part	28.00			195.00
*Salt and pepper, ftd., pr.	65.00		900.00	
44 ▸ Sandwich server, center handle	6,000.00			
9 ▸ Saucer with cup ring	225.00			
Saucer, 6" (sherbet plate)	3.00	2.00	90.00	2.00
7 ▸ Sherbet, 3⅛", molded	15.00	35.00	75.00	
Sherbet, 3⅛", blown	16.00		75.00	
14 ▸ Sherbet, 4⅞"	30.00	100.00	135.00	
25 ▸ Sugar, 3¼"	16.00	20.00		
Sugar, 4¼"	25.00		125.00	
15 ▸ Tumbler, 3¾", 5 oz., juice	30.00		90.00	
16 ▸ Tumbler, 4", 9 oz., water	24.00		80.00	10.00
Tumbler, 4¾", 10 oz., flat	26.00		95.00	
46 ▸ Tumbler, 5", 11 oz., flat	30.00	80.00	110.00	
45 ▸ Tumbler, 5¼", 15 oz.	70.00	350.00	135.00	
Tumbler, 3 oz., footed, juice	70.00		135.00	
17 ▸ Tumbler, 5", 9 oz., footed	26.00	18.00	115.00	
19 ▸ Tumbler, 5¾", 11 oz., ftd.	60.00		135.00	
Tumbler, 6⅜", 15 oz., ftd.	650.00			
Vase, 5¾"	295.00			
Vase, 8"	40.00			
Water bottle (dark green) Whitehouse vinegar	30.00			

* Beware reproductions
** Same as flat cake plate

Cameo

Experimental item

42

43

30

27

44

45

46

CHERRYBERRY, U.S. Glass Company, Early 1930s

Colors: pink, green, crystal; some iridized

Cherryberry is one of several patterns that have stayed on the periphery of glass collecting. It is so similar to Strawberry that it is often confused even by collectors looking for that pattern. Neither berry has been picked in vast numbers due, in part, to its short supply. Because there was a Cherry Blossom pattern already being hunted, the Cherryberry name was coined to differentiate it from the already accepted Strawberry.

As is the case of other U.S. Glass patterns, Cherryberry has no cup, saucer, or designed butter base. Only the top of the butter carries the motif. All of the U.S. Glass Depression era patterns are from similar moulds but Strawberry and Cherryberry are twins. You can only distinguish them with careful examination.

Meticulous collectors have always found fault with most U. S. Glass patterns which have protruding mould seams and color inconsistencies. For instance, green hues can be found from a very yellow tint to a blue one. There is not as much color variation with the pink, but there are some pieces that are conspicuously pale. If you consider the standards used in the manufacture of this older glassware (less controlled than today), then the resulting burned out or poor quality color matches were an inherent part of this and should be of little concern. However, if you are a collector who is bothered by various color tones, Cherryberry may not be for you.

Although most U.S. Glass patterns do not have as full a complement of pieces as do those of other companies, there are various collector fields contending for the same items. Carnival glass followers look for iridized pitchers, tumblers, and butters which are precious pieces in their world. Then, too, there are "item" collectors for butter dishes and pitchers who also acquire those. Today, there appear to be fewer item collectors than in the past, but those there are have done a great job of eliminating certain items from the marketplace.

Crystal Cherryberry can be found occasionally, and is doubtless rare, but there is little demand for it, and thus, prices are unaffected.

		Crystal, Iridescent	Pink, Green
	Bowl, 4", berry	6.50	12.00
5 ▸	Bowl, 5⅛"	25.00	
	Bowl, 6¼", 2" deep	50.00	140.00
1 ▸	Bowl, 6½", deep, salad	20.00	25.00
	Butter dish and cover	130.00	150.00
	Butter dish bottom	60.00	80.00
	Butter dish top	70.00	70.00
	Comport, 5¾"	18.00	25.00
4 ▸	Creamer, small	11.00	20.00
	Creamer, 4⅝", large	16.00	35.00
	Olive dish, 5", one-handled	9.00	18.00
	Pickle dish, 8¼", oval	9.00	18.00
	Pitcher, 7¾"	165.00	165.00
2 ▸	Plate, 6", sherbet	6.00	9.00
	Plate, 7½", salad	7.50	12.00
	Sherbet	6.50	8.00
3 ▸	Sugar, small, open	11.00	20.00
	Sugar, large	15.00	20.00
	Sugar cover	25.00	40.00
	Tumbler, 3⅝", 9 ounce	20.00	33.00

CHERRY BLOSSOM, Jeannette Glass Company, 1930 – 1939
Colors: pink, green, Delphite (opaque blue), crystal, Jadite (opaque green), and red (See Reproduction Section.)

Cherry Blossom collectors have been one of the remaining bright spots in Depression glass. Although prices have adjusted somewhat downward in the present economy, pieces are selling. Over the years Cherry Blossom has had its ups and downs. It started in the 70s when reproductions first appeared and prices plummeted for a few years. After a while, everyone was well informed and reproductions were ignored. If you are a beginner, turn to the Reproduction Section in the back of the book and educate yourself on Cherry Blossom reproductions. (See pages 244 – 245.)

Collectors are always capricious and Cherry Blossom seems to emphasize their quirks. Prices began diminishing five or six years ago on basic dinnerware items, but not the harder to find pieces. That development has persisted and cups, saucers, and dinner plates can now be purchased at prices of years ago. Supply outweighs the demand and collectors are noticing and beginning to buy the ever popular Cherry Blossom once again.

That 9" platter remains the most difficult piece to find (after genuine pink shakers). A badly chipped one just sold on an Internet auction for $22.50. Chipped glass is usually ignored, unless rare. Only a couple of green 9" platters have materialized. (Measure this platter outside edge to outside edge.) The commonly found 11" platter measures 9" from the inside to inside rim and there is quite a price difference. Mugs have become a bit more common than in the past due to Internet exposure. Mugs still remain on collectors' "most wanted" lists.

Other Cherry Blossom items that are hard to attain include flat iced teas, soup or cereal bowls, and the 10" green grill plate. (That larger grill plate has never even been found in pink.) Mint condition grill plates are a prize. Mint is the operative word since damaged ones are available. All Cherry Blossom is subject to inner rim chips, nicks, or those famous "chigger bites" as auctioneers call them. Inner rim roughness (irr) was caused as much from stacking glass together as from using it. You can carefully store dishes (bowls or plates) with paper plates/bowls between them. This is specifically true at glass shows or antique malls where stacks of items are mishandled and clanged together repeatedly.

Keep in mind that only two pairs of original pink Cherry Blossom shakers were ever documented and as far as we know, have never resurfaced for sale after being sold into collections in the past 30 years. (Original ones are pictured on page 35.) We have lost count, but several dozen times we've received calls or e-mails about that third pair being "found." None of these were real. The country has been absolutely flooded with reproduction Cherry shakers with their squared, jut wing collars. We do request that if you solicit us for verification, that you trust our judgment of 40 years experience. More than once, we have given our honest opinion only to be told we are wrong. If you do not want to know, please don't ask.

Cherry Blossom was made for 10 years and there were many experimental colors and items made. Today, there is not the demand for these pieces as there was 20 or 30 years ago. They are rare, but demand has lessened; so has the price. Some known experimental pieces of Cherry Blossom include a pink cookie jar, pink five-part relish dishes, green covered casserole, orange with green trim slag bowls, and amber children's pieces. Note the opaque red bowl with yellow rim pictured. A few red (both opaque and transparent) and yellow pieces have surfaced, but the reproduction transparent red wiped out most collectors' desire to own the beautiful old transparent red. Original transparent red was glossy. You can see most of these pieces pictured in our *Treasures of Very Rare Depression Glass*.

AOP in our listings and advertisements stands for "all over pattern" on the footed tumblers and pitchers. The large, footed tumblers and the AOP pitcher come in two styles. One style has a scalloped or indented foot while the other is merely round with no indentations. Sherbets are also found like that. PAT stands for "pattern at the top," illustrated by the flat-bottomed tumblers and pitchers.

We used to list two sizes of flat PAT pitchers in earlier books, and somehow between third and fourth edition the 36 oz. pitcher was omitted. This time we are displaying them side by side so you can see there is a difference in shape. Also note the experimental pink pitcher, which looks like Jeannette first started to make a footed, round, PAT pitcher.

Experimental pitcher

		Pink	Green	Delphite
23 ▸	Bowl, 4¾", berry	13.00	16.00	16.00
	Bowl, 5¾", cereal	45.00	50.00	
	Bowl, 7¾", flat soup	90.00	80.00	
10 ▸	*Bowl, 8½", round berry	45.00	48.00	40.00
	Bowl, 9", oval vegetable	40.00	40.00	40.00
6 ▸	Bowl, 9", 2-handled	40.00	75.00	25.00
	**Bowl, 10½", 3-leg, fruit	80.00	90.00	
11 ▸	Butter dish and cover	75.00	110.00	
	Butter dish bottom	15.00	20.00	
	Butter dish top	60.00	90.00	
13 ▸	Cake plate (3 legs), 10¼"	32.00	35.00	
17 ▸	Coaster	10.00	12.00	
20 ▸	Creamer	15.00	16.00	16.00
9 ▸	Cup	15.00	17.00	17.00
15 ▸	Mug, 7 oz.	400.00	375.00	
19 ▸	‡Pitcher, 6¾", AOP, 36 ounce scalloped or round bottom	70.00	60.00	70.00
2 ▸	Pitcher, 7¼", PAT, 42 ounce, flat	70.00	70.00	
	Pitcher, 7¾", PAT, 36 ounce, footed	70.00	70.00	
1 ▸	Pitcher, PAT, 36 ounce, flat	70.00	70.00	
	Plate, 6", sherbet	7.00	9.00	8.00
	Plate, 7", salad	20.00	20.00	
22 ▸	‡‡Plate, 9", dinner	1.00	20.00	20.00
3 ▸	§Plate, 9", grill	25.00	28.00	
	Plate, 10", grill		100.00	
	Platter, 9", oval	950.00	1,100.00	
16 ▸	Platter, 11", oval	40.00	50.00	35.00
	Platter, 13"	50.00	80.00	
	Platter, 13", divided	60.00	70.00	
4 ▸	Salt and pepper (scalloped bottom)	1,300.00	1,100.00	
12 ▸	Saucer	2.00	3.00	3.00
8 ▸	Sherbet	14.00	16.00	15.00
19 ▸	Sugar	11.00	14.00	16.00
	Sugar cover	18.00	18.00	
14 ▸	Tray, 10½", sandwich	24.00	30.00	20.00
18 ▸	Tumbler, 3¾", 4 ounce, footed, AOP	14.00	20.00	20.00
7 ▸	Tumbler, 4½", 9 ounce, round, footed, AOP	32.00	35.00	18.00
5 ▸	Tumbler, 4½", 8 ounce, scalloped, footed, AOP	32.00	35.00	18.00
	Tumbler, 3½", 4 ounce, flat, PAT	18.00	28.00	
	Tumbler, 4¼", 9 ounce, flat, PAT	16.00	22.00	
	Tumbler, 5", 12 ounce, flat, PAT	65.00	75.00	

* Yellow	$395.00	‡‡ Translucent green $225.00
** Jadite	$325.00	§ Jadite $85.00
‡ Jadite	$325.00	

CHERRY BLOSSOM — CHILD S JUNIOR DINNER SET

		Pink	Delphite
	Creamer	25.00	22.50
	Sugar	25.00	22.50
	Plate, 6" (design on bottom)	5.00	5.00
24 ▸	Cup	25.00	22.50
25 ▸	Saucer	2.00	3.00
	14 piece set	180.00	175.00

Original box sells for $35.00 extra with pink sets.

15

4

6

Experimental item

CHINEX CLASSIC, MacBeth-Evans Division of Corning Glass Works, Late 1930s – Early 1940s

Colors: ivory, ivory w/decal decoration

Chinex Classic collectors are few and far between. Few collect plain, undecorated ivory pieces; so if you like that color, you could purchase a small useable set as inexpensively as buying currently made dinnerware. If compared to other patterns, prices remain inexpensive even for the harder to find pieces. There are not the thousands seeking Chinex so collectors can be choosy about their purchases.

For some reason, this pattern has never caught on as well as others. The multitude of decorations and scarcity in finding them are likely culprits. If you find a decoration you like, start with that. Even pieces offered on Internet auctions do not cause bidding wars; so there is one place you can shop for Chinex.

You will have trouble matching florals found on ivory tint and related Cremax ware. We have been told that the undecorated scroll designed Chinex Classic works well in the microwave, but we have not tried it. Nor have we heard what happens to decaled items used that way.

Collectors are fond of the Windsor castle decals but there, too, a problem exists with different shades of colors. Darker blue trims appear to be more admired than the lighter blue or brown. They are, also, more tricky to unearth. The brown Windsor castle comes with or without a brown trim as pictured. We see "more" brown decorated wares, but that is somewhat misleading as only a dozen or so pieces are offered for sale at shows each year. We understand brown is an "in" color, of late in the fashion world.

We see more Chinex in the Pittsburgh and eastern Pennsylvania area since MacBeth Evans was located near there. There is a large reasonably priced set in an antique mall that has sat for at least three years. Sometimes it makes more sense to price pieces individually than to try to sell 120 pieces to one buyer. Marketing glassware is not a science, but more collectors have $20.00 to spend than have $500.00.

The most recent sightings have been made in Canada where Corning was a mainstay in glass production. Chinex was made to challenge chinaware that crazed and chipped. It was promoted as resistant to crazing and chipping which helps explain its comparatively excellent condition, today, and was a good marketing point. You may find a few pieces marked Corning on the back, but not many.

Butter tops and bottoms are becoming scarce as more collectors are involved in buying older glassware. Matching Chinex tops to bottoms is a considerable chore if you are lucky enough to spot a butter part. The butter bottom looks like the Cremax (pie crust) pattern on the edge rather than Chinex. The butter tops have the scroll-like design that distinguishes Chinex, but this scroll design is missing from the butter bottoms. The floral or castle designs will be inside the base of the butter, and ostensibly surrounding the knob of the top if the top is floral decorated.

		Browntone or Plain Ivory	Decal decorated	Castle decal
1 ▶	Bowl, 5¾", cereal	4.00	6.00	15.00
11 ▶	Bowl, 6¾", salad	10.00	16.00	30.00
	Bowl, 7", vegetable	12.00	20.00	30.00
	Bowl, 7¾", soup	11.00	16.00	30.00
6 ▶	Bowl, 9", vegetable	9.00	20.00	30.00
	Bowl, 11"	14.00	30.00	35.00
	Butter dish	45.00	60.00	120.00
8 ▶	Butter dish bottom	10.00	20.00	30.00
7 ▶	Butter dish top	35.00	40.00	90.00
9 ▶	Creamer	5.00	10.00	18.00
12 ▶	Cup	4.00	6.00	10.00
4 ▶	Plate, 6¼", sherbet	2.00	3.00	6.00
10 ▶	Plate, 9¾", dinner	4.00	8.00	12.00
5 ▶	Plate, 11½", sandwich or cake	7.00	12.00	20.00
13 ▶	Saucer	1.50	2.00	3.00
2 ▶	Sherbet, low footed	6.00	10.00	20.00
3 ▶	Sugar	5.00	10.00	18.00

Chinex Classic

CIRCLE, Hocking Glass Company, 1930s
Colors: green, pink, and crystal

Green Circle is the only color that can be collected in large sets over time. Where did all five sizes of bowls disappear? Prices for bowls have steadily increased due to demand being placed on that small supply. Demand is usually the determining factor in higher prices; but rarity comes into play with Circle's bowls. From time to time, a piece is so rare that few care; but that is not the case with Circle.

Excluding those bowls, Circle is sensibly priced, but not so simply found. Pink apparently appears only as a luncheon set. We are having trouble finding pink in any quantity. Many pieces thought to be common in the early days of collecting are not. If you have a piece of pink not in the listing, please let us know.

Crystal occurs only as stems; and most crystal stems are found with green tops. Bi-colored green stems with crystal tops are more easily found than entirely green stems. In many Elegant patterns, two-toned stems are more expensive and avidly sought. This has not yet proven true for Circle. The good news is that you can buy these inexpensively should you desire the two-tone effect.

Kitchenware collectors (specifically reamer collectors) are aware of Circle. They treasure that 80-ounce pitcher which is found with a reamer top. Color variations between the pitcher and reamers make buying them separately, "iffy" at best. There seems to be more of the darker green pitchers found, but the reamers are usually found in the lighter green shade.

There are three different small bowls pictured to show you the differences. They range from 4½" to 5¼" with the flared one measuring 5", but it is clearly a darker shade of green when compared with the other pieces.

Both the 9⅜" and 5¼" green bowls pictured have ground bottoms. With Hocking patterns, ground bottoms and a darker shade of green usually suggest early production. Those ground bottoms and dark green color can often be found in Cameo pieces also.

Quirks in Circle are further demonstrated by two different styles of cups. A flat-bottomed style fits only a saucer/sherbet plate while the rounded cup takes an indented saucer. Pink is found in both styles, but not easily.

		Green	Pink
15 ▸	Bowl, 4½", deep	17.50	
8 ▸	Bowl, 5¼"	28.00	
9 ▸	Bowl, 5", flared, 1¾" deep	30.00	
12 ▸	Bowl, 8"	35.00	
	Bowl, 9⅜"	40.00	
8 ▸	Creamer	7.00	25.00
3 ▸	Cup (2 styles)	5.00	10.00
	Goblet, 4½", wine	10.00	
	Goblet, 8 ounce, water	9.00	
	Pitcher, 60 ounce	65.00	
5 ▸	Pitcher, 80 ounce	35.00	
10 ▸	Plate, 6", sherbet/saucer	2.00	5.00
	Plate, 8¼", luncheon	5.00	10.00
	Plate, 9½"	10.00	
6 ▸	Plate, 10", sandwich	12.00	
	Saucer w/cup ring	2.50	3.00
13 ▸	Sherbet, 3⅛"	4.00	10.00
1 ▸	Sherbet, 4¾"	6.00	
7 ▸	Sugar	6.00	25.00
	Tumbler, 3½", 4 ounce, juice	8.00	
	Tumbler, 4", 8 ounce, water	9.00	
2 ▸	Tumbler, 5", 10 ounce, tea	15.00	
	Tumbler, 15 ounce, flat	28.00	

CLOVERLEAF, Hazel-Atlas Glass Company, 1930 – 1936
Colors: pink, green, yellow, crystal, and black

The Cloverleaf pattern is easy to identify. Even the non-collecting public notices the "good luck" symbols on the glass and exclaims over it when displayed. However, you may well need the "luck of the Irish" to find the bowls in this pattern no matter the color. All bowls, in any color, as well as grill plates and tumblers are becoming extremely difficult to garner.

Collectors of green Cloverleaf have a broad assortment of pieces from which to choose. Luckily, it is the most wanted color. Again, the 5" cereal, straight-sided 8" bowl, and tumblers are rarely offered for sale. Of the three styles of tumblers pictured, it is the flat, straight-sided, cylinder shaped one, available only in green, which is often missing in collections.

If you wish a dinner-sized plate, the grill (three-part) will have to suffice, since the luncheon plate is only 8". Collectors of yellow will find the candy dish, shakers, and bowls in short supply. We have only found one yellow cereal bowl in our travels and few of the other sized bowls.

Very few collectors hunt the elusive pink or crystal. Besides a luncheon set in pink, a berry bowl and a flared, 10 ounce tumbler can be found. That pink tumbler was meagerly circulated and has not yet been discovered in crystal.

Prices for the used-to-be-exciting Deco black Cloverleaf have begun to slip over the last few years due to supply outweighing demand. Once enticing small ashtrays are often ignored; but the larger ones still sell occasionally. For a while, there were collectors seeking all cigarette items and one nationally known author on antiques touted them as the new trend of collectibles. As with other movements, that fad appears to have waned, although there are collectors still searching for tobacco collectibles, just not as many as there once were.

We need to draw attention to the sherbet plate and saucer being the same size. The saucer has no Cloverleaf design in the center, but the sherbet plate does. Because sherbet plates sporadically are found in stacks of saucers, you should check each one. In 1972, we ordered a saucer to go with an odd cup. When it arrived, it was different from our other saucers. Thus the sherbet plate became a new listing.

It does not make any difference if the Cloverleaf pattern is inside or outside. In order for the black to show the pattern, moulds had to be designed with the pattern on the top or outside of pieces; otherwise, it looked like unadorned black. On transparent pieces, the pattern could be on either side and it would still show. Over the years, transparent pieces were made using the moulds designed for the black; thus, you now find pieces with the pattern on either the top or bottom.

		Pink	Green	Yellow	Black
	Ashtray, 4", match holder in center				50.00
	Ashtray, 5¾", match holder in center				60.00
3 ▸	Bowl, 4", dessert	20.00	40.00	40.00	
2 ▸	Bowl, 5", cereal		58.00	55.00	
4 ▸	Bowl, 7", deep salad		80.00	100.00	
8 ▸	Bowl, 8"		110.00		
1 ▸	Candy dish and cover		65.00	115.00	
12 ▸	Creamer, 3⅝", footed		13.00	20.00	10.00
10 ▸	Cup	8.00	8.00	10.00	10.00
6 ▸	Plate, 6", sherbet		12.00	8.00	25.00
5 ▸	Plate, 8", luncheon	10.00	8.00	12.00	12.00
7 ▸	Plate, 10¼", grill		30.00	30.00	
13 ▸	Salt and pepper, pair		40.00	125.00	75.00
11 ▸	Saucer	2.00	2.00	3.00	4.00
17 ▸	Sherbet, 3", footed	9.00	8.00	10.00	10.00
9 ▸	Sugar, 3⅝", footed		10.00	20.00	10.00
16 ▸	Tumbler, 4", 9 ounce, flat		60.00		
15 ▸	Tumbler, 3¾", 10 ounce, flat, flared	30.00	50.00		
14 ▸	Tumbler, 5¾", 10 ounce, footed		30.00	35.00	

COLONIAL, "KNIFE AND FORK," Hocking Glass Company, 1934 – 1936

Colors: pink, green, crystal, and Vitrock (white)

Green Colonial is still the color of choice for collectors. Rapid price escalations have become a thing of the past, so now might be the right time to buy pieces you have been putting off. Prices for pink Colonial are comparable to those of green due to scarcity more than demand. Were pink as hunted as green, prices would leap ahead of the green. Crystal Colonial collecting would be a great starting place for a beginner that will not drain your bank account. If you like the look of older pattern glass, this is for you. There is speculation that the name was chosen since this pattern was designed to look like older glassware.

Collecting Colonial has been consistent. New admirers begin and older ones sell their collections; so a supply replenishes itself. Rarer pieces are disappearing into long-time collections. Prices of rare items may shock beginners, but today's high price may turn out to be tomorrow's bargain.

Only one pink and one green beaded top pitcher have been unearthed, although it is doubtful only one of each was made. Both of these have been pictured in previous books. We buy rare items to photograph, and then pass them on to ardent collectors. Thus, you get to see rarely found items that you may never encounter in your travels.

There are three sizes of footed tumblers and five different stems in Colonial. Do not confuse the footed tumblers with stems. Review our legend of pieces to tell the difference.

The cheese dish consists of a wooden board with an indented groove upon which the glass lid rests as can be seen in crystal.

Coveted Colonial mugs are rarely found. The 11-ounce Colonial tumbler measures 2¾" across the top while the 12 ounce measures exactly 3". These two tumblers are often confused with each other. There is a price difference, although not as great as once was. It is more uncomplicated to measure across the top than to measure the contents if you are out shopping. The spooner is 5½" tall, while the sugar without a lid is only 4½". Rarely is that inch difference as mistaken today as in the past.

Colonial soup bowls (both cream and flat), cereals, and unscratched dinner plates remain difficult to obtain in any color. The pronounced ridges on Colonial pieces have a tendency to damage; so look at those ridges first when buying and stack with paper plates between them when owning. Always take the top off any shaker to check for damage. There may be a big surprise of missing glass under that top if you do not check before buying. Been there, done that.

Vitrock (white) Colonial items are showing up more frequently. So far, we have seen cream soups and liners, water pitchers, cups, saucers (two styles), luncheon plates, creamers, and sugar bowls. No top has been spotted for that sugar. Vitrock has been largely ignored in the past due to its limited availability, but now a small set might be feasible.

1

33

	Pink	Green	Crystal
7 ▶ Plate, 8½", luncheon	9.00	10.00	5.00
28 ▶ *Plate, 10", dinner	50.00	55.00	20.00
26 ▶ *Plate, 10", grill	25.00	25.00	15.00
12 ▶ *Platter, 12", oval	25.00	25.00	20.00
6 ▶ Salt and pepper, pair	130.00	110.00	50.00
33 ▶ Saucer/sherbet plate, white $3	5.00	7.00	3.00
Sherbet, 3"	25.00		
2 ▶ Sherbet, 3⅜"	11.00	14.00	7.00
25 ▶ *Spoon holder or celery, 5½"	120.00	120.00	75.00
10 ▶ *Stem, 3¾", 1 oz., cordial		25.00	15.00
15 ▶ *Stem, 4", 3 oz., cocktail		20.00	11.00
32 ▶ *Stem, 4½", 2½ oz., wine		20.00	11.00
21 ▶ *Stem, 5¼", 4 oz., claret		20.00	17.00
34 ▶ *Stem, 5¾", 8½ oz., water		24.00	20.00
30 ▶ *Sugar, 4½"	25.00	15.00	6.00
31 ▶ *Sugar cover	65.00	25.00	15.00
9 ▶ Tumbler, 3", 5 oz., juice	18.00	20.00	12.00
4 ▶ **Tumbler, 4", 9 oz., water	17.00	18.00	12.00
8 ▶ Tumbler, 5⅛" high, 11 oz.	30.00	36.00	18.00
Tumbler, 12 oz., iced tea	42.00	42.00	18.00
19 ▶ *Tumbler, 15 oz., lemonade	55.00	65.00	35.00
13 ▶ *Tumbler, 3¼", 3 oz., footed	18.00	22.00	8.00
Tumbler, 4", 5 oz., footed	32.00	38.00	16.00
14 ▶ ‡Tumbler, 5¼", 10 oz., footed	50.00	50.00	22.00
23 ▶ *Whiskey, 2½", 1½ oz.	14.00	14.00	9.00

	Pink	Green	Crystal
17 ▶ *Bowl, 3¾", berry	60.00		
18 ▶ *Bowl, 4½", berry	18.00	12.00	8.00
16 ▶ *Bowl, 5½", cereal	60.00	85.00	30.00
1 ▶ Bowl, 4½", cream soup, white $60	65.00	75.00	55.00
Bowl, 7", low soup	65.00	70.00	30.00
3 ▶ Bowl, 9", large berry	26.00	28.00	20.00
11 ▶ *Bowl, 10", oval vegetable	38.00	35.00	20.00
24 ▶ Butter dish and cover	650.00	55.00	40.00
*Butter dish bottom	400.00	35.00	25.00
Butter dish top	250.00	20.00	15.00
27 ▶ *Cheese dish		250.00	
29 ▶ *Cream/milk pitcher, 5", 16 oz.	60.00	25.00	18.00
Cup, white $8	8.00	12.00	5.00
Mug, 4½", 12 oz.	600.00	800.00	
5 ▶ +Pitcher, 7", 54 oz.	45.00	50.00	30.00
20 ▶ *+Pitcher, 7¾", 68 oz., white $300	60.00	70.00	35.00
Plate, 6", sherbet/saucer	5.00	7.00	3.00

*Beaded top $1,250.00 ‡Royal ruby $175.00
**Royal ruby $125.00 +With or without ice lip

43

COLONIAL FLUTED, "ROPE," Federal Glass Company, 1928 – 1933

Colors: green and crystal

Federal's "F" in a shield is regularly embossed in the center of Colonial Fluted pieces. This symbol was used by Federal Glass Company to designate their glass, but was not on every piece. That "F" does not stand for Fire-King as we so often see items labeled. While here, let's state that H over A is Hazel Atlas Glass Company's mark and not Anchor-Hocking's. Many white Federal kitchenware items are similar to Fire-King products. More Federal Glass is shown in *Florences' Ovenware from the 1920s to the Present*.

There has not been a single different item in the Colonial Fluted pattern since we started writing in 1972. Usually a new find or color enlivens our writing, but not so with Colonial Fluted.

Colonial Fluted used to be a basic set for beginning collectors who wanted a reasonably priced green pattern to use. Currently, collectible quantities are so lacking that new collectors become discouraged looking for it. There are pieces of Colonial Fluted being found, but scratched and mutilated best describe those finds. Most flat pieces have heavy wear. Knife cuttings erode the surface of glassware and scratched plates in Colonial Fluted are evidence of that. It apparently was well used.

Bowls are very scarce and all are holding their prices. Apparently, these were not sold with basic luncheon sets and today their paucity is shown by their market price.

There is no dinner plate in the Colonial Fluted pattern, but there is a dinner-sized plate made by Federal that goes with this very well. It has the roping around the outside of the plate, but not the fluting. There is also a grill plate you could use with the pattern. It has no roping, but flutes. Both of these pieces can expand the number of items in your set. Federal made those items mentioned, therefore they match in color and many are even marked.

Colonial Fluted was sold as a bridge set. Poker is the card game of choice today and bridge parties are not the rage they were in the 1930s. Crystal decorated pieces with hearts, spades, diamonds, and clubs are very collectible — but infrequently spotted. These decorations are decals which may have worn off through the years.

		Green
	Bowl, 4", berry	12.00
2 ▸	Bowl, 6", cereal	15.00
	Bowl, 6½", deep (2½") salad	30.00
8 ▸	Bowl, 7½", large berry	20.00
4 ▸	Creamer	6.00
9 ▸	Cup	5.00
1 ▸	Plate, 6", sherbet	2.00
11 ▸	Plate, 8", luncheon	6.00
10 ▸	Saucer	1.00
12 ▸	Sherbet	6.00
7 ▸	Sugar	6.00
6 ▸	Sugar cover	14.00

* 3, 5 "go with" items

44

COLUMBIA, Federal Glass Company, 1938 – 1942
Colors: crystal, some pink

The butter dish in Columbia is the one piece of this pattern that proliferates today. This Federal product was profusely produced for dairy premiums in the Midwest with an assortment of decorations such as satinized and with flashed colors and/or floral patterns. Additional Columbia items are less frequently seen. You may well find Columbia water tumblers with advertisements for dairy products printed on them. These were commonly used as containers for cottage cheese.

Columbia tumblers were never easy to find; but, currently, there are other quandaries to sort out. Tumblers actually made include a 2⅞", four-ounce juice and a nine-ounce water. A "comparable" water tumbler has shown up which is marked "France" on the bottom. Collectors of Columbia need to be cognizant of this before shelling out for a foreign-made replica. We stress that any glassware marked France is not Depression glass and has been made in the last 20 years.

Pink Columbia sells remarkably well for a pattern that only has four known pieces, albeit prices for pink have slowed. Remember a few years ago when enough could not be found to keep up with collectors' requests?

The previously obscure (except in Colorado) snack tray has begun to turn up more often, causing the price to drop quite a bit. Many collectors have not known what to look for, since it is atypical and shaped unlike most Columbia. Our pictures in recent editions have shown the tray so well that collectors are finding these to the point that supply is overrunning demand right now. These snack plates were found packed with Columbia cups in a Federal Glass Company's boxed snack set over 30 years ago in northern Ohio. Snack trays are also being found with Federal cups other than the Columbia pattern, which is probably why so many are being located after all these years. We should point out that there are bowls and snack sets that are patterned like the Columbia snack tray. They do not have the raised center motif but do have the "winged" tab handles. These are being found in original Federal boxes identified as Homestead.

Satinized, pastel-banded, and floral-decaled luncheon sets in Columbia have surfaced. These sets are scarce and there are some collectors, who adore them.

		Crystal	Pink				Crystal	Pink
5 ▶	Bowl, 5", cereal	11.00				Butter dish top	11.00	
1 ▶	Bowl, 8", low soup	18.00		12 ▶	Cup	6.00	20.00
10 ▶	Bowl, 8½", salad	16.00		6 ▶	Plate, 6", bread & butter	3.00	12.00
4 ▶	Bowl, 10½", ruffled edge	16.00		9 ▶	Plate, 9½", luncheon	8.00	30.00
	Butter dish and cover	15.00		8 ▶	Plate, 11", chop	11.00	
3 ▶	Ruby flashed	22.00		11 ▶	Saucer	1.00	8.00
	Other flashed	21.00		13 ▶	Snack plate	16.00	
	Butter dish bottom	4.00		2 ▶	Tumbler, 2⅞", 4 ounce, juice	20.00	
				7 ▶	Tumbler, 9 ounce, water	20.00	

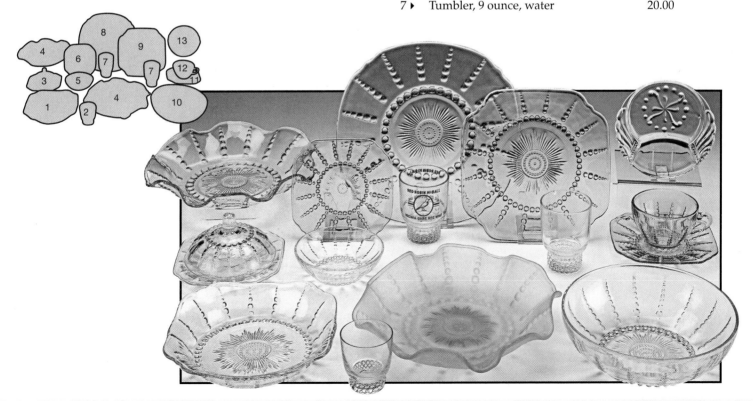

45

CORONATION, "BANDED RIB," "SAXON," Hocking Glass Company, 1936 – 1940
Colors: pink, green, crystal, and Royal Ruby

Anchor Hocking, in the late 1990s, made a pattern called Annapolis in pink and crystal that is based upon the Coronation design. Some pieces are shown on the right. We bought two pink iced teas noticing the resemblance to Coronation though something seemed awry. We packed them away determined to see what we could find out. On a buying trip we saw several crystal pieces and one was marked with Anchor Hocking's anchor symbol. Since then we have found catalog information picturing bowls and plates besides several sizes of tumblers, both footed and flat. Our teas were not marked. So if you see a piece not in our listings, consider it to be Annapolis and not Coronation.

Coronation was launched in 1936 and probably named for the coronation going on in England at that time. America was captivated since an American was involved with British royalty.

Many collectors are introduced to Coronation because of the tumbler's similarity to rarely found Old Colony ("Lace Edge") tumblers. There are many Old Colony collectors searching for elusive tumblers and some of them have bought Coronation tumblers by mistake. Others acquired them because they were cheaper and that demand raised the price on Coronation's tumblers. They have often been offered for sale as Old Colony. Please note the row of fine ribs above the middle of the Coronation tumbler. These ribs are missing on the Old Colony footed tumbler. Look on page 154 to see the differences with those shown on page 47. Both are the same shape and color and made by the same manufacturer. Just don't accidentally confuse the two since there is quite a price disparity.

Royal Ruby Coronation cups were sold with crystal, non-indented saucers. Those crystal saucer/sherbet plates are the only common crystal pieces found in Coronation. Recently, crystal saucers with an indented cup ring have been discovered, but no crystal cups for them. Only the crescent salad plate causes excitement in crystal. No Royal Ruby Coronation saucer or sherbet plates have ever been seen. Royal Ruby is the patented name of the red glass that was made by Hocking beginning in 1938. Only Hocking's red glassware can be called Royal Ruby.

The handles on Royal Ruby Coronation bowls are open; handles on the pink are closed. Two rarely found bowls in pink have emerged without handles. They measure 4¼" and 8", just like the established rare green ones. The items pictured in green Coronation are shown thanks to Anchor Hocking. Additional green pieces have been found including a luncheon plate and large and small berry bowls. That green crescent salad plate is a rather interesting item for Depression glass. Crescent salads are more prevalent in elegant patterns. Only a few of these have been found in crystal and pink.

Some novice dealers price commonly found Royal Ruby handled Coronation berry bowls extraordinarily high and label them "pigeon blood." We have seen them priced as high as $22.00, but they are a tough sell in the $8.00 range.

Coronation pitchers are rarely offered for sale. Notice the one photographed, so you will recognize it, if you see it.

		Pink	Royal Ruby	Green
8 ▶	Bowl, 4¼", berry, handled	5.00	8.00	
9 ▶	Bowl, 4¼", no handles	100.00		60.00
2 ▶	Bowl, 6½", nappy, handled	7.00	18.00	
3 ▶	Bowl, 8", large berry, handled	15.00	15.00	
	Bowl, 8", no handles	225.00		200.00
6 ▶	*Cup	4.00	6.00	
12 ▶	Pitcher, 7¾", 68 ounce	695.00		
7 ▶	Plate, 6", sherbet/saucer	2.00		
5 ▶	Plate, 8½", luncheon	6.00		70.00
10 ▶	Plate, crescent salad	100.00		175.00
	Saucer w/indent (crystal only)		3.00	
1 ▶	Sherbet	9.00		110.00
4 ▶	Tumbler, 5", 10 ounce, footed	18.00		225.00
11 ▶	Tumbler, 5⁷⁄₁₆", 14½ ounce, experimental	N/A	N/A	N/A

*Crystal $4.00

CRACKLE, various companies (L.E. Smith, McKee Glass, MacBeth-Evans, Federal Glass, U.S. Glass, et. al.), c. 1924

Colors: amber, amethyst, blue, canary, crystal, green, pink, satin (frosted) colors, crystal with color trims

There were so many companies that made crackle in some form or another that even we had trouble distinguishing who made a particular piece. We were finally convinced to add it to the book after talking to some zealous collectors who told us they didn't care which company made what they bought as long as they liked the piece. There are two styles — cold water, reheated crackle, and the moulded type. There seems to be more collectors interested in the moulded type. One collector told Cathy, "It would be nice to know what is available and what kind of prices I should be paying." Well, we're trying to report prices we see, but you must decide what you are willing to pay.

We hope that by consolidating every moulded piece we can find into a list, then that will help collectors. Feel free to supply additional pieces to our listing. Again, we're only looking for the moulded, crackled appearing wares that were advertised throughout the late 1920s and early 1930s as making liquids "look like cracked ice."

Ice was a precious commodity in this era, so many companies jumped onto this "suggestion of ice" effect in their glassware lines, particularly in beverage sets; and judging by the available pieces found in markets today, so did the buying public. A 1927 Sears catalogue shows an 18 piece tumbler assortment of six each (5 oz. juice, 9 oz. table, and 12 oz. tea) for 98¢. For 98¢ you could also buy 10 tall footed sherbets, six cone shape sherbets with 6¼" liners, or eight 10 oz. tall footed goblets. There was also a lidded bedroom pitcher and glass on a tray in rose or green for $2.10 and a water tankard with six glasses for 95¢. From a psychological aspect, did the crackle effect truly make the drink seem cooler?

For now, we're pricing only crystal, using prices observed in the market. Colored crackle will fetch 20% – 25% more, except for canary, which will fetch up to double the prices listed.

		*Crystal				*Crystal				*Crystal
	Bottle, water	18.00	15 ▸	Compote, cheese (for cracker)	12.50		Sherbet, octagon rim	10.00
10 ▸	Bowl, 6", ruffled	10.00	14 ▸	Compote, 6", candy	12.00	12 ▸	Sherbet, round rim	8.00
	Bowl, console	20.00		Cup	10.00		Tray, 3-footed, flat	20.00
	Bowl, flare rim on black base	35.00		Jar, screw threads	22.00		Tumbler, 4¾", footed cone	8.00
7 ▸	Bowl, footed, small vegetable	20.00	3 ▸	Pitcher, bulbous middle, water, no lid	28.00		Tumbler, 5 oz., bowed middle, juice	10.00
	Bowl, ruffled, vegetable	18.00					
	Bowl, hexagon, cereal	12.00		Pitcher, 64 oz., bulbous, w/lid	45.00	2 ▸	Tumbler, 9 oz., bowed middle, water	8.00
	Butter, small (powder jar style)	25.00		Pitcher, 9", cone, footed	48.00			
	Caddy, center handle, 6 holder	12.00		Pitcher, water, slant edge, flat	30.00		Tumbler, 12 oz., bowed middle, tea	9.00
	Caddy, center handle, 4 holder	10.00	11 ▸	Plate, dessert, round or octagon	8.00			
9 ▸	Candle, 1¾"	9.00		Plate, salad, round or octagon	9.00		Tumbler, juice, straight side	8.00
	Candle, cone	22.00	5 ▸	Plate, 8", round or octagon	10.00		Tumbler, tea, straight side	6.00
6 ▸	Candle, sq. base	15.00	1 ▸	Plate, cloverleaf, snack	14.00		Tumbler, water, straight side	8.00
	Candy box, hexagonal lid	28.00		Plate, cracker w/center rim	17.00	4 ▸	Vase, 8", bulbous w/ruffled rim	30.00
8 ▸	Candy, footed, round, dome lid	25.00		Plate, server, 2-handle	20.00	13 ▸	Vase, squat, bulbous w/flat rim	15.00

* Colors add 20 – 25%, except canary, add 50%

CREMAX, MacBeth-Evans Division of Corning Glass Works, Late 1930s – Early 1940s
Colors: Cremax, Cremax with fired-on colored trim or decals

Cremax is regularly dubbed "pie crust" by non-collectors; it is also a term used for those tableware patterns that were produced in the light ivory glass coloring (called Cremax). Some patterns used the color itself as part of the pattern name. For example, there was Cremax Bordette line, with pink, yellow, blue, and green borders; Cremax Rainbow line with pastel pink and green borders; the Cremax Windsor line, with Windsor brown, blue, and green castle decals; and an unadorned ware simply called Cremax. Decals included were a hexagon-sided center floral called Princess Pattern and a floral spray known as Flora.

Blue or pink-bordered trims with a center of red roses have attracted more collectors than do the non-colored border items. You may also find "Mountain Flowers" which is customarily found as a Petalware decoration. Prices for plain Cremax remain reasonable and there would be little competition in gathering a set if you desire. Cremax vied for china dinnerware dollars and was promoted as resilient to chips and warranted to be useable for years. What is found now is usually still in great shape, except for worn decals.

Blue Cremax (in three distinctly different shades, although cobalt is rarely found) has ensnared the most appreciation for this pattern. Blue is normally found in Canada and bordering states of Michigan and New York. You can see two shades of blue in the lower left corner of the picture below. A cobalt creamer is shown above. Internet auctions have exposed blue pieces to anyone wishing to collect it.

We have learned the lighter "robin's egg" blue was sold by Corning almost exclusively in Canada. Price both shades of blue about the same as the pieces with decals. Gathering a set of either blue will be quite a task, but not impossible.

Cremax Bordette demitasse sets were marketed in sets of eight. Some sets have been found on a wire rack. The typical composition of these sets has been two sets each of four color trims: pink, yellow, blue, and green.

		Cremax	*Blue, decal decorated			Cremax	*Blue, decal decorated
	Bowl, 5¾", cereal	3.00	11.00	6 ▸	Plate, 9¾", dinner	4.00	10.00
1 ▸	Bowl, 7¾", soup	7.00	20.00	7 ▸	Plate, 11½", sandwich	5.00	15.00
	Bowl, 9", vegetable	11.00	18.00	3 ▸	Saucer	1.00	2.50
	Creamer	4.00	8.00	8 ▸	Saucer, demitasse	2.00	
2 ▸	Cup	3.00	4.00	10 ▸	Sugar, open	4.00	8.00
9 ▸	Cup, demitasse	7.00					
5 ▸	Egg cup, 2¼"	10.00					
4 ▸	Plate, 6¼", bread and butter	2.00	3.00				

*Add 50% for castle decal

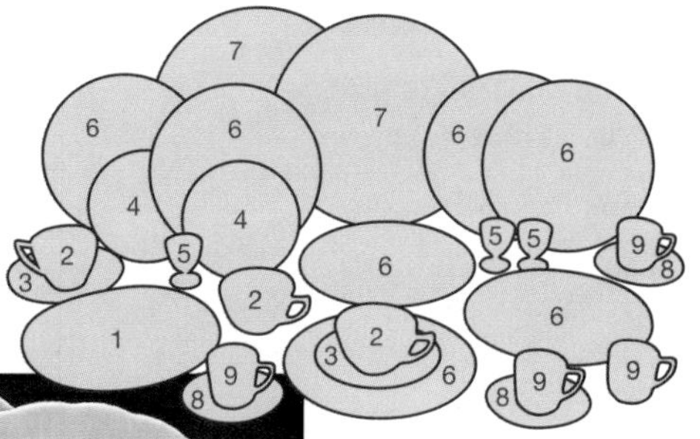

"CROW'S FOOT," Line 412 & Line 890, Paden City Glass Company, 1930s

Colors: amber, amethyst, black, cobalt blue, crystal, pink, Ruby red, white, and yellow

Paden City's "Crow's Foot" moulds were used for various etchings, but the blanks themselves are sought in unembellished Ruby and cobalt blue. "Crow's Foot" is found on two separate, but distinct shapes. Line #412 is a squared mould shape with fans usually inside the rim, and Line #890 is round with fans at rim. Price is a factor in amassing "Crow's Foot" since not everyone can afford those admired Paden City etched patterns like "Cupid," "Orchid," or "Peacock & Wild Rose."

New collectors using the Internet have made red and cobalt blue "Crow's Foot" tricky for dealers to keep in stock, because little is being uncovered. Often, the initial lure in collecting glass is color rather than the pattern. Note that some "Crow's Foot" devotees who search for only round or square items are willing to mix serving pieces which are so few and far between.

There is less demand for amber, crystal, or yellow; but small sets can be accumulated in these colors for a modest expense. Neither black nor white is frequently seen. You need to consider purchasing white items if you find them reasonably priced. Note the rarely seen footed white cake plate below.

One problem with Paden City's Ruby pieces is consistency in color. Many items are found in an amberina color (especially tumblers). Amberina is a collectors' term for the yellowish hue remaining on pieces that were issued as red. It was initially a manufacturing (heating) mistake, not the color that they were intending to make. Today, amberina itself is fascinating to some collectors who now seek it for that specific bi-color effect.

You may find ornamented silver accoutrements, but these were most likely added by another decorating firm. Silver decorated designs on Ritz blue or Ruby are frequently found appealing by people who are not "Crow's Foot" collectors.

		Ruby Red	Black, Ritz Blue	Other colors
1 ▸	Bowl, 4⅞", square	20.00	25.00	10.00
	Bowl, 8¾", square	40.00	45.00	20.00
	Bowl, 6", deep	30.00	30.00	12.00
6 ▸	Bowl, 6½", rd., 2½" high, 3½" base	35.00	40.00	18.00
	Bowl, 8½", square, 2-handle	45.00	55.00	22.00
	Bowl, 10", footed	65.00	65.00	30.00
	Bowl, 10", square, 2-handle	65.00	65.00	30.00
	Bowl, 11", oval	35.00	40.00	20.00
8 ▸	Bowl, 11", square	50.00	60.00	30.00
	Bowl, 11", square, rolled edge	55.00	65.00	32.50
	Bowl, 11½", 3 footed, round console	75.00	80.00	40.00
	Bowl, 11½", console	65.00	70.00	37.50
14 ▸	Bowl, cream soup, footed/flat	20.00	22.00	10.00
	Bowl, Nasturtium, 3 footed	140.00	150.00	65.00
	Bowl, whipped cream, 3 footed	45.00	55.00	25.00
	Cake plate, square, 2", pedestal foot	65.00	75.00	38.00
16 ▸	Cake stand, 4½" high	70.00	70.00	40.00
	Candle, round base, tall	50.00	55.00	30.00
	Candle, square, mushroom	32.00	35.00	18.00

		Ruby Red	Black, Ritz Blue	Other colors
7 ▸	Candlestick, 5¾", sq. based	25.00	28.00	12.50
15 ▸	Candy w/cover, 6½", 3 part (2 styles)	75.00	85.00	35.00
	Candy, 3 footed, rd., 6⅛" wide, 3¼" high	120.00	135.00	60.00
	Cheese stand, 5"	30.00	28.00	12.50
11 ▸	Comport, 3¼" tall, 6¼" wide	30.00	32.00	15.00
	Comport 4¾" tall, 7⅜" wide	40.00	50.00	25.00
	Comport, 6⅝" tall, 7" wide	45.00	55.00	25.00
	Creamer, flat	14.00	16.00	8.00
9 ▸	Creamer, footed	14.00	16.00	8.00
17 ▸	Cup, footed or flat	12.00	16.00	8.00
	Gravy boat, flat, 2 spout	60.00	70.00	40.00
	Gravy boat, pedestal	125.00	135.00	50.00
10 ▸	Mayonnaise, 3 footed	40.00	50.00	22.00
13 ▸	Plate, 5¾"	5.00	6.00	1.50
	Plate, 8", round	11.00	13.00	4.50
5 ▸	Plate, 8½", square	12.00	14.00	3.50
	Plate, 9¼", round, small dinner	25.00	25.00	12.50
	Plate, 9½", round, 2-handle	50.00	60.00	25.00
	Plate, 10⅜", round, 2-handle	40.00	50.00	22.00
	Plate, 10⅜", square, 2-handle	50.00	50.00	20.00
	Plate, 10½", dinner	60.00	65.00	25.00
4 ▸	Plate, 11", cracker	40.00	45.00	18.00
	Platter, 12"	30.00	35.00	12.00
2 ▸	Punch set w/12 Roly Polys as pictured	500.00	500.00	
	Relish, 11", 3 part	65.00	70.00	35.00
	Sandwich server, round, center-handle	45.00	55.00	25.00
	Sandwich server, square, center-handle	40.00	45.00	17.50
	Saucer, 6", round	4.00	5.00	1.00
18 ▸	Saucer, 6", square	4.50	6.00	1.50

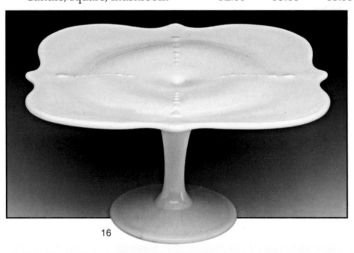

16

	Ruby Red	Black, Ritz Blue	Other Colors
Sugar, flat	12.00	15.00	5.50
12 ▸ Sugar, footed	12.00	15.00	5.50
3 ▸ Tumbler, 4¼"	60.00	70.00	30.00
Vase, 4⅝" tall, 4⅛" wide	70.00	75.00	35.00
Vase, 10¼", cupped	110.00	125.00	45.00
Vase, 10¼", flared	100.00	115.00	32.50
Vase, 11¾", flared	165.00	175.00	50.00

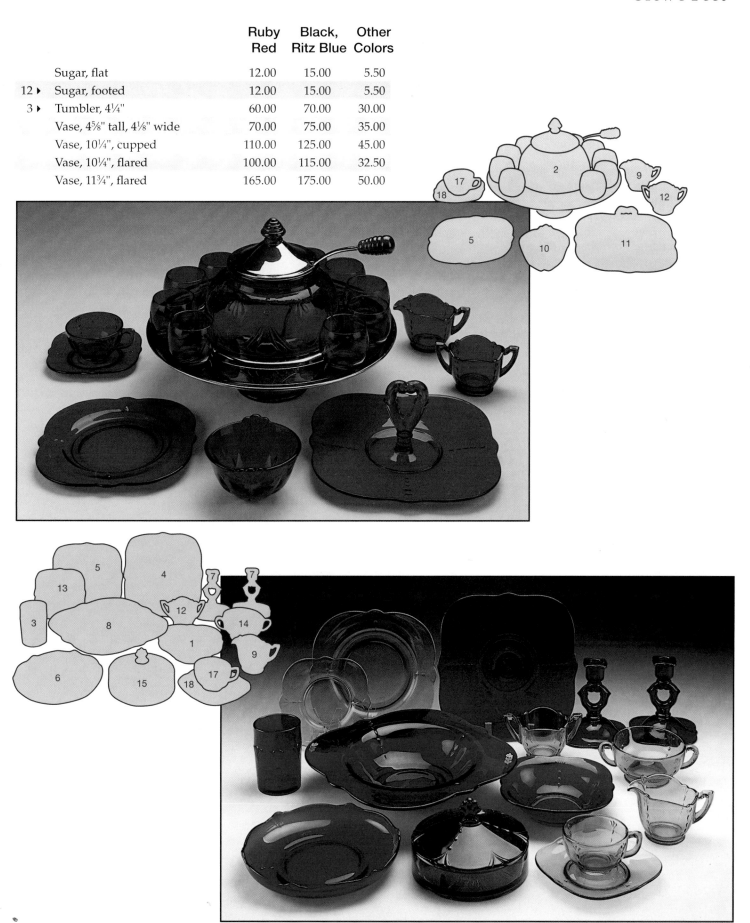

CUBE, "CUBIST," Jeannette Glass Company, 1929 – 1933
Colors: pink, green, crystal, Ultra Marine, canary yellow, and blue

Jeannette's Cube was a poor man's copy of Fostoria's American which had been in production since 1915. American was produced mostly in crystal, so it is possible Jeannette hoped to lure buyers seeking color for their tableware.

Chances are excellent that any green or pink Cube you find will not be Fostoria.

We mention that because Indiana's Whitehall pattern was produced in colors of pink and green along with others. We used to get letters regularly about new found colors or pieces of "Cube." Indiana's Whitehall was produced in the 1980s and 1990s. Their colored Cube-like pitchers are shaped differently than the ones we picture. If the pitcher is not moulded like the pink or green pitchers on page 53, then they are not Jeannette's Cube. Today, we get e-mails, and the Whitehall bandwagon has now switched over to being Fostoria rather than Jeannette. It is still a mistake. Unfortunately, these have been advertised and auctioned on the Internet as "rare" Cube or Fostoria. They are neither, and especially not rare.

Only three Cube pieces (small sugar, creamer, and round tray) were produced in crystal, but they are actually a production of Hazel-Atlas and not Jeannette. You may also spot these in amber or milk white. They are also Hazel-Atlas.

Cube tumblers are always flat as pictured, and were made in only one size. If you spot colored, footed tumblers of any shape or size, they are Whitehall, not Jeannette or Fostoria.

Cube tumblers are difficult to find in either color, especially in mint condition. They frequently have chips on some of the many points or are often water stained. Rarely do you see the heavy top rim chipped. Although pitchers are seldom found, most collectors attain the pitcher before securing four, six, or eight tumblers.

Cube is another Jeannette pattern where unstable hues of pink or green crop up, a problem when buying on the Internet. The answer is to attend a Depression glass show and handle what you are buying. As a matter of fact, you might be willing to pay a little more for that pleasure. Be assured, "pleasure" it is.

All Cube powder jars are three-footed with a rounded, flattened top. (The other pointed Cube lid is interchangeable with the sugar and candy jar.) Experimental colors of powder jars have turned up such as canary yellow and two shades of blue. Sporadically, these jars are found with celluloid or plastic lids. Powder jars were produced with glass tops. These others may have been replacements when tops were broken. Another possibility is that left-over powder bottoms were sold to some company who affixed celluloid lids to match brush, mirror, or comb handles for sets they sold. In any case, prices below are for intact, original glass lids. The powder jars with other types of lids sell for half or less as glass tops are harder to find. A celluloid lid is better than no lid at all — and for collectors of celluloid items, it's most likely better than a glass one.

		Pink	Green
	Bowl, 4½", dessert, pointed edge	12.00	12.00
	*Bowl, 4½", deep	8.00	
19 ▸	Bowl, 5", tab hdld.	75.00	
	**Bowl, 6½", salad	12.00	12.00
	*Bowl, 7¼", pointed edge	18.00	20.00
	*Butter dish and cover	60.00	55.00
	Butter dish bottom	20.00	15.00
	Butter dish top	40.00	40.00
2 ▸	Candy jar and cover, 6½"	25.00	25.00
7 ▸	Coaster, 3¼"	7.00	8.00
18 ▸	* ‡ Creamer, 2⅝"	3.00	
8 ▸	Creamer, 3⁹⁄₁₆"	9.00	10.00
5 ▸	Cup	6.00	8.00
9 ▸	Pitcher, 8¾", 45 ounce	235.00	255.00
	*Plate, 6", sherbet	2.00	2.00
14 ▸	*Plate, 8", luncheon	7.00	8.00
3 ▸	Powder jar and cover, 3 legs	25.00	30.00
1 ▸	Salt and pepper, pair	32.00	35.00
6 ▸	Saucer	2.00	2.00
13 ▸	*Sherbet, footed	8.00	9.00
17 ▸	‡ Sugar, 2⅜"	3.00	
11 ▸	*Sugar, 3"	5.00	6.00
10 ▸	*Sugar/candy cover	15.00	15.00
	Tray for 3⁹⁄₁₆" creamer and sugar, 7½" (crystal only)	4.00	
15 ▸	*Tumbler, 4", 9 ounce	70.00	80.00

19

*Ultra Marine $50.00   **Ultra Marine $90.00
‡ Amber or white (Hazel-Atlas) $3.00; crystal $1.00

"CUPID," Paden City Glass Company, 1930s
Colors: pink, green, light blue, peacock blue, black, canary yellow, amber, and crystal

"Cupid" was one of the first patterns that appealed to Cathy when we started buying Depression glass in 1970. At that time there was no book which listed "Cupid" as a pattern, so we bought what we could find. Even then, competition was rearing its head. Too, we found that any time someone saw us buying a particular pattern, word got around quickly.

A few years ago, the Internet auctions introduced "Cupid" to people who found it as captivating as we did. As a result, prices for "Cupid" spiraled and buying was brisk. Suddenly, previously unimaginable prices reigned on the auctions and some long-time collectors let go of their sets. Many Paden City etchings increased at least 20% to 30% and rare items doubled. Then came the economic downturn and more pieces were being offered than were being bought. Today, those stratospheric prices are in the past. Ice buckets and tubs, bowls, and candles have all suffered setbacks in price from that frenzied heyday. Some outrageous prices are still being asked, but there seem to be few buyers at those heights. If you like this pattern, now would be a good time to buy it because bargaining is possible.

Prices are the most difficult part of writing this book. Even with all the help from other dealers around the country, prices never please everyone. If you own a piece, you want it to be highly priced; if you want to buy the same piece, you want the price to be low. Keep in mind that one sale at a high price does not mean that everyone would be willing to pay that. That is especially true of rare glass and any outrageous sums obtained at auctions. If two people want something and have the money (or if one person simply does not want the other to get the item cheaply), then there may be an exorbitant price paid. That does not mean that that identical item will sell for that price the next time, or ever again. Only you can determine what a piece of glass is worth to you. If a price is more than you wish to pay, walk away. There will always be other pieces you want, and hopefully, at a price you like.

"Cupid" cups and saucers are still in demand. They have only been found in pink, although we had a report of a cup in green that was never verified. A bottom to a tumble-up (water bottle) has been seen, but so far, no reports of a tumbler have surfaced. Several pink and green casseroles have been found on the West Coast, but only two casseroles in black with silver overlay.

Two styles of samovars are found infrequently and are a magnet of attention when they are displayed. One style has the spout in the surrounding metal frame, while the other is drilled and pours out of the glass itself. To be a "Cupid" samovar, the "Cupid" pattern has to be etched on it. Mould shape alone does not make the pattern. We once had a beautiful, expensive, but plain, samovar shipped to us as "Cupid"; so we speak of this from experience.

New reports of "Cupid's" design found on silver overlay vases marked "Made in Germany" keep arriving. To our knowledge, these vases have been found in cobalt, orange, and lavender. Our last report involves a silver overlay vase marked "Made in Czechoslovakia."

Our help turned the green candle holders upside down in the photo. Since they are often displayed thus at markets, we decided these might help with recognition. See those in pink for their proper display angle.

		Green, Pink	Blue
2 ▸	Bowl, 8½", oval, footed	200.00	
14 ▸	Bowl, 9¼", footed fruit	210.00	
17 ▸	Bowl, 9¼", center-handled	200.00	
18 ▸	Bowl, 10¼", fruit	155.00	300.00
13 ▸	Bowl, 10½", rolled edge	140.00	
	Bowl, 11", console	140.00	
	Bowl, 13½", console	155.00	
	Cake plate, 11¾"	160.00	
	Cake stand, 2" high, footed	160.00	
8 ▸	Candlestick, 5" wide, pair	150.00	425.00
16 ▸	Candy w/lid, footed, 5¼" high	300.00	
1 ▸	Candy w/lid, 3 part, flat	225.00	
	*Casserole, covered	795.00	
12 ▸	Comport, 6¼"	150.00	300.00
	Creamer, flat	150.00	
6 ▸	Creamer, 4½", footed	110.00	
	Creamer, 5", footed	110.00	
	Cup	225.00	
3 ▸	Ice bucket, 6"	175.00	
9 ▸	Ice tub, 4¾"	185.00	
	**Lamp, silver overlay	495.00	

*Black (silver overlay) $75.00
**Possibly German

		Green, Pink	Blue
7 ▸	Mayonnaise, 6" diameter, fits on 8" plate, spoon, 3 pc.	160.00	350.00
	Plate, 10½"	135.00	250.00
15 ▸	Samovar	1,100.00	
	Saucer	50.00	
	Sugar, flat	150.00	
5 ▸	Sugar, 4¼", footed	110.00	
	Sugar, 5", footed	110.00	
10 ▸	Tray, 10¾", center-handled	135.00	
11 ▸	Tray, 10⅞", oval-footed	210.00	
4 ▸	Vase, 8¼", elliptical	595.00	
	Vase, fan-shaped	525.00	
	Vase, 10"	335.00	
	Water bottle w/tumbler	850.00	

DAISY AND BUTTON W/NARCISSUS, Line 124, Indiana Glass Company, c. 1910
Colors: crystal and with colored stains; Sunset (amberina) and Ruby for Tiara Exclusives

Pattern glass books (including our *American Pattern Glass Table Sets*) designate this as Line 124. Supposedly Daisy and Button w/Narcissus was found in a 1932 Indiana Glass catalog by Barbara Shaffer and Vel Hinchliffe. That would certainly make the pattern Depression era even though it was produced as early as 1910. That's why we are including the pattern here. Another author is said to have found a piece of this advertised in a 1918 Sears catalog. There may be more items to be found than those in our listing and we would appreciate you letting us know what you uncover.

Indiana remanufactured a decanter and tray with six wines in crystal and their amberina (Sunset) and Ruby color for Tiara Exclusives home party ware division after Tiara's opening in the 1970s. The original wine tray was scalloped as can be seen in a 1927 Sear's catalog advertisement. Then it was touted as a grape juice set and sold for $1.35. Indiana's recent tray has paneled edging and a flattened rim. Remember that all amberina and Ruby colored wares were made in the last 30 years and should be priced accordingly. Cathy remembers spotting a wine set with faint cranberry stained flowers which would've been a beginning production. Staining techniques were used in the early part of the twentieth century to enhance basic crystal glassware. Many of these stains have deteriorated through the years and finding one without erosion is uncommon.

This is a pattern that has withstood the passage of almost 100 years rather well.

		Crystal
2 ▶	Bowl, 4⅛", salad (Indiana's designation)	7.00
4 ▶	Bowl, 4⅛", 3-toed fruit	12.00
	Bowl, 5½", ftd. bonbon	14.00
	Bowl, round vegetable	22.00
	Bowl, 9½", oval, ftd.	25.00
	Butter w/cover	35.00
	Compote, 4½", ftd. jelly	12.50
	Cup, custard	8.00
	Creamer	11.00
1 ▶	Decanter w/stop, 12½"	40.00
	Goblet, water	12.50
6 ▶	Goblet, 4⅝", wine	12.50
	Pitcher	65.00
	Sugar	11.00
3 ▶	Tray, 10⅜"	25.00
5 ▶	Tumbler, 4⅜", water	13.00

1   6   3   5   4   2

DELLA ROBBIA, #1058, Westmoreland Glass Company, Late 1920s – 1940s
Colors: crystal, crystal w/applied lustre colors, milk glass, pink, purple slag, and opaque blue

Della Robbia is Westmoreland's pattern #1058. We previously have shown catalog pages that had some other lines shown along with Della Robbia items. The ball candles and bowl pictured there are not #1058, so are not Della Robbia although we continue to see them advertised and pictured as such.

Della Robbia was made in crystal, crystal with applied lustre colors, pink, opaque blue, green, and milk glass. That is an unusual decoration on the plate pictured on page 58. Notice that the fruit on each piece of Della Robbia depicts red apple, yellow pear, and purple grape. Two color variations occur in the fruit decorations on crystal. All apples are red; pears, yellow; and grapes, purple; but the darker shaded fruits are most wanted. The quandary with this darker color is that the applied lustre scratches and rubs off easily. Scuffs are prominent on the darker hue. Most collectors choose not to mix the two tinted wares. However, we have never seen a punch set in the darker adaptation, though they supposedly were made.

Similar patterns to Della Robbia exist, but they include a banana in the design. If there is a banana, it's most likely Indiana's #301 pattern. Be sure to see Indiana's version in our 9th edition of *Collectible Glassware from the 40s, 50s, 60s....*

Prices for Della Robbia dinner plates have finally backed down from their ever-ascending spiral, if you can find one. They were used and show strong evidence of that. Should you find serving pieces, vigilantly inspect them for wear. Remember the prices listed are for mint condition pieces and not ones that are worn or scuffed. One of the reasons prices for mint condition pieces are high is that there are worn pieces around for sale, but few perfect ones.

Della Robbia pitcher and tumbler moulds were recycled to make some carnival colored water sets in the 1970s. These were made for the Levay Company just as were pieces of red English Hobnail. They can be seen in light blue and amethyst carnival. We have been informed that some Westmoreland collectors seek them; but no collector of Della Robbia has ever asked us about them.

		Crystal w/ lustre colors				Crystal w/ lustre colors
	Basket, 9"	150.00	11 ▶	Pitcher, 32 ounce		235.00
15 ▶	Basket, 12"	195.00	5 ▶	Plate, 6", finger liner		8.00
	Bowl, 4½", nappy	28.00	14 ▶	Plate, 6⅛", bread & butter		8.00
	Bowl, 5", finger	35.00		Plate, 7¼", salad		12.00
2 ▶	Bowl, 6", one-handle heart	35.00	10 ▶	Plate, 9", luncheon		30.00
8 ▶	Bowl, 6", nappy, bell	32.00	16 ▶	Plate, 10½", dinner		125.00
1 ▶	Bowl, 6½", one-handle nappy	32.00		*Plate, 14", torte		75.00
	Bowl, 7½", nappy	42.00		Plate, 18"		160.00
	Bowl, 8", nappy, bell	60.00		Plate, 18", upturned edge, punch bowl liner		210.00
	Bowl, 8", bell, handle	75.00		Platter, 14", oval		195.00
	Bowl, 8", heart, handle	110.00		Punch bowl set, 15 piece		995.00
6 ▶	Bowl, 9", nappy	100.00		Salt and pepper, pair		60.00
	Bowl, 12", footed	135.00		Salver, 14", footed, cake		135.00
	Bowl, 13", rolled edge	95.00		Saucer		10.00
7 ▶	Bowl, 14", oval, flange	225.00		Stem, 3 ounce, wine		24.00
	Bowl, 14", punch	335.00	12 ▶	Stem, 3¼ ounce, cocktail		18.00
	Bowl, 15", bell	225.00		Stem, 5 ounce, 4¾", sherbet, high foot		14.00
	Candle, 4"	30.00	13 ▶	Stem, 5 ounce, sherbet, low foot		14.00
	Candle, 4", 2-lite	110.00		Stem, 6 ounce, champagne		16.00
	Candy jar w/cover, scalloped edge	110.00	19 ▶	Stem, 8 ounce, 6", water		20.00
9 ▶	Candy, round, flat, chocolate	75.00	18 ▶	Sugar, footed		15.00
3 ▶	Comport, 6½", 3⅝" high, mint, footed	40.00		Tumbler, 5 ounce, ginger ale		22.00
	Comport, 8", sweetmeat, bell	110.00		Tumbler, 8 ounce, footed		25.00
	Comport, 12", footed, bell	130.00		Tumbler, 8 ounce, water		20.00
	Comport, 13", flanged	135.00		Tumbler, 11 ounce, iced tea, footed		32.00
17 ▶	Creamer, footed	15.00		Tumbler, 12 ounce, iced tea, bell		35.00
	Cup, coffee	18.00	4 ▶	Tumbler, 12 ounce, iced tea, bell, footed		35.00
	Cup, punch	15.00		Tumbler, 12 ounce, 5³⁄₁₆", iced tea, straight		38.00

*Pink $150.00

16

DIAMOND QUILTED, "FLAT DIAMOND," Imperial Glass Company, Late 1920s – Early 1930s
Colors: pink, blue, green, crystal, black; some red and amber

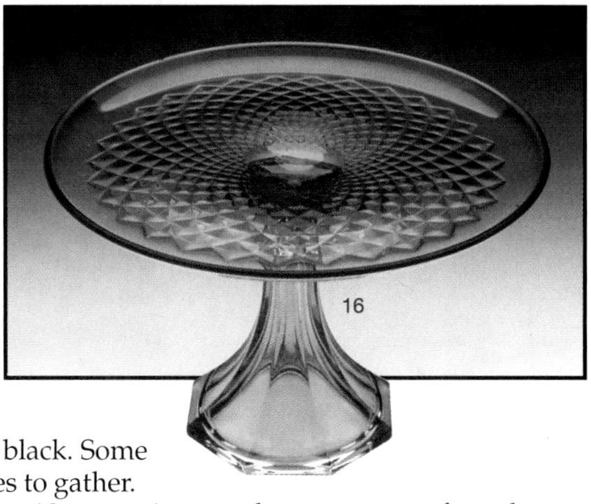

Imperial's Diamond Quilted can be collected in sets of pink or green with time and patience. Other colors are occasionally available including blue, black, red, and amber. Red is purchased by more collectors of red glass than by Diamond Quilted collectors since so few pieces were made in that color. It is a strong red color unlike the amberina found in Imperial's famous Candlewick and Cape Cod lines. Speaking of those patterns, Diamond Quilted does not get as much recognition in the glass collecting world as they do.

Black Diamond Quilted often goes unrecognized unless you realize that the pattern occurs on the outside of pieces. That means that no design shows when flat pieces are displayed unless turned upside down as in our photo. It will take time to gather a luncheon set in black, but a few try. Blue Diamond Quilted was highly prized by early collectors, so little is found today unless a collection is sold. There is a comparable Fenton Diamond Optic pattern found in black. Some collectors combine the Fenton and Imperial which gives a wider diversity of pieces to gather.

Punch bowl sets are the item missing from most collections. It has been over 10 years since we have seen one for sale at a show. Unfortunately, green punch bowls are usually a darker shade of green than the cups. The regular cup was used for the punch set, but those are already in short supply. We rarely see cups for sale, but prices are modest for their scarcity.

Lack of a dinner plate used to be a detriment to collecting patterns; but today, Depression glass is often used as accents. We've observed that some use luncheon plates for serving snacks or hors d'oeuvres and we're told people dieting like the smaller sized luncheon plates — to make their smaller portions more visually palatable. Cathy received compliments on her mixed pattern luncheon plates used for serving snacks at a shower. So, Depression glass luncheon sized plates can definitely be fashionable once again.

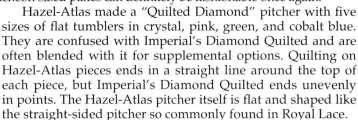

16

Hazel-Atlas made a "Quilted Diamond" pitcher with five sizes of flat tumblers in crystal, pink, green, and cobalt blue. They are confused with Imperial's Diamond Quilted and are often blended with it for supplemental options. Quilting on Hazel-Atlas pieces ends in a straight line around the top of each piece, but Imperial's Diamond Quilted ends unevenly in points. The Hazel-Atlas pitcher itself is flat and shaped like the straight-sided pitcher so commonly found in Royal Lace.

The original sales advertisement shows console sets at 65¢ and a dozen candy dishes in assorted colors for $6.95. Those candy jars are rarely seen today, indicating they were heavily used and discarded or did not sell well at the time. This ad is from a 1930 catalog.

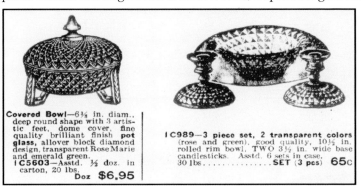

Covered Bowl—6⅜ in. diam., deep round shape with 3 artistic feet, dome cover, fine quality brilliant finish **pot glass**, allover block diamond design, transparent Rose Marie and emerald green.
1C5603—Asstd. ½ doz. in carton, 20 lbs.
Doz $6.95

1C989—3 piece set, 2 transparent colors (rose and green), good quality, 10½ in. rolled rim bowl, TWO 3½ in. wide base candlesticks. Asstd. 6 sets in case. 30 lbs. . . . . SET (3 pcs) **65c**

		Pink, Green	Amber, Blue, Black
10 ▶	Bowl, 4¾", cream soup	12.00	22.00
	Bowl, 4¾", finger, 2½" deep	14.00	20.00
	Bowl, 5", cereal	10.00	15.00
15 ▶	Bowl, 5½", one handle	9.00	22.00
3 ▶	Bowl, 7", crimped edge	12.00	22.00
8 ▶	Bowl, 7", straight	10.00	14.00
	Bowl, 10½", rolled edge console	35.00	60.00
16 ▶	Cake salver, tall, 10" diameter	110.00	
9 ▶	Candlesticks (2 styles), pair	25.00	30.00
4 ▶	Candy jar and cover, footed	75.00	
14 ▶	Compote, 6" tall, 7¼" wide	40.00	
	Compote and cover, 11½"	95.00	125.00
1 ▶	Creamer	10.00	12.00
6 ▶	Cup	8.00	17.50
	Goblet, 1 ounce, cordial	15.00	
	Goblet, 2 ounce, wine	14.00	
	Goblet, 3 ounce, wine	14.00	
	Goblet, 6", 9 ounce, champagne	12.00	
13 ▶	Ice bucket	45.00	75.00

		Pink, Green	Amber, Blue, Black
12 ▶	Mayonnaise set: ladle, plate, comport	40.00	60.00
	Pitcher, 64 ounce	55.00	
	Plate, 6", sherbet	3.00	6.00
	Plate, 7", salad	5.00	10.00
5 ▶	Plate, 8", luncheon	8.00	12.00
	Punch bowl and stand	650.00	
	Plate, 14", sandwich	15.00	
	Sandwich server, center handle	25.00	50.00
7 ▶	Saucer	4.00	6.00
11 ▶	Sherbet	10.00	16.00
2 ▶	Sugar	10.00	12.00
	Tumbler, 9 ounce, water	9.00	
	Tumbler, 12 ounce, iced tea	9.00	
	Tumbler, 6 ounce, footed	8.50	
	Tumbler, 9 ounce, footed	12.50	
	Tumbler, 12 ounce, footed	15.00	
	Vase, fan, dolphin handles	55.00	75.00
	Whiskey, 1½ ounce	10.00	

DIANA, Federal Glass Company, 1937 – 1941
Colors: pink, amber, and crystal

Pink Diana remains the trendy color to collect. Price increases of the late 1990s are now a thing of the past with only the candy jars, shakers, and tumblers holding steady. There has been some price adjustment for many Depression glass patterns in the market. Diana is no exception even though many pieces are rarely seen.

Diana tumblers may be rarer in crystal than pink, but there are not as many searchers for crystal. Amber is also not as sought by collectors.

Pictured here is a crystal, gold trimmed cake set which is reasonably priced should you find it attractive. The red stained children's set was found with tumblers to match. Usually, you only see the flashed red demitasse which sells in the $10.00 to $12.00 range; but someone added tumblers to make this a child's set. How uncommon these are is only a guess, but this is the only one we have seen. Demand for pink demitasse cup and saucer sets has slowed causing prices to slip a bit. We ran into one demitasse collector who said that Diana is what got her started in collecting them, and her collection now numbered several hundred.

Prices recorded below are valid selling prices for Diana and not advertised or wished-for prices. There is a major difference between an advertised price and the price being accepted by both buyer and seller. Rarely have we heard of something selling for more than advertised (except houses on the West Coast), but often we have heard of less. Today, dealers coast to coast are providing prices for us to peruse. That's been a big help to us as we work to keep pricing up to date in our books. The Internet, though a new source for estimates, has to be considered with some healthy skepticism and not taken too factually. We attend as many Depression glass shows as possible and spend many hours checking prices and talking to dealers about what is, and what is not selling, and for what price. Unfortunately, we are discussing more of what is not selling than we ever did.

Satinized (frosted) pieces of Diana show up in crystal and pink occasionally. The 11" bowl has been found frosted and drilled to be used for ceiling or lamp globes.

Remember, the centers of Federal's Diana pieces are swirled where the centers of most other swirled patterns are plain.

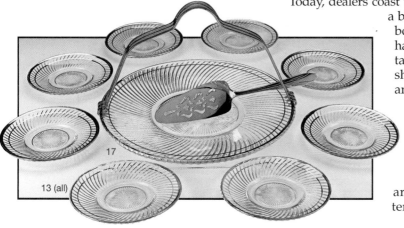

		Crystal	Pink	Amber
	*Ashtray, 3½"	2.50	3.50	
5 ▸	Bowl, 5", cereal	6.00	8.00	14.00
2 ▸	Bowl, 5½", cream soup	12.00	25.00	20.00
	Bowl, 9", salad	12.00	20.00	18.00
9 ▸	Bowl, 11", console fruit	16.00	32.00	18.00
	Bowl, 12", scalloped edge	16.00	25.00	20.00
6 ▸	Candy jar and cover, round	16.00	30.00	30.00
11 ▸	Coaster, 3½"	2.50	8.00	10.00
3 ▸	Creamer, oval	9.00	13.00	9.00
14 ▸	Cup	6.00	18.00	8.00
	Cup, 2 ounce demitasse and 4½" saucer set	9.00	30.00	
13 ▸	Plate, 6", bread & butter	2.00	4.00	2.00
4 ▸	Plate, 9½"	6.00	16.00	9.00
17 ▸	Plate, 11¾", sandwich	9.00	20.00	10.00
8 ▸	Platter, 12", oval	12.00	30.00	15.00
10 ▸	Salt and pepper, pair	30.00	75.00	75.00
15 ▸	Saucer	1.50	5.00	2.00
12 ▸	Sherbet	3.00	10.00	12.00
1 ▸	Sugar, open oval	9.00	13.00	8.00
7 ▸	Tumbler, 4⅛", 9 ounce	30.00	45.00	25.00
16 ▸	Junior set: 6 demitasse cups & saucers with round rack	70.00	240.00	

* Green $3.00

DOGWOOD, "APPLE BLOSSOM," "WILD ROSE," MacBeth-Evans Glass Company, 1929 – 1932
Colors: pink, green, some crystal, Monax, Cremax, and yellow

Dogwood maintains its status as one of the leading collectible Depression patterns, though it has experienced some softening of prices, a too frequent trend of late. Pink is the color preferred, which is fortunate since pink is most often found. Green Dogwood is available in much smaller quantities; but there are fewer collectors, so it all works out.

Luncheon plates are plentiful and anyone looking for Dogwood will almost certainly see these first. Larger dinner plates are exceedingly hard to find especially without scratches or scuffs. Larger is a matter of relativity, as they are only 9¼" and have a rim that forces everything to the center. We collected Dogwood in the 1970s and used the divided grill plates for our meals. Pink grill plates occur in two styles. Some have the Dogwood pattern all over the plate, and others have the pattern only around the rim. Green grills have only been found with a rim pattern.

The elusive large fruit bowl and platter are almost extinct and typically enter the market today through collections being sold.

One reason that large fruit bowls are in short supply is that they were marketed by some company that satinized the bowls, bored a hole in the center, and made ceiling fixtures out of them. Those shades sell in the $100.00 range in pink or green which is quite a bit less than conventional bowls would bring.

Tumblers and pitchers have to be silk screened with Dogwood pattern to be Dogwood. Shape does not define the pattern; and the mould blanks made by MacBeth-Evans go with plain, no design tumblers that were sold separately with various pink sets. If there is no silk screen pattern, then the price is not going to be those shown below. However, some collectors purposely purchase the plain blanks to use with their sets because they are less costly.

The thin, flat style creamer and sugar are shown in green while the thick, footed-style Dogwood sugar and creamer are pictured in pink. Pink sugar/ creamer sets are found in both styles, but green is only found in that thin version. Additionally, there are thin green cups, but thick and thin pink cups. There is only one style saucer for both.

Dogwood sherbets are found with a Dogwood blossom etched on the bottom or plain. Though from different moulds, prices are the same.

Rarely unearthed green pitchers and water tumblers are pricey. Iced teas are scarce and the pink juice tumbler, once rare, now has supplies outpacing demand since most collectors only buy one.

The top photo shows "go with" items.

"go with" items

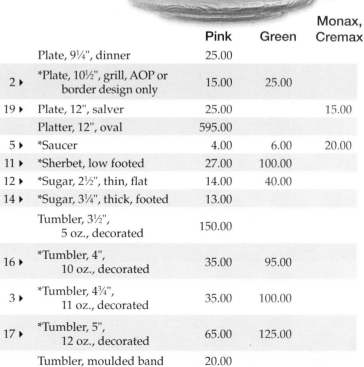

		Pink	Green	Monax, Cremax
13 ▶	*Bowl, 5½", cereal	28.00	32.00	15.00
1 ▶	*Bowl, 8½", berry	50.00	110.00	40.00
6 ▶	**Bowl, 10¼", fruit	595.00	275.00	125.00
	Cake plate, 11", heavy solid foot	1,295.00		
7 ▶	*Cake plate, 13", heavy solid foot	135.00	95.00	195.00
	Coaster, 3¼"	695.00		
10 ▶	*Creamer, 2½", thin, flat	14.00	40.00	
15 ▶	*Creamer, 3¼", thick, footed	15.00		
18 ▶	*Cup, thick	15.00		45.00
4 ▶	*Cup, thin	14.00	35.00	
9 ▶	*Pitcher, 8", 80 oz., decorated	195.00	495.00	
	Pitcher, 8", 80 oz. (American Sweetheart Style)	650.00		
8 ▶	*Plate, 6", bread and butter	7.00	8.00	22.00
	*Plate, 8", luncheon	6.00	9.00	

		Pink	Green	Monax, Cremax
	Plate, 9¼", dinner	25.00		
2 ▶	*Plate, 10½", grill, AOP or border design only	15.00	25.00	
19 ▶	Plate, 12", salver	25.00		15.00
	Platter, 12", oval	595.00		
5 ▶	*Saucer	4.00	6.00	20.00
11 ▶	*Sherbet, low footed	27.00	100.00	
12 ▶	*Sugar, 2½", thin, flat	14.00	40.00	
14 ▶	*Sugar, 3¼", thick, footed	13.00		
	Tumbler, 3½", 5 oz., decorated	150.00		
16 ▶	*Tumbler, 4", 10 oz., decorated	35.00	95.00	
3 ▶	*Tumbler, 4¾", 11 oz., decorated	35.00	100.00	
17 ▶	*Tumbler, 5", 12 oz., decorated	65.00	125.00	
	Tumbler, moulded band	20.00		

* yellow $75.00   ** Lampshade $150.00

DORIC, Jeannette Glass Company, 1935 – 1938

Colors: pink, green, some Delphite, Ultra Marine, and yellow

Collectors of green Doric will find a shortage of pitchers and cream soups. The green, 48-ounce pitcher, with or without ice lip, is nearly a fantasy for collectors to own. Green cereal bowls and all tumblers are only spotted infrequently. Those pieces in pink are not commonly seen either, but they can all be located with determined searching, save for the cream soup, never yet found in pink. Cream soups, or consommés as some companies called them, have two handles. Cereal bowls have no handles but are often offered for sale as cream soups.

Green Doric is found in Florida, but is often cloudy ("sick") glass. Apparently, well water created mineral deposits that react with the glass. You could make a fortune if you could figure out a way to easily remove these deposits. I know I have heard of everything from Zud to Efferdent tablets. As far as I know, this cloudiness cannot be expunged short of professionally polishing it out over a span of time. Do not be hoodwinked into buying cloudy glass unless it is inexpensive, you plan to use and wash it in your dishwasher regularly, or you have that elusive magic cure. Harsh dishwater detergents will also cloud your glass over time.

Doric has become an enjoyable challenge to collectors, and may require years to finish a set. Collectors tell us they do not care how difficult a pattern is to acquire because the hunt fascinates them almost as much as the glass itself. In addition, some collectors aren't even trying for complete sets in today's market. They're blending patterns and colors into rainbow settings.

Mould seam roughness is the norm on Doric, especially on those hard-to-find footed tumblers or cereals. This discourages fussy collectors who look for perfection. Factory irregularities shouldn't stop you from owning these pieces if you see them for sale. Keep in mind that Depression glass was relatively inexpensive or give-away glass. Mint condition, though desirable in glass collecting, can be carried to ludicrous extremes. Magnifying glasses to look for flaws and black (ultraviolet) lights to check for repairs are seen at shows today. At least glass collecting doesn't have people being paid to determine quality and grades for glass as in other collecting fields — or at least, not yet.

Only one yellow Doric pitcher is known to exist; but it is improbable that the factory made only one. Former workers have advised me that even experimental color runs commonly consisted of 30 to 50 items.

The 48-ounce Doric pitchers come with or without an ice lip, but the 32-ounce flat pitcher is only found without a lip. Oddly, candy and sugar lids in this Jeannette pattern are not interchangeable as is true for most of their wares. The candy lid is taller and more domed.

Sherbet and cloverleaf candies are commonly found in Delphite. All other Delphite pieces are scarce in Doric and the price is still inexpensive for that rare color. Only the Delphite pitcher creates much of a pricing disturbance and that is not too great considering its scarcity. Jeannette made mostly kitchenware items in Delphite, rather than dinnerware.

An iridescent, three-part candy was made in the 1970s and sold for 79 cents in our local dish barn. Sometimes an Ultra Marine candy is found within a piece of hammered aluminum hollowed for the candy to fit. I recently saw a 1950s ad showing that Everlast Metal Products Corp. made that 12" piece of aluminum. I pass that along for whatever worth it may be to the growing number of collectors for 50s aluminum wares.

		Pink	Green	Delphite				Pink	Green	Delphite
10 ▸	Bowl, 4½", berry	11.00	12.00	40.00			Plate, 6", sherbet	5.00	6.00	
	Bowl, 5", cream soup, 2 hdld.		595.00			7 ▸	Plate, 7", salad	22.00	22.00	
	Bowl, 5½", cereal	60.00	95.00			6 ▸	Plate, 9", dinner, serrated	195.00	18.00	18.00	
13 ▸	Bowl, 8¼", large berry	30.00	35.00	150.00		5 ▸	Plate, 9", grill	24.00	24.00	
	Bowl, 9", 2-handled	26.00	35.00				Platter, 12", oval	30.00	32.00	
18 ▸	Bowl, 9", oval vegetable	40.00	50.00			19 ▸	Relish tray, 4" x 4"	14.00	12.00	
2 ▸	Butter dish and cover	64.00	90.00			17 ▸	Relish tray, 4" x 8"	22.00	18.00	
	Butter dish bottom	20.00	25.00				Salt and pepper, pair	30.00	35.00	
	Butter dish top	50.00	65.00			12 ▸	Saucer	4.00	5.00	
	Cake plate, 10", 3 legs	20.00	22.00			8 ▸	Sherbet, footed	12.00	15.00	8.00
	Candy dish and cover, 8"	33.00	38.00			3 ▸	Sugar	12.00	12.00	
1 ▸	*Candy dish, 3-part	10.00	10.00	10.00		4 ▸	Sugar cover	18.00	28.00	
15 ▸	Coaster, 3"	15.00	15.00			9 ▸	Tray, 10", handled	25.00	28.00	
16 ▸	Creamer, 4"	15.00	14.00				Tray, 8" x 8", serving	35.00	35.00	
11 ▸	Cup	10.00	12.00			20 ▸	Tumbler, 4½", 9 oz.	65.00	100.00	
	Pitcher, 5½", 32 oz., flat	45.00	50.00	1,500.00			Tumbler, 4", 10 oz., footed	60.00	90.00	
	Pitcher, 7½", 48 oz., footed, yellow at $2,000.00	695.00	1,200.00				Tumbler, 5", 12 oz., footed	85.00	125.00	

Candy in metal holder $40.00, iridescent made in the 70s, ultra marine $18.00.

Doric

DORIC AND PANSY, Jeannette Glass Company, 1937 – 1938
Colors: Ultra Marine; some crystal and pink

Today the supply of Ultra Marine (teal) Doric and Pansy far out weighs the demand for it. In the early 70s, we believed the teal butter, sugar, creamer, salt, and pepper were very rare; they were, within the United States. No one thought to look further than our boundaries for American-made glassware. We have discovered that much Depression era glassware was shipped overseas. Rarely found items of yesteryear in Ultra Marine Doric and Pansy are no longer rare today. Importers of English wares began receiving Doric and Pansy, Royal Lace, Floral, and Fostoria's American glass as "fill" in their containers of imported furniture. Today, English use of the Internet has cut out the middle man. Were it not for shipping costs, we suspect there would be a lot more of these patterns "coming home."

Also, Australia and New Zealand dealers are selling their American Depression finds there through the Internet. At least we now know Depression glass was distributed throughout the world and we ship quite a few books to worldwide dealers wanting to know its value.

Doric and Pansy tumblers and berry bowls are not being found in the supplies abroad; so prices are fairly consistent on them. There are two tumblers pictured. The common one (shaped like the flat Doric tumbler) has a flared top. Only two straight-sided, heavy, darker colored, 4¼", 10 oz. tumblers have been unearthed. Both turned up in California and no others have since emerged.

Take heed of poorly patterned shakers. These should be valued less (50% to 60%). If color and shape are the only clues that it is a Doric and Pansy shaker, do not purchase it unless it is seriously under priced. Weak patterns and cloudiness ruin many shakers. Hazy shakers are not worth mint prices. Cloudiness is caused by a chemical reaction between the glass and its contents of salt or pepper. Salt often corroded original metal shaker tops and while those are desirable, new lids are adequate and available.

Color inconsistencies trouble everyone buying Jeannette's Ultra Marine. Some pieces have a noticeably green tint instead of blue. Fewer collectors seek the greener shade, but it is often priced inexpensively.

Berry bowls and children's sets are found in pink. Strangely, there have been no reports of children's sets or pink Doric and Pansy found in England or Canada. Prices for children's sets have taken a price hit recently since so many have surfaced on Internet auctions.

Luncheon sets in crystal can be obtained, and a few collectors have caught on to that and the price is rising on these rarely observed items.

		Ultra Marine	Pink, Crystal				Ultra Marine	Pink, Crystal
1 ▸	Bowl, 4½", berry	18.00	12.00			Plate, 7", salad	40.00	
	Bowl, 8", large berry	90.00	25.00	11 ▸	Plate, 9", dinner	35.00	25.00
	Bowl, 9", handled	40.00	22.00	6 ▸	Salt and pepper, pr.	350.00	
13 ▸	Butter dish and cover	295.00		16 ▸	Saucer	5.00	5.00
	Butter dish bottom	35.00		7 ▸	Sugar, open	90.00	100.00
	Butter dish top	260.00		8 ▸	Tray, 10", handled	35.00	
2 ▸	Cup	15.00	20.00	9 ▸	Tumbler, 4½", 9 ounce	75.00	
12 ▸	Creamer	90.00	100.00	10 ▸	Tumbler, 4¼", 10 ounce	495.00	
5 ▸	Plate, 6", sherbet	6.00	7.00					

DORIC AND PANSY
"PRETTY POLLY PARTY DISHES"

		Ultra Marine	Pink
3 ▸	Cup	30.00	25.00
4 ▸	Saucer	4.00	3.00
5 ▸	Plate, 6"	6.00	7.00
15 ▸	Creamer	30.00	25.00
14 ▸	Sugar	30.00	25.00
	14-piece set	220.00	190.00

"ELLIPSE," "SHERATON," "TWITCH," Line No. 92, Bartlett-Collins, c. Late 1930s

Colors: crystal, and with applied primary colors (yellow, red, blue, and green) and decaled or hand painted patterns; green

We finally found an Ellipse 61 ounce jug, but it wasn't easy. Note all the flashed colored cups below. We seem to see cups, but are not finding saucers to go with them. With most patterns it's the other way around. Notice that the cups are similarly shaped to Hocking's Colonial and one style of Pillar Optic. We find Ellipse when we travel to Oklahoma and Texas shows. Of course, it was made in that area of the Midwest.

Catalogs do not list some items or colors we are showing. We presume you can help us supplement these listings. Cathy was so excited by finding several colored pieces in a mall that she failed to notice a rarely found item in the same booth. That Rose Point piece more than paid for the Ellipse pieces when we sold it.

At present, there appear to be few collectors searching for this, a consequence of its seldom being seen, no doubt. We have yet to find a green decorated item, but it would not surprise us.

		All Colors
	Bowl, 4½", hdld.	10.00
6 ▸	Bowl, 8", vegetable, hdld.	25.00
5 ▸	Creamer	10.00
1 ▸	Cup	10.00
7 ▸	Goblet, 14 oz,. ftd. tea	18.00
	Jug, 24 oz.	40.00
	Jug, 61 oz., 7½"	60.00
	Plate, 8½"	7.00
	Salt shakers, 3", pr.	40.00
2 ▸	Saucer	3.00
8 ▸	Sherbet	9.00
4 ▸	Sugar, open	10.00
	Tumbler, 5 oz., juice	10.00
3 ▸	Tumbler, 9 oz., water	10.00
	Tumbler, 12 oz., tea	12.00

ENGLISH HOBNAIL, Line #555, Westmoreland Glass Company, 1917 – 1940s; few items through 1980s

Colors: pink, turquoise/ice blue, cobalt blue, green, lilac, red, opal trimmed blue, red flashed, black, blue, amber, and milk

English Hobnail is often confused with Hocking's Miss America, a comparable design, possibly made to compete with this popular Westmoreland pattern. English Hobnail pieces have rays of different distances in the center of the piece. Notice the photographs illustrating this six-point star effect. In Miss America, shown on page 131, the center rays all end uniformly from the center. The hobs on English Hobnail are more curved and feel smoother to the touch; goblets flare and the hobs go directly into a plain rim area around the top. Miss America's hobs are sharper to touch and the goblets do not flare at the rim. All goblets and tumblers of Miss America have three sets of concentric rings above the hobs before entering a plain glass rim. If you have a candy jar that measures more or less than Miss America's 11½" including the cover, then it is probably English Hobnail which occurs in several sizes, both smaller and larger.

Westmoreland's Line #555, English Hobnail, was produced sporadically for over 70 years. Initially, it was christened Early American and was undoubtedly Westmoreland's most expansive line. The foremost production period ran from 1926 through the early 1940s. During those years, it was promoted as English Hobnail. Two dissimilar shapes arise in the pattern, round and square. These profiles expand to the bases on stems so that round based pieces match round plates and bowls, etc. Black footed (c.1929), flashed red, and gold-trimmed items are intermittently found, but are mostly thought of as novelties except by a few passionate collectors.

Due to space limits, we have combined crystal, amber, Westmoreland's 1960s "Golden Sunset" color, and others into the *Collectible Glassware from the 40s, 50s, 60s…* and are listing Depression era and collected colors in this book. We are cognizant that crystal was made from the early teens and darker amber in the late 1920s; but crystal was a major impetus by the company in the WWII years, when chemicals for color production were less available. We have shown quite a few catalog pages from Westmoreland's later years in earlier editions of *Collectible Glassware from the 40s, 50s, 60s…* should you be interested.

Pricing has been grouped into pink or green and turquoise/ice blue. A piece in cobalt blue or black will bring 40% to 50% more than the turquoise prices listed. Very little cobalt English Hobnail is being exposed and even fewer pieces in black. The black pieces are totally black and not crystal trimmed in black.

It took us at least five years to gather enough turquoise/ice blue items for our photo. Extra turquoise items were produced in the 1970s. These later items appear to have a deeper color when put side by side with older pieces.

Shakers are found round or square footed. Most of the ones found in color have round feet. Flat shakers are rarely seen; turquoise blue ones are a treasure.

Compilations of pink or green English Hobnail can be accumulated with time and determination. This pattern does have major color inconsistencies, doubtless due to various times of manufacture. Pink is the most abundant color, but in two dissimilar shades. Not only that, but there are three different greens, from a light, yellow-green to a deep, dark green.

		Pink, Green	Turquoise/ Ice Blue				Pink, Green	Turquoise/ Ice Blue
12 ▸	Ashtray, 3"	20.00				Bowl, 8", footed	60.00	
	Ashtray, 4½"		22.50			Bowl, 8", hexagonal footed, 2-handled	95.00	165.00
	Ashtray, 4½", square	25.00				Bowl, 8", pickle	30.00	
	Bonbon, 6½", handled	25.00	40.00	16 ▸		Bowl, 8", round nappy	35.00	
18 ▸	Bottle, toilet, 5 ounce	35.00	50.00			Bowl, 9", celery	32.00	
13 ▸	Bowl, 3", cranberry	20.00		30 ▸		Bowl, 10", flared	40.00	
	Bowl, 4", rose	50.00				Bowl, 11", rolled edge	50.00	80.00
15 ▸	Bowl, 4½", finger	15.00				Bowl, 12", celery	40.00	
	Bowl, 4½", round nappy	13.00	30.00			Bowl, 12", flange or console	50.00	
	Bowl, 4½", square footed, finger	15.00	35.00			Candlestick, 3½", round base	25.00	35.00
	Bowl, 5", round nappy	15.00	40.00			Candlestick, 9", round base	45.00	55.00
8 ▸	Bowl, 6", crimped dish	18.00				Candy dish, 3 footed	65.00	
1 ▸	Bowl, 6", round nappy	16.00		17 ▸		Candy, ½ lb. and cover, cone shaped	55.00	100.00
14 ▸	Bowl, 6", square nappy	16.00				Cigarette box and cover, 4½" x 2½"	35.00	55.00
	Bowl, 6½", grapefruit	22.00		21 ▸		Cigarette jar w/cover, round	50.00	60.00
	Bowl, 6½", round nappy	20.00				Compote, 5", round, footed	25.00	
	Bowl, 7", round nappy	22.00				Compote, 6", honey, round, footed	30.00	
	Bowl, 8", cupped, nappy	30.00				Compote, 8", ball stem, sweetmeat	60.00	
				7 ▸		Creamer, hexagonal footed	22.50	45.00
						Creamer, square footed	42.50	
				2 ▸		Cup	18.00	25.00
						Cup, demitasse	55.00	

English Hobnail

	Pink, Green	Turquoise/ Ice Blue			Pink, Green	Turquoise/ Ice Blue
4 ▶ Ice tub, 4"	50.00	100.00	10 ▶ Shaker, pair, round footed	75.00	
Ice tub, 5½"	75.00	135.00	Stem, 2 oz., square footed, wine	30.00	60.00
Lamp, 6¼", electric	60.00		26 ▶ Stem, 3 oz., round footed, cocktail	20.00	40.00
Lamp, 9¼", electric	100.00		Stem, 5 oz., sq. footed, oyster cocktail	16.00	
Marmalade w/cover	60.00	85.00	Stem, 8 oz., sq. footed, water goblet	30.00	50.00
Mayonnaise, 6"	20.00		Stem, sherbet, round foot, low		12.00
9 ▶ Nut, individual, footed	20.00		Stem, sherbet, square footed, low	12.00	
Pitcher, 23 ounce, rounded	150.00		Stem, sherbet, round high foot	15.00	30.00
Pitcher, 32 ounce, straight side	185.00		Stem, sherbet, square footed, high	15.00	35.00
Pitcher, 38 ounce, rounded	225.00		22 ▶ Stem, water, round foot		30.00
Pitcher, 60 ounce, rounded	295.00		6 ▶ Sugar, hexagonal footed	22.50	45.00
11 ▶ Pitcher, 64 ounce, straight side	300.00		Sugar, square footed	45.00	
Plate, 5½", round	9.50		Tidbit, 2 tier	45.00	85.00
Plate, 6", square finger bowl liner	9.00		Tumbler, 5 ounce, ginger ale	18.00	
Plate, 6½", round	10.00		19 ▶ Tumbler, 8 ounce, water	22.00	
Plate, 6½, round finger bowl liner	9.50		Tumbler, 10 ounce, ice tea	25.00	
5 ▶ Plate, 8", round	12.50		Tumbler, 12 ounce, ice tea	30.00	
Plate, 8½", round	15.00	25.00	Urn, 11", w/cover (15")	295.00	
Plate, 10", round	37.00	85.00	Vase, 7½", flip	90.00	
Plate, 14", round torte	60.00		Vase, 7½", flip jar w/cover	135.00	
20 ▶ Puff box, w/ cover, 6", round	50.00	77.50	27 ▶ Vase, 8½", flared top	145.00	250.00
Saucer, demitasse, round	15.00		Vase, 10" (straw jar)	125.00	
3 ▶ Saucer, round	4.00	5.00			
Shaker, pair, flat	150.00	250.00			

FANCY COLONIAL, #582, Imperial Glass Company, c. 1914

Colors: crystal, pink, green, teal, some iridized Rubigold and Ice (rainbow washed crystal)

Fancy Colonial, first introduced in crystal, was advertised as "everything for the table in the same design" and was "kept in open stock like a china dinnerware pattern." Some pieces carried the cut star bottom, some didn't.

Pink, their Rose Marie color, was introduced in 1926 and is the color most prevalent. Early pieces sometimes show the Imperial cross marking whereas two letters of the word Imperial are in each quadrant of the cross.

Carnival collectors refer to #582 as Optic and Buttons and value the dozen or so Marigold and Clambroth (some Smoke) iridized items. Other collector names include "Button & Flute" and "Pillar and Optic."

		All colors*
	Bonbon, 5½", handle	20.00
	Bottle, water, no stop	70.00
	Bowl, 3½", nappy	10.00
	Bowl, 4½", nappy	12.00
	Bowl, 4½", rim foot berry	12.00
	Bowl, 5", nappy or olive	12.00
	Bowl, 5", footed, 2 handle	20.00
	Bowl, 5", nut or lily (cupped rim)	20.00
	Bowl, 5", rim foot berry	18.00
4 ▸	Bowl, 6", nappy	18.00
	Bowl, 7", nappy or rim foot berry	30.00
	Bowl, 7", lily	40.00
	Bowl, 8", 2-handle berry	60.00
	Bowl, 8", nappy or salad	35.00
	Bowl, 8", spoon tray (hump edge)	35.00
13 ▸	Bowl, 8", lily (cupped)	40.00
	Bowl, 8", rim foot berry	35.00
	Bowl, 9", rim foot berry	35.00
	Butter & cover	70.00
	Celery, 12", oval	45.00
	Comport, 4", footed	25.00
5 ▸	Comport, 5½", footed	30.00
	Comport, 6¼", footed	35.00

		All colors*
8 ▸	Creamer, footed	20.00
	Cup, custard, flare edge	15.00
	Cup, punch, straight edge	12.00
	Goblet, egg cup, low foot, deep	25.00
	Goblet, low foot, caf parfait	25.00
	Mayo w/liner, flat	45.00
	Oil bottle w/stopper, 6¼ oz.	60.00
	Oil bottle, 5½ ounce, bulbous, w/stopper	70.00
10 ▸	Pickle, 8", oval	30.00
	Pitcher, 3 pint	150.00
	Plate, 5¾"	8.00
	Plate, 7½", salad	15.00
	Plate, 10½", cake	35.00
	Plate, mayonnaise liner	12.00
	Salt & pepper, pair	75.00
3 ▸	Salt, table or footed almond, handled	20.00
	Saucer	5.00
	Sherbet, 3¼", low ft., flare rim or not	20.00
	Sherbet, 4¼", low foot	20.00
	Sherbet, 4¾", footed jelly	22.00
	Spoon (flat open sugar)	20.00
11 ▸	Stem, 1 oz., cordial, deep	30.00
	Stem, 2 oz., wine, deep	25.00

		All colors*
	Stem, 3 oz., cocktail, shallow	18.00
	Stem, 3 oz., port, deep	25.00
6 ▸	Stem, 4½ oz., cocktail, shallow	18.00
	Stem, 4 oz., burgundy, deep	25.00
	Stem, 5 oz., claret, deep	25.00
	Stem, 6 oz., champagne, deep	18.00
7 ▸	Stem, 6 oz., saucer/ champagne, shallow	15.00
	Stem, 8 oz., goblet, deep	20.00
	Stem, 10 oz., goblet, deep	20.00
14 ▸	Sugar w/lid	30.00
	Tumbler, 2 oz., whiskey	20.00
	Tumbler, 4 oz.	12.00
	Tumbler, 5 oz., belled rim or not	12.00
	Tumbler, 6 oz.	12.00
	Tumbler, 8 oz.	15.00
	Tumbler, 10 oz.	15.00
	Tumbler, 12 oz., iced tea	16.00
	Tumbler, 14 oz., iced tea	20.00
	Vase, 8", low foot, flare	65.00
	Vase, 10" flat, bead base, ruffled rim	85.00
	Vase, 12" flat, bead base, ruffled rim	110.00

* Crystal subtract 25%; teal add 25%

FIRE-KING DINNERWARE "PHILBE," Hocking Glass Company, 1937 – 1938
Colors: blue, green, pink, and crystal

Where has all the Fire-King dinnerware gone? It has always been taxing to collect. Finding previously unknown pieces has not been as much of a problem as finding items that we already know should be turning up. Today, collectors would appreciate finding one piece of this obscure Hocking pattern.

Note the vivid blue color of Fire-King dinnerware, often called "Philbe" by collectors. This name was derived from a factory worker, Philip Bee, who was helpful to authors learning about older Hocking glassware. It does not refer to the paler blue ovenware made by Hocking although it is a label often erroneously used for that ware.

We added Fire-King dinnerware to our *Anchor Hocking's Fire-King & More* book and collectors of Fire-King who had never read our Depression glass books were enthralled by it. We received dozens of letters and e-mails inquiring "Where do I find a piece?" The only place in the country that this seems to turn up is in central Ohio near Lancaster where it was made. There was a monthly flea market in Washington Court House where dozens of pieces used to be displayed regularly. At that time, we didn't know what the pattern was; simply that it had mould shapes like Cameo, and thus was Hocking. A pink juice pitcher was displayed for two years priced at $6.00 until a collector finally bought it for his pitcher collection. In 1972, on a first research trip to Anchor Hocking there was a large set of this blue dinnerware displayed in an outer office window. We were writing our first book and didn't know what it was and neither did anyone we asked at the factory. It was from the morgue and a pattern they made in the 1930s. Years later, when visiting the morgue again, there were only a few pieces left. We wonder where they are today.

Some blue pieces have a platinum trim but few other Hocking patterns received that treatment. In fact, only small luncheon sets of Princess with a trim is all that comes to mind.

If there is such a thing as a usually seen piece of blue, it is the footed ice tea since more of these have been found than any other piece. That tea is not as rare as the water, so that is why the water is priced higher. Blue items are more easily found than other colors. It is also the most preferred color. However, collectors will buy any color "Philbe" found, including crystal.

Oval vegetable bowls and the 10½" salver are items most found in pink. Oval bowls can be found in green and crystal, but supply is extremely limited. The green grill or luncheon plates will be the next easiest pieces to obtain. All colored 6" saucer/sherbet plates are exceptionally hard to locate. You should watch for this pattern even if you don't collect it. Were you to spot a piece, it's a certainty that someone wants it.

As a rule, Fire-King dinnerware is found on Cameo shaped blanks; but some pieces, including footed tumblers, nine-ounce water goblets, and the high sherbets appear on Mayfair type blanks.

		Crystal	Pink, Green	Blue				Crystal	Pink, Green	Blue
	Bowl, 5½", cereal	35.00	50.00	75.00	4 ▸	Plate, 10½", grill	40.00	75.00	95.00
10 ▸	Bowl, 7¼", salad	50.00	80.00	100.00	5 ▸	Plate, 11⅝", salver	50.00	62.50	95.00
6 ▸	Bowl, 10", oval vegetable	75.00	95.00	175.00	13 ▸	Platter, 12", closed handles	75.00	150.00	195.00
	Candy jar, 4", low, with cover	300.00	750.00	850.00		Saucer, 6" (same as sherbet plate)	40.00	65.00	95.00
11 ▸	Cookie jar with cover	600.00	995.00	1,500.00	8 ▸	Sherbet, 3¾", no stem	75.00		550.00
	Creamer, 3¼", footed	75.00	150.00	175.00		Sherbet, 4¾", stemmed		300.00	350.00
	Cup	60.00		195.00	2 ▸	Sugar, 3¼", footed	75.00	150.00	175.00
	Goblet, 7¼", 9 ounce, thin	115.00	195.00	250.00		Tumbler, 4", 9 oz., flat water	40.00	105.00	130.00
12 ▸	Pitcher, 6", 36 oz., juice	495.00	695.00	895.00		Tumbler, 3½", footed, juice	40.00	150.00	175.00
	Pitcher, 8½", 56 oz.	495.00	995.00	1,250.00	9 ▸	Tumbler, 5¼", 10 oz., footed	40.00	100.00	150.00
3 ▸	Plate, 6", sherbet	40.00	65.00	95.00	7 ▸	Tumbler, 6½", 15 oz., footed, iced tea	50.00	100.00	125.00
1 ▸	Plate, 8", luncheon	20.00	50.00	60.00					
	Plate, 10", heavy sandwich	40.00	100.00	125.00					
	Plate, 10½", salver	65.00	95.00	110.00					

11

12

13

FLORAL, "POINSETTIA," Jeannette Glass Company, 1931 – 1935

Colors: pink, green, Delphite, Jadite, crystal, amber, red, black, custard, and yellow

"Poinsettia" was the name most often heard for this pattern before we started writing. Collectors thought it looked like poinsettia leaves, but one letter we received from someone who knew the plant better than we did suggested it had to be hemp. One of the first younger dealers said he knew for a fact that it was. After that, a botanist provided evidence from drawings and several pages of information that the design depicted is a passion flower (Passiflora), not a poinsettia or hemp. Passion flower might have been an apt name since collectors for this pattern are definitely passionate in their regard for it. The name bestowed by Jeannette was Floral.

We bought a set of pink Floral that a collector had been trying to sell for several years. Dealers buy sets; collectors usually buy a few pieces at a time. The pursuit is a part of the fun of collecting, and buying an entire set eliminates the stimulus of the hunt. Not only that, but a large set usually involves a prohibitive outlay at one time. In the set we purchased some of the harder to find pieces (which included the lemonade pitcher and tumblers) sold very fast. On the other hand, some of the common pieces are still in our inventory because most collectors of pink Floral already have them. It takes new collectors to buy basic items like cups, saucers, and dinner plates. You can still find these with little trouble, and usually for less than a few years ago. It's the rarely found items that may elude you. You can still find basic Depression glass to collect.

Rare green Floral pieces have been unearthed in England and Canada including all vases, rose bowls, flat pitchers, and flat tumblers. Most of those items found in the United States began appearing in inventories of furniture dealers who imported from England. Today, some dealers have buyers in England searching for American-made glassware along with those fine European antiques. Minor deviations of color and design are present on these items. They are commonly a lighter green color, slightly paneled, and have ground bottoms. The green cups found in England have ground bottoms and are slightly footed. The base of the cup is larger than the normally found saucer indentation. We are shipping more and more books to England as well as Australia and New Zealand; so they definitely realize our glass can be found there.

Prices have dropped slightly on green Floral, flat-bottomed pitchers and tumblers since there are more being found than collectors wanting them. Only the lemonade pitcher and tumbler are holding steady prices. Floral sugar and candy lids are interchangeable, as are most Jeannette lids. Floral designs can be found on the under side of lids and on the base of square Jadite kitchenware/refrigerator storage containers made by Jeannette in the mid-1930s.

One unpleasant reminder is that the smaller, footed Floral shakers have been reproduced in pink, cobalt blue, red, and a very dark green color. Only the pink is of concern since those other colors were never made by Jeannette. The darker green will not glow under a black (ultraviolet) light, as does the old. The new pink shakers, however, are an excellent reproduction of pattern and color. The best way to differentiate the Floral reproduction is to take the top off and look at the threads where the lid screws onto the shaker. On the old, two parallel threads end right before the side mould seams. The new Floral has one continuous line/thread that starts on one side and continues around the shaker until it ends above the beginning line on the other side. There is approximately one inch of overlapped thread making two lines for that inch; but the whole thread is one continuous line and not two separate ones as on the old. To our knowledge, no other Floral reproductions have been made as of May 2007.

		Pink	Green	Delphite	Jadite
1 ▶	Bowl, 4", berry	18.00	20.00	50.00	
	Bowl, 4", berry, ruffled	75.00			
	Bowl, 5½", cream soup	750.00	750.00		
25 ▶	*Bowl, 7½", salad, ruffled $150.00 (23)	26.00	26.00	60.00	
21 ▶	Bowl, 8", covered vegetable	40.00	60.00	75.00 (no cover)	
10 ▶	Bowl, 9", oval vegetable	22.00	25.00		
22 ▶	Butter dish and cover	90.00	100.00		
	Butter dish bottom	25.00	25.00		
	Butter dish top	65.00	75.00		
	Canister set: coffee, tea, cereal, sugar, 5¼" tall, each				135.00
	Candlesticks, 4", pair	75.00	90.00		
4 ▶	Candy jar and cover	38.00	40.00		
2 ▶	Creamer, flat, Cremax $160.00	15.00	18.00	77.50	
18 ▶	Coaster, 3¼"	10.00	12.00		
3 ▶	Comport, 9", ruffled or plain rim	1,000.00	1,025.00		
15 ▶	‡Cup	13.00	11.00		
	Dresser set		1,250.00		
	Frog for vase, also crystal $500.00		725.00		
	Ice tub, 3½", high, oval	950.00	995.00		
	Lamp	325.00	325.00		
	Pitcher, 5½", 23 or 24 ounce		400.00		
	Pitcher, 8", 32 ounce, footed, cone	35.00	40.00		
	Pitcher, 10¼", 48 ounce, lemonade	265.00	295.00		
11 ▶	Plate, 6", sherbet	5.00	6.00		
	Plate, 8", salad	11.00	12.00		

Floral

		Pink	Green	Delphite	Jadite
20 ▸	**Plate, 9", dinner	16.00	18.00	150.00	
	Plate, 9", grill		325.00		
8 ▸	Platter, 10¾", oval	20.00	24.00	150.00	
	Platter, 11" (like Cherry Blossom)	75.00			
17 ▸	Refrigerator dish and cover, 5" square		60.00	95.00	50.00
14 ▸	‡Relish dish, 2-part oval	18.00	20.00	160.00	
	‡‡Salt and pepper, 4", footed, pair	35.00	40.00		
	Salt and pepper, 6", flat	48.00			
16 ▸	‡Saucer	8.00	8.00		
19 ▸	Sherbet	15.00	16.00	85.00	
24 ▸	Sherbet, ruffled	100.00			
5 ▸	Sugar, Cremax $160.00	10.00	12.00	72.50 (open)	
6 ▸	Sugar/candy cover	15.00	18.00		
12 ▸	Tray, 6", square, closed handles	25.00	30.00		
	Tray, 9¼", oval for dresser set		195.00		
	Tumbler, 3½", 3 ounce, footed		150.00		
13 ▸	Tumbler, 4", 5 ounce, footed, juice	18.00	20.00		
	Tumbler, 4½", 9 ounce, flat		110.00		
9 ▸	Tumbler, 4¾", 7 ounce, footed, water	21.00	22.00	195.00	
7 ▸	Tumbler, 5¼", 9 ounce, footed, lemonade	50.00	55.00		
	Vase, 3 legged rose bowl		525.00		
	Vase, 3 legged, flared (also in crystal)		495.00		
	Vase, 6⅞" tall (8 sided), crystal $275.00		425.00		

* Cremax $125.00
** These have now been found in amber and red.
‡ This has been found in yellow.
‡‡ Beware reproductions.

FLORAL AND DIAMOND BAND, U.S. Glass Company, Late 1920s

Colors: pink, green; some iridescent, black, and crystal

Floral and Diamond is the name that was used for this pattern when we first started this adventure of writing about Depression glass in 1972. Observe the 1927 ad on the right which called it the opposite — Diamond and Floral.

Characteristic U. S. Glass rough mould seams are found on most Floral and Diamond Band pieces. This earlier, thick seamed pattern was not as polished as later patterns. This irregularity is standard for Floral and Diamond Band and not regarded as a detriment by long-time collectors who have come to accept it. Difficulty in gathering Floral and Diamond Band is compounded by inconsistent hues of green and pink. Some green has a distinctive blue tint and some pink tends to be very light or lean toward a slight hint of orange. Our smaller photo does not reveal this as our pieces match fairly well.

Luncheon plates, sugar lids, pitchers, and iced tea tumblers (in both pink and green) are limited in supply. Six tumblers were advertised in that 1927 catalog for 85¢. The pitcher and six tumblers were $1.15; that pitcher added only 30 cents to your bill. Today, finding a pitcher for less than $75.00 would be quite a bargain.

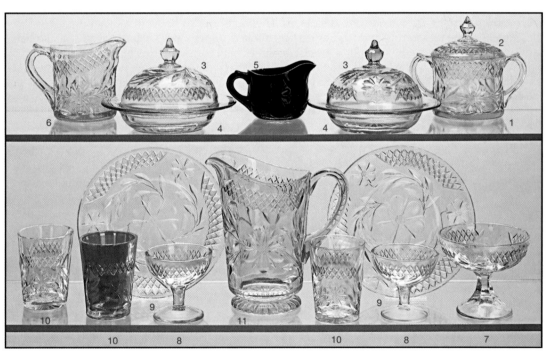

Floral and Diamond Band butter tops may be easier to find than the bottoms since many have been pilfered over the years to be used with tops from more expensive U.S. Glass patterns such as Strawberry and Cherryberry. This transpired because these U.S. Glass butter bottoms are plain and, thus, compatible, since the pattern motifs are positioned only on the top. Dealers were especially guilty of buying all the Floral and Diamond Band butters they could find solely for those plain bottoms. Today, there is a dearth of bottoms for all the tops found.

Small Floral and Diamond Band creamers and sugars have been found in black with ground bottoms, but nothing else in black. That small sugar and creamer, in various colors, is often found with a cut flower over the top of the customary moulded flower. That further idea of cut over moulded seems odd today. That cutting may have made it more commercially accepted at a time when moulded glass wasn't as treasured as cut.

Floral and Diamond Band pitchers, tumblers, and butter dishes with luminous iridescent color bring premium prices from carnival glass collectors as a pattern they dubbed "Mayflower." Sadly, most iridescent pitchers are often weakly colored and unwanted by carnival glass buyers. Glassware collecting overlaps categories and eras and, sometimes attains greater prices from one faction of collectors than it does others.

		Pink	Green				Pink	Green
	Bowl, 4½", berry	8.00	10.00	11 ▶	*Pitcher, 8", 42 ounce		100.00	110.00
	Bowl, 5¾", handled, nappy	12.00	12.00	9 ▶	Plate, 8", luncheon		30.00	30.00
	Bowl, 8", large berry	16.00	16.00	8 ▶	Sherbet		6.00	7.00
	*Butter dish and cover	115.00	105.00		Sugar, small		10.00	10.00
4 ▶	Butter dish bottom	80.00	80.00	1 ▶	Sugar, 5¼"		10.00	10.00
3 ▶	Butter dish top	35.00	25.00	2 ▶	Sugar lid		45.00	55.00
7 ▶	Compote, 5½", tall	16.00	20.00	10 ▶	Tumbler, 4", water		18.00	20.00
5 ▶	Creamer, small	10.00	10.00		Tumbler, 5", iced tea		40.00	45.00
6 ▶	Creamer, 4¾"	15.00	16.00					

* Iridescent $275.00; Crystal $125.00

79

FLORENTINE NO. 1, OLD FLORENTINE, "POPPY NO. 1,"

Hazel-Atlas Glass Company, 1932 – 1935
Colors: pink, green, crystal, yellow, and cobalt blue (See Reproduction Section.)

Differentiating Florentine No. 1 and Florentine No. 2 remains the only mystery for many who list auctions on the Internet. Study the shapes. The serrated edged pieces are hexagonal (six sided) on each flat piece of Florentine No. 1. Additionally all footed pieces including tumblers, shakers, or pitchers have that serrated edging around the base. In Florentine No. 2, all pieces have plain circular edges as can be seen as the next pattern. Florentine No. 1 was even promoted as Hexagonal and Florentine No. 2 was advertised as Round. However, both patterns were sold in mixed pattern sets. Over the years, that practice confused buyers when they found sets with mixed patterns. Today, some collectors still combine both patterns giving them opportunity for extra pieces.

Confusion reigns over the 48 ounce, flat-bottomed pitcher since it was sold with both Florentine No. 1 and No. 2 sets. Original catalogs show this as 54 ounces, but it typically holds six ounces less on ones we have measured. Capacities vary due to the shape of the hand-formed lip as to how many ounces it will hold before liquid runs out. Our inclination is to list this pitcher only with Florentine No. 1 using the handle shape as the deciding factor. However, this pitcher was regularly found with flat-bottomed Florentine No. 2 tumblers which persuades us to list it with both.

Some flat tumblers have moulded, ridged interiors. This style was usually discovered with Florentine No. 1 pitchers. These paneled tumblers should be Florentine No. 1 rather than Florentine No. 2. That determination is for diehard collectors who seem troubled about the panels. Paneled flat tumblers are tough to find, so few need to worry about this difference.

Pink footed tumblers, covered oval vegetable bowls, and butter dishes are practically unavailable now in mint condition. If used, chips and flakes flourished around the uneven edging. Collectors pursuing mint items have quite a chore. Be sure to look underneath as well as on top when you pick a piece to buy. More damage is found underneath the edge than on top. You can gather sets in green or crystal, but yellow and pink are doubtful at this time unless you find someone selling a set collected long ago.

Cobalt blue Florentine No. 1 pitchers have appeared a couple of times over the years. However, do not mistake one of these with the cone shaped, reproduction cobalt No. 2 pitcher turning up regularly.

Florentine No. 1 shakers have been copied in pink and cobalt blue. Other colors may exist, but we have not seen them. The reproduction pink shaker is somewhat problematic. When comparing a reproduction shaker to a couple of old pairs, the older shakers have a major open blossom on each side. There is a top circle on this blossom with three smaller circles down each side. Thus, there are seven circles forming the outside of the blossom. The reproduction blossom looks more like a strawberry and has no circles forming the outside of the blossom. The threading test mentioned under Floral will not work for the Florentine No. 1 shakers although the same company out of Georgia imports these. The threads are correct on this reproduction pattern. The copied design we have seen as of May 2007 has been badly formed, but that could be corrected. Kitchenware item reproductions seem to be the newest target.

Fired-on colors have appeared in Florentine luncheon sets. Sugars, creamers, cups, and saucers are snatched up in unusual colors. You can find all sorts of decorations and colored bands on crystal. A drawback to these banded colors is finding enough to put a set together, although they do add charm to regular crystal sets.

		*Green	Yellow	Pink	Cobalt Blue
	Ashtray, 5½"	20.00	28.00	30.00	
9 ▶	Bowl, 5", berry	12.00	16.00	16.00	25.00
11 ▶	Bowl, 5", cream soup or ruffled nut	30.00		15.00	50.00
	Bowl, 6", cereal	25.00	32.00	45.00	
15 ▶	Bowl, 8½", large berry	26.00	32.00	35.00	
12 ▶	Bowl, 9½", oval vegetable and cover	55.00	75.00	75.00	
17 ▶	Butter dish and cover	110.00	150.00	140.00	
	Butter dish bottom	40.00	75.00	70.00	
	Butter dish top	70.00	75.00	70.00	
	Coaster/ashtray, 3¾"	20.00	22.00	30.00	
	Comport, 3½", ruffled	45.00		15.00	55.00
16 ▶	Creamer	10.00	20.00	18.00	
3 ▶	Creamer, ruffled	40.00		30.00	55.00
	Cup	8.00	12.00	10.00	85.00
	Pitcher, 6½", 36 oz., footed	40.00	55.00	45.00	895.00
	Pitcher, 7½", 48 oz., flat, ice lip or none	75.00	135.00	230.00	
8 ▶	Plate, 6", sherbet	5.00	6.00	6.00	

		*Green	Yellow	Pink	Cobalt Blue
	Plate, 8½", salad	9.00	12.00	10.00	
5 ▶	Plate, 10", dinner	20.00	25.00	30.00	
6 ▶	Plate, 10", grill	14.00	20.00	22.00	
	Platter, 11½", oval	25.00	30.00	25.00	
10 ▶	‡ Salt and pepper, footed	32.00	50.00	50.00	
	Saucer	3.00	4.00	5.00	17.00
13 ▶	Sherbet, 3 oz, footed	10.00	14.00	14.00	
1 ▶	Sugar	9.00	12.00	12.00	
2 ▶	Sugar cover	18.00	30.00	30.00	
4 ▶	Sugar, ruffled	40.00		30.00	35.00
7 ▶	Tumbler, 3¼", 4 oz., footed	15.00			
	Tumbler, 3¾", 5 oz., footed, juice	15.00	25.00	25.00	
	Tumbler, 4", 9 oz., ribbed	15.00		20.00	
14 ▶	Tumbler, 4¾", 10 oz., footed, water	20.00	25.00	25.00	
	Tumbler, 5¼", 12 oz., footed, iced tea	25.00	30.00	30.00	
	Tumbler, 5¼", 9 oz., lemonade (like Floral)			150.00	

*Crystal 20 to 30% less   ‡ Beware reproductions

Read about the differences between the two Florentines on page 80. Try mixing them, a practice the company itself engaged in since boxed sets have turned up over the years including both patterns. This blending of patterns is further demonstrated by the ruffled nut, cream soup, and comport. These pieces meet the standards of Florentine No. 1 because they go with the ruffled creamer and sugar which have serrated bottoms.

The rarer yellow, footed, 6¼", 24-ounce cone-shaped Florentine No. 2 pitcher is hardly ever confused with the footed pitcher that is 7½" tall. Few of the smaller pitchers are discovered. Speaking of that 7½" pitcher, we must report that it and a footed water tumbler have been reproduced in an extremely dark cobalt blue, amber, pink, and a dark green. Originally, the pitcher and tumblers were not made in those colors. If you spot a pink pitcher, realize it is new. They are reproductions.

The 10" Florentine relish dish comes in three styles. The most commonly found is the "Y" style where the divider forms a "Y." The unusual style has two curved divisions, one on each side. The undivided (plain) is the most difficult to attain in all colors. Grill plates with a round indent for the cream soup have been found in green, crystal, and yellow. The indent accommodates the bottom of the cream soup and is too large for the cup.

Crystal Florentine is scarce; hence, prices are similar. Amber, shown in earlier editions, is the rarest Florentine color. Just realize that the footed pitcher and tumblers in that color are new.

A Florentine candy lid measures 4¾" in diameter, the butter lid 5", although similarly shaped. These lids are interchangeable between No. 1 and No. 2.

Custard cups remain the most obscure piece in Florentine No. 2. The custard plate is flat with a larger indentation than the bottom of a regular cup; the saucer curves up on the edges.

27   28

		*Green	Pink	Yellow	Cobalt Blue
2 ▸	Bowl, 4½", berry	*14.00	15.00	20.00	
23 ▸	Bowl, 4¾", cream soup	15.00	16.00	20.00	
	Bowl, 5½"	35.00		45.00	
21 ▸	Bowl, 6", cereal	33.00		42.00	
	Bowl, 7½", shallow			100.00	
	Bowl, 8", large berry	28.00	30.00	38.00	
	Bowl, 9", oval vegetable with cover	30.00		40.00 / 85.00	
	Bowl, 9", flat	35.00			
	Butter dish and cover	100.00		150.00	
	Butter dish bottom	25.00		70.00	
	Butter dish top	75.00		80.00	
17 ▸	Candlesticks, 2¾", pair	45.00		65.00	
	Candy dish and cover	90.00	125.00	140.00	
16 ▸	Coaster, 3¼"	12.00	15.00	20.00	
25 ▸	Coaster/ashtray, 3¾"	15.00		30.00	
	Coaster/ashtray, 5½"	20.00		32.00	
7 ▸	Comport, 3½", ruffled	45.00	15.00		55.00
28 ▸	Creamer	9.00		12.00	
9 ▸	Cup, amber 50.00	8.00		10.00	
	Custard cup or jello	55.00		85.00	
19 ▸	Gravy boat			50.00	
	Pitcher, 6¼", 24 oz., cone-footed			135.00	135.00
13 ▸	**Pitcher, 7½", 28 oz., cone-footed	35.00		35.00	
	Pitcher, 7½", 48 ounce	75.00	135.00	230.00	
	Pitcher, 8¼", 76 ounce	95.00	195.00	395.00	
24 ▸	Plate, 6", sherbet	3.00		5.00	

		*Green	Pink	Yellow	Cobalt Blue
	Plate, 6¼", with indent	30.00		25.00	
6 ▸	Plate, 8½", salad	9.00	8.50	8.00	
	Plate, 10", dinner	14.00		14.00	
12 ▸	Plate, 10¼", grill	16.00		18.00	
	Plate, 10¼", grill w/ cream soup ring	45.00			
22 ▸	Platter, 11", oval	15.00	15.00	22.00	
20 ▸	Platter, 11½", for gravy boat			50.00	
26 ▸	Relish dish, 10", 3-part or plain	28.00	30.00	35.00	
8 ▸	‡ Salt and pepper, pair	40.00		45.00	
10 ▸	Saucer, amber $15.00	3.00		4.00	
	Sherbet, ftd., amber $40.00	9.00		10.00	
27 ▸	Sugar	9.00		10.00	
	Sugar cover	15.00		25.00	
	Tray, round, condiment for shakers, creamer/sugar			70.00	
3 ▸	Tumbler, 3⅜", 5 oz., juice	12.00	12.00	20.00	
1 ▸	Tumbler, 3⁹⁄₁₆", 6 oz., blown	15.00			
14 ▸	‡‡ Tumbler, 4", 9 oz., water	12.00	16.00	18.00	60.00
15 ▸	Tumbler, 5", 12 oz., blown	20.00			
	‡‡ Tumbler, 5", 12 oz., tea	33.00		50.00	
18 ▸	Tumbler, 3¼", 5 oz., footed	14.00		18.00	
11 ▸	Tumbler, 4", 5 oz., footed	15.00		14.00	
4 ▸	Tumbler, 5", 9 oz., footed	30.00		26.00	
5 ▸	Vase or parfait, 6"	35.00		50.00	

* Crystal 20 to 30% less   ** Ice Blue $595.00   ‡ Fired-on red, orange, or blue, Pr. $42.50   ‡‡ Amber $75.00

FLOWER GARDEN WITH BUTTERFLIES, "BUTTERFLIES AND ROSES," BROCADE,

U.S. Glass Company, Factory R, Tiffin Plant, c. 1924
Colors: pink, green, blue-green, canary yellow, crystal, amber, blue, and black

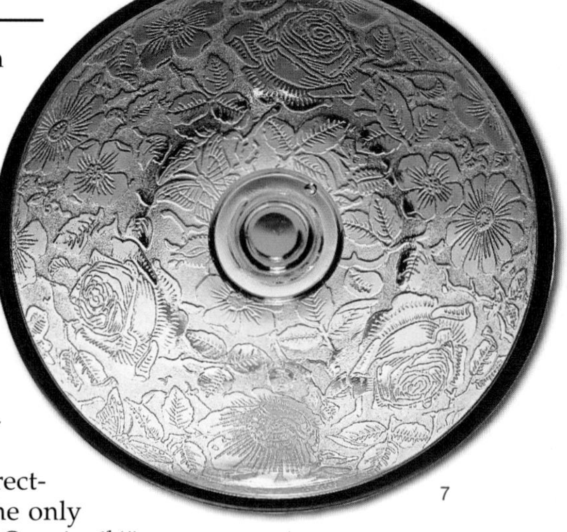

After collecting Flower Garden with Butterflies for over 20 years, in a moment of madness, we sold our set. Earlier editions showed a much larger grouping because of our collection. Now, we are having trouble finding pieces and can better identify with people who search for it.

Tiffin catalog pages continue to be unearthed from all over the country, so we are fortunate to learn things about our glassware that pioneer authors didn't know. The original name for this pattern was Brocade. It is understood to have been in production for about a 10-year period, though evidently not continuously considering the deficiency of items available today.

This pattern is found so rarely that few new collectors are attempting it. Over the years, Brocade collections have been assembled and today, only materialize on the market when complete sets are sold. Yet, this is one pattern that lends itself extremely well for a one-piece display. Please know that even one piece of any pattern you like can give you visual pleasure with every glance.

There are three styles of powder jars, which may explain why oval and rectangular dresser trays are easily found. Dresser trays and luncheon plates are the only consistently found items in the pattern. Two different footed powders exist. One is 6½" high; but the taller stands 7½". Luckily the lids for these footed powders are the same. The flat powder jar is 3½" in diameter. We never found a blue, flat powder while we were collecting, though we feel certain there must be some out there.

The search for butterflies on each piece is entertaining. Sometimes they are prominently displayed, but often not. We owned a black candlestick that only had the end of a butterfly antenna on it. You really had to search to find that little piece of butterfly. The other candlestick of the pair had half a butterfly. Will an item turn up where the butterfly flew away entirely?

A crystal cologne with black stopper turned up for us after we had earlier photographed a black cologne sans stopper. We missed the opportunity to photograph them together. Possibly the black one had a crystal stopper originally, but we are not sure. Check the dauber in the perfumes. Many of them are broken off or ground down to hide the broken end. Daubers are much harder to find than the bottles themselves; take that into consideration when buying only the bottle. That is true for any perfume/cologne in any pattern. The piece handled most often usually suffered the damage and was tossed away. However, if the lone bottle gives you pleasure, corks are available.

There is a semi-circular, footed glass dresser box which holds five wedge (pie shaped) bottles that is often advertised as Flower Garden because it has flower designs on it. Labels found intact on bottles promoted the New York/Paris affiliation of "Charme Volupté." One bottle contained cold cream, another vanishing cream, and three others once held parfumes. There are dancing girls at either end of the box, and flowers abound on the semi-circle. There are no dancing girls on Brocade. Other not-to-be-mistaken-for Flower Garden pieces include the 7" and 10" trivets with flowers all over them made by U.S. Glass. They were also used as mixing bowl covers and they do not have butterflies.

		Amber, Crystal	Pink, Green, Blue-Green	Blue, Canary			Amber, Crystal	Pink, Green, Blue-Green	Blue, Canary
	Ashtray, match-pack holders	125.00	150.00	155.00		Mayonnaise, footed, 4¾" h. x 6¼" w., w/7" plate & spoon	75.00	95.00	135.00
	Candlesticks, 4", pair	40.00	55.00	85.00					
	Candlesticks, 8", pair	65.00	125.00	140.00		Plate, 7"	12.00	18.00	25.00
	Candy w/cover, 6", flat		130.00	155.00		Plate, 8", two styles	12.00	15.00	20.00
	Candy w/cover, 7½", cone-shaped	60.00	110.00	125.00		Plate, 10"		42.50	48.00
						Plate, 10", indent for 3" comport	32.00	40.00	45.00
9 ▶	Candy w/cover, heart-shaped		1,250.00	1,400.00		Powder jar, 3½", flat		60.00	
	*Cologne bottle w/stopper, 7½"		225.00	350.00	4 ▶	Powder jar, footed, 6¼" h.	65.00	125.00	150.00
	Comport, 2⅞" h.		23.00	28.00		Powder jar, footed, 7½" h.	65.00	125.00	150.00
	Comport, 3" h., fits 10" plate	20.00	23.00	28.00	3 ▶	Sandwich server, center handle	50.00	60.00	80.00
7 ▶	Comport, 4¼" h. x 4¾" w.			50.00	2 ▶	Saucer		15.00	
6 ▶	Comport, 4¾" h. x 10¼" w.	48.00	65.00	85.00		Sugar		55.00	
	Comport, 5⅞" h. x 11" w.	55.00		95.00		Tray, 5½" x 10", oval	55.00	60.00	
5 ▶	Comport, 7¼" h. x 8¼" w.	60.00	80.00			Tray, 11¾" x 7¾", rectangular	50.00	60.00	70.00
	Creamer		55.00			Tumbler, 7½"	175.00		
1 ▶	Cup		55.00		8 ▶	Vase, 6¼"	75.00	100.00	175.00
	* Stopper, if not broken off, ½ price of bottle					Vase, 10½"		135.00	235.00

PRICE LIST FOR BLACK ITEMS ONLY

Bonbon w/cover, $6\frac{5}{8}$" diameter	200.00
Bowl, $7\frac{1}{4}$", w/cover, flying saucer	325.00
Bowl, $8\frac{1}{2}$", console, w/base	140.00
Bowl, 9", rolled edge, w/base	175.00
Bowl, 11", footed orange	175.00
Bowl, 12", rolled edge console w/base	175.00
Candlestick 6" w/$6\frac{1}{2}$" candle, pair	495.00
Candlestick, 8", pair	250.00
Cheese and cracker, footed, $5\frac{3}{8}$" h. x 10" w.	195.00
Comport and cover, $2\frac{3}{4}$" h. (fits 10" indented plate)	175.00
Cigarette box & cover, $4\frac{3}{8}$" long	140.00
Comport, tureen, $4\frac{1}{4}$" h. x 10" w.	195.00
Comport, footed, $5\frac{7}{8}$" h. x 10" w.	195.00
Comport, footed, 7" h.	140.00
Plate, 10", indented	75.00
Sandwich server, center-handled	95.00
Vase, $6\frac{1}{4}$", Dahlia, cupped	125.00
Vase, 8", Dahlia, cupped	175.00
Vase, 9", wallhanging	395.00
Vase, 10", 2-handled	195.00
Vase, $10\frac{1}{2}$", Dahlia, cupped	210.00

"FLUTE & CANE," "SUNBURST & CANE," "CANE," "HUCKABEE,"
SEMI-COLONIAL, NO. 666 & 666½, Imperial Glass Company, c. 1921
Colors: crystal, pink, green, Rubigold (marigold), Caramel slag

Does anyone have a large accumulation of "Flute & Cane"? If you'll be kind enough to let us know what you've turned up, we'd be most appreciative and will make an effort to pass it along to collectors. Cathy convinced me to include this pattern with the unfortunate "devil's" line number. She finds the cane look intriguing. We were informed by an Imperial devotee that the half number beside Imperial's line numbers indicated the less expensively made glassware sold in places like F.W. Woolworth, Sears, Montgomery Wards, et. al. The slag being found is from the 70s, near the time of Imperial's demise.

There was a sugar and creamer displayed in slag when we visited the factory in the 80s, though it is not in any of the catalogs they offered then for research. As was Imperial's (and other glass companies) wont, they launched a few items from older moulds into their wares from time to time, and in whatever colors they were running. Since our catalog information doesn't comprise Imperial's entire history, we can't be positive what other colors you'll find in "Flute and Cane."

Many of the Rubigold pieces are quite rare and highly prized by carnival glass collectors. Notice we have not found any to display. The tall, slender pitcher, tumblers, cups, 6" plates, and goblets are considered enviable items to own. Nevertheless, various bowls are what we usually find. The 6" plate was marketed in several ways, with the sherbet as an ice cream set, with the molasses as an underliner, and with the custard cup as a saucer. There ought to be quite a few of those available; but that doesn't seem to be the case. There is a very cane-like candle in the picture that legitimately goes with the Amelia #671 line, shown on page 10. Trying to photograph dozens of patterns over a week or so sometimes presents problems unseen until too late such as a wrong piece in the photo — as here. You actually need to read the text from time to time and not always trust just an author's photo.

Cathy believes she saw some blue long before we decided to put #666 in our book. If you have some, it will help document another color.

		Crystal*			Crystal*			Crystal*
8 ▸	Bowl, 4½", fruit	10.00		Celery, 8½", oval	22.00	3 ▸	Pitcher, tall/slender	65.00
	Bowl, 6½", oval, pickle	16.00		Celery, tall, 2 handle	40.00		Plate, 6"	20.00
	Bowl, 6½", square	15.00		Compote, 6½", oval, ftd., 2-hdl.	30.00		Salt & pepper	45.00
1 ▸	Bowl, 7½", ruffled	28.00		Compote, 7½", stem w/bowl	25.00	6 ▸	Sherbet, 3½", stem	12.00
5 ▸	Bowl, 7½", salad	25.00		Compote, 7½", stem, flat	25.00		Spooner (open sm. sug)	15.00
	Bowl, 8½", large fruit	30.00	2 ▸	Compote, ruffled top	25.00		Stem, 1 ounce, cordial	25.00
4 ▸	Bowl, créme soup, 5½", ftd.	22.00		Creamer	15.00		Stem, 3 ounce, wine	18.00
	Butter w/lid, small (powder box look)	35.00		Cup, custard	12.00		Stem, 6 ounce, champagne	15.00
				Molasses, nickel top	70.00		Stem, 9 ounce, water	18.00
	Butter, dome lid	55.00		Oil bottle w/stopper, 6 oz.	45.00	7 ▸	Sugar w/lid	20.00
	Candle, 8"	20.00		Pitcher, 22 ounce, 5¼"	40.00		Tumbler, 9 ounce	25.00
9 ▸	Candlestick (Amelia)	25.00		Pitcher, 51 ounce	55.00	10 ▸	Vase, 6"	37.50

* add 50% for colors

86

FORTUNE, Hocking Glass Company, 1937 – 1938
Colors: pink and crystal

The Fortune covered candy is the most often spotted candy in Depression era glass even though you might not think so from our photo. A few years ago, a lady approached us to ask about replacing her mom's candy that she had accidentally broken. We had one in our photography box, so we shipped it to her and keep forgetting to replace it. That fortune candy makes a fantastic gift for a beginning collector and remains one of the most economically priced pink candy dishes in Depression glass.

Luncheon plates are costly, and you ordinarily find them only one at a time. Time and a little luck can help you still assemble a set of pink Fortune. Occasionally, you will find a crystal piece or two, but not enough to complete a set — even a small one.

Fortune tumblers have been acquired by collectors of Queen Mary and Old Colony to use with those sets because they were inexpensive compared to their patterns' tumblers. Given that Hocking made all three patterns, the colors do match and Fortune blends well with both patterns. Prices for Fortune tumblers still lag behind those other patterns; so it is still realistic to use them with other sets. We see tumblers and small berry bowls when we spot Fortune. Other items are not so easily found. The 7¾" large berry has become a nemesis.

We receive a few letters every so often from someone who thinks they have spotted a Fortune pitcher. It is a Hocking pitcher similar to Fortune and some collectors are buying them for use with their sets since no true Fortune pitcher has yet been found. These "go-with" juice pitchers are usually offered in the $30.00 to $50.00 range.

		Pink, Crystal
1 ▸	Bowl, 4", berry	8.00
	Bowl, 4½", dessert	8.00
	Bowl, 4½", handled	8.00
5 ▸	Bowl, 5¼", rolled edge	15.00
	Bowl, 7¾", salad or large berry	25.00
	Candy dish and cover, flat	20.00
6 ▸	Cup	10.00
4 ▸	Plate, 6", sherbet	6.00
	Plate, 8", luncheon	25.00
7 ▸	Saucer	4.00
3 ▸	Tumbler, 3½", 5 ounce, juice	7.00
2 ▸	Tumbler, 4", 9 ounce, water	10.00

FRANCES, Central Glass Works, Late 1920s – Early 1930s
Colors: amber, black, blue, crystal, green, pink

We added the Frances pattern from Central Glass Works to our book last time, and right after it went to press we ran into an amber pitcher which we had failed to list. Frances has been noticed by a few for years, but the Internet exposed it to thousands more. Usually spotted items include bowls, sandwich servers, and vases. Amber is one color ignored in other patterns, but the vivid amber is attractive in Frances. It's often labeled as "Deco" in antique malls.

We amassed some duplicate pieces while purchasing Frances for photography. After the photo session, we priced the extras for sale. Most sold at the first show we displayed them. The last pink bowl we placed in our booth in a mall only sat three days before it left. Buyers were not collectors of Frances per se. They just found the pieces attractive and "must have."

Blue and black items are rarely seen which makes that blue powder/candy special. We bought it several years ago thinking it was Hocking's Gem since the color appeared the same and the pattern similar. Research revealed it to be a piece of Frances.

		*All colors
	Ashtray, 5", 2-piece	75.00
	Bowl, 6", round	15.00
	Bowl, 8", round	35.00
4 ▸	Bowl, 9½" round	40.00
8 ▸	Bowl, 10", 3-ftd., two-sided, fluted	50.00
	Bowl, 10", 3-ftd., round	50.00
	Bowl, 10", 3-ftd., triangular, fluted	50.00
1 ▸	Bowl, 12", console	50.00
6 ▸	Cake plate, 12", 3-ftd.	65.00
	Candle stick, 3½"	35.00
	Celery, 7½" high, 2-hdld., ftd.	40.00

		*All colors
	Celery, 10¼", 4-ftd	35.00
	Comport, 5¼" high	30.00
7 ▸	Creamer, ftd.	30.00
9 ▸	Pitcher	65.00
	Plate, 6¼"	10.00
3 ▸	Powder/candy jar w/tab knobbed lid	100.00
2 ▸	Sugar, ftd., 2 styles	30.00
	Tray, 10¼", center handled server	35.00
	Tumbler, 10 oz.	30.00
5 ▸	Vase, 8½" to 10½" high	60.00

* Crystal 30 – 35% less, black or blue 50% morea

FRUITS, Hazel-Atlas and other glass companies, 1931 – 1935

Colors: pink, green, some crystal, and iridized

Fruits pattern suffers from a lack of recognition by collectors who do not search for pieces not so readily found. Fruits pitchers have only cherries in the pattern along the top and on the bottom. They are often misidentified as Cherry Blossom flat-bottomed pitchers. Notice that the handle is moulded like that of flat Florentine pitchers (Hazel-Atlas Company) and not like Cherry Blossom (Jeannette Glass Company) flat pitchers. Crystal Fruits pitchers sell for less than half the price of green and other crystal pieces are usually ignored. Both crystal pitchers and tumblers are obtainable should you want an antique 80 year old, economically priced, beverage set.

Fruits water tumblers (4") are commonly found. Iridescent "Pears"-only tumblers are bountiful. Federal Glass Company probably made these carnival-colored tumblers at the same time they were making iridescent Normandie and a few pieces in Madrid in the late 1930s. Water tumblers with cherries or a combination of fruits are found in pink.

Fruits green water tumblers are found infrequently; but the 3½" (5 ounce) juice and 5" (12 ounce) iced tea tumblers have joined the large and small berry bowls as the choice pieces of green to discover. We have only owned one iced tea and no juice tumblers. The Cherry Blossom flat juice tumbler is sometimes mistaken as a Fruits juice. Cherry Blossom juices have blossoms along the top edge whereas Fruits have cherries. However, prices are softer on these rarely seen items as there is little demand for them at this time. Previous collectors gave up on finding them and are doing without.

Fruits berry bowls (in both sizes) are among the most challenging "finds" in all Depression glass. Given that Fruits is not one of the most collected patterns with thousands of admirers, the inadequacy of both sizes of bowls has only become apparent in recent years.

We have never found a pink pitcher or juice and tea tumblers, though we once inadvertently listed them. In the earlier books, we only showed one price for all Fruits colors. The price of green escalated quicker than pink due to more collecting pressure. When we separated prices into two colors no one comprehended that the apparently imaginary pink juice and tea tumblers were shrouded under that "all colors" categorization. It took a while for us to realize that those pink items were not to be found; so, we dropped them.

		Green	Pink			Green	Pink
7 ▸	Bowl, 4½", berry	30.00	22.00	5 ▸	Sherbet	12.00	13.00
3 ▸	Bowl, 8", berry	85.00	50.00		Tumbler, 3½", juice	60.00	
1 ▸	Cup	7.00	9.00	9 ▸	*Tumbler, 4" (1 fruit)	18.00	16.00
6 ▸	Pitcher, 7", flat bottom	100.00		10 ▸	Tumbler, 4" (combination of fruits)	30.00	22.00
4 ▸	Plate, 8", luncheon	10.00	10.00	8 ▸	Tumbler, 5", 12 ounce	125.00	
2 ▸	Saucer	4.00	4.00		*Iridized $8.00		

GEM, "KALEIDOSCOPE," Hocking Glass Company, c. 1933

Colors: Mayfair blue, crystal, green, and pink

"Kaleidoscope" was our given name for this ware when we added it to our book six years ago since no name could be found in any of our Hocking records or catalogs. We searched high and low, and as much as we have frowned on naming patterns in the past, Cathy suggested "Kaleidoscope" and so it became for a time.

Late that year, a former Anchor-Hocking employee's wife gave him our book for Christmas. When he saw our new listing for "Kaleidoscope," he sent us documentation to show this was definitely a Hocking pattern as we had surmised. He sent copies of designs and drawings of pieces which were unnamed; however, he owned a labeled piece designating it as Gem. It is not a plentiful pattern, but there are enough basic pieces to pursue a nice table setting if you wish.

Blue turns up more in our travels and may be the most available color; but pieces in pink, green, and even crystal can be unearthed. The pink celery is the only pink piece we have come across. Crystal and cobalt blue are pictured for the first time. Crystal was made for Woolworth's which should make it easier to find — but not for us. Of note is a blue coaster with raised rays like those on Hocking's Miss America coaster. That is pictured, but a crystal cup was placed on top of it so the rays may just as well be invisible. We have only found the divided relish in crystal, but the undivided celery has been found in every color.

The cobalt plate with its squared divider may have been used as a snack plate, but what fits the square raised rim is a mystery. Several sets of the light blue were spotted years ago when we were not looking for photography items. They are out there somewhere. Keep searching.

		Blue	*Green, Pink				Blue	*Green, Pink
	Bowl, 5", berry	25.00	15.00	4 ▶	Plate, 9½", dinner		35.00	25.00
1 ▶	Bowl, flat soup	50.00	35.00	10 ▶	Plate, 9½", grill		35.00	20.00
	Bowl, oval vegetable w/tab hdls.	75.00	55.00		Platter, oval w/tab handles		90.00	75.00
8 ▶	Celery, tab handles	60.00	50.00	2 ▶	Relish, 11½", divided, tab hdls.			45.00
11 ▶	Coaster	30.00		7 ▶	Saucer		20.00	15.00
9 ▶	Creamer	60.00	35.00		Stem, 6 ounce, sherbet		25.00	20.00
6 ▶	Cup	90.00	75.00	3 ▶	Stem, 10 ounce, water		50.00	35.00
	Plate, 6", bread	12.00	10.00		Sugar		60.00	35.00
5 ▶	Plate, 8" salad w/indent (cobalt)	60.00						

*Crystal 50%

GEORGIAN, "LOVEBIRDS," Federal Glass Company, 1931 – 1936
Colors: green, crystal, and amber

Federal Glass Company's Georgian pattern exhibits two lovebirds (or parakeets, as an ornithologist reader enlightened us) sitting side by side with a hanging basket alternating with the birds around most pieces. Those lovebirds distinguish Georgian for most items; however, there are a few pieces of this pattern without birds. Both sizes of tumblers, the hot plate, and a few dinner plates have only baskets. Few collectors seek dinner plates without birds; so, that basket (only) style plate sells for less.

You can occasionally find a good buy on tumblers if the owner does not recognize that Georgian tumblers have no birds. The tumblers are so rarely found that a long-time dealer friend once called about them. He was looking at a reasonably priced Georgian set with tumblers, but worried that there were no birds on the tumblers. We have mentioned this in every book we have written, so somehow we are not getting through to you.

Basic pieces of Georgian are available. Berry bowls, cups, saucers, sherbets, sherbet plates, and luncheon plates can be found without difficulty. So, yes, this pattern can still be collected. Georgian tumblers (no birds) are tricky to acquire. Prices for iced teas have softened and waters have reduced about 20%. Supplies of waters keep turning up, but not so the iced teas. We have owned at least a dozen Georgian waters for every iced tea to give you an idea of how difficult teas are to unearth. Several boxed sets of 36 water tumblers were found stored in the Chicago area, where a newspaper gave the tumblers away to subscribers in the 1930s. Evidently, subscribers were not found to deplete that supply. We also heard of an antique mall opening in northern Ohio where six water tumblers were purchased for around $30.00. That was quite a find; but surprisingly, upon returning a few days later, those tumblers had been supplanted with six additional ones for the same price. Unfortunately, that dozen was all there was; but it was pleasurable surprise while it lasted.

The lack of new collectors searching for Georgian has caused some reduction on the prices of items offered for less than $50.00. Rarely seen items usually hold their own when price downturns occur, but items once rarely seen are becoming less so with all the new sellers on the Internet worldwide searching basements, attics, garages, and even old dumps.

Georgian serving pieces were heavily utilized; so be cautious of mint pricing for pieces that are scratched and worn from use. You may pay a premium for mint condition, but make sure it is mint. Keep in mind that all prices listed in this book are for mint condition pieces. Damaged or scratched and worn pieces should go for less depending upon the degree of damage and deterioration. If you are gathering this glass to use, some defects may not make as much difference as collecting for eventual reselling. At this time, chipped and damaged glass is not even bringing 20 – 25% of mint as they used to do. Mint condition glass will always sell faster and for a much better price if you ever are inclined to part with your collection.

Georgian Lazy Susans (cold cuts servers as shown below) are more rarely seen than the Madrid ones that turn up, infrequently, at best. Walnut trays have surfaced in southern Ohio and northern Kentucky with original decal labels reading "Kalter Aufschain Cold Cuts Server Schirmer Cincy." These wooden Lazy Susans are made of walnut and are 18½" across with seven 5" openings for holding the hot plates. These 5" so-called hot plates may be a misnomer since they are found on a cold cuts server. These cold/hot plates have only the center motif design and can also be found in crystal.

There is a round, thin plate made by Indiana Glass having two large parakeets as its center design, covering nearly the whole plate. This is not Georgian, but can be found in green as well as amber and canary. All Georgian plates are thick.

15

Georgian

		Green				Green
	Bowl, 4½", berry	8.00	7 ▸	*Hot plate, 5", center design	90.00
1 ▸	Bowl, 5¾", cereal	16.00		**Plate, 6", sherbet	4.00
8 ▸	Bowl, 6½", deep	48.00	6 ▸	Plate, 8", luncheon	7.00
	Bowl, 7½", large berry	45.00	12 ▸	Plate, 9¼", dinner	18.00
	Bowl, 9", oval vegetable	45.00	5 ▸	Plate, 9¼", center design only	12.00
	Butter dish and cover	65.00		Platter, 11½", closed-handled	48.00
	Butter dish bottom	40.00	10 ▸	Saucer	2.00
	Butter dish top	25.00	11 ▸	Sherbet	10.00
15 ▸	Cold cuts server, 18½", wood with seven 5" openings for 5" coasters	895.00	3 ▸	Sugar, 3", footed	7.00
				Sugar, 4", footed	14.00
2 ▸	Creamer, 3", footed	8.00	4 ▸	Sugar cover for 3"	35.00
	Creamer, 4", footed	14.00	14 ▸	Tumbler, 4", 9 ounce, flat	48.00
9 ▸	Cup	7.00	13 ▸	Tumbler, 5¼", 12 ounce, flat	110.00

*Crystal $30.00   **Amber $40.00

92

GLADES, Line #215, New Martinsville, c. 1930s

Colors: amber, amethyst, crystal and w/etches, cobalt, ruby, green, blue, black

Glades, as we know it, is Paden City's Line #215. The linear design has a very strong Deco look, prevalent at the time. While we were searching for pieces of Glades to photograph, we ran across a large amethyst set in an antique mall. Although the owner had no idea what it was, the prices were prohibitive. One of each piece is illustrated. Amethyst items pictured have ground bottoms, which is indicative of earlier, hand-finished glassware.

Not long ago, we found a gorgeous ruby, platinum decorated, whiskey set consisting of a decanter, ice tub, and six footed cocktails all on a mirrored tray. We felt it to be a prized, intact, 30s find.

Canton Glass was still making Glades as late as 1954 from Paden City moulds. You will doubtless find additional pieces and perhaps other colors than those listed.

		*Crystal			*Crystal
	Bowl, 4½", tab hdld., fruit	10.00		Ice tub, 4" high x 6⅜" diameter	75.00
	Bowl, 4¾", cream soup	12.50		Plate, 6½", tab hdld.	5.00
	Bowl, 5", tab hdld., flare rim, cereal	12.50		Plate, 7"	6.00
7 ▸	Bowl, 6", cereal, deep	18.00		Plate, 8"	7.50
	Bowl, 6", tab hdld., shallow	15.00		Plate, 9¼"	12.50
	Bowl, 6", tab hdld., bonbon	15.00		Plate, 10"	15.00
	Bowl, 7"	12.50	6 ▸	Plate, 11½", serving	20.00
	Bowl, 7¼", gravy	30.00		Plate, 12"	20.00
5 ▸	Bowl, 8⅝"	35.00		Relish, 4 part, tab hdld	32.50
	Bowl, 10", tab hdld., oval	50.00		Relish tray, 12¾", 2 hdld., 2 part	40.00
	Bowl, 3 toe, 12½", flat rim, console	45.00		Server, center-hdle. w/round, lined center knob	35.00
1 ▸	Candle, 5", double light	35.00		Saucer	2.50
	Cocktail, 8", 30 oz.; w/metal lid, 11"	40.00		Shaker, 2⅛", round, pr.	30.00
	Cocktail, double cone shape, 3 oz.	13.00		Sugar, 7 oz.	12.50
	Comport, 3½" high	27.50		Tray, 11", oval celery	20.00
	Comport, 7⅝" high, indented top	37.50	4 ▸	Tumbler, 3 oz., flat whiskey	12.50
2 ▸	Creamer, 7 oz.	12.50		Tumbler, 3½ oz.	17.50
	Cup	13.00	3 ▸	Tumbler, 4", 8 oz.	17.50
	Decanter, 6½", 12 oz., tilt w/handle, cordial	55.00		Tumbler, 5¼", 12 oz., tea	20.00

* Add 50% for blue, red, black;
10 – 15% with etching or amethyst

GOTHIC GARDEN, Paden City Glass Company, 1930s

Colors: amber, pink, green, black, yellow, and crystal

Gothic Garden is a Paden City etched pattern that is mostly found on their Line #411 (square shapes with the corners cut off), which is also known as "Mrs. B" line. It also crops up on other Paden City blanks.

Cups and saucers are rare in all etched patterns of this company. A dearth of cups and saucers has not hurt collecting Paden City's patterns. For now, we are only listing one price for all colors found; add 25% for black and subtract 25% or more for crystal. What little crystal we have seen has been gold trimmed which, with good gold, will attract some attention.

When we see Gothic Garden at antique shows, pieces usually have overpriced stickers. However, since we keep seeing those same pieces offered for sale, we feel Gothic Garden etch has not caught on with collectors to the magnitude of those excessive prices.

Amazingly, most of the essential designs of 1930s glassware decorations (including birds, flowers, scrolls, garlands, and urns) are found in Gothic Garden pattern. It should be the most sought-after etch ever made in that period, but, regrettably, it is not. There is an uncomfortable posture by the bird in the design. The bird's body faces outward on either side of the designed medallion, but its head turns rearward in relation to the center floral motif. It is evocative of a Phoenix bird, that mythological bird that rose from the ashes. A number of Paden City patterns feature birds.

Measurements may fluctuate up to an inch due to the degree of the hand-turned up edges on bowls; do not take our listings as absolute gospel. All measurements listed are ones from the pieces we measured ourselves.

We saw a flat, yellow Gothic Garden square candy like the one pictured in "Peacock Reverse" on page 169. Since it was more esteemed by the seller, he still owns it — two years later.

		All colors			All colors
2 ▸	Bowl, 9", 2-handle	65.00		Ice bucket	125.00
1 ▸	Bowl, 10", footed	85.00	8 ▸ Mint tray, 8½", footed	65.00
	Bowl, 10⅛", handled	95.00		Plate, 11", tab handle	60.00
	Bowl, 10½", oval, handled	110.00	5 ▸ Server, 9¾", center handled	85.00
	Bowl, 11½", squared	65.00	7 ▸ Sugar	40.00
9 ▸	Cake stand, 10½", footed	90.00		Vase, 6½"	110.00
	Candy, flat	130.00	3 ▸ Vase, 8"	125.00
	Comport, tall, deep top	65.00	4 ▸ Vase, 9½"	135.00
6 ▸	Creamer	40.00			

GRAPE, Cut #6, Standard Glass Manufacturing Company, 1932 – 1936
Colors: crystal, green, pink, and topaz

For years, we have been questioned as to why we haven't added this Grape cutting to our repertoire of patterns. At long last, we were able to finalize a listing from some old Hocking catalogs. Most of the pieces are shaped like the well-known Cameo or Mayfair. There were always a few collectors gathering Grape, but with supplies of many popular patterns drying up, some are turning to less documented 1930s patterns such as this. Amassing a set of Grape is not simply done due to lack of mass productions that popular mould etched patterns enjoyed. Rewards of finding pieces are just as satisfying, however.

Grape was produced at the Standard Glass plant even after they were acquired by Hocking. All Hocking orders for cut patterns were sent to the Standard plant for years. The mid-1930 Hocking catalogs have pages dedicated to cut patterns with Standard Glass Company's name still shown at the bottom of each page.

Grape was produced predominantly in green and pink, but some Topaz (yellow) can occasionally be found. There are a few pieces being found in crystal, but mostly stems. Pitchers and numerous sizes of tumblers were heavily publicized in the 1936 catalog and they indubitably sold well as they are the pieces spotted today. Few cup and saucer sets are located. The handles on the cup, creamer, and sugar are the ones found on Cameo and Block Optic identified as "fancy" handles.

Our listing is taken from several Hocking catalogs. There are two older terminologies listed. In one catalog, the 57 oz. jug is listed, but later jugs are referred to as pitchers. The 4¾, 7 ounce goblet is listed as sundae in one and high sherbet in another. Neither place is it called a saucer champagne as in White Band which was a same time frame Hocking pattern shown later in this book. The grapes cut number from the top, three, four, three, two, one.

		*All colors				*All colors
4 ▸	Creamer	15.00			Sherbet, 6 oz.	7.00
	Cup	10.00		3 ▸	Sugar	15.00
	Goblet, 3 oz., cocktail	15.00			Tumbler, 3½ oz., ftd., juice	12.00
1 ▸	Goblet, 7 oz., sundae or high sherbet	10.00		7 ▸	Tumbler, 5 oz., juice	7.00
2 ▸	Goblet, 9 oz., water	18.00			Tumbler, 9 oz., barrel	18.00
	Pitcher, jug, 57 oz.	35.00			Tumbler, 9 oz., table	10.00
	Pitcher, 80 oz., ice lip	40.00			Tumbler, 10 oz., ftd., water	11.00
5 ▸	Pitcher, 80 oz., no lip	45.00			Tumbler, 10 oz., shell	9.00
	Plate, 6", sherbet	3.00			Tumbler, 10 oz., table	9.00
	Plate, 8", luncheon	8.00			Tumbler, 10 oz., water	9.00
	Salt and pepper, pr.	35.00		6 ▸	Tumbler, 12 oz., iced tea	14.00
	Saucer	2.50			Tumbler, 15 oz., ftd tea	16.00

* 25% less for crystal

HEX OPTIC, "HONEYCOMB," Jeannette Glass Company, 1928 – 1932

Colors: pink, green, Ultra Marine (late 1930s), and iridescent in 1950s

Jeannette's Hex Optic was one of the earliest Depression glass patterns having started production in 1928. Advertised in new brilliant green and wild rose colors, Hex Optic made an impact on the patrons of that time. It was a historic glass fabrication, concocted in one of the first fully automated glassmaking facilities of the era. Hex Optic was developed for everyday dinnerware and kitchenware; most pieces found today are chipped, scratched, or damaged from use. Hex Optic supplied a homemaker's total glass needs as it could be amassed in matching products. It was innovative and different in an industry just moving from making glass by hand into an age of automation.

Hex Optic is acknowledged by kitchenware collectors more than any other pattern of Depression glass because of the various kitchenware pieces it incorporates. Sugar shakers, bucket reamers, mixing bowls, refrigerator stacking sets, and butter dishes were designed in green and pink. Actually, were it not for kitchenware collectors becoming passionate about Hex Optic, it might have been ignored in the glass-collecting sphere.

Hex Optic's cups, sugars, and creamers have inventive solid handles which make them risky to pick up with wet fingers. You might see some creamers and sugars with a floral cutting. That cutting was done outside of Jeannette's factory. Some early pieces of Jeannette's glass were embossed with a J in a triangle trademark.

There are two styles of pitchers, one being footed and having the Deco cone shape and the other, a flat-bottomed, cylindrical shape. That 8" tall, 70-ounce, flat-bottomed version is found in both colors, although green is harder to spot. It often turns up in Minnesota and Wisconsin where they were dairy premiums according to one reader. The footed pitcher is hard to garner now, having quietly disappeared into collections. Price may not reflect just how hard it is since demand is rather soft at present.

Note that Jeannette's Hex Optic pitcher is thick as are the other pieces. Other companies' honeycomb pitchers are thin; so keep that in mind when you see an inexpensive thin one.

Iridescent oil lamps, both style pitchers, and tumblers were all made during Jeannette's iridized obsession of the late 1950s. The Ultra Marine tumblers were probably a product of the late 1930s when the company was making Doric and Pansy.

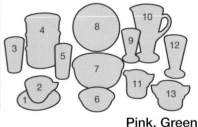

		Pink, Green
6 ▸	Bowl, 4¼", ruffled berry	8.00
7 ▸	Bowl, 7½", ruffled large berry	15.00
	Bowl, 7¼", mixing	15.00
	Bowl, 8¼", mixing	18.00
	Bowl, 9", mixing	20.00
	Bowl, 10", mixing	25.00
	Bucket reamer	70.00
	Butter dish and cover, rectangular, 1 pound size	90.00
11 ▸	Creamer, 2 style handles	6.00
2 ▸	Cup, 2 style handles	8.00
	Ice bucket, metal handle	30.00
	Pitcher, 5", 32 ounce, sunflower motif in bottom	17.00
10 ▸	Pitcher, 9", 48 ounce, footed	35.00
	Pitcher, 8", 70 ounce, flat	75.00
	Plate, 6", sherbet	2.00

		Pink, Green
8 ▸	Plate, 8", luncheon	5.00
	Platter, 11", round	15.00
	Refrigerator dish, 4" x 4"	18.00
4 ▸	Refrigerator stack set, 4 piece	85.00
	Salt and pepper, pair	30.00
1 ▸	Saucer	2.00
13 ▸	Sugar, 2 styles of handles	6.00
	Sugar shaker	250.00
	Sherbet, 5 ounce, footed	6.00
5 ▸	Tumbler, 3¾", 9 ounce	4.00
3 ▸	Tumbler, 5", 12 ounce	7.00
9 ▸	Tumbler, 4¾", 7 ounce, footed	8.00
12 ▸	Tumbler, 5¾", footed	9.00
	Tumbler, 7", footed	10.00
	Whiskey, 2", 1 ounce	9.00

HOBNAIL, Hocking Glass Company, 1934 – 1936
Colors: crystal, crystal w/red trim, and pink

Hobnail patterns were made by numerous glass companies during the Depression glass era. What differentiates Hocking's is the mould shapes which are like those found in Miss America and Moonstone. In reality, the 1940s Anchor-Hocking Moonstone pattern is basically Hocking's Hobnail design with a further white accent to the hobs and edges. You can locate the Moonstone pattern in our *Collectible Glassware from the 40s, 50s, 60s...* book.

Finding Hobnail serving pieces is not an easy chore, but beverage and decanter sets are abundant. It's fairly inexpensive when you find it for sale. This is a pattern that many dealers do not carry to shows. You might need to ask if they have inventory on hand.

Hobnail exhibits well when placed on dark colored backgrounds and is also one Hocking pattern that you rarely find chipped. Most collectors have been captivated by the red-trimmed pieces usually spotted on the West Coast. The decanter and footed juices/wines are about the only red-trimmed pieces we spot in our travels in the eastern half of the country. This was a well utilized pattern and the red trim did not hold up well. The red-trimmed pieces always disappear quickly when we put them out for sale.

Hocking made only four pieces in pink Hobnail with the 6" plate serving as both saucer and sherbet plate. That was a standard procedure of Hocking and saved them from making a separate mould for saucers. Another pink Hobnail pattern, such as one made by MacBeth-Evans, can coexist with this Hocking pattern; that way, you can add a pitcher and tumblers, something unavailable in Hocking's ware. Many other companies' Hobnail patterns will blend with Hocking's crystal Hobnail.

Footed juice tumblers were sold with the decanter as a wine set; consequently, it was also a wine glass until the preacher dropped in. Terminology had a lot to do with tumblers and stems during this era. During Prohibition, wine glasses were sold as juices and the champagnes as high sherbets or sundaes. Wine glasses during that era routinely held around three ounces. Now, people believe the 8 – 10 ounce water goblets from the Depression era are wine goblets; today's wine drinkers want larger glasses. Dealers should verify size with customers when they ask for wines since they may really be wishing for water goblets. This is not a big problem in Depression glass, but a major problem in Elegant glassware patterns of that era.

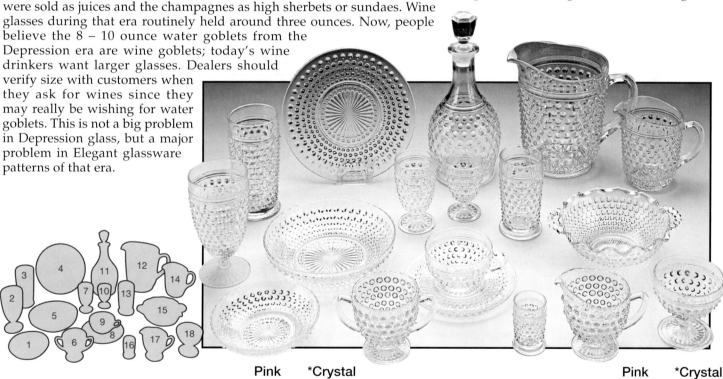

		Pink	*Crystal				Pink	*Crystal
1 ▸	Bowl, 5½", cereal		4.00	4 ▸	Plate, 8½", luncheon	6.00	5.00
15 ▸	Bowl, 6½", crimped, hdld.		15.00	8 ▸	Saucer/sherbet plate	3.00	1.50
5 ▸	Bowl, 7", salad		5.00	18 ▸	Sherbet	6.00	3.00
9 ▸	Cup	5.00	4.00	6 ▸	Sugar, footed		9.00
17 ▸	Creamer, footed		8.00		Tumbler, 5 ounce, juice		4.00
11 ▸	Decanter and stopper, 32 ounce		35.00	13 ▸	Tumbler, 9 ounce, 10 oz., water		5.00
2 ▸	Goblet, 10 ounce, water		8.00	3 ▸	Tumbler, 5¼", 15 ounce, iced tea		14.00
	Goblet, 13 ounce, iced tea		10.00	10 ▸	Tumbler, 3 oz., footed, wine/juice		5.00
14 ▸	Pitcher, 18 ounce, milk		18.00	7 ▸	Tumbler, 5 oz., footed, cordial		6.00
12 ▸	Pitcher, 67 ounce		25.00	16 ▸	Whiskey, 1½ ounce		7.00
	Plate, 6", sherbet	3.00	1.50		*Add 20 – 25% for red trimmed pieces		

HOMESPUN, "FINE RIB," Jeannette Glass Company, 1939 – 1949

Colors: pink and crystal, fired-on colors

All sizes of Homespun bowls have tab handles which have a propensity to develop nicks and chips from use. Sherbets (non-stemmed) are encountered with inner rim roughness (irr), but are hard to track down. Buy them as soon as you catch sight of them. There is no child's teapot in the crystal and no sugars or creamers in the sets.

Homespun has nine tumblers, which is surprising for a pattern so small that officially it does not include a pitcher. For years we have noted the large Fine Rib pitcher, made by Hazel-Atlas as being originally packaged by some unknown company for use with Homespun tumblers and 13½ ounce, band-at-top iced teas. This pitcher has similar narrow bands around the neck and matches in color, but has no waffling design. However, a pitcher and tumbler set now have been found with an official Jeannette label. We had to pay an arm and a leg to get these to show you, but it solves one mystery regarding a Homespun pitcher existing. As to the difference between this pitcher and the Fine Rib one made by Hazel-Atlas, we will have to get back to you on that as at a glance they seem the same.

There is no true Homespun sugar lid. The lid occasionally presented on the sugar is a Fine Rib powder jar top.

Band-at-top tumblers are harder to find; but most collectors seek the ribbed to the top edge. You need to specify no stem or slight stem on the 15 ounce footed teas. There is an ⅛" disparity.

		Pink, Crystal				Pink, Crystal
14 ▶	Bowl, 4½", closed handles	15.00	15 ▶	Sherbet, low flat		20.00
16 ▶	Bowl, 5", cereal, closed handles	35.00	17 ▶	Sugar, footed		11.00
12 ▶	Bowl, 8¼", large berry, closed handles	30.00	2 ▶	Tumbler, 3⅞", 7 ounce, straight		18.00
10 ▶	Butter dish and cover	55.00	4 ▶	Tumbler, 4⅛", 8 ounce, water, flared top		18.00
	Coaster/ashtray	5.00	19 ▶	Tumbler, 4¼", 9 ounce, band at top		18.00
1 ▶	Creamer, footed	11.00	3 ▶	Tumbler, 4⁵⁄₁₆", 9 ounce, no band		18.00
8 ▶	Cup	9.00	18 ▶	Tumbler, 5⅜", 12½ ounce, iced tea		25.00
	Plate, 6", sherbet	5.00	20 ▶	Tumbler, 5⅞", 13½ ounce, iced tea, band at top		25.00
7 ▶	Plate, 9¼", dinner	20.00	11 ▶	Tumbler, 4", 5 ounce, footed		6.00
13 ▶	Platter, 13", closed handles	18.00	5 ▶	Tumbler, 6¼", 15 ounce, footed		25.00
9 ▶	Saucer	4.00	6 ▶	Tumbler, 6⅜", 15 ounce, footed		25.00

HOMESPUN CHILD'S TEA SET

		Pink	Crystal			Pink	Crystal
21 ▶	Cup	30.00	20.00	24 ▶	Teapot cover	100.00	
22 ▶	Saucer	7.00	5.00		Set: 14-pieces	395.00	
	Plate	10.00	8.00		Set: 12-pieces	340.00	135.00
23 ▶	Teapot	50.00					

INDIANA CUSTARD, "FLOWER AND LEAF BAND," Indiana Glass Company, 1930s; 1950s
Colors: ivory or custard, early 1930s; white, 1950s

Indiana Custard is becoming difficult to sell due to a lack of new collectors and the dearth of rarely seen items frustrating long-time collectors. Even if you live in central Indiana, new discoveries are not forthcoming. You can count on enough pieces for a basic set, but the color seems to have fallen out of favor at the present time.

On the other hand, at an antique show, a dealer had around 100 pieces displayed. There were no sherbets, but most everything else was there. He told us that he was having trouble selling it. Once again, marketing a large set is difficult at best. He could sell some of the pieces were he to separate it out, but he was stuck in the "sell it all or bust" mode. One problem with this set is varying shades on the cups and saucers, a minor annoyance. Some of the pieces are more yellow and translucent than the beige of others. When promoted as a set, these varying shades stick out vividly and could be a reason for the lack of a customer. On top of that, there is often an extra premium for being a set — something that seldom works with glass. Sets are not worth more than the sum of the pieces. Few people buy complete sets unless they are dealers buying wholesale. In our experience, individual pricing of items will often see an entire set sell in a shorter time than trying to market an entire set.

Indiana Custard is the only Depression-era pattern where cups and sherbets are the most elusive items to find. Cups are being found more regularly than sherbets. Some collectors consider the sherbet overpriced; but those who have searched for years without owning one would contradict that. On the other hand, if you can find a sherbet, it may be priced less than a few years ago due to fewer now paying the price that was asked then. We have found sherbets in groups of six or eight (twice) and the cups one or two at a time.

Indiana made this pattern in white in the 1950s under the name Orange Blossom. So far, there is only minor demand for white, though it is a lovely, pristine white. Orange Blossom can be found in our *Collectible Glassware from the 40s, 50s, 60s...* and we do get requests for Orange Blossom at shows.

		French Ivory			French Ivory
13 ▸	Bowl, 5½", berry	8.00		Plate, 7½", salad	12.00
11 ▸	Bowl, 6½", cereal	20.00		Plate, 8⅞", luncheon	15.00
2 ▸	Bowl, 7½", flat soup	20.00		Plate, 9¾", dinner	22.00
	Bowl, 9", 1¾" deep, large berry	22.00	5 ▸	Platter, 11½", oval	30.00
1 ▸	Bowl, 9½", oval vegetable	26.00	4 ▸	Saucer	4.00
8 ▸	Butter dish and cover	40.00	10 ▸	Sherbet	75.00
12 ▸	Cup	28.00	7 ▸	Sugar	8.00
9 ▸	Creamer	10.00	6 ▸	Sugar cover	17.00
3 ▸	Plate, 5¾", bread and butter	5.00			

INDIANA SILVER, Indiana Glass Company, c. 1918
Color: crystal w/sterling silver overlay

Indiana Silver began manufacture before most of the patterns listed in this book, but production ran through the Depression glass years. It combined the past Art Nouveau influence (flowered scrolls) with the upcoming simple, linear Deco look. Attaching silver to the glass also unified it with the silver decorating craze of that time and marked it as exclusive merchandise. Much of the glass we come across nowadays is missing most or all of the silver; but the outstanding motif is still present. If you decide to collect this, worry about silver condition once you find the pieces, and then swap them as you can. Please note that the plate was termed a calling card tray — something definitely from another time. Of all the pieces, sherbets and footed vases seem to turn up regularly. One customer told us that she was buying vases to use as glasses with her pieces, as she plucked one from our show booth.

We have found some promotional material for this pattern which was offered back then to retail stores, a 130-pound, 13 dozen-piece "Sensation" assortment and a 100-pound "Sterling dining assortment." The dining assortment selling prices were to be $1.25 – $1.50 each — which was a dear price then, considering most wares in their other lines were designed to be sold for 10¢ to 25¢.

		Item	Price			Item	Price
		Bowl, 4½", dessert	8.00			Goblet, wine	15.00
2 ▸		Bowl, 5½", ftd., bonbon	12.00	4 ▸		Plate, 7½", card tray	8.00
6 ▸		Bowl, 8½", berry	20.00			Pitcher, ½ gal.	45.00
		Butter w/cover	35.00	3 ▸		Sherbet, ftd.	7.00
7 ▸		Cup, custard	10.00			Spooner	15.00
		Compote, ftd., jelly	12.00			Sugar w/cover, large	20.00
9 ▸		Creamer, small berry	10.00	8 ▸		Sugar, open, small, berry	10.00
		Creamer, large	15.00	1 ▸		Tumbler	16.00
		Goblet, water	20.00	5 ▸		Vase, 6½", ftd.	30.00

IRIS, "IRIS AND HERRINGBONE," Jeannette Glass Company, 1928 – 1932; 1950s; 1970s

Colors: crystal, iridescent; some pink and green; recently bi-colored red/yellow and blue/green combinations, and white
(See Reproduction Section.)

Iris has been hard hit both by the economy and the reproduction scoundrels looking to make an easy buck. It has also been broadly collected and beloved. However, reproduction Iris has been overshadowing Iris for the previous few years. We are relentlessly asked what is being made now or what do I do about my collection? Our answer to that is to sit tight, that this too will pass, but may take a few years. In the meantime, truth is that prices are adjusting — unfortunately, not up. The last reproduction that we can confirm is the cocktail which joins the reproduction dinner plates, iced teas, flat tumblers, and coasters that have previously been unloaded into our market. See the Reproduction section in the back of this book for telltale signs between old and new.

Do not panic. This has happened before to Cherry Blossom and other major patterns and they have recovered. All the new crystal is exceedingly clear. If you place old crystal Iris on a white background it will appear to have a gray or even slightly yellow tint. The new is very clear without a tinge of color of any sort and looks like more expensive crystal. The new flat tumblers have no herringbone on the bottom — just Iris. The coaster is more than half-full of glass when you look from the side. Page 247 has details.

Sellers on Internet auctions have intensified sales of these reproductions. If it is so cheap you can't believe the price — beware. Check Internet sellers to see if they sell other reproductions – an excellent clue. Jeannette is often used as "certification" in the wording of Internet auctions. Sometimes the ploy is that the items were bought at an estate sale or auction and they don't know how old they are. Reproduced items get on the Internet first as "old" and unsuspecting bidders pay high prices before word gets out in the collecting world. Most of these sellers know their products are new; so if bidding, ask about their return policy before you bid. Reputable sellers will offer refunds or returns.

Prices for iced teas, dinner plates, coasters, and flat water tumblers have been whacked hard. Several large collections are having a tough time finding buyers right now because owners want pre-reproduction prices. If you have to sell, be aware that prices are down. Now may be the time to buy harder-to-find pieces from established, reputable dealers.

Original crystal production for Iris began in 1928. Some was made in the late 1940s and 1950s; candy bottoms and vases emerged as late as the 1970s. All these were made by Jeannette. The crystal Iris decorated with red and gold that keeps turning up was called Corsage and styled by Century in 1946, information obtained from a card attached to a 1946 wedding gift.

Satinized (frosted) plates and bowls usually had hand-colored or painted irises on them. It wears off easily and pieces do not sell well unless the original decoration is still bright. Those rarely seen 8" crystal luncheon plates may be scarce because many more of them were frosted than were not. In any case, the frosted ones are a tough sell at $25.00, but you can find them priced much higher. You may affix a label with any price on it you want, but obtaining that price is a whole new proposition. Get realistic if you are trying to sell your Iris pattern now.

Iridescent candy bottoms are another product of the early '70s when Jeannette also made crystal bottoms flashed with two-tone colors of red/yellow or blue/green. These were sold as vases; and, over time, the colors have peeled off or been purposely stripped to make them, again, crystal candy bottoms. These later issues lack rays on the foot which were on all earlier candy bottoms. White or painted white vases sell around $12.00 – 15.00. These are not rare. The exceedingly rare vase is transparent pink and not pink painted over white.

Iris

		Crystal	Iridescent	Green, Pink
18 ▶	Bowl, 4½", berry, beaded edge	35.00	5.00	
28 ▶	Bowl, 5", ruffled sauce	6.00	18.00	
11 ▶	Bowl, 5", cereal	75.00		
22 ▶	Bowl, 7½", soup	135.00	50.00	
	Bowl, 8", berry, beaded edge	60.00	20.00	
14 ▶	Bowl, 9½", ruffled salad	10.00	10.00	200.00
23 ▶	Bowl, 11½", ruffled fruit	10.00	14.00	
1 ▶	Bowl, 11", fruit, straight edge	60.00		
7 ▶	Butter dish and cover	30.00	30.00	
	Butter dish bottom	10.00	10.00	
	Butter dish top	20.00	20.00	
3 ▶	Candlesticks, pair	28.00	25.00	
30 ▶	Candy jar and cover	100.00		
	‡ Coaster	40.00		
15 ▶	Creamer, footed	11.00	10.00	150.00
31 ▶	Cup	13.00	12.00	
16 ▶	*Demitasse cup	35.00	150.00	
17 ▶	*Demitasse saucer	110.00	250.00	
2 ▶	Fruit or nut set	100.00	150.00	
	Goblet, 4", wine		20.00	

		Crystal	Iridescent	Green, Pink
	‡Goblet, 4½", 4 oz., cocktail	16.00		
8 ▶	Goblet, 4½", 3 oz., wine	12.00		
13 ▶	Goblet, 5½", 4 oz.	15.00	495.00	
6 ▶	Goblet, 5½", 8 oz.	18.00	295.00	
	**Lamp shade, 11½"	75.00		
27 ▶	Pitcher, 9½", footed	25.00	25.00	
	Plate, 5½", sherbet	10.00	11.00	
5 ▶	Plate, 8", luncheon	65.00		
3 ▶	‡ Plate, 9", dinner	30.00	35.00	
	Plate, 11¾", sandwich	22.00	32.00	
32 ▶	Saucer	6.00	6.00	
21 ▶	Sherbet, 2½", footed	20.00	10.00	
12 ▶	Sherbet, 4", footed	18.00	295.00	
33 ▶	‡‡ Sugar	9.00	9.00	150.00
34 ▶	Sugar cover	10.00	10.00	
	‡ Tumbler, 4", flat	65.00		
	Tumbler, 6", footed	14.00	12.00	
4 ▶	‡ Tumbler, 6½", footed	18.00		
	Vase, 9"	20.00	18.00	225.00

* Ruby, blue, amethyst priced as iridescent
** Colors, $85.00
‡ Has been reproduced
‡‡ Yellow, $195.00

JUBILEE, Lancaster Glass Company, Early 1930s
Colors: yellow, crystal, and pink

The traditional Jubilee cut (#1200) on Lancaster blanks contains a 12-petal, open centered flower. We mention that for readers who keep asking if any glassware with an open center, 12-petal flower is Jubilee. No, it is not. We need to emphasize that the cut design has to be on the Lancaster blank. Plain, uncut, exactly the same shape items are not Jubilee either — merely the blank used for Jubilee cutting. Cups, saucers, luncheon plates, creamers, and sugars are being found at rates that presently oversupply demand and prices reflect that.

Misunderstandings with Jubilee transpire when you get Standard Glass Company's paneled blanks with a #1200 cut. An earlier author called these "Tat"; but people seeing these pieces over the years said, "Ah! Jubilee!" and corralled them with that pattern. This development caused some Standard items to be accepted as Jubilee pattern. Further confusion arises when people find Standard Glass Company's closed center, 12-petal flower cut (#89) on paneled blanks, which Standard promoted as Martha Washington pattern.

Basic pieces of Lancaster's Jubilee were cut on smooth blanks (no optic panels). Standard's #1200 was presented on optic paneled blanks. Martha Washington came on optic paneled blanks, with rayed footed tumblers and fancy handled cups.

Both Lancaster and Standard showed companion-serving wares for these patterns using the same petal edged, fancy handled blanks. To further confuse things, Standard had both #200 and a #28 cut, very like #1200, which had the same flower with more cut branches. These were cut on those same type serving pieces, with some petal blank, three-toed bowls and trays additionally made. Other similar cuts incorporated a mayo bowl with 16 petals and a cutting with 12 petals, but having a smaller petal in between the larger ones. Frankly, most collectors are happy to buy any of these pieces as Jubilee pattern to enhance their sets. Ultimately, you have to decide how much of a purist you wish to be and there are quite a few who will accept nothing except Jubilee.

After all the detailed information above, we ought to point out that two pieces of Jubilee only have 11 petals, those being the 3", 8 ounce, non-stemmed sherbet and the three-footed covered candy. Having only 11 petals on the candy and sherbet apparently came from cutting problems experienced when using the typical 6" cutting wheel. The foot of the sherbet and the knob on the candy were in the way when trying to cut a petal of the 12-petal design. The glass cutter had to move over to the side in order to cut a petal and only 11 could be provided.

The #889 liner plate for the #890 mayo has a raised rim for the mayo to sit inside the raised circle, making that liner plate scarcer than the mayo. Some mayonnaise sets have 16 petals on the bowl and plate.

Jubilee

		Pink	Yellow
	Bowl, 8", 3-footed, 5⅛" high	195.00	175.00
	Bowl, 9", handled fruit		125.00
	Bowl, 11½", flat fruit	155.00	135.00
6 ▸	Bowl, 11½", 3-footed	195.00	175.00
	Bowl, 11½", 3-footed, curved in		175.00
	Bowl, 13", 3-footed	195.00	175.00
16 ▸	Candlestick, pair	160.00	160.00
	Candy jar, w/lid, 3-footed	250.00	250.00
	Cheese & cracker set	175.00	175.00
1 ▸	Creamer	27.50	15.00
10 ▸	Cup	22.00	11.00
	Mayonnaise & plate	175.00	165.00
	w/original ladle	195.00	185.00
18 ▸	Plate, 7", salad	15.00	10.00
5 ▸	Plate, 8¾", luncheon	20.00	10.00
	Plate, 13½", sandwich, handled	60.00	40.00
	Plate, 14", 3-footed		165.00
11 ▸	Saucer, two styles	6.00	3.00
	Sherbet, 3", 8 oz.		65.00
	Stem, 4", 1 oz., cordial		250.00
	Stem, 4¾", 4 oz., oyster cocktail		65.00

		Pink	Yellow
9 ▸	Stem, 4⅞", 3 oz., cocktail		85.00
8 ▸	Stem, 5½", 7 oz., sherbet/champagne	60.00	50.00
13 ▸	Stem, 7½", 11 oz.		150.00
2 ▸	Sugar	27.50	14.00
14 ▸	Tray, 11", 2-handled cake	55.00	40.00
7 ▸	Tumbler, 5", 6 oz., footed, juice		75.00
4 ▸	Tumbler, 6", 10 oz., water	55.00	27.50
3 ▸	Tumbler, 6⅛", 12½ oz., iced tea		125.00
17 ▸	Tray, 11", center-handled sandwich	135.00	135.00
	Vase, 12"	175.00	210.00

20 ▸ Jubilee cut on other mould blanks

Standard Glass items.

LACED EDGE, "KATY BLUE," Imperial Glass Company, Early 1930s
Colors: blue w/opalescent edge and green w/opalescent edge, et al.

Imperial's Laced Edge pattern was produced for many years in a vast assortment of colors. However, only their opalescent blue and green dinnerwares are being dealt with in this book since that is where collector interest lies. Imperial unveiled this white decoration as "Sea Foam." The Sea Foam treatment fluctuates from barely coating the edge of pieces to others having a ½" of prominent, opalescent edging. Most of the colors without the white edge were made into the 1950s and later; so, they missed the time restriction (pre-1940) for this book.

Early pioneers in the business called opalescent blue "Katy Blue"; that extended to calling the green, "Katy Green." Blue and green pieces without the white edge sell for less than half of the prices shown if a buyer can be found; few collectors seek those. There is little interest in crystal pieces, which are often spied in malls with big prices. Our theory is that if it is still there, no one has been willing to pay the price wanted. The undivided, oval vegetable bowl is missing from the ad shown, as well as many collections today. Notice the divided bowl and the platter were the most expensive pieces to earn with coupons.

Some traditionalists do not acknowledge the 12" cake plate (luncheon plate in Imperial catalog) or the 9" vegetable bowl (salad in ad on next page) as Laced Edge because the edges are more open than those of the other items. We didn't make them, just report what we find.

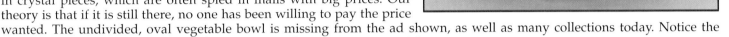

A Laced Edge collector from Illinois let us borrow an original ad (page 106) showing an extravagant retail price along with the cost in coupons (product) for Laced Edge pieces. We assume most folks used the coupons.

Spouts for creamers often have dissimilar shapes due to their being individually formed using a tool. Cereal, berry, and soup bowls vary as much as ⅜" depending upon the edge. Some edges go straight up while others are horizontally correct. Collectors will accept these minor discrepancies in order to have enough bowls. Stacking these bowls, however, is sometimes difficult due to the minor size differences.

		Opalescent				Opalescent
	Basket bowl	235.00	2 ▶	Mayonnaise, 3-piece		110.00
9 ▶	Bowl, 4⅜"–4¾", fruit	22.00		Plate, 6½", bread & butter		10.00
17 ▶	Bowl, 5"	30.00	3 ▶	Plate, 8", salad		22.00
6 ▶	Bowl, 5½"	30.00	4 ▶	Plate, 10", dinner		65.00
12 ▶	Bowl, 5⅞"	30.00		Plate, 12", luncheon (per catalog description)		75.00
	Bowl, 7", soup	65.00	5 ▶	Platter, 13"		150.00
	Bowl, 9", vegetable	95.00	11 ▶	Saucer		8.00
1 ▶	Bowl, 11", divided oval	100.00	8 ▶	Sugar		30.00
	Bowl, 11", oval	130.00		Tidbit, 2-tiered, 8" & 10" plates		100.00
15 ▶	Candlestick, double, pair	150.00	7 ▶	Tumbler, 9 ounce		30.00
10 ▶	Cup	26.00	18 ▶	Vase, flower bowl		300.00
16 ▶	Creamer	30.00				

Laced Edge

6 FOOTED TUMBLERS
27 COUPONS
Retail Value $1.20

SALAD BOWL
13 COUPONS
Retail Value 60c

3 SAUCE DISHES
14 COUPONS
Retail Value 60c

3 CUPS AND SAUCERS
25 COUPONS
Retail Value $1.20

3 PIECE
MAYONNAISE
SET
15 COUPONS
Retail Value 60c

3 SALAD PLATES
20 COUPONS
Retail Value 90c

PLATTER
(13 INCH)
30 COUPONS
Retail Value $1.25

3 BREAD
AND BUTTERS
14 COUPONS
Retail Value 75c

3 SOUP DISHES
20 COUPONS
Retail Value 90c

3 CEREAL DISHES
14 COUPONS
Retail Value 75c

SUGAR AND
CREAMER
14 COUPONS
Retail Value 50c

DIVIDED VEGETABLE DISH
30 COUPONS   Retail Value $1.25

CAKE PLATE (12 INCH)
18 COUPONS   Retail Value 75c

3 DINNER PLATES
33 COUPONS   Retail Value $1.50

LAKE COMO, Hocking Glass Company, 1934 – 1937
Color: Vitrock with blue scene; some with red scene

No other red Lake Como pieces have been reported except the creamer and sugar pictured. We seriously doubt only those two items exist.

This smaller pattern has just 13 different pieces. All are shown below. Save for the shakers and large bowl, most are hardly ever seen today. Indeed, some collectors tell us they never see it. It would appear that this design did not satisfactorily survive years of washings. Prices below are for mint condition Lake Como (full bright pattern). You should be able to buy worn Lake Como at 60% to 80% of the prices listed depending upon the amount of wear. If the pattern is missing, it is not Lake Como — just Vitrock. We were once told by a former factory worker that getting added colors to stay put had consumed early technicians.

One couple told us that they were buying less than mint Lake Como in order to have some of the harder-to-find pieces. They would replace those pieces as they found items more to their liking. When offered for sale, "like new" Lake Como sells swiftly.

The flat soup has a floral embossed decoration on the edge (like the normally found Vitrock soup) instead of being painted in blue. Only the center of the soup has the design and if ever used, the design has usually gone astray. You will find platters almost as difficult to find as soup bowls; but most collectors are looking for only one platter, but at least two or more soups.

Several small reserves of vegetable bowls have been found in the last few years; thus, the price has lessened a bit on them. Finding either style cup in mint condition will be a headache. If you are willing to buy worn cups, then no problem exists.

4 ▸	Bowl, 6", cereal	20.00		7 ▸	Plate, 9¼", dinner	30.00
6 ▸	Bowl, 9¾", vegetable	40.00		2 ▸	Platter, 11"	75.00
5 ▸	Bowl, flat soup	75.00		3 ▸	Salt & pepper, pair	20.00
11 ▸	Creamer, footed	20.00		9 ▸	Saucer	7.00
8 ▸	Cup, regular	20.00		13 ▸	Saucer, St. Denis	7.00
12 ▸	Cup, St. Denis	25.00		10 ▸	Sugar, footed	20.00
1 ▸	Plate, 7¼", salad	15.00				

LARGO, LINE #220, Paden City Glass Company, Late 1937 – 1951; Canton Glass company, 1950s
Colors: amber, amethyst, cobalt blue, crystal, crystal w/ruby flash, light blue, red

Our first introduction to Paden City's Largo occurred about 25 years ago in an antique mall in Ohio. There was a set of a couple of dozen pieces labeled and priced as Cambridge blue Caprice. We knew it wasn't Caprice, but did not know what it was until we did some research. Even now, it wouldn't fetch the prices being asked then. The mall closed and we have often wondered where that set ended up.

Paden City's Largo was not as widely distributed as Cambridge's Caprice, something which causes us to look high and low for Largo today. We have found more red than blue. Several colored, divided candy bottoms appeared in our travels, but never a Largo top, though they do exist.

Collectors of sugar and creamer sets have put a hole in that skimpy supply. There are few four- footed sugars and creamers in other collectible patterns of that day; so these stand out. Most four-toed ones are found in older pattern glass. We, personally, have found several Paden City etchings on Largo items, but have not found corresponding collectors for them. Most apparently prefer the unadorned blank.

All blue cups we have found have been with the non-indented 6⅝" plates. Though supposedly made, we wonder about the existence of blue saucers, so if you have one…?

Please note that Largo pieces have four half circle ridged lines while its sister pattern, Maya (#221) has a bristle haired thistle ball in the design. Because of like colors and similar items, these patterns are sometimes mistaken for each other, although there seem to be more searchers for Largo than Maya.

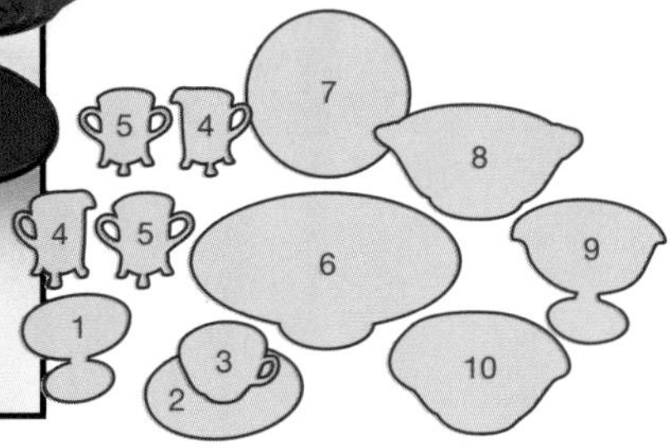

		Amber, Crystal	Blue, Red				Amber, Crystal	Blue, Red
	Ashtray, 3", rectangle	14.00	25.00	9 ▸	Comport, double spout, pedestal		30.00	70.00
	Bowl, 5"	14.00	22.00		Comport, fluted rim, pedestal		30.00	70.00
	Bowl, 6", deep	15.00	32.00		Comport, 6½" x 10", plain rim, pedestal		28.00	60.00
	Bowl, 7½"	18.00	35.00					
10 ▸	Bowl, 7½", crimped	20.00	40.00	4 ▸	Creamer, footed		18.00	35.00
8 ▸	Bowl, 9", tab-handled	25.00	60.00	3 ▸	Cup		12.00	24.00
	Bowl, 11⅝", 3½" deep, tri-footed, flared rim	32.00	70.00		Mayonnaise, toed		22.00	50.00
					Plate, 6⅝"		6.00	12.00
	Bowl, 12¾", 4¾" deep, tri-footed, flat rim	40.00	70.00	7 ▸	Plate, 8"		8.00	16.00
					Plate, 10¾", cheese w/indent		18.00	35.00
6 ▸	Cake plate, pedestal	28.00	75.00	2 ▸	Saucer		4.00	10.00
	Candleholder	22.00	50.00	5 ▸	Sugar, footed		18.00	35.00
	Candy, flat w/lid, 3-part	32.00	85.00		Tray, 11", center handle			50.00
	Cigarette box, 4" x 3¼" x 1½"	22.00	55.00		Tray, 13¾", tri-footed, serving		22.00	65.00
1 ▸	Comport, cracker	10.00	22.00	11 ▸	Tray, 14", five-part, relish		45.00	

LAUREL, McKee Glass Company, 1930s
Colors: French Ivory, Jade Green, White Opal, Poudre Blue, and various colors of decorated rims

McKee's Jade Laurel has surpassed the Poudre (powder) Blue in popularity. For years Poudre Blue was the color to own, but it was not as plentiful. There were collectors of Jade and to some extent French Ivory, but there was a wealth of Jade Green around; however, few early collectors noticed it. That has changed with the popularity of Fire-King's Jade-ite on the Internet. Collecting of other Jadite colors followed, leading to Laurel's Jade Green. Prices nearly doubled on every piece and suddenly, shortages of some items were exposed. French Ivory attracts few collectors; prices there have remained fairly stable.

The short sugar and creamer have finally been found in Poudre Blue; and thanks to an Ohio dealer, you can see them pictured.

All colors of serving pieces are inadequate for demand. That trend is slowly but surely raising its ugly head in many Depression patterns. Serving pieces, priced separately, were not originally in basic sets. They were too large to pack in products as premiums; and few people were willing to spend the extra money for serving items to match what they received free, or bought as a basic set.

Laurel children's tea sets, once thought scarce, are being offered on the Internet and prices are slipping as more and more appear. Sets are found with edged trims of red, green, or orange. Watch for wear on these colored trims; it appears many children did, in fact, play with these dishes. You wonder if the Internet had not come along, what would have happened to all this suddenly available glass with no exposure to collectors or dealers. The Scottie dog decal children's sets were produced in Jade Green or French Ivory colors. Collectors of Scottie items had elevated the prices on these sets to levels where few collectors tried to buy full sets. Now, prices have slipped somewhat with so many single pieces being auctioned. Many are satisfied just to acquire one piece.

Laurel has two styles of candlesticks. The 4" style is available, but the three-footed variety is rare. The footed style is pictured in green.

		Jade or Decorated Rims	White Opal, French Ivory	Poudre Blue				Jade or Decorated Rims	White Opal, French Ivory	Poudre Blue
14 ▶	Bowl, 4¾", berry	15.00	8.00	15.00			Plate, 6", sherbet	16.00	10.00	10.00
2 ▶	Bowl, 5½"	35.00					Plate, 7½", salad	20.00	10.00	16.00
15 ▶	Bowl, 6", cereal	28.00	14.00	28.00	4 ▶	Plate, 9⅛", dinner, 2 styles	20.00	15.00	30.00
	Bowl, 6", three legs	28.00	15.00		8 ▶	Plate, 9⅛", grill, round or scalloped	25.00	15.00	
1 ▶	Bowl, 7⅞", soup, 2 styles	45.00	35.00	85.00		Platter, 10¾", oval	55.00	30.00	60.00
3 ▶	Bowl, 9", large berry	45.00	28.00	55.00		Salt and pepper	90.00	45.00	
	Bowl, 9¾", oval vegetable	55.00	30.00	55.00	17 ▶	Saucer	4.50	3.00	7.50
	Bowl, 10½", three legs	60.00	40.00	70.00	11 ▶	Sherbet	20.00	12.00	
	Bowl, 11"	60.00	40.00	85.00		Sherbet/champagne, 5"	80.00	50.00	
	Candlestick, 4", pair	65.00	30.00		5 ▶	Sugar, short	25.00	10.00	50.00
6 ▶	Candlestick, 3 footed	150.00				Sugar, tall	25.00	11.00	35.00
9 ▶	Cheese dish and cover	110.00	55.00			Tumbler, 3⅜", 7 ounce, flat		30.00	
23 ▶	Creamer, short	25.00	12.00	50.00		Tumbler, 4½", 9 ounce, flat	75.00	30.00	
7 ▶	Creamer, tall	25.00	15.00	40.00		Tumbler, 5", 12 ounce, flat		50.00	
16 ▶	Cup	15.00	7.00	22.50					

CHILDREN'S LAUREL TEA SET

		French Ivory	Jade or Decorated Rims	Scotty Dog Jade	Scotty Dog Ivory
21 ▶	Creamer	30.00	100.00	260.00	130.00
19 ▶	Cup	25.00	50.00	100.00	50.00
22 ▶	Plate	10.00	20.00	80.00	40.00
18 ▶	Saucer	8.00	12.50	75.00	37.50
20 ▶	Sugar	30.00	100.00	260.00	130.00
	14-piece set	235.00	530.00	1,550.00	775.00

Laurel

LINCOLN INN, Line No. 1700, Fenton Glass Company, Late 1920s

Colors: amber, amethyst, black, cobalt, crystal, green, green opalescent, jade (opaque), light blue, pink, and red

Lincoln Inn Tumblers are not as easy to find as the omnipresent stems, but acquiring an old pitcher to use with them in any color is threatening the impossible. Fenton made an iridized, dark carnival colored pitcher and tumblers in the 1980s. Any other iridescent piece you might see in this pattern is of recent production comparatively speaking to the Depression glass era. All original light blue pitchers surfaced in the South, but none that we've heard of in 20 years.

Lincoln Inn plates are illustrated in a 1930s catalog with a fruit design (intaglio) in the center. Besides the plates we have seen a 9" and 7½" crystal bowl with the fruit center. Additional pieces of intaglio may exist, but that is all we can corroborate. There have never been any reports of this intaglio in colored wares.

Stems must have been abundantly produced since they are the only pieces of the pattern you can view with any regularity and the champagne/sherbet leads the pack. If someone asks us for Lincoln Inn, it is usually prefaced with, "I don't need stems, but…." A small collection of stems for serving desserts or champagne could be made in a multitude of colors without destroying your budget. Stemware was sold to accompany china.

Today, you might possibly obtain a setting in crystal, but colors are less certain, even using the Internet. In spite of the fact that tableware was advertised in at least eight of the above listed colors in 1929, little color other than red and the several shades of blue are accumulated today. Serving pieces are extremely scarce. This pattern definitely lends itself to rainbow collecting and blending trends so common today.

Lincoln Inn shakers are inadequate for even a small demand, including crystal ones. Collectors of shakers tell us that Lincoln Inn ones may not be the most expensive ones in our book, but they are among the most challenging to find. Red and black shakers are the preferred colors; do not bypass any color in your travels. Years ago, a red pair were found sitting with Royal Ruby in a dark corner of a store. They were priced as red shakers and not Lincoln Inn. You need to check every little corner when you shop.

Red Lincoln Inn pieces are often amberina in color. For novices, amberina is red glass that has some yellow hues in it. Some older glass collectors reject amberina pieces for their collections as unfit to own. However, there are some devotees actually searching for amberina glass. There is a growing fascination for all two-toned glassware; and amberina certainly fits that mode.

		Cobalt Blue, Red	**All other colors
	Ashtray	17.50	12.00
	Bonbon, handled, square	15.00	12.00
	Bonbon, handled, oval	18.00	12.00
	Bowl, 5", fruit	15.00	9.00
10 ▶	Bowl, 5¾", footed	30.00	
8 ▶	Bowl, 6	28.00	
	Bowl, 6", cereal	25.00	10.00
	Bowl, 6", crimped	18.00	8.50
	Bowl, 9", shallow		23.00
	Bowl, 9¼", footed	80.00	30.00
16 ▶	Bowl, 9½", crimped	55.00	35.00
	Bowl, 10½", footed	80.00	35.00
	Bowl, handled olive	18.00	9.50
9 ▶	Bowl, finger	22.00	12.50
	Candy dish, footed, oval	45.00	20.00
	Comport	30.00	14.50
15 ▶	Creamer	22.50	14.50
5 ▶	Cup	12.00	10.00
1 ▶	Goblet, water	30.00	15.50
2 ▶	Goblet, wine	32.00	16.50

		Cobalt Blue, Red	**All other colors
	Nut dish, footed	25.00	12.00
	Pitcher, 7¼", 46 ounce	800.00	600.00
	Plate, 6"	9.00	4.50
14 ▶	Plate, 8"	12.00	8.00
4 ▶	Plate, 9¼"	42.00	11.50
	Plate, 12"	60.00	15.50
	*Salt/pepper, pair	225.00	150.00
	Sandwich server, center handle	175.00	110.00
6 ▶	Saucer	5.00	3.50
	Sherbet, 4½", cone shape	22.00	11.50
12 ▶	Sherbet, 4¾"	20.00	11.00
	Sugar	20.00	14.00
	Tumbler, 4 ounce, flat, juice	30.00	9.50
	Tumbler, 9 ounce, flat, water		19.50
7 ▶	Tumbler, 5 ounce, footed	30.00	11.00
	Tumbler, 9 ounce, footed	28.00	14.00
3 ▶	Tumbler, 12 ounce, footed	50.00	19.00
	Vase, 9¾"	165.00	85.00
11 ▶	Vase, 12", footed	250.00	125.00

* Black $300.00   ** w/fruits, add 20 – 25%

LINE #555, Paden City Glass Company, Late 1930s – 1951; Canton Glass Company, 1950s
Colors: crystal, light blue, red

Paden City's Line #555 mould shape was used for several diverse etches and cuttings. The Gazebo pattern depicted in our *Elegant Glassware of the Depression Era* is the pattern most collected. Further pieces of Line #555 not shown here are portrayed with the Gazebo etching. Evidently, there were many careless users of the heart-shaped candy dishes as bottoms abound. The bottom is divided into three sections and if the lids survived, you need to check carefully as many have been clanged against those heavy bottoms over the years. Rounded lids have an inclination to slip from your grasp if you try to pick them up. Many of these candy lids have etchings or cuttings on them including a cupid with a bow.

The candles, both single and double, appear in many candlestick collections since they are an eye-catching creation.

A tray is pictured with the creamer and sugar, but was also sold independently. Canton Glass bought many Paden City moulds and continued making pieces of Line #555 during the early 1950s. We have a 1954 Canton catalog which notes color could be special ordered although crystal was the standard being made.

"Pearls and Teardrops" pattern was what one older lady called our display of pieces at a show. We had never heard that name, but it does seem apropos.

		*Crystal				*Crystal
	Bowl, 6", 2-part nappy	12.00			Plate, 6"	5.00
	Bowl, 6", nappy	12.00			Plate, 8"	10.00
	Bowl, 9", 2-handled	20.00			Plate, 12½", 2-handled	18.00
	Bowl, 14", shallow	22.00			Plate, 16", salad or punch liner	26.00
	Cake stand, pedestal foot	25.00			Punch bowl	65.00
5 ▸	Candlestick, 1-light	15.00			Punch cup	5.00
	Candlestick, 2-light	18.00			Relish, 7½", square, 2-part	12.00
1 ▸	Candy, w/lid, heart	40.00			Relish, 9¾", rectangular, 3-part	18.00
	Candy, w/lid, 10¼", pedestal foot	25.00	6 ▸	Relish, 10½", round, 5-part	20.00
	Candy, w/lid, 11", pedestal foot	28.00			Relish, 11", round, 3-part	20.00
7 ▸	Comport, 7"	20.00			Saucer	2.00
3 ▸	Creamer	8.00	2 ▸	Sugar	8.00
	Cup	8.00	4 ▸	Tray, creamer/sugar	8.00
	Mayonnaise liner	7.50			Tray, 9"	12.00
	Mayonnaise	15.00			Tray, 11", center handle	20.00

* Double price for colors

"LITTLE JEWEL," DIAMOND BLOCK, Line #330, Imperial Glass Company,
Late 1920s – Early 1930s
Colors: black, crystal, green, iridescent, pink, red, white, yellow

"Little Jewel" is a miniscule pattern that is attracting people in general, not just collectors. Seldom do customers consider it as Depression-era glass. They are only buying it because it appeals to them. This appreciation for the pattern makes owning a piece or two pleasing rather than acquiring it as a set. "Little Jewel" does not cause sticker shock, another alluring attribute. Blue and black items are the fastest selling colors for us when we display them at shows. Keep that in mind when you see "Little Jewel" for sale.

Imperial dubbed this Line #330 or Diamond Block, but in a 1920s catalog it was advertised for sale under the "Little Jewel" label. This name caught on instead of the Diamond Block given by Imperial.

Colored items are the most popular; unfortunately little color is being found. Red, black, and yellow are rarely seen, but blue is the color generally grabbed first by collectors. Still, even crystal with this delightful design can make a first-rate enhancement to your table.

A collector sent pictures confirming two sizes of lily bowls.

		White Crystal	Colors*
5 ▶	Bowl, 5½", square, honey dish	9.00	18.00
9 ▶	Bowl, 5", lily	9.00	15.00
	Bowl, 6", lily	15.00	
3 ▶	Bowl, 6½"	9.00	15.00
4 ▶	Bowl, 7½", berry	14.00	20.00
6 ▶	Celery, 8½", tray	16.00	22.50
8 ▶	Creamer	8.00	15.00
7 ▶	Jelly, 4½", handle	8.00	15.00
	Jelly, 5", footed	10.00	15.00
	Jug, pint tankard	25.00	50.00
1 ▶	Pickle dish, 6½", 2 handles	15.00	22.50
2 ▶	Sugar	8.00	15.00
10 ▶	Vase, 6", bouquet	12.00	20.00

* add 25% for blue or black

"LOIS," Line #345 et al., United States Glass Company, c. 1920s
Colors: crystal, green, and pink

"Lois" was a Depression glass pattern that we continually received pictures and questions about, so we added it to our book several years ago. We recently had an e-mail picture from a lady who had inherited a set of pink glass which she could not find in any book. After we documented it as "Lois," she happily bought the book it was in and later wrote back to say she had over $2,000.00 worth of "Lois." It was a lucky legacy which paid for her book several times over.

"Lois" was generally etched on Line #345, which consists of octagonal shaped pieces. It was initially presented to commercial establishments as a selection package. "Assortments," as they were labeled, were normally confined to 6 to 15 items, and in the case of etchings, they could be found on various mould lines. Sometimes assortment packages were compiled around a theme, such as table settings, bridge sets, or serving items; but, often as not, they were just various wares put in a grouping. Probably, they were inducement prices to move old stock or slow selling items. It often took several assortments to stock an entire line. Doubtless some pieces are lacking today because stores did not stock all assortments. These were early promotional techniques used by companies to wholesale their wares; and we know from old catalogs "Lois" was thus advertised.

You should find other items than those in the listing and some of them will be on other than octagon shape #345. Let us know what you find.

		All Colors
9 ▸	Bowl, 8¼", octagon, soup	30.00
	Bowl, 10", fruit, pedestal foot, octagon	50.00
	Bowl, 10", salad, flat rim	35.00
	Bowl, 12", console, rolled edge	40.00
	Cake, salver, pedestal foot	55.00
2 ▸	Candle, 2¼", short, single	20.00
	Candy box, octagonal lid	70.00
	Candy jar w/lid, cone shape	60.00
	Comport, cheese	20.00
	Creamer, footed	25.00
1 ▸	Ice bucket	75.00
	Mayonnaise or whipped cream w/ladle	45.00
	Pitcher, milk	55.00
4 ▸	Plate, 10", cracker	25.00
	Plate, 10", dinner, octagon	40.00
10 ▸	Plate, 10¼", small center, octagon	30.00
3 ▸	Server, 10¼", center handled, octagon	40.00
7 ▸	Stem, 4¼", cocktail	22.00
6 ▸	Stem, 4⅝", champagne	30.00
8 ▸	Stem, 5", wine	25.00
	Sugar, footed	25.00
5 ▸	Tumbler, 4½", footed	30.00
	Vase, 9¼"	85.00

LORAIN, "BASKET," No. 615, Indiana Glass Company, 1929 – 1932
Colors: green, yellow, and some crystal

Last summer we photographed Lorain and then took it to a Depression glass show. A customer spotted it and bought every yellow piece. He was disappointed we only had one of each in the basic items, but was tickled to get all of the harder to find bowls at one time. The green was slower to find its way home with collectors. They are beginning to turn to the green Lorain because of price and availability. Green is less expensive and more easily found. A few pieces are surfacing in crystal, but completing a set might not be possible. Many items aren't available in crystal, but you could use them to supplement your colored Lorain.

Yellow Lorain, fawned upon by early collectors, is in very short supply today. When you do locate it, you almost certainly will have to settle for mould roughness on the seams of the pieces. If you are determined about totally mint condition glassware, then you should focus on some other non-Indiana pattern.

Speaking from nearly 40 years of experience, we have several observations about Lorain. First, you should purchase any cereal bowls you can uncover. Scrutinize inner rims closely; they chip and flake. The 8" deep berry is the hardest to find piece. Most collectors only want one, but they often wait years to find it. Dinner plates are almost as scarce as cereals, but scratches are the bugaboo for these. After all, these were every day dishes. Have you looked at your daily dishes for scratches recently? Oval vegetable bowls are uncommon in all colors. Saucers are harder to track down than cups because of mould roughness and wear on them over the years. Dealers used to decline to buy saucers in any pattern unless there were cups with them. Today, many of these once disdained saucers are willingly bought even without cups. There are several patterns of Depression glass where saucers are more difficult to find than cups, and this is one of them.

Some crystal snack trays are found with fired-on colored borders of red, yellow, green, and blue. You can see a blue one pictured below. This tray is made from the platter mould with an added ring for a cup. Those trimmed in yellow or green do not seem to be offered at any price. Collectors have added these to their sets and they did a good job of gathering them. Crystal cups came trimmed in the four colors to match the snack trays; but sometimes they are crystal with no trim.

We have had e-mails and letters concerning goblets with a basket design similar to Lorain. These are likely an early Tiffin product. If you want to use them with Lorain, do so. There is also a heavy Hazel-Atlas green goblet comparable in shape to Colonial Block that has a basket etching. There were copious basket designs in the 1920s and 1930s. There is no known Lorain goblet; so, if you want a goblet, feel free to mix these with your set. These are known in the trade as "go-with" items, rather than being the actual pattern.

		Crystal, Green	Yellow
2 ▶	Bowl, 6", cereal	50.00	85.00
1 ▶	Bowl, 7¼", salad	50.00	65.00
10 ▶	Bowl, 8", deep berry	125.00	195.00
16 ▶	Bowl, 9¾", oval vegetable	50.00	55.00
4 ▶	Creamer, footed	18.00	22.00
11 ▶	Cup	10.00	12.00
13 ▶	Plate, 5½", sherbet	8.00	10.00
	Plate, 7¾", salad	12.00	12.00
15 ▶	Plate, 8⅜", luncheon	20.00	22.00
6 ▶	Plate, 10¼", dinner	65.00	75.00
3 ▶	Platter, 11½"	30.00	40.00
9 ▶	Relish, 8", 4-part	23.00	27.50
12 ▶	Saucer	4.00	5.00
8 ▶	Sherbet, footed	22.00	27.50
14 ▶	Snack tray, crystal/trim	35.00	
5 ▶	Sugar, footed	18.00	22.00
7 ▶	Tumbler, 4¾", 9 ounce, footed	25.00	28.00

LOTUS, Pattern #1921, Westmoreland Glass Company, 1921 – 1980
Colors: amber, amethyst, black, blue, crystal, green, milk, pink, red, and various applied color trims; satinized colors

Westmoreland's pattern #1921, Lotus, was in production off and on for 60 years. Several companies had their own renderings of a Lotus design on their glassware and china during this same period. We even ran across one collector who gathered any Lotus decorations — china or glass. We've met collectors of Daffodil and Fuchsia who gathered any form of those also. You do not have to be confined to one glass pattern unless you want it that way.

We traveled coast to coast in our quest to acquire different pieces and colors of Westmoreland's Lotus; and after a massive three hour photo session, we packed three chicken boxes of Lotus for sale. We had less than a box left after the first show. Some customers asked what that pattern was since it was unknown to them. We had such an array of colors that lookers were fascinated by the flower shaped pieces just as Cathy had been, when she was captivated by it. In a way it was sad to see it go, but "our" Lotus finds brought joy to others, a rewarding feeling in itself.

Allegedly, candles with a domed foot were made near the end of Westmoreland's demise. Candles with a more flattened foot are an indication of an earlier mould. Red was a later color and most of it is inclined to be amberina (yellow tint in the red).

Infrequently found pieces of Lotus include a lamp, tumbler, cologne bottle, and puff box, although colognes found are of later manufacture. They are still desirable. The elusive tumbler is crystal with a colored petal foot. The only one we have seen has a green foot (pictured).

		Satinized colors, Amber, Crystal, White	Blue, Green, Pink	Cased colors			Satinized colors, Amber, Crystal, White	Blue, Green, Pink	Cased colors
	Bowl, 6", lily (flat mayonnaise)	12.00	20.00	40.00	7 ▸	Creamer	22.00	30.00	40.00
5 ▸	Bowl, 9", cupped	50.00	85.00	110.00	19 ▸	Lamp	195.00	295.00	
	Bowl, 11", belled	60.00	95.00	125.00		Lamp with metal rod	35.00		
	Bowl, oval vegetable	30.00	85.00	110.00		Mayonnaise, 4", ftd., flared rim	15.00	25.00	30.00
25 ▸	Candle, 3", twist stem	15.00			1 ▸	Mayonnaise, 5", footed, bell rim	20.00	30.00	35.00
3 ▸	Candle, 4", single	15.00	35.00	40.00	2 ▸	Plate, 6", mayonnaise	6.00	9.00	12.00
24 ▸	Candle, 4", twist stem	15.00			15 ▸	Plate, 8½", salad	10.00	35.00	40.00
9 ▸	Candle, 9" high, twist stem	50.00	65.00	100.00		Plate, 8¾", mayonnaise	9.00	15.00	15.00
10 ▸	Candle, triple	20.00	50.00		6 ▸	Plate, 13", flared	35.00	50.00	65.00
	Candy jar w/lid, ½ pound	65.00	100.00	135.00	11 ▸	Puff box, 5", w/cover	110.00	145.00	
	Coaster	12.00	15.00	20.00	12 ▸	Salt, individual	15.00	20.00	25.00
	Cologne, ½ ounce	85.00	110.00	145.00	18 ▸	Shaker	30.00	45.00	
22 ▸	Comport, 2½", mint, twist stem	30.00			4 ▸	Sherbet, tulip bell	18.00	28.00	35.00
	Comport, 6½", honey	20.00	30.00	45.00	8 ▸	Sugar	22.00	30.00	40.00
14 ▸	Comport, 5" high, twist stem	30.00	40.00	50.00	13 ▸	Tray, lemon, 6", handle	30.00	40.00	53.00
	Comport, 8½" high, twist stem	55.00	80.00	100.00	20 ▸	Tumbler, 10 ounce		50.00	

Lotus

LUCY, #895, Paden City Glass Company, c. 1935
Colors: crystal, amber, Cheriglo, Royal Blue, Ruby

Paden City's Lucy was first listed in a 1935 trade journal according to Jerry Barnett who first wrote a Paden City book in 1978. We only seem to find amber and crystal colors, the latter usually with an etching. Trying to match etchings found might be a problem as we rarely see the same one twice. One of the first pieces we bought was the crystal center-handled bowl with silver overlay around an etch. Today, we still haven't found a name for that etch.

Ruby and Royal Blue are the colors that excite Paden City collectors, but knowledgeable ones are more fascinated when Cheriglo (pink) appears. We have only come across two footed bowls in pink. Have you other pieces? Notice their different treatment from the mould, edge flared and edge crimped. Cheriglo is among the rarest colors and is priced with the Ruby and Royal Blue due to its scarcity.

There is a double candle having a fan-like center that stands 5⅛" high and is almost 6" wide which may belong to this line, according to recent information. It has been identified with several different patterns over the years which may have been the intent of Paden City as a sort of "one size fits all" motif. Remember, moulds were costly and the glass relatively inexpensive. Volumes had to be sold to pay for thousands spent on moulds. If several functions could be gotten from a single mould, that was money saved. With its look of several patterns, it can be used with each without a problem.

		Amber Crystal	Pink/Ruby Royal Blue			Amber Crystal	Pink/Ruby Royal Blue
	Bowl, 6¾"	8.00	18.00	9 ▸	Compote, 2⅞", cheese	9.50	17.50
2 ▸	Bowl, 9", 2-hdld.	25.00	65.00		Compote, 5", low foot	25.00	55.00
4 ▸	Bowl, 9½", ftd., crimped	40.00	80.00		Compote, 7", high ft.	25.00	50.00
3 ▸	Bowl, 9½", ftd.	35.00	75.00		Gravy, 5"x7¼"	35.00	60.00
1 ▸	Bowl, 9¾", center hdld.	30.00	65.00		Ice tub, 5⅝"	50.00	90.00
6 ▸	Bowl, 9⅞", flared	30.00	60.00	8 ▸	Mayonnaise, 3⅞", w/liner	30.00	55.00
	Bowl, 10", 3-ftd., crimped	40.00	85.00		Plate, 6¼"	5.00	12.00
7 ▸	Bowl, 11½", 3-ftd.	40.00	75.00		Plate, 10½", cracker	15.00	35.00
5 ▸	Cake salver, 11¾" x 2⅛" high	40.00	75.00		Plate, 13¾", 2-hdld.	25.00	50.00
	Candlestick, 5"	35.00			Relish, 10¾"x7¼", 3-part	40.00	90.00
	Candlestick, 5⅛", double	30.00	65.00		Server, 10⅝", center hdld.	32.00	60.00

121

MADRID, Federal Glass Company, 1932 – 1939; Indiana Glass Company, 1980s
Colors: green, pink, amber, crystal, and Madonna blue (See Reproduction Section.)

Madrid was once one of the easiest found and most beloved Depression glass patterns. Blue was especially cherished although green and amber were found more frequently. You couldn't visit a flea market or a show without seeing it on dealers' tables. In this day and age, you rarely see a piece of the old, soft "Madonna" blue Madrid. Unfortunately, what you see outside of shows from malls to the Internet are blue reproductions. Collectors are avoiding the blue today, since so little old is available. Green was never reproduced but is not found with regularity; it is difficult to gather a large green set. Amber, however, is still very available in today's marketplace, and is being collected even though there have been thousands of pieces of the newer amber Madrid dumped in the market since 1976. Prices have remained inexpensive on all but rare pieces; so if you like amber colored ware, you can still find 1930s Madrid.

Amber Madrid has been subject of dialogue and debate since 1976 when the Federal Glass Company reintroduced this pattern for the Bicentennial under a new name, "Recollection" glassware. Other companies resurrected wares from past lines during this period also, not just Federal. Each piece of "Recollection" was embossed '76 in the design. The mistake, here, was that it was remade in an amber color comparable to the original which caused trepidation for collectors of the older amber Madrid. Collectors were well informed about "Recollection," and many noncollectors purchased boxed sets believing they would someday be collectible as Bicentennial products and they eventually may. Regrettably, Indiana Glass purchased the Madrid moulds when Federal went out of business, removed the '76 date and added crystal and amber without the '76 mark. The older crystal butter was selling for several hundred dollars and the new one sold for $2.99. Prices nose-dived. Next, they made pink; and even though it was a lighter pink than the original, prices dipped in the collectibles market for the old pink. Later, Indiana made blue; it was a brighter, harsher blue than the beautiful, soft blue of the original Madrid; still, it had a negative effect on the value of the 1930s blue. All pieces made in new pink have now also been produced in shades of teal blue. Original blue pieces are priced in our listings and if you find something not priced, then it is new.

The rarely seen Madrid gravy boats and platters have generally been found in Iowa. They must have been premiums for some product there, but no one has yet found solid evidence of that.

Mint condition sugar lids in any color Madrid are difficult to find due to the protruding points around the lid. That holds true for butter dish tops also. Footed tumblers are harder to locate than flat ones, with juice tumblers almost non-existent. Amber footed shakers are less available than flat ones, but the supply is holding up to any demand. Footed shakers are the only style found in blue. Any heavy, flat shakers you spot are new.

The wooden Lazy Susan is like the Georgian one pictured on page 91 only with Madrid inserts. Madrid insert prices jumped after a few went for some serious money on Internet auctions, but sobriety has once again reigned and prices have fallen to previous levels.

We keep observing the later-made, lightly colored pink Madrid sugar and creamers with high prices at flea markets and antique malls. Originally, there were no pink sugars and creamers made. Check my list for pieces made in pink. If no price is listed, then it was not made in the 1930s. (See the new pink in the Reproduction Section in the back.)

All original blue pieces are pictured except the sauce bowl and juice tumbler.

		Amber	Pink	Green	Blue				Amber	Pink	Green	Blue
6 ▸	Ashtray, 6", square	395.00		395.00			Pitcher, 8½", 80 oz., ice lip	60.00		225.00	
	Bowl, 4¾", cream soup	15.00				25 ▸	Plate, 6", sherbet	3.00	3.50	4.00	8.00
	Bowl, 5", sauce	8.00	10.00	9.00	30.00	23 ▸	Plate, 7½", salad	8.00	9.00	9.00	22.00
	Bowl, 7", soup	15.00		16.00		20 ▸	Plate, 8⅞", luncheon	8.00	7.00	9.00	18.00
9 ▸	Bowl, 8", salad	14.00		17.50	50.00	21 ▸	Plate, 10½", dinner	50.00		40.00	60.00
	Bowl, 9⅜", large berry	20.00	20.00				Plate, 10½", grill	9.50		20.00	
	Bowl, 9½", deep salad	35.00					Plate, 10¼", relish	15.00	14.00	16.00	
2 ▸	Bowl, 10", oval veg.	18.00	15.00	22.50	40.00		Plate, 11¼", round cake	16.00	12.00		
18 ▸	*Bowl, 11", low console	12.00	12.00			17 ▸	Platter, 11½", oval	14.00	14.00	16.00	24.00
	Butter dish w/lid	65.00		90.00		10 ▸	Salt/pepper, 3½", footed, pair	90.00		90.00	125.00
	Butter dish bottom	20.00		40.00							
	Butter dish top	45.00		50.00		11 ▸	Salt/pepper, 3½", flat, pair	30.00		50.00	
	*Candlesticks, 2¼", pr.	20.00	20.00								
19 ▸	Cookie jar w/lid	50.00	30.00			5 ▸	Saucer	2.00	4.00	4.00	8.00
3 ▸	Creamer, footed	8.00		12.50	20.00	1 ▸	Sherbet, two styles	6.00		11.00	17.50
4 ▸	Cup	6.00	9.00	9.00	16.00	15 ▸	Sugar	6.00		14.00	15.00
	Gravy boat	1,000.00				14 ▸	Sugar cover	50.00		60.00	225.00
	Gravy platter	1,000.00					Tumbler, 3⅞", 5 oz.	14.00		28.00	30.00
	Hot dish coaster	120.00		100.00		7 ▸	Tumbler, 4¼", 9 oz.	14.00	17.00	20.00	30.00
	Hot dish coaster w/indent	120.00		100.00		24 ▸	Tumbler, 5½", 12 oz., 2 styles	15.00		22.00	40.00
12 ▸	Jam dish, 7"	25.00		20.00	40.00	22 ▸	Tumbler, 4", 5 oz., footed	38.00		40.00	
	Jello mold, 2⅛", tall	9.00				13 ▸	Tumbler, 5½", 10 oz., footed	26.00		45.00	
	Pitcher, 5½", 36 oz., juice	35.00									
8 ▸	**Pitcher, 8", sq., 60 oz.	40.00	30.00	125.00	160.00		Wooden Lazy Susan, cold cuts coasters	1,000.00			
	Pitcher, 8½", 80 oz.	50.00		185.00							

* Iridescent priced slightly higher   ** Crystal $150.00

MANHATTAN, "HORIZONTAL RIBBED," Anchor Hocking Glass Company, 1938 – 1943
Colors: crystal, pink; some green, ruby, and iridized

If you find a piece of Manhattan that does not match the measurements in the list below, then you may have a piece of Anchor Hocking's newer line, Park Avenue. Several claims of older Manhattan measuring the same as listings for Park Avenue plates have created some controversy. These statements came from knowledgeable collectors who owned Manhattan before Park Avenue was made in 1987. Be aware that there may be some 8" Manhattan plates previously listed as 8½" below. You can see Park Avenue listings in our book *Anchor Hocking's Fire-King & More, Third Edition*.

Some collectors of Manhattan bought this new pattern to augment their Manhattan or for daily use. One Park Avenue piece is generating discussions. A martini glass has been designed which is similar to the old comport. That older comport has four wafers on the stem while the new one has five. It was only made in crystal.

Comport price jumps in Manhattan and several other patterns can be frankly accredited to margarita and/or martini drinkers. Originally, comports were proposed for candy or mints, but ardent drinkers used these for mixed drinks and the new Park Avenue piece was definitely made for that purpose.

Manhattan's pricing has not been influenced in a bad way by the making of Park Avenue; however, the new line has caused some chaos with Manhattan cereal bowls. The older 5¼" cereals are rarely seen, particularly in mint condition; Park Avenue line lists a small bowl at 6" and the height is a hair over 2" The original cereal only measures 1¹⁵⁄₁₆" high. You need an accurate ruler to check this. Once you have seen the new, it will be more easily recognized because that silly ¹⁄₁₆" looks so much bigger that you'll wonder why you were worried. Be particularly cautious if the bowl is mint since old ones rarely are. Manhattan cereals do not have handles.

Pink Manhattan cups, saucers, and dinner plates are real, but are rarely seen. The saucer/sherbet plates of Manhattan are like many of Hocking's saucers; they have no cup ring. The juice pitcher has been found in Royal Ruby and four or five large pitchers have been seen in Jade-ite. The Manhattan juice pitcher has been reproduced in Jade-ite. Originally, only crystal, pink, and Royal Ruby were made; so beware of any other color.

Manhattan sherbets have a beaded bottom edge like the tumblers, but the center insert to the relish tray does not have these beads, rather vertical ribs along the bottom edge. Sherbets are often used as center inserts. Relish tray inserts can be found in crystal, pink, and Royal Ruby; but the center insert is always crystal on these trays.

Manhattan is one pattern that is augmented by some look-alike pieces that can be used with it. Some collectors buy Hazel-Atlas shakers to use with Manhattan since they are round rather than the original squared ones that Hocking made. In fact, one such domed candy is in the listing. One piece that is often labeled Manhattan is the "eared" flat piece shown below. It may be from another line, but it is not a Hocking piece from the Manhattan line.

		Crystal	Pink
1 ▸	*Ashtray, 4", round	9.00	
10 ▸	Ashtray, 4½", square	14.00	
7 ▸	Bowl, 4½", sauce, closed handles	9.00	
11 ▸	Bowl, 5⅜", berry w/closed handles	18.00	15.00
	Bowl, 5¼", cereal, no handles	110.00	225.00
	Bowl, 7½", large berry	20.00	
3 ▸	Bowl, 8", closed handles	30.00	25.00
	Bowl, 9", salad	28.00	
	Bowl, 9½", fruit, open handle	30.00	40.00
12 ▸	Candlesticks, 4½", square, pair	18.00	
	Candy dish, 3 legs, 6¼"		12.00
	**Candy dish and cover	37.50	
	Coaster, 3½"	15.00	
	Comport, 5¾"	35.00	42.00
21 ▸	Creamer, oval	10.00	15.00
16 ▸	Cup	14.00	295.00
8 ▸	‡‡Pitcher, 24 ounce	25.00	50.00

		Crystal	Pink
13 ▸	Pitcher, 80 ounce, tilted	35.00	55.00
17 ▸	Plate, 6", sherbet or saucer	5.00	75.00
20 ▸	Plate, 8½", salad	15.00	
14 ▸	Plate, 10¼", dinner	15.00	250.00
	Plate, 14", sandwich	25.00	
18 ▸	Relish tray, 14", 5-part	20.00	
5 ▸	Relish tray, 14", with inserts	75.00	85.00
2 ▸	Relish tray, center	10.00	14.00
6 ▸	‡Relish tray insert	4.00	7.00
	Salt & pepper, 2", square, pair	18.00	35.00
17 ▸	Saucer/sherbet plate	5.00	75.00
4 ▸	Sherbet	10.00	18.00
15 ▸	Sugar, oval	10.00	15.00
9 ▸	§Tumbler, 10 ounce, footed	18.00	25.00
19 ▸	Vase, 8"	25.00	
	**Wine, 3½"	3.00	

*Add for Hocking ad $15.00; add for others $12.50   **Look-Alike
‡ Ruby $4.00   ‡‡ Ruby $695.00   § Green or iridized $20.00

Paden City's Maya (#221) pattern can be distinguished from Largo (#220) by the thistle (ball) in its design. That same fascinating pointed thistle/ball component is designed into the knobs of the candy and cheese dishes as well as the top of the center-handled server. The cheese dish with its plain top and thistle knob seems to be the most sought piece of Maya. The bottom plate has a raised rim for the top to fit inside. One is pictured in red.

Maya's flat sugars and creamers show up even less frequently than those of Largo. Sugar and creamer collectors also prize them. We finally found a pair, but they didn't make it to the photography session on time.

The Maya candy is flat and divided into three parts like Largo's. Cuttings and etchings are not found on Maya as often as on Largo. Red Maya appears to be scarce, although we do have the elusive cheese dish.

		Crystal	Colors
	Bowl, 7", flared rim	18.00	30.00
3 ▸	Bowl, 9½", flared, tri-footed	28.00	50.00
	Bowl, 11⅝", 3½" deep, tri-footed, flared rim	30.00	70.00
2 ▸	Bowl, 12¾", 4¾" deep, tri-footed, flat rim	30.00	70.00
	Cake plate, pedestal	30.00	70.00
	Candleholder	15.00	40.00
1 ▸	Candy, footed w/lid, 3-part	40.00	125.00
5 ▸	Cheese dish w/lid	75.00	175.00
7 ▸	Comport, fluted rim, pedestal	30.00	70.00

		Crystal	Colors
8 ▸	Comport, 6½" x 10", plain rim, pedestal	30.00	70.00
	Creamer, flat	15.00	50.00
	Mayonnaise, tri-footed	14.00	35.00
6 ▸	Mayonnaise, tri-footed, crimped	18.00	40.00
	Plate, 6⅝"	6.00	12.00
	Plate, 7", mayonnaise	8.00	18.00
	Sugar, flat	15.00	50.00
4 ▸	Tray, 13¾", tri-footed, serving	25.00	70.00
	Tray, tab-handled	25.00	60.00

MAYFAIR, Federal Glass Company, 1934

Colors: crystal, amber, and green

Federal deliberately altered their Mayfair glass moulds into what eventually became the Rosemary pattern since Hocking had copyrighted the name Mayfair several years before. We are showing only the old Federal Mayfair pattern before it was changed. You will have to refer to an earlier edition to see the transitional period glassware made between the old Federal Mayfair pattern and what was to become Rosemary pattern. These transitional pieces have arching in the bottom of each piece rather than the waffle design, and there is no waffling between the top arches. If you turn to Rosemary (page 197), you will see that the design under the arches is entirely plain also. Collectors regard the transitional pieces a part of Federal Mayfair rather than Rosemary and that is why it is priced here.

Federal's Mayfair was an extremely limited production (before limited productions were used as a selling scheme). Amber and crystal are the colors that can be collected (in the true Mayfair form). Amber cream soups have been found in small numbers and platters in even fewer. Federal's crystal Mayfair can be collected as a set and it will be reasonably priced when you find it. We had a letter about a large set of eight selling for less than $100.00 on the Internet, but postage was more than half of the selling price. You need to factor in postage and insurance to really see if you are getting a so-called bargain. Green can only be bought in transitional style and the prices here are for that and not true Mayfair. We don't believe the pure form of green Mayfair exists.

Generally, you will find several pieces of Mayfair together, rather than a piece here and there. We used to see sets here in Florida, but in recent years, it has been numerous sets of amber Rosemary instead.

		Transitional Green	Amber	Crystal				Transitional Green	Amber	Crystal
6 ▶	Bowl, 5", sauce	10.00	7.00	6.50			Plate, 6¾", salad	8.00	5.00	4.50
	Bowl, 5", cream soup	22.00	18.00	15.00			Plate, 9½", dinner	13.00	9.00	9.00
2 ▶	Bowl, 6", cereal	22.00	15.00	10.00			Plate, 9½", grill	13.00	15.00	8.50
3 ▶	Bowl, 10", oval vegetable	35.00	22.00	18.00	9 ▶		Platter, 12", oval	32.00	25.00	20.00
					8 ▶		Saucer	3.00	3.00	2.50
5 ▶	Creamer, footed	18.00	11.00	10.50	4 ▶		Sugar, footed	18.00	11.00	11.00
7 ▶	Cup	10.00	8.00	5.00	1 ▶		Tumbler, 4½", 9 oz.	35.00	28.00	18.00

MAYFAIR, "OPEN ROSE," Line No. 2000, Hocking Glass Company, 1931 – 1937
Colors: ice blue, pink; some green, yellow, and crystal (See Reproduction Section.)

Hocking's Mayfair is probably the most popular and well distributed 1930s Depression glass pattern in the country. Many families still have treasured pieces passed down from grandma or even great-grandma. The pink cookie jar is regularly recognized. Cookie jars were premiums with "store bought" cookies and soaps. (Remember, this was during a time when people still made their own cookies and soap at home.) Buying products often meant you kept the container as a bonus. We have been endlessly asked if we have a spare pink Mayfair cookie jar lid for sale. Sadly, lids are rarely offered for sale by themselves. We have always recommended that customers buy a complete cookie and use the old bottom for some other purpose that doesn't need a lid. Blue cookie tops are even more difficult to find than pink as their distribution was more limited. We should note that the Mayfair cookie jar has been reproduced, so check the Reproduction section (page 249) for information on the differences between old and new.

A 1937 distributor's catalog depicts 10 items of No. 2000 line pink Mayfair "exquisitely etched (painted) with rose floral design" that could be bought by the dozen for under $1.75 to use as premiums. The least expensive item was the cereal bowl for 37¢ a dozen. The most expensive was the 80-ounce pitcher for $1.75 a dozen. This demonstrates how economically a shop owner could obtain this pattern to help promote his products and attract people to his store. This particular promotion was satinized using camphoric acid and hand painted decorations. Collectors repeatedly disregarded satin pieces in the past; but a few, today, try to find mint examples of this hand-painted pattern. Note the deep fruit bowl pictured which has been satinized and a hole drilled in it to use as a lamp or ceiling fixture. Many large bowls from an assortment of Depression glass patterns were utilized for shades.

Pink Mayfair has one of the larger selections of pieces found during this era. There are numerous stems and tumblers possible. A setting for four with all the serving pieces is pricey. However, if you do not buy the whole gamut, you can put a small set together for about the same cost as most other patterns. Price depends upon how many assorted stems or tumblers you wish as well as whether you want to own a sugar lid or the expensive, rarely seen, three-footed bowl.

All yellow Mayfair is rare and all green except for five large pieces which sell in the ballpark of $45.00. You can tell rarity by the prices listed. If no price is shown, it means that that piece has not been found in that color. Pieces in these colors are rarely seen and very expensive in mint condition; most collectors strive to own only one piece of yellow or green. A set would be a dream in today's market, a challenge to find, and a goodly sum to purchase.

A few crystal creamers and a covered sugar are known but few collectors search for crystal Mayfair. The juice pitcher, shakers, butter bottom (only), and the divided platter are commonly found. The platter is often found in a fitted metal holder and a reader wrote that the divided platter was given as a premium with the purchase of coffee or spices in late 1930s. Although some crystal items are rare, with little demand, they do not presently mandate big prices.

Blue Mayfair is strikingly beautiful and regrettably, nearly all gone from the market today. In the early days of collecting, a large set could be assembled. Today, you might have to settle for a smaller set as few accumulations are being found in basements or attics. Now, already collected sets being sold have to satisfy demand and that seldom happens. We received a listing of a large set for sale at around $20,000. This collector wanted about 90% of book prices which is not a good marketing ploy. Dealers will not pay anything close to 90% and few collectors want to buy a complete set especially in that price range. Lack of accessibility of blue Mayfair in the market is currently preventing its rise in price and to some extent is causing some drop in price. We collected a blue set, but sold it in 1972 to have money to buy other patterns for the first book. That was a pure financial risk which we don't regret today, as we work on this eighteenth book.

There are a few fine points about Mayfair that you need to know. Some stems have a plain foot while others are rayed. The 10" celery measures 11½" handle to handle and the 9" one measures 10½" handle to handle. (The measurements in this book do not include handles unless so noted.) Footed iced teas vary in height. Some teas have a short stem above the foot and others have almost none. This causes the heights to vary. It is just a mould variation, which may account for capacity differences, too. Note under measurements on page 2 the listings of tumblers that we have taken from old Hocking catalogs and how they vary from year to year.

		*Pink	Blue	Green	Yellow
8 ▶	Bowl, 5", cream soup	48.00			
30 ▶	Bowl, 5½", cereal	28.00	48.00	85.00	85.00
6 ▶	Bowl, 7", vegetable	28.00	50.00	175.00	175.00
	Bowl, 9", 3⅛ high, 3-leg console	5,500.00		5,500.00	
	Bowl, 9½", oval vegetable	34.00	70.00	125.00	135.00
28 ▶	Bowl, 10", vegetable	30.00	65.00		135.00

*Frosted or satin finish items slightly lower if paint is worn or missing

		*Pink	Blue	Green	Yellow
	Bowl, 10", same covered	125.00	130.00		995.00
12 ▶	Bowl, 11¾", low flat	55.00	60.00	40.00	225.00
7 ▶	Bowl, 12", deep, scalloped fruit	55.00	90.00	40.00	255.00
	Butter dish and cover or 7", covered vegetable	70.00	250.00	1,300.00	1,300.00
	Butter bottom with indent				250.00
	Butter dish top	42.00	245.00	1,150.00	1,150.00
	Cake plate, 10", footed	30.00	60.00	150.00	
23 ▶	Candy dish and cover	55.00	295.00	595.00	495.00
	Celery dish, 9", divided			195.00	195.00
	Celery dish, 10"	45.00	70.00	125.00	125.00
	Celery dish, 10", divided	265.00	65.00		
5 ▶	Cookie jar and lid	48.00	250.00	595.00	895.00
11 ▶	Creamer, footed	28.50	50.00	225.00	225.00
2 ▶	Cup	16.00	50.00	155.00	155.00
	Cup, round	350.00			
15 ▶	Decanter and stopper, 32 ounce	195.00			
22 ▶	Goblet, 3¾", 1 ounce cordial	995.00		995.00	
	Goblet, 4⅛", 2½ ounce	795.00		950.00	
	Goblet, 4", 3 ounce, cocktail	80.00		395.00	
	Goblet, 4½", 3 ounce, wine	90.00		450.00	
	Goblet, 5¼", 4½ ounce, claret	795.00		950.00	
	Goblet, 5¾", 9 ounce, water	65.00		495.00	
	Goblet, 7¼", 9 ounce, thin	225.00	275.00		
4 ▶	**Pitcher, 6", 37 ounce	50.00	135.00	600.00	600.00
	Pitcher, 8", 60 ounce	60.00	195.00	650.00	500.00
24 ▶	Pitcher, 8½", 80 ounce	125.00	240.00	800.00	850.00
	Plate, 5¾" (often substituted as saucer)	12.00	18.00	90.00	90.00
10 ▶	Plate, 6½", round sherbet	14.00			
19 ▶	Plate, 6½", round, off-center indent	20.00	30.00	135.00	135.00
29 ▶	Plate, 8½", luncheon	24.00	55.00	85.00	85.00

Mayfair

		*Pink	Blue	Green	Yellow
	Plate, 9½", dinner	55.00	85.00	150.00	150.00
	Plate, 9½", grill	45.00	55.00	85.00	125.00
	Plate, 11½", handled grill				125.00
26 ▸	Plate, 12", cake w/handles	40.00	65.00	35.00	
	Plate, 12", with tab handles				175.00
	‡Platter, 12", oval, open handles	32.00	65.00	175.00	
	Platter, 12½", oval, 8" wide, closed handles			235.00	235.00
25 ▸	Relish, 8⅜", 4-part	35.00	70.00	165.00	165.00
	Relish, 8⅜", non-partitioned	195.00		295.00	295.00
31 ▸	‡‡Salt and pepper, flat, pair	55.00	325.00	1,100.00	875.00
	Salt and pepper, footed	10,000.00			
	Sandwich server, center handle	45.00	75.00	32.00	135.00
	Saucer (cup ring)	28.00			150.00
3 ▸	Saucer (same as 5¾" plate)	12.00	18.00	90.00	90.00
20 ▸	Sherbet, 2¼", flat	195.00	195.00		
27 ▸	Sherbet, 3", footed	16.00			
21 ▸	Sherbet, 4¾", footed	65.00	65.00	165.00	165.00
1 ▸	Sugar, footed	28.50	50.00	210.00	210.00
2 ▸	Sugar lid	2,750.00		1,500.00	1,500.00
	Tumbler, 3½", 5 ounce, juice	40.00	100.00		
17 ▸	Tumbler, 4¼", 9 ounce, water	29.00	85.00		
	Tumbler, 4¾", 11 ounce, water	175.00	125.00	225.00	225.00
14 ▸	Tumbler, 5¼", 13½ ounce, iced tea	55.00	225.00		
	Tumbler, 3¼", 3 ounce, footed, juice	85.00			
	Tumbler, 5¼", 10 ounce, footed	36.00	150.00		225.00
13 ▸	Tumbler, 6½", 15 ounce, footed, iced tea	36.00	210.00	300.00	
9 ▸	Vase (sweet pea)	160.00	95.00	325.00	
16 ▸	Whiskey, 2¼", 1½ ounce (w/split stem)	100.00			

* Frosted or satin finish items slightly lower if paint is worn or missing   ‡ Divided Crystal $12.50
** Crystal $15.00   ‡‡ Crystal $17.50 pair — Beware reproductions.

MISS AMERICA (DIAMOND PATTERN), Line #2500, Hocking Glass Company, 1935 – 1938
Colors: crystal, pink; some green, ice blue, Jade-ite, and Royal Ruby (See Reproduction Section.)

Miss America brings more to mind than Depression glass. It is a glass beauty that is sought at Depression glass shows and is often seen at flea markets and antique malls. New collectors need to know to check the pointed edges carefully on the design when buying. Often, the tips of these points are missing, particularly underneath where most damage occurs. Also, inspect candy jar knobs to make certain they have not been glued back on. We have seen more than a dozen glued knobs over the last few years. Glue for repairing glass is becoming better grade without discoloration to make it stand out.

All Miss America tumblers and stems have three parallel lines below the plain glass rim as depicted in our photos of pink. The green tumbler on page 132 has been ground down and does not exhibit that trait. We often buy inexpensive damaged glass to photograph in order to keep our cost down. Westmoreland's English Hobnail pattern, which was made earlier and continued production past that of Miss America, is often incorrectly labeled as Miss America. Check the differences by reading the comparison of the two under that pattern on page 70. Because of marketing schemes promoting Hocking's inexpensive wares, Miss America surpassed English Hobnail's position with the public during the late 1930s. The last Miss America color made was Royal Ruby (c. 1938). We have pictured a Royal Ruby grouping in the previous editions. This particular set went home with a factory worker and we later bought it from his heirs. A few pieces turn up occasionally as did the plate on page 132.

Some reproductions tarnished Miss America for a while, but it has recovered very well over the years. A reproduction butter dish emerged in several colors in the late 1970s; but the red ones were an amberina red. No original red, blue, or green butter has been discovered and those you may spot are reproductions. Additional reproductions have appeared in Miss America pattern since the early 1970s. Please refer to page 251 for a listing and facts regarding these aggravations. The Internet exposed reproductions to a newer collecting public that had not kept informed by buying books; many of them were duped into buying these copies. Today, more informed collectors have learned how to tell old from new; so, it hardly causes a ripple in collector circles. Remember, if the price seems too good to be true, then there may be a reason for that.

Some pieces of Miss America are found with metal lids. The relish (four-part dish shown) and cereal bowl are often found that way. These glass pieces were sold to another company who made lids to fit. They are not original factory lids. The cereal is the same as a butter bottom. The metal lid adds around $10 to the price of the cereal and not hundreds of dollars as some Internet sellers might have you believe.

If a glass pattern were made for several years, it is likely that similar pieces will differ slightly in size. In talking to former Anchor Hocking mould makers, we learned that moulds were "cut down" when they deteriorated. Therefore, some pieces deviated in size a little each time the moulds were reworked and cut away to sharpen the design. If the mould were reworked several times, the sizes of a piece could vary up to $\frac{1}{16}$".

There are two styles of Miss America shakers. Shakers that are fatter toward the foot are the better ones to buy, since that style has not been reproduced. Narrow, thinner bottomed reproduction shakers are everywhere. Read how to tell the difference on page 251.

A few pieces of Jade-ite, light blue, and flashed-on amethyst, red, or green turn up occasionally, but not enough to collect a set. These colors have been shown in earlier editions of this book and in our *Treasures of Very Rare Depression Glass*.

Miss America

		Crystal	Pink	Green	Royal Ruby
18 ▶	Bowl, 4½", berry			18.00	
17 ▶	Bowl, 6¼", cereal	10.00	30.00	22.00	
6 ▶	Bowl, 8", curved in at top	38.00	85.00		695.00
	Bowl, 8¾", straight, deep fruit	32.00	85.00		
7 ▶	Bowl, 10", oval vegetable	14.00	40.00		
	Bowl, 11", shallow				950.00
12 ▶	*Butter dish and cover	195.00	595.00		
	Butter dish bottom	10.00	30.00		
	Butter dish top	185.00	565.00		
1 ▶	Cake plate, 12", footed	25.00	60.00		
	Candy jar and cover, 11½"	55.00	145.00		
13 ▶	Celery dish, 10½", oblong	14.00	38.00		
2 ▶	Coaster, 5¾"	12.00	32.00		
20 ▶	Comport, 5"	13.00	30.00		
	Creamer, footed	10.00	20.00		250.00
14 ▶	Cup	7.00	20.00	15.00	325.00
	Goblet, 3¾", 3 oz., wine	20.00	110.00		325.00
24 ▶	Goblet, 4¾", 5 oz., juice	22.00	110.00		325.00
	Goblet, 5½", 10 oz., water	15.00	50.00		295.00
	Pitcher, 8", 65 ounce	40.00	150.00		
	Pitcher, 8½", 65 ounce, w/ice lip	55.00	195.00		
3 ▶	**Plate, 5¾", sherbet	4.00	10.00	8.00	60.00
19 ▶	Plate, 6¾"			14.00	
4 ▶	Plate, 8½", salad	6.00	24.00		175.00
5 ▶	‡Plate, 10¼", dinner	12.00	33.00		
11 ▶	Plate, 10¼", grill	10.00	25.00		
	Platter, 12¼", oval	12.00	40.00		
21 ▶	Relish, 8¾", 4-part	10.00	22.50		
22 ▶	Relish, 11¾", round, divided, 5-part	20.00	6,995.00		
23 ▶	Salt and pepper, pair	30.00	60.00		
15 ▶	Saucer	2.00	5.00		75.00
16 ▶	**Sherbet	5.00	12.00		165.00
	Sugar	7.00	20.00		250.00
10 ▶	Tumbler, 4", 5 oz., juice	12.00	75.00		235.00
9 ▶	Tumbler, 4½", 10 oz., water	11.00	38.00	28.00	
8 ▶	Tumbler, 5¾", 14 oz., iced tea	22.00	100.00		

*Absolute mint price   **Also in Ice Blue $50.00   ‡Also in Ice Blue $225.00

132

MODERNISTIC, "COLONIAL BLOCK," Hazel-Atlas Glass Company, Early 1930s
Colors: green, crystal, black, pink, and rare in cobalt blue; white in 1950s

"Colonial Block" is the name collectors have used for this pattern for nearly 40 years, but the name it was promoted under was Modernistic. We found numerous little tidbits like this while researching our *Hazel-Atlas Glass Identification and Price Guide* book. If you want to find out more about Hazel-Atlas productions besides dinnerware patterns, we have a book for you.

Most pieces of Modernistic are marked HA, but not all. The H is on top of the A, which confuses some people who assume that this is the symbol for Anchor Hocking. The anchor was a symbol used by Anchor Hocking and that was not used until after the 1930s.

Green Modernistic is the color sought. You may infrequently find a crystal piece or white creamer and sugar sets. A few black and frosted green Modernistic powder jars are being seen. You might use any of these to supplement your collection, but there is not enough available to do more than that.

A cobalt blue Modernistic creamer is shown in our Hazel-Atlas book with Shirley Temple's image in white. (Hazel-Atlas also made a different creamer, a mug, and cereal bowl with that same Shirley image which have now been reproduced.) That Modernistic style however, is so rare, the copycat artists probably couldn't find one to know it even existed. The cobalt creamer itself, when found, sells in the $300.00 range and the one with Shirley Temple's image in excess of $1,000; so watch for them. They are not merely scarce but truly rare.

U.S. Glass made a pitcher similar in style to Hazel-Atlas's Modernistic. There is little difference save for handle shape and most Hazel-Atlas pitchers are marked. The handle on the Hazel-Atlas pitcher is shaped like those of the creamer and sugar. Collectors today are not as inflexible in their collecting principles as they previously were. Many will buy either pitcher to go with their set. That is why items that are similar to a pattern, but not actually a part of it, are referred to as "go-with" or "look-alike" pieces. In general, these items are more reasonably priced.

The green 4" and 7" bowls, butter tub, and the pitcher are the pieces often absent from collections. The five-ounce footed juice is the rarest piece of green Modernistic. Some of those hard-to-find pieces may well have been premiums for some marketed product that did not sell well.

		Crystal	Pink, Green	White				Crystal	Pink, Green	White
1 ▸	Bowl, 4"	3.00	10.00		7 ▸	Goblet	5.00	12.50	
6 ▸	Bowl, 7"	10.00	20.00		8 ▸	Pitcher	25.00	50.00	
10 ▸	Butter dish	24.00	25.00			*Powder jar w/lid	12.00	17.50	
	Butter dish bottom	4.00	6.00		9 ▸	Sherbet	4.00	7.00	
	Butter dish top	20.00	19.00		2 ▸	Sugar	7.00	10.00	8.00
4 ▸	Butter tub	20.00	40.00		3 ▸	Sugar lid	8.00	15.00	7.50
5 ▸	Candy jar w/cover	20.00	35.00			Tumbler, 5¼", 5 oz., footed		85.00	
11 ▸	Creamer	5.00	10.00	8.00					

133

MODERNTONE, Hazel-Atlas Glass Company, 1934 – 1942; Late 1940s – Early 1950s
Colors: amethyst, cobalt blue; some crystal, pink, and Platonite fired-on colors

Moderntone is most esteemed for its rich colorings of blue and amethyst and for its simplistic style. Reasonable pricing compared to other Depression glass patterns is its most redeeming value. At present, prices have dipped some and stocking up might be an idea. It is the only cobalt colored pattern that can be collected in a setting for six or eight for less than $500.00. Originally Moderntone was priced about the same as other 1930s patterns. A 36-piece set of cobalt Moderntone could be bought for $2.38 plus freight costs for 24 pounds as long as you sent two yellow coupons or four blue coupons from Blair's Best or White Fox flour. That was not difficult since baking was an everyday thing at that time. Realize that $2.38 was a somewhat large sum then, more than a day's wages for workers making 20 cents to a dollar a day.

There was no designated tumbler for the Moderntone set. Tumblers sold, today, as Moderntone were just advertised on the same page with this pattern, but they were never sold as an essential to the set. There are two unlike style tumblers that have been accepted. Some water and juice tumblers are paneled and have a rayed bottom, while another juice is not paneled and has a plain bottom and is marked H over top A, the Hazel-Atlas trademark. Either tumbler is acceptable, but most collectors choose the circled, paneled one since it is more abundant in most areas of the country. All sizes of tumblers are hard to find in cobalt or amethyst except for the water. Green, pink, or crystal tumblers were produced, but there is little demand for these except for the whiskey glass that is being snatched by a developing clique of collectors buying all the shot glasses that can be found.

The butter bottom and sugar were evidently marketed to another company who made metal tops. Several other Hazel-Atlas patterns including both Florentines can be found with similar metal tops. Lids appear with black, red, or blue knobs, but red ones are the most visible. No one knows which knob is the "real thing," so all colored knobs are accepted. By attaching a metal notched lid and adding a spoon, mustards were made from the handle-less custard. Speaking of that custard, there is a punch set being sold as Moderntone, which uses a Hazel-Atlas mixing bowl and either the plain, cobalt, roly-poly cups found with the Royal Lace toddy set or Moderntone custard cups. This was not Hazel-Atlas assembled; but some embrace it to "go-with" Moderntone. It may have been designed by the same company making lids for sugar and butter dishes. Our thoughts are that the handle-less cups rather than roly-poly cups should be accepted as Moderntone.

In past editions, we have shown a boxed child's set with crystal Moderntone shot glasses in a metal holder that came with a Modernistic creamer. (You can see a set in our book on Hazel-Atlas.) These boxed children's sets used to sell in the $100.00 range, but so many have turned up on Internet auctions that the demand has dwindled, and they are bringing about half the previous price if they sell at all. The major attraction to this set was the group of whiskey glasses and the nostalgia factor — both of which are waning.

There are a few collectors hunting crystal Moderntone. It brings about half the price of amethyst. Flat soups are rare in any color except crystal. They are hard to find, but not in comparison to the colored ones. Today's collectors blend colors; so, crystal soups may become more popular and pricey as they are used in place of the rarer and more costly colored ones.

Ruffled cream soup prices have exceeded those of sandwich plates. Sandwich plates are costly in mint condition because finding one not heavily scraped or worn is a problem. When you pick up a blue plate that looks white in the center from years of use, it might be advisable to pass it by.

The cheese dish remains the highest priced piece of Moderntone. This cheese dish is fundamentally a salad plate with a metal cover and wooden cutting board inside. Evidently, those cutting boards were tossed and few are found today.

Finding any Moderntone bowl without inner rim roughness (irr) is a difficult task. Bowls, themselves, are not rare; mint condition bowls are. Prices are for mint condition pieces. That is why bowls are so highly priced. Used, nicked, and bruised bowls are the norm and should be priced half or less or leave them alone.

Platonite Moderntone has been switched to Collectible *Glassware from the 40s, 50s, 60s...* since it better fits the period of time covered by that book.

		Cobalt	Amethyst				Cobalt	Amethyst
	*Ashtray, 7¾", match holder in center	150.00		17 ▸	Plate, 7¾", luncheon	11.00	9.00
9 ▸	Bowl, 4¾", cream soup	20.00	20.00	6 ▸	Plate, 8⅞", dinner	15.00	12.00
21 ▸	Bowl, 5", berry	30.00	22.00	18 ▸	Plate, 10½", sandwich	40.00	35.00
15 ▸	Bowl, 5", cream soup, ruffled	65.00		20 ▸	Platter, 11", oval	45.00	35.00
12 ▸	Bowl, 6½", cereal	85.00	65.00	5 ▸	Platter, 12", oval	80.00	40.00
1 ▸	Bowl, 7½", soup	125.00	90.00	19 ▸	Salt and pepper, pair	28.00	28.00
16 ▸	Bowl, 8¾", large berry	45.00	35.00	8 ▸	Saucer	3.00	2.00
19 ▸	Butter dish with metal cover	100.00		11 ▸	Sherbet	11.00	10.00
24 ▸	Cheese dish, 7", with metal lid	295.00		2 ▸	Sugar	12.00	10.00
4 ▸	Creamer	12.50	10.00	23 ▸	Sugar lid (metal)	37.50	
7 ▸	Cup	10.00	8.00	22 ▸	Tumbler, 5 ounce	65.00	35.00
13 ▸	Cup (handle-less) or custard	18.00	13.00	10 ▸	Tumbler, 9 ounce	30.00	25.00
3 ▸	Plate, 5⅞", sherbet	5.00	4.00		Tumbler, 12 ounce	110.00	80.00
	Plate, 6¾", salad	8.00	8.00	14 ▸	**Whiskey, 1½ ounce	35.00	

* Pink $50.00; green $75.00
** Pink or green $17.50

MONTICELLO, Later WAFFLE, #698, Imperial Glass Company, c. 1920 – 1960s

Colors: crystal, Rubigold, milk, clambroth, teal

Imperial introduced Monticello in the early 1920s in crystal and Rubigold which was Imperial's name for their marigold (iridescent) colored carnival glass. It was evidently a profitable pattern for Imperial since they continued making it off and on for over 40 years. Over 60 pieces were produced during its history. We typically see crystal items, but carnival collectors search for the Rubigold which we rarely see.

Monticello was later dubbed Waffle by Imperial, which is what it was being called at markets in the late 1960s and 1970s when we first started shopping for glassware.

Fortunately, or unfortunately as the case may be for collectors, Imperial reissued a variety of bits and pieces from this line throughout their production years in whatever colors were most important at that moment. So, it's to be expected you may find other, later colors than those listed above. We are pricing only crystal for now. Colors will increase the listed prices, with teal and clambroth bringing the most. Pricing for Rubigold will double on choice items, but collectors of carnival glass seem to differ on how important a pattern Monticello is to their collecting fraternity.

		Crystal		Crystal			Crystal
4 ▸	Basket, 10"	20.00	Bowl, 8", shallow	17.00		Plate, 8", salad	9.00
	Bonbon, 5½", 1 handle	12.00	Bowl, 9", round	20.00		Plate, 9", dinner	20.00
	Bowl, 4½", finger	10.00	Bowl, 9", shallow	17.50	6 ▸	Plate, 10½", square	25.00
	Bowl, 4½", fruit, 2 styles	7.00	Bowl, 10", belled	22.00		Plate, 12", round	35.00
	Bowl, 5½", créme soup	12.50	Bowl, 10", shallow	22.00		Plate, 16", cupped	50.00
2 ▸	Bowl, 5", lily	18.00	Bowl, 12", deep	25.00		Plate, 16½", round	80.00
	Bowl, 5", fruit	10.00	Buffet set, 3-pc. (mayo, spoon, 16½" rnd. plate)	85.00		Plate, 17", flat	55.00
	Bowl, 6½", belled	12.00				Punch bowl, belled rim	40.00
	Bowl, 6", lily	20.00	Butter tub, 5½"	35.00	5 ▸	Punch cup	4.00
	Bowl, 6", round	10.00	Celery, 9", oval	20.00		Relish, 8¼", divided	16.00
	Bowl, 7½", square	17.50	Cheese dish and cover	75.00		Salt & pepper w/glass tops	20.00
	Bowl, 7½", belled	15.00	Coaster, 3¼"	8.00		Saucer	3.00
	Bowl, 7", flower (w/flower grid)	40.00	9 ▸ Compote, 5¼"	12.50	8 ▸	Sherbet	10.00
			Compote, 5¾", belled rim	15.00		Stem, cocktail	12.50
	Bowl, 7", lily	25.00	1 ▸ Creamer	12.50		Stem, water	15.00
	Bowl, 7", nappy	12.50	Cup	10.00	3 ▸	Sugar, open	12.50
	Bowl, 7", round	12.50	Cuspidor	65.00		Tidbit, 2-tier (7½" & 10½")	40.00
	Bowl, 8½", belled	17.50	Mayo set, 3-piece	35.00		Tumbler, 9 oz., water	12.00
	Bowl, 8", lily (cupped)	30.00	7 ▸ Pickle, 6", oval	17.00		Tumbler, 12 oz., tea	15.00
	Bowl, 8", round veg.	25.00	Pitcher, 52 oz., ice lip	65.00		Vase, 6"	20.00
	Bowl, 8", round	17.00	Plate, 6", bread	5.00		Vase, 10½", flat	40.00

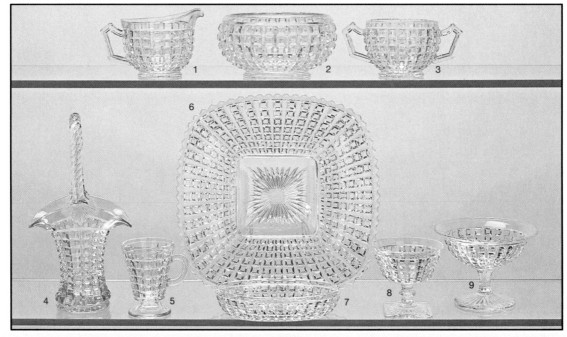

MOONDROPS, New Martinsville Glass Company, 1932 – 1940
Colors: amber, pink, green, cobalt, ice blue, red, amethyst, crystal, dark green, light green, Jadite, smoke, and black

Red and cobalt blue Moondrops are the preferred color choices; but little is being found except for creamers and sugars which are more abundant than previously thought. Red Moondrops dominates Internet auctions, but only rare items are selling at normal prices. High priced listings are receiving very little response.

Every antique shop and mall dealer knows that red and cobalt blue glass are expensive colors; consequently, prices are generally high even if they are not familiar with Moondrops. In contrast, other colors evade scrutiny; you may find a bargain in them. Rarely found items are recognized in collecting circles. Amber is the least preferred color and even rarely seen items are difficult to sell in that. Not only Moondrops, but other amber patterns are not finding favor with enough collectors to raise prices. We do feel Moondrops amber is better than most.

Perfume bottles, powder jars, mugs, gravy boats, and triple candlesticks are indicative of more elegant glassware; those items are eliminated from the market quickly. Bud vases, decanters, and popular "rocket style" stems command extraordinary prices. Five colors of "rocket style" decanters and other unusual pieces are pictured in our *Treasures of Very Rare Depression Glass*.

Apparently, New Martinsville or their glass distributors deliberately mismatched some Moondrops colors. We have found two powder jars with crystal bottoms and cobalt blue tops in antique malls in Ohio and Florida, so they were probably marketed that way. We have never found a complete blue powder jar, but we have seen a complete cobalt perfume.

The butter has to have a Moondrops glass top with fan finial to realize the prices listed below. There is a metal top with a bird finial found on some butter bottoms which sells for about $35.00. However, a metal top with a fan finial sells for double that. Both fan finials are not easily found. Collectors have a predilection for glass tops on their butter dishes.

		Blue, Red	Other Colors			Blue, Red	Other Colors
	Ashtray	25.00	15.00	22 ▸	Bowl, 13", console with wings	120.00	42.00
15 ▸	Bowl, 4¼", cream soup	50.00	20.00		Butter dish and cover	425.00	250.00
	Bowl, 5¼", berry	15.00	8.00		Butter dish bottom	25.00	10.00
	Bowl, 5⅜", 3-footed, tab handle	70.00	30.00		Butter dish top (glass)	400.00	210.00
16 ▸	Bowl, 6¾", soup	60.00			Candles, 2", ruffled, pair	45.00	25.00
	Bowl, 7½", pickle	30.00	15.00	7 ▸	Candles, 4½", sherbet style, pair	25.00	18.00
	Bowl, 8⅜", footed, concave top	40.00	25.00		Candlesticks, 5", ruffled, pair	35.00	22.00
	Bowl, 8½", 3-footed divided relish	36.00	20.00	3 ▸	Candlesticks, 5", wings, pair	110.00	50.00
29 ▸	Bowl, 9½", 3-legged, ruffled	65.00			Candlesticks, 5¼", triple light, pair	150.00	75.00
	Bowl, 9¾", oval vegetable	60.00	45.00		Candlesticks, 8½", metal stem, pair	50.00	30.00
6 ▸	Bowl, 9¾", covered casserole	250.00	145.00		Candy dish, 8", ruffled	35.00	18.00
27 ▸	Bowl, 9¾", handled, oval	50.50	36.00		Cocktail shaker with or without handle, metal top	60.00	35.00
	Bowl, 11", boat-shaped celery	32.00	23.00				
8 ▸	Bowl, 12", round, 3-footed console	70.00	30.00		Comport, 4"	25.50	15.00

Moondrops

		Blue, Red	Other Colors
	Comport, 11½"	75.00	40.00
	Creamer, 2¾", miniature	15.00	9.00
	Creamer, 3¾", regular	15.00	9.00
17 ▸	Cup	15.00	6.00
	Decanter, 7¾", small	55.00	30.00
	Decanter, 8½", medium	60.00	35.00
	Decanter, 11¼", large	90.00	45.00
	Decanter, 10¼", rocket	495.00	325.00
12 ▸	Goblet, 2⅞, ¾ oz., cordial	20.00	15.00
13 ▸	Goblet, 3¾, ¾ oz., metal stem cordial	55.00	35.00
1 ▸	Goblet, 4", 4 oz., cocktail	18.00	12.00
20 ▸	Goblet, 4½", 3 oz., wine	22.00	18.00
21 ▸	Goblet, 4¾", rocket, wine	50.00	30.00
	Goblet, 4¾", 5 oz.	20.00	12.00
4 ▸	Goblet, 5¾", 8 oz.	20.00	18.00
	Goblet, 5⅛", 3 oz., metal stem, wine	14.00	10.00
5 ▸	Goblet, 5½", 4 oz., metal stem, wine	16.00	10.00
	Goblet, 6¼", 9 oz., metal stem, water	20.00	14.00
	Goblet, 6½", 9 oz.	60.00	30.00
2 ▸	Grapefruit, 4¾"	60.00	35.00
	Gravy boat	165.00	80.00
	Mayonnaise, 5¼"	50.00	30.00
	Mug, 5⅛", 12 oz.	40.00	20.00
	Perfume bottle, rocket	275.00	175.00
	Pitcher, 6⅞", 22 oz., small	150.00	75.00
	Pitcher, 8⅛", 32 oz., medium	60.00	95.00
	Pitcher, 8", 50 oz., large, with lip	170.00	95.00
19 ▸	Pitcher, 8⅛", 53 oz., large, no lip	160.00	100.00

		Blue, Red	Other Colors
	Plate, 5⅞"	8.00	6.00
11 ▸	Plate, 6⅛", sherbet	5.00	3.00
	Plate, 6", round, off-center sherbet indent	10.00	7.00
	Plate, 7⅛", salad	10.00	6.00
	Plate, 8½", luncheon	12.00	10.00
	Plate, 9½", dinner	28.00	16.00
23 ▸	Plate, 14", round sandwich	40.00	18.00
	Plate, 14", 2-handled sandwich	50.00	22.00
	Platter, 12", oval	40.00	20.00
28 ▸	Powder jar, 3-footed	295.00	175.00
18 ▸	Saucer	3.00	2.00
	Sherbet, 2⅝"	14.00	9.00
	Sherbet, 4½"	20.00	12.00
	Sugar, 2¾"	14.00	8.00
9 ▸	Sugar, 3½"	15.00	9.00
	Tumbler, 2¾", 2 oz., shot	18.00	9.00
	Tumbler, 2¾", 2 oz., handled shot	16.00	12.00
24 ▸	Tumbler, 3¼", 3 oz., footed juice	18.00	11.00
26 ▸	Tumbler, 3⅝", 5 oz.	18.00	10.00
	Tumbler, 4⅜", 7 oz.	16.00	10.00
25 ▸	Tumbler, 4⅜", 8 oz.	20.00	10.00
	Tumbler, 4⅞", 9 oz., handled	30.00	16.00
10 ▸	Tumbler, 4⅞", 9 oz.	18.00	12.00
14 ▸	Tumbler, 5⅛", 12 oz.	30.00	14.00
	Tray, 7½", for mini sugar/creamer	30.50	15.00
	Vase, 7¾", flat, ruffled top	55.00	40.00
	Vase, 8½", rocket bud	295.00	195.00
	Vase, 9¼", rocket style	295.00	165.00

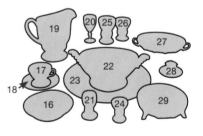

MT. PLEASANT, "DOUBLE SHIELD," L. E. Smith Glass Company, 1920s – 1934
Colors: black amethyst, amethyst, cobalt blue, crystal, pink, green, and white

Mt. Pleasant is routinely purchased for its cobalt blue or black colors more than for its being Depression glass. Prices have dipped due to the lack of new collectors. Five or six years ago, Cathy pointed out to me that TV shows were emphasizing getting rid of anything you haven't used in a year. That hardly lends itself to collecting. Yet, those same type shows often go to great lengths to "feature" such items when found in a home.

The "Double Shield" refers to the moulded design on most pieces. Years before names were known, collectors called this pattern "Double Shield" and it stuck. Crystal with striped colors is rarely seen. We have had sporadic reports of pink and green items, generally, sugars and creamers. We picture a green double candle in our second *Glass Candlesticks of the Depression Era* book. A few pink plates turn up intermittently, suggesting a luncheon set might be attainable.

Cobalt blue Mt. Pleasant was prevalent in the Midwest and in northern New York. We understand that Mt. Pleasant was displayed and awarded as premiums in hardware stores in those areas. Black overshadows other colors in some areas of the country, but we have not found evidence that black was also used as premiums.

Pieces of both colors are discovered with a platinum (silver) band trim. This decorated band fades away with use. Prices should be less for worn decorations. It's a documented fact that gold and silver trims deteriorate quickly with dishwasher/lemon soap exposure; so, you should hand wash items with those trims in non-lemon soap, if you care to preserve them.

		Pink, Green	Amethyst, Black, Cobalt			Pink, Green	Amethyst, Black, Cobalt
	Bonbon, 7", rolled-up, handle	14.00	20.00		Leaf, 11¼"		30.00
	Bowl, 4" opening, rose	18.00	24.00	12 ▶	Mayonnaise, 5½", 3-footed, 2 styles	18.00	25.00
7 ▶	Bowl, 4⅞", square, footed, fruit	13.00	22.00	5 ▶	Mint, 6", center handle	16.00	22.00
14 ▶	Bowl, 6", 2-handle, square	13.00	18.00		Plate, 7", 2-handle, scalloped	9.00	14.00
	Bowl, 7", 3-footed, rolled out edge	16.00	25.00	9 ▶	Plate, 8", scalloped or square	8.00	12.00
	Bowl, 8", scalloped, 2-handle	18.00	32.00	6 ▶	Plate, 8", 2-handle	11.00	20.00
	Bowl, 8", square, 2-handle	19.00	22.00		Plate, 8¼", square, w/indent for cup		16.00
	Bowl, 9", scalloped, 1¾" deep, ftd.		32.00		Plate, 9", grill		20.00
	Bowl, 9¼", square, footed, fruit	19.00	32.00	2 ▶	Plate, 10½", cake, 2-handle, 2 styles	12.00	20.00
	Bowl, 10", scalloped fruit		40.00		Plate, 10½", 1¼" high, cake		40.00
	Bowl, 10", 2-handle turned-up edge		22.00		Plate, 12", 2-handle	16.00	26.00
	Cake plate, 10½", footed, 1¼" high		35.00		Salt and pepper, 2 styles	22.00	40.00
	Candlestick, single, pair	18.00	25.00		Sandwich server, center-handle		25.00
	Candlestick, double, pair	35.00	35.00	3 ▶	Saucer	2.50	5.00
11 ▶	Creamer	18.00	15.00		Sherbet, 2 styles	10.00	13.00
	Cup (waffle-like crystal)	4.50		1 ▶	Sugar	18.00	15.00
4 ▶	Cup	9.50	13.00	8 ▶	Tumbler, footed		15.00
10 ▶	Leaf, 8"		15.00		Vase, 7¼"		25.00

MT. VERNON, Later WASHINGTON, #699, Imperial Glass Company, Late 1920s – 1970s

Colors: crystal, red, green, yellow, milk, iridized, red flash

Imperial's Mt. Vernon pattern is often confused with Tiffin's Williamsburg made in the late 20s in crystal and in the 50s in colors. Williamsburg has a rayed star bottom design; Mt. Vernon's pattern shows a waffle type designed bottom and extended tip handle augmentation, exhibited by the white oil bottle.

Mt. Vernon was a trendy, prismatic design, in sync with its deco roots. This pattern adopts square, round, triangle, and cubist forms, along with novelty handle protrusions and wafer-like stems.

Mt. Vernon exists by and large in crystal; but limited pieces of color emerged from time to time, as is typical with Imperial moulds that were occasionally reintroduced throughout their production years. Cobalt and emerald items were made in a last ditch effort to raise money to "save Imperial Glass." You should be able to gather a set of crystal now without breaking the bank. The tall celery becomes a pickle by adding a lid; both styles of sugar bowls, the 5¾" two-handled bowl, and the 69-ounce pitcher were sold with or without lids which makes finding lids for them even more difficult than normal.

		Crystal				Crystal			Crystal
1 ▸	Bonbon, 5¾", one-handle	10.00		Creamer, large	10.00		Saucer	2.00
	Bowl, 5", finger	12.00		Cup, coffee	8.00		Shaker, pair	20.00
	Bowl, 5¾", two-handle	10.00	7 ▸	Cup, custard or punch	5.00		Spooner	20.00
	Bowl, 5¾", two-handle, w/cover	20.00		Decanter	38.00	3 ▸	Stem, 2 ounce, wine	12.00
	Bowl, 6", lily	15.00	11 ▸	Oil bottle, 6 ounce	30.00	4 ▸	Stem, 3 ounce, cocktail	8.00
10 ▸	Bowl, 7", lily	18.00		Pickle jar, w/cover	35.00		Stem, 5 ounce, sherbet	6.00
	Bowl, 8", lily	20.00	13 ▸	Pickle, tall, two-handle	22.00		Stem, 9 ounce, water goblet	9.00
	Bowl, 10", console	25.00		Pickle, 6", two-handle	15.00		Sugar lid, for individual	8.00
	Bowl, 10", 3-footed	25.00		Pitcher top, for 69 ounce	30.00		Sugar lid, for large	12.00
6 ▸	Bowl, punch	30.00	14 ▸	Pitcher, 54 ounce	35.00	2 ▸	Sugar, individual	8.00
	Butter dish, 5"	30.00		Pitcher, 69 ounce, straight edge	40.00		Sugar, large	12.00
9 ▸	Butter dish, dome top	35.00					Syrup, 8½ ounce, w/cover	45.00
	Butter tub, 5"	15.00		Plate, 6", bread and butter	4.00		Tidbit, two-tier	30.00
	Candlestick, 9"	22.00		Plate, 8", round	9.00		Tumbler, 7 ounce, old fashioned	10.00
	Celery, 10½"	22.00	12 ▸	Plate, 8", square	9.00			
	Compote, 5½"	20.00	15 ▸	Plate, 11", cake	18.00		Tumbler, 9 ounce, water	8.00
	Compote, tri-stem knob	25.00		Plate, 12½", sandwich	20.00		Tumbler, 12 ounce, iced tea	12.50
5 ▸	Creamer, individual	8.00		Plate, 13¼", torte	25.00	16 ▸	Vase, 6"	18.00
			8 ▸	Plate, 18", liner for punch	25.00		Vase, 10", orange bowl	50.00

NEW CENTURY, Hazel-Atlas Glass Company, 1930 – 1935
Colors: green; some crystal, pink, amethyst, and cobalt

New Century has captivated glass hunters for years, but not in the multitudes of other Hazel-Atlas patterns like Royal Lace or the Florentines. Green is the only color in which to find sets. A few pieces are found in crystal, but not enough to compile a set. Crystal prices have been comparable to green due to rarity, but that is changing due to a lack of interest in crystal. You can find crystal powder jars made from a sugar lid set atop a sherbet. The knob of the sherbet often has decorative glass marbles or beads attached by a wire. We believe these were a legitimate product of the 30s since so many have been discovered over the years. Powder jars in most patterns could be assembled in this fashion. We once saw a "rare" one in Cherry Blossom priced around $300.00, but collectors in the know only got a chuckle from this display. Hopefully, the seller was having some fun that day.

Pink, cobalt, and amethyst New Century have only materialized in pitchers and several sizes of flat tumblers. An occasional cup or saucer has been found in those colors. Incidentally, in doing some other research, we found that most beverage sets in the 30s were priced around a $1.00 and were often used as sales promotions. If you shopped the sales at a store, you could buy a seven-piece beverage set for 79¢ to a $1.00. This classic "pillow optic" design, as it was promoted in a Butler Brothers catalog, has definitely withstood the test of time.

New Century bowls, unfortunately, are all but impossible to find. Nor have we seen a 4½" berry bowl at market in years. That Butler Brothers ad mentioned those sold for 37¢ a dozen, and they were packed three dozen to a carton. Surely, some sold at that price, but they are not easily uncovered now. The larger 8" bowl can be spotted occasionally, but that too, is missing from many collections.

Casseroles, whiskeys, wines, decanters, grill plates, and cocktails are driving collectors to early cocktail hours. Cream soups are finally showing up, but not regularly enough for all. As in Adam, the casserole bottom is more challenging to find than the top. We recently examined a badly chipped casserole lid priced for $10.00; the seller informed us that all Depression glass lids were worth way more than that. Well, not really; and especially not badly damaged ones.

		Green, Crystal	Pink, Cobalt, Amethyst
5 ▸	Ashtray/coaster, 5⅜"	22.00	
1 ▸	Bowl, 4½", berry	25.00	
12 ▸	Bowl, 4¾", cream soup	20.00	
21 ▸	Bowl, 8", large berry	28.00	
2 ▸	Bowl, 9", covered casserole	75.00	
	Butter dish and cover	40.00	
13 ▸	Cup	12.00	20.00
25 ▸	Creamer	15.00	
3 ▸	Decanter and stopper	75.00	
20 ▸	Goblet, 3¼ ounce, cocktail	35.00	
27 ▸	Pitcher, 7¾", 60 ounce, with or without ice lip	35.00	35.00
	Pitcher, 8", 80 ounce, with or without ice lip	40.00	42.00
	Plate, 6", sherbet	7.00	
7 ▸	Plate, 7⅛", breakfast	11.00	
26 ▸	Plate, 8½", salad	13.00	
8 ▸	Plate, 10", dinner	18.00	
23 ▸	Plate, 10", grill	18.00	
6 ▸	Platter, 11", oval	25.00	
22 ▸	Salt and pepper, pair	36.00	
14 ▸	Saucer	3.00	7.50
11 ▸	Sherbet, 3"	12.00	
24 ▸	Sugar	10.00	
10 ▸	Sugar cover	18.00	
	Tumbler, 3½", 5 ounce	18.00	12.00
	Tumbler, 3½", 8 ounce	30.00	
	Tumbler, 4", 5 ounce, footed	22.00	
18 ▸	Tumbler, 4¼", 9 ounce	22.00	12.00
4 ▸	Tumbler, 4⅞", 9 ounce, footed	25.00	
9 ▸	Tumbler, 5", 10 ounce	22.00	15.00
	Tumbler, 5¼", 12 ounce	30.00	18.00
	Whiskey, 2½", 1½ ounce	20.00	

NEWPORT, "HAIRPIN," Hazel-Atlas Glass Company, 1936 – 1940
Colors: cobalt blue, amethyst; some pink, Platonite white, and fired-on colors

Newport's cobalt blue is the choice color in this pattern. Let's admit it; cobalt blue is admired in any pattern. We rarely see amethyst offered for sale but a few weeks ago, there was a large setting for eight with everything except tumblers being offered at a reasonable price. While looking it over, we noticed that many pieces were chipped and scratched. Appealing, but not for resale in today's market.

Small amounts of pink Newport are found today; so the 32-piece set on the next page that was free, excluding collect shipping charges may not have increased seed sales much. That seems like a good deal today for only ordering a $4.00 packet of seeds. That was a lot of seeds and $4.00 was a tidy sum in those days. We usually see berry bowls and little else in pink. Price pink half or less of amethyst prices due to few people looking for it.

Unless an old collection is sold or split up, cereal bowls, sandwich plates, large berry bowls, and tumblers are not appearing in the marketplace in any color. In a couple of months of watching Internet auctions, only a damaged Newport dinner plate and one tumbler have been offered. Neither sold.

There is a 5/16" difference between a purported "larger" dinner and a luncheon plate. At any rate, the larger dinner plate measures 8¹³⁄₁₆" while the luncheon plate measures 8½"; and, honestly, after that first occasion of the differences being pointed out, few collectors really seem to care and opt for the cheaper one. It was originally noticed because of problems with mail orders and Internet auctions. ("The plates you sent me were smaller than the ones I have!") The only official listing we have lists plates of 6", 8½", and 11½". However, after obtaining several of these plates, we found actual measurements differ as you can see from our listing below. One of the problems with catalog measurements is that they were not always accurate. Measurements were rounded off or sometimes seem to have been estimated instead of measured. Maybe the difference occurred when worn moulds were "cut down" to re-use. In any case, there are discrepancies in plate sizes, so be aware of it.

		Cobalt	Amethyst			Cobalt	Amethyst
2 ▸	Bowl, 4¾", berry	18.00	15.00	12 ▸	Plate, 8¹³⁄₁₆", dinner	25.00	20.00
1 ▸	Bowl, 4¾", cream soup	15.00	15.00		Plate, 11¾", sandwich	40.00	33.00
4 ▸	Bowl, 5¼", cereal	40.00	30.00	7 ▸	Platter, 11¾", oval	48.00	40.00
8 ▸	Bowl, 8¼", large berry	45.00	40.00	11 ▸	Salt and pepper	40.00	35.00
10 ▸	Cup	12.00	10.00	9 ▸	Saucer	4.00	4.00
13 ▸	Creamer	15.00	12.00	15 ▸	Sherbet	10.00	10.00
16 ▸	Plate, 5⅞", sherbet	8.00	6.00	14 ▸	Sugar	15.00	12.00
5 ▸	Plate, 8½", luncheon	10.00	12.00	6 ▸	Tumbler, 4½", 9 ounce	40.00	35.00

NEWPORT, New Martinsville, c. 1930s
Colors: cobalt, red, green, amber

Cobalt blue Newport does not seem to be in our stars. Have you any pieces? Red seems to be the color offered for sale in our travels although some green occasionally comes into view.

The New Martinsville Newport we chance upon is usually priced out of range due to its colors and not necessarily for any knowledge of the pattern or manufacturer. We added amber to the listing after finding a small luncheon set in that color in an antique mall in Ohio. The owner had no idea what he had and listed it only as pretty amber glass. Amber is a seldom sought color today; consequently, prices below need to be reduced to half those listed to be more in line with the selling price of that particular color. Because there's so much amber available in various 1930s patterns, it was apparently beloved in that period. There are enthusiasts for it today, but they are few.

		Amber, Green	Red, Cobalt
4 ▸	Creamer	12.00	22.00
1 ▸	Cup	12.00	20.00
5 ▸	Plate, 8"	10.00	12.00
2 ▸	Saucer	3.00	4.00
3 ▸	Sugar	12.00	22.00
6 ▸	Tray, 13½", round torte	35.00	45.00

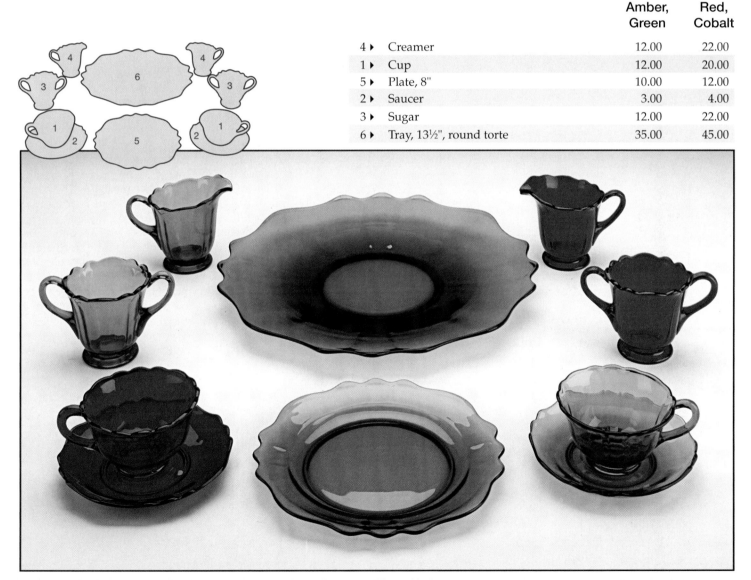

NORMANDIE, "BOUQUET AND LATTICE," Federal Glass Company, 1933 – 1940

Colors: Sunburst (iridescent), amber, pink, and crystal

Normandie was identified as "Bouquet and Lattice" by carnival glass collectors before its actual name was uncovered. Pink became the most preferred color as many Depression glass collectors bought anything pink when they started and that penchant stuck through the years. Normandie was also made in amber and Sunburst (iridescent), which you will have a better chance of collecting today. Sunburst was accomplished by spraying color over crystal and re-firing the wares. We met a collector who informed us he bought every piece of Sunburst Normandie he found, so that someday when it was hard to find, he would be rich. Not long ago he said he had over 5,000 pieces and was fast on his way to poverty instead of riches. That may prove how much Sunburst Normandie can be bought today.

Pink Normandie has been a strain to purchase for several years; but amber juice and tea tumblers, sugar lids, and dinner-sized plates have scant supplies too. Should you discover any pink Normandie tumblers, prices are rapidly approaching those of American Sweetheart. Most pink Normandie pitchers are already hidden away in older collections. Over the years, our shop only owned two pink Normandie pitchers to give you some perspective on how hard they are to obtain.

Buy any hard-to-find Normandie items first, or anytime you see them. That recommendation goes for collecting any pattern. Rarer, harder-to-find items have always increased in price quicker than commonly found ones. Also, if you unearth pieces of pink except cups, saucers, sherbets, small bowls, and luncheon plates grab them; someone will want them.

All rare pieces of pink have held their value in the latest downward pricing trend; we have not seen a pink dinner plate for sale in over six years. Actually, we have only owned one of those in over 38 years of selling.

Some Sunburst Normandie is still being offered for sale at Depression glass shows, but there are not enough buyers to raise the prices for now. Sunburst is realistically priced in comparison to pink and amber and is actually rather striking in this particular pattern. A console bowl and candlesticks (frequently found with sets of Sunburst Normandie) are actually Madrid pattern. These were manufactured about the same time as Normandie and apparently sold along with Normandie in sets. That does not make them Normandie; they are still Madrid. The design on the glass determines pattern, not the color. We have received a letter and an e-mail recently asking why we did not list Normandie candles as they had bought candles in a set of iridescent Normandie. See Madrid for pricing of these console sets.

We should mention that there is a new pink glassware set based on the mould shapes of Normandie, but having a heart as its center design, that was sold through the Cracker Barrel chain of restaurants. It is no threat to Depression ware and is actually rather attractive and fitting to those surroundings. The pitcher we saw was heavier and a brighter pink color.

		Amber	Pink	Iridescent
3 ▶	Bowl, 5", berry	7.00	9.00	4.00
8 ▶	*Bowl, 6½", cereal	20.00	50.00	8.00
13 ▶	Bowl, 8½", large berry	25.00	38.00	14.00
	Bowl, 10", oval vegetable	18.00	38.00	16.00
6 ▶	Creamer, footed	8.00	14.00	8.00
2 ▶	Cup	6.00	8.00	5.00
12 ▶	Pitcher, 8", 80 ounce	80.00	195.00	
16 ▶	Plate, 6", sherbet	3.00	6.00	2.00
	Plate, 7¾", salad	10.00	14.00	
15 ▶	Plate, 9¼", luncheon	8.50	15.00	12.00
14 ▶	Plate, 11", dinner	30.00	150.00	11.50
	Plate, 11", grill	11.00	25.00	6.00

		Amber	Pink	Iridescent
11 ▶	Platter, 11¾"	20.00	48.00	12.00
	Salt and pepper, pair	45.00	80.00	
1 ▶	Saucer	1.50	2.50	1.50
7 ▶	Sherbet	4.00	8.00	5.00
10 ▶	Sugar	8.00	12.00	7.00
9 ▶	Sugar lid	95.00	195.00	
	Tumbler, 4", 5 ounce, juice	25.00	90.00	
5 ▶	Tumbler, 4¼", 9 ounce, water	20.00	60.00	
4 ▶	Tumbler, 5", 12 ounce, iced tea	38.00	110.00	

* Mistaken by many as butter bottom

No. 610, "PYRAMID," Indiana Glass Company, 1926 – 1932
Colors: green, pink, yellow, white, crystal, blue, or black in 1974 – 1975 by Tiara

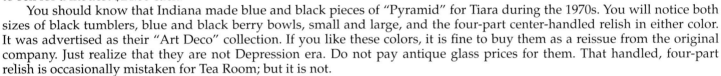

"Pyramid," as Indiana's pattern No. 610 is called by collectors, has finally slowed its price climb. Two reasons have caused this slow down. First, little mint condition of this deco looking ware is being found in the market; and secondly, high prices have prevented new admirers from even looking for it. Art Deco devotees as well as Depression glass collectors have pushed prices for years, but additional supplies are needed to rejuvenate sales.

Mint condition "Pyramid" is bringing premium prices when it does appear. Chips do downgrade the price — even more on rare items. The prices below are for mint condition glassware; any with a "ding" or two should sell for less. "Pyramid" was, and still is, easily damaged on its points. Be sure to examine all the ridged panels and corners on each piece. You will be amazed how often a chipped or cracked piece of "Pyramid" is offered as mint. About eight months ago we bought a yellow pitcher and eight tumblers that were supposedly mint. The pitcher and five good tumblers sold, but we still have three tumblers with very small nicks on a corner that we have been unable to sell for a modest $24.00 each.

You should know that Indiana made blue and black pieces of "Pyramid" for Tiara during the 1970s. You will notice both sizes of black tumblers, blue and black berry bowls, small and large, and the four-part center-handled relish in either color. It was advertised as their "Art Deco" collection. If you like these colors, it is fine to buy them as a reissue from the original company. Just realize that they are not Depression era. Do not pay antique glass prices for them. That handled, four-part relish is occasionally mistaken for Tea Room; but it is not.

The legitimate sugar/creamer stand (tray) has squared indentations on each side to fit the squared bottoms of the sugar and creamer. Stands with round indentions were common in an assortment of patterns, but it takes one with square indentations for it to truly be "Pyramid."

"Pyramid" crystal pitchers and tumblers are priced higher than all but yellow, even though yellow ones are seen more often. Crystal pitchers are truly rare and only a handful have turned up over the years. There are so many collectors of yellow "Pyramid" that prices have kept steady. Ice buckets turn up often, even in yellow. However, it is the yellow lid to the ice bucket that is nearly unattainable. No lids have yet been found for any other colored "Pyramid" ice buckets.

"Pyramid" oval bowls and pickle dishes are often confused because both measure 9½". The oval bowl has pointed edges; the pickle dish has rounded edges with open tab handles.

		Crystal	Pink	Green	Yellow
11 ▶	Bowl, 4¾", berry	18.00	22.00	25.00	38.00
8 ▶	Bowl, 8½", master berry	25.00	50.00	55.00	75.00
6 ▶	Bowl, 9½", oval	30.00	40.00	45.00	65.00
3 ▶	Bowl, 9½", pickle, 5¾" wide, handled	30.00	35.00	40.00	55.00
7 ▶	Creamer	20.00	30.00	28.00	35.00
	Ice tub	125.00	135.00	175.00	200.00
	Ice tub lid				700.00
5 ▶	Pitcher	495.00	395.00	250.00	550.00
1 ▶	Relish tray, 4-part, handle	25.00	50.00	55.00	60.00
9 ▶	Sugar	17.50	30.00	28.00	35.00
10 ▶	Tray for creamer and sugar	25.00	30.00	30.00	55.00
2 ▶	Tumbler, 8 ounce, footed, 2 styles	50.00	50.00	50.00	70.00
4 ▶	Tumbler, 11 ounce, footed	80.00	60.00	80.00	85.00

No. 610, "Pyramid"

No. 612, "HORSESHOE," Indiana Glass Company, 1930 – 1933
Colors: green, yellow, pink, and crystal

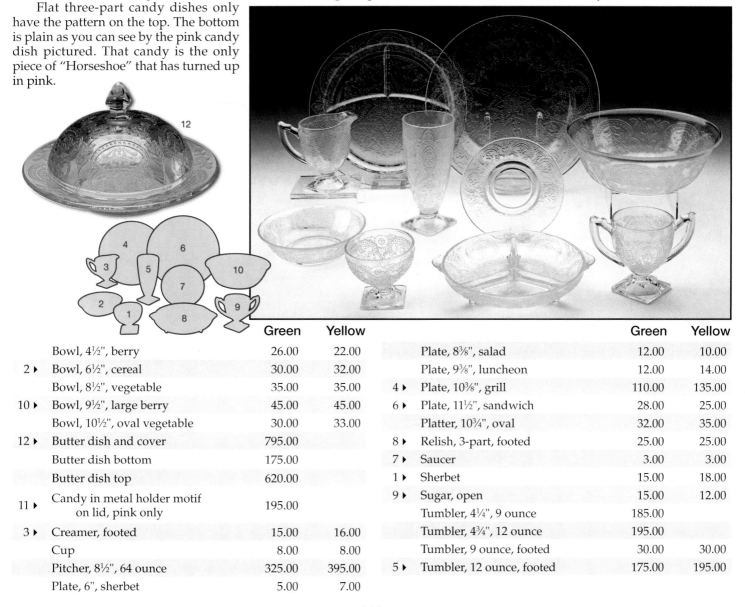

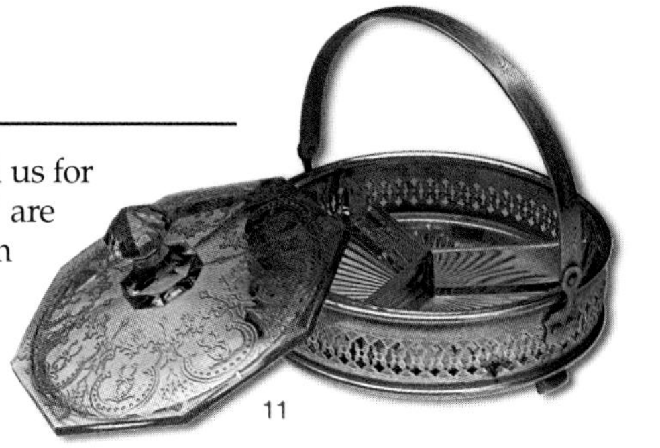

Why Indiana's pattern No. 612 has been called "Horseshoe" by collectors has intrigued us for years. That design does not fit any form of horseshoe ever made. Prices for "Horseshoe" are inclined to shock new collectors. If you genuinely like something, even a piece or two can offer gratification. You don't have to buy it all, just buy what you can afford — and enjoy.

The green "Horseshoe" butter dish rarely turns up, although supplies of tumblers, both flat and footed tea, grill plates (which not all collectors want), and pitchers are also inadequate for demand. We have been fortunate enough to find two butters in the last few years and both went galloping out of our booth at the first show exhibited. On the other hand, there are a couple of butters traveling all over the country with prices no one will pay. It's one thing to be proud of your glass; but as a dealer, selling is necessary.

The "Horseshoe" butter dish has always been highly priced. If you can find a first edition of this book, the butter dish was $90.00 in 1972. That was big money for a butter dish back then. There was a collector/dealer who traveled every well known flea market and shop in a five state area looking for a "Horseshoe" butter top. He had a bottom and wanted a top. He bought another bottom from us explaining that way someone else wouldn't be searching for a top if they were to purchase our bottom. Makes sense to me.

No. 612 creates problems for collectors of yellow, also. There is no butter dish; and pitchers, grill plates, and footed iced teas are insufficient for those wanting them. There are a few crystal pieces popping up including creamer, sugar, and plates. Even that seemingly invisible grill plate has appeared in crystal. The grill in yellow or green is notorious for having inner rim roughness (irr) but most collectors will accept some roughness just to own one.

Platters come both plain in the center, or with the regular pattern. Be aware of scuffs on these. They were used.

Flat three-part candy dishes only have the pattern on the top. The bottom is plain as you can see by the pink candy dish pictured. That candy is the only piece of "Horseshoe" that has turned up in pink.

		Green	Yellow				Green	Yellow
	Bowl, 4½", berry	26.00	22.00		Plate, 8⅜", salad		12.00	10.00
2 ▸	Bowl, 6½", cereal	30.00	32.00		Plate, 9⅜", luncheon		12.00	14.00
	Bowl, 8½", vegetable	35.00	35.00	4 ▸	Plate, 10⅜", grill		110.00	135.00
10 ▸	Bowl, 9½", large berry	45.00	45.00	6 ▸	Plate, 11½", sandwich		28.00	25.00
	Bowl, 10½", oval vegetable	30.00	33.00		Platter, 10¾", oval		32.00	35.00
12 ▸	Butter dish and cover	795.00		8 ▸	Relish, 3-part, footed		25.00	25.00
	Butter dish bottom	175.00		7 ▸	Saucer		3.00	3.00
	Butter dish top	620.00		1 ▸	Sherbet		15.00	18.00
11 ▸	Candy in metal holder motif on lid, pink only	195.00		9 ▸	Sugar, open		15.00	12.00
					Tumbler, 4¼", 9 ounce		185.00	
3 ▸	Creamer, footed	15.00	16.00		Tumbler, 4¾", 12 ounce		195.00	
	Cup	8.00	8.00		Tumbler, 9 ounce, footed		30.00	30.00
	Pitcher, 8½", 64 ounce	325.00	395.00	5 ▸	Tumbler, 12 ounce, footed		175.00	195.00
	Plate, 6", sherbet	5.00	7.00					

No. 616, "VERNON," Indiana Glass Company, 1930 – 1932
Colors: green, crystal, yellow

Over the last 36 years, No. 616 has given every photographer we have had a headache trying to capture this busy, thinly designed pattern so that it magically becomes visible on the printed page. Light passes through it without picking up the design well. This one pattern is definitely better seen "in person" than viewed through a photographer's lens. Indiana's No. 616 pattern was pigeonholed as "Vernon" in honor of another glass author's spouse.

No. 616 was one of the first patterns we used as everyday dishes after purchasing most of a set in the late 60s. It was attractive; but we warn you from experience that there are rough mould lines protruding from the seams of the tumblers. This thorny problem comes from extra glass on the mould seam and not chips or flakes. After a cut lip or two from using the tumblers, this set was added to our sale box. If you place No. 616 on a patterned cloth, the design appears to vanish.

Crystal No. 616 is still found today and some pieces are trimmed in platinum (silver). These decorated pieces seldom have worn platinum. Obviously, Indiana's process for attaching this silver border was top quality when compared to other companies which wore easily.

The 11½" sandwich plate makes a great dinner or barbecue plate when grilling out. We used grill plates more than the luncheon plates for serving when we used this glassware. Those 8" luncheon plates are excellent for those dieting and reducing food amounts. Do realize that sharp knives will damage glass rather easily.

Sets of yellow and green No. 616 are no longer easy to complete; but there is even less green than yellow available.

		Green	Crystal	Yellow
7 ▸	Creamer, footed	25.00	10.00	25.00
2 ▸	Cup	15.00	8.00	15.00
1 ▸	Plate, 8", luncheon	6.00	4.00	6.00
6 ▸	Plate, 11½", sandwich	22.00	10.00	22.00
3 ▸	Saucer	3.00	2.00	3.00
4 ▸	Sugar, footed	25.00	10.00	20.00
5 ▸	Tumbler, 5", footed	40.00	18.00	40.00

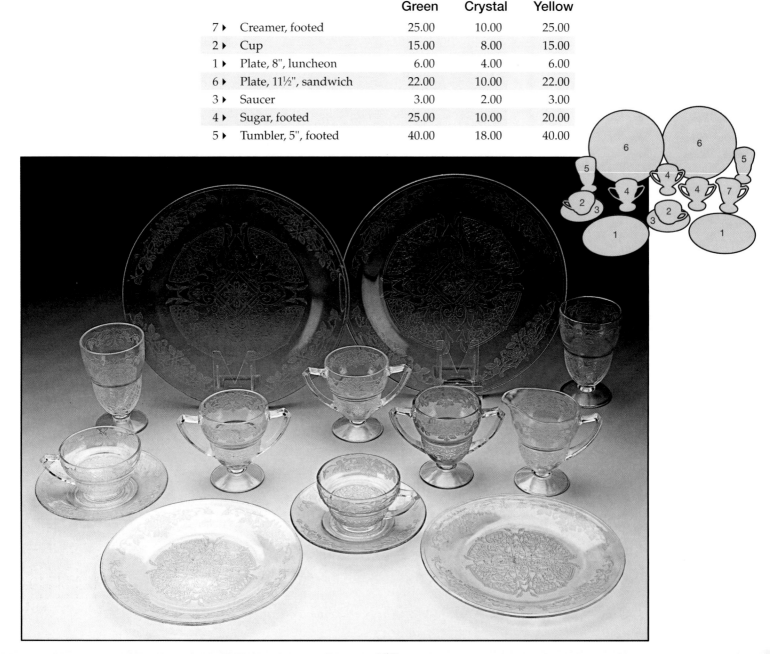

No. 618, "PINEAPPLE & FLORAL," Indiana Glass Company, 1932 – 1937

Colors: crystal, amber; some fired-on red, green, milk white; late 1960s, avocado; 1980s pink, cobalt blue, etc.

Indiana's No. 618 was first produced in 1932 but "Pineapple and Floral" is the only name used for this pattern. The diamond-shaped comports and 7" salad bowls were re-issued in the late 80s and early 90s in a multitude of sprayed-on colors but also, regrettably, in crystal. Sadly, prices for older crystal comports and salad bowls have not yet recovered. No other items have been remade as of May 2007. Amber and fired-on red are safe colors to buy since they were not remade.

"Pineapple and Floral" crystal (excluding the comport and salad bowl) is not easily acquired; but it is not out of the question. Tumblers, cream soups, platters, and sherbets are difficult to find. As with most of Indiana's patterns, there is continual mould roughness on the seams. This roughness comes from too much glass and not missing glass. Always try to acquire the harder-to-find pieces first. This pattern is surprisingly attractive when pieces are displayed together.

Amber No. 618 is not collected as often as crystal since there is so little available. Only dinner plates have been found in light green. These are old and will glow under ultraviolet light.

		Crystal	Amber, Red			Crystal	Amber, Red
	Ashtray, 4½"	12.00			Plate, 11½", w/indentation	25.00	
	Bowl, 4¾", berry	12.00	12.00		Plate, 11½", sandwich	14.00	12.00
	Bowl, 6", cereal	15.00	15.00	1 ▶	Platter, 11", closed handle	12.00	15.00
17 ▶	*Bowl, 7", salad	2.00	10.00	16 ▶	Platter, relish, 11½", divided	20.00	
	Bowl, 10", oval vegetable	18.00	18.00	10 ▶	Saucer	2.00	2.00
	*Comport, diamond-shaped	1.00	8.00		Sherbet, footed	12.00	15.00
7 ▶	Creamer, diamond-shaped	7.00	8.00	2 ▶	Sugar, diamond-shaped	7.00	8.00
15 ▶	Cream soup	18.00	18.00	13 ▶	Tidbit, 2-tier	35.00	
11 ▶	Cup	7.00	7.00	12 ▶	Tumbler, 4¼", 8 ounce	12.50	22.00
14 ▶	Plate, 6", sherbet	2.00	3.00		Tumbler, 5", 12 ounce	35.00	
4 ▶	Plate, 8⅜", salad	6.00	6.00		Vase, cone-shaped	30.00	
5 ▶	**Plate, 9⅜", dinner	8.00	8.00		Vase holder, metal	30.00	

* Reproduced in several colors
** Green $45.00

151

OLD CAFE, Hocking Glass Company, 1936 – 1940
Colors: pink, crystal, and Royal Ruby

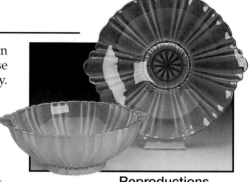

Reproductions

Several pieces of Old Café have been remade with a satin-like finish. You can see ones we have found pictured on the right and #10 below. We are assuming these are from Anchor-Hocking moulds but they were not marked or labeled in any way. Just be aware that they exist and do not be duped into buying them as rare Old Cafe because they are unlisted in most present day books.

As with other smaller patterns, prices have lessened somewhat. Fewer new collectors want to buy smaller patterns. Old Cafe has always had admirers from the older collecting fraternity even though it is a relatively minor pattern. Several pieces were efficiently dispersed 60 years ago and thus it had the "recognition factor" with older collectors. You seldom go antiquing without spotting a piece (usually the low candy or two-handled bowl). Old Cafe lamps, pitchers, and dinner plates are in very short supply in today's market. These pieces are expensive when compared to prices for the rest of the pattern. Pitchers, shown in earlier editions, have alternating large panels with two smaller panels, the make-up of all Old Cafe pieces. The pitcher often misidentified as Old Cafe can be seen under Hocking's Pillar Optic on pages 177 – 178. Some collectors are mistakenly buying Pillar Optic (evenly spaced panels) for Old Cafe because Internet auctions often list them as such. A little time spent in a good book could save you money. The juice pitcher is shaped like the Mayfair juice pitcher, again with a large panel alternating with two smaller panels.

Some pink and Royal Ruby lamps were concocted by drilling through a normal vase to allow for a cord, but the real ones were constructed with ball feet to raise it enough to allow the cord to pass under the edge. The 5" bowl has an open handle while the 4½" bowl has tab handles, as does the 3¾" berry. There are two sherbets, footed and flat, which measure 3¾". The footed one is harder to locate.

You need to know that Royal Ruby Old Cafe cups were made with crystal saucers. No Old Cafe Royal Ruby saucers have ever been seen. The 5½" crystal candy turn ups with a Royal Ruby lid but no Royal Ruby bottom is known.

Hocking made a cookie jar (a numbered line) which is an excellent "go-with" piece. It is ribbed up the sides similar to Old Cafe but is found with a cross-hatched lid that does not match anything thing else in Old Cafe.

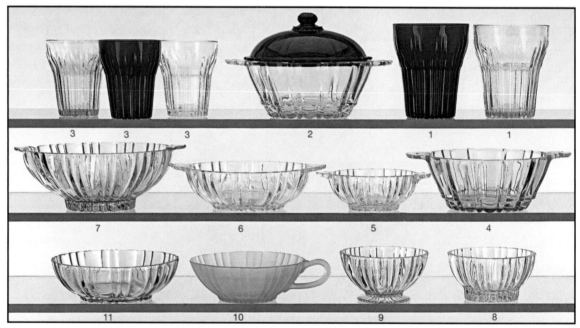

		Crystal, Pink	Royal Ruby			Crystal, Pink	Royal Ruby
5 ▸	Bowl, 3¾", berry, tab handles	10.00	9.00		Pitcher, 6", 36 oz.	140.00	
11 ▸	Bowl, 5½", cereal, no handles	32.00	30.00		Pitcher, 80 ounce	175.00	
6 ▸	Bowl, 5½", closed handles	12.00			Plate, 6", sherbet	7.00	
4 ▸	Bowl, 6½", open handles	16.00			Plate, 10", dinner	52.00	
7 ▸	Bowl, 9", closed handles	30.00			Saucer	3.00	
	Candy dish, 8", low, tab handles	12.00	14.00	9 ▸	Sherbet, 3¾", low ftd.	10.00	10.00
2 ▸	Candy jar, 5½", crystal with ruby cover		25.00	8 ▸	Sherbet, 3¾", no ft.	15.00	
				3 ▸	Tumbler, 3", juice	12.00	16.00
	Cup	10.00	10.00	1 ▸	Tumbler, 4", water	16.00	25.00
	Lamp	100.00	150.00		Vase, 7¼"	50.00*	55.00
	Olive dish, 6", oblong	9.00			* Crystal $10.00		

OLD COLONY "LACE EDGE," "OPEN LACE," Hocking Glass Company, 1935 – 1938

Colors: pink and some crystal and green

The Internet has exposed hordes of previously unknown quantities of popular Old Colony. There have been over 400 Internet listings in the last three weeks. Granted only about 75% are truly Old Colony, but supply is passing demand and even the rarer pieces such as footed tumblers, three-footed bowls, and candles are now being sold for less than 10 years ago. However, many of these sellers have no idea how to inspect this pattern. Old Colony's "lace" needs to be scrutinized carefully around the edge and underneath. Be sure to look for cracks running from each opening to the next. The "lace" damaged easily and still does. Plates and bowls should be stacked carefully, preferably with a paper plate between each piece.

Mint condition candlesticks, console bowls, and vases are limited, but are available with chips, nicks, or cracks. Many of these were satinized and sometimes painted with floral designs. We recently found frosted cereal bowls. Satinized or frosted pieces currently sell for a fraction of the cost of their unfrosted counterparts. Lack of demand is the reason. Possibly vases and candlesticks are rare because so many candles and vases were satinized. That said, if satinized pieces still have the original painted floral decorations, they will fetch up to 25% more than the prices for plain satin. So far, only a few collectors think frosted Old Colony beautiful; but we are noticing that more are buying it because of its less expensive price.

A flower bowl with crystal frog converts to a candy jar when a cover is added in place of the frog. It was advertised and sold both ways. That cover also fits the butter dish or bonbon as Hocking actually cataloged it. The 7" comport becomes a footed candy with a cookie lid added. This piece was listed as a covered comport; but today, many dealers call it a footed candy jar. Since both these lids fit two separate items, it does not take a genius to realize why there is a severe lid shortage now. Interchangeable lids saved making separate expensive moulds. It was purely an economic practice for getting as many pieces from as few moulds as possible.

There are two styles of 7¾" and 9½" bowls, ribbed or not. The smaller, non-ribbed salad bowl serves as a butter bottom. Both sizes of ribbed bowls are harder to find than their non-ribbed counterparts. The larger ribbed bowl is falling out of favor with collectors and is selling for less than the non-ribbed one; but the price for the ribbed 7¾" bowl is double the plain one.

Ribs on the footed tumbler reach roughly half way up the side as they do on the cup. This tumbler is often confused with the Coronation tumbler that has a comparable shape and design. See the Coronation photograph (page 46) and read there. Notice the fine ribbed effect from the middle up on the Coronation tumbler. Upper ribbing is missing on Old Colony tumblers.

The actual 9" wide comport in Old Colony has a rayed base. There is a similar comport that also measures 9". This "pretender" has a plain foot and was most likely made by Standard or Lancaster Glass. Both Lancaster and Standard had similar designs. If the piece is not shown in my listing, or is in any color other than pink or crystal, the likelihood of your having an unknown Old Colony piece is doubtful.

Old Colony "Lace Edge"

<table>
<tr><td colspan="2"></td><td>Pink</td></tr>
<tr><td>3 ▶</td><td>*Bowl, 6⅜", cereal</td><td>16.00</td></tr>
<tr><td></td><td>Bowl, 7¾", plain</td><td>25.00</td></tr>
<tr><td></td><td>Bowl, 7¾", ribbed, salad</td><td>60.00</td></tr>
<tr><td></td><td>Bowl, 8¼", crystal</td><td>12.00</td></tr>
<tr><td></td><td>Bowl, 9½", plain</td><td>25.00</td></tr>
<tr><td></td><td>Bowl, 9½", ribbed</td><td>22.00</td></tr>
<tr><td>15 ▶</td><td>**Bowl, 10½", 3 legs, frosted $65.00</td><td>235.00</td></tr>
<tr><td>14 ▶</td><td>Butter dish or bonbon with cover</td><td>65.00</td></tr>
<tr><td></td><td>Butter dish bottom, 7¾"</td><td>28.00</td></tr>
<tr><td></td><td>Butter dish top</td><td>37.00</td></tr>
<tr><td></td><td>**Candlesticks, pair, frosted $95.00</td><td>450.00</td></tr>
<tr><td></td><td>Candy jar and cover, ribbed</td><td>45.00</td></tr>
<tr><td></td><td>Comport, 7"</td><td>25.00</td></tr>
<tr><td>9 ▶</td><td>Comport, 7", and cover, footed</td><td>45.00</td></tr>
<tr><td></td><td>Comport, 9"</td><td>995.00</td></tr>
<tr><td>10 ▶</td><td>Cookie jar and cover, frosted $60.00</td><td>65.00</td></tr>
<tr><td>2 ▶</td><td>Creamer</td><td>18.00</td></tr>
<tr><td>11 ▶</td><td>Cup</td><td>20.00</td></tr>
<tr><td></td><td>Fish bowl, 1 gallon, 8 ounce (crystal only)</td><td>40.00</td></tr>
</table>

* Officially listed as cereal or cream soup, green $75.00

<table>
<tr><td colspan="2"></td><td>Pink</td></tr>
<tr><td></td><td>Flower bowl, crystal frog</td><td>30.00</td></tr>
<tr><td></td><td>Plate, 7¼", salad</td><td>20.00</td></tr>
<tr><td></td><td>Plate, 8¼", luncheon</td><td>16.00</td></tr>
<tr><td></td><td>Plate, 10½", dinner</td><td>20.00</td></tr>
<tr><td></td><td>Plate, 10½", grill</td><td>20.00</td></tr>
<tr><td></td><td>Plate, 10½", 3-part relish</td><td>20.00</td></tr>
<tr><td></td><td>Plate, 13", solid lace</td><td>60.00</td></tr>
<tr><td></td><td>Plate, 13", 4-part, solid lace</td><td>45.00</td></tr>
<tr><td></td><td>Platter, 12¾"</td><td>36.00</td></tr>
<tr><td>7 ▶</td><td>Platter, 12¾", 5-part</td><td>32.00</td></tr>
<tr><td>5 ▶</td><td>Relish dish, 7½", 3-part, deep</td><td>88.00</td></tr>
<tr><td>12 ▶</td><td>Saucer</td><td>6.00</td></tr>
<tr><td></td><td>**Sherbet, footed</td><td>100.00</td></tr>
<tr><td>4 ▶</td><td>Sugar</td><td>18.00</td></tr>
<tr><td>6 ▶</td><td>Tumbler, 3½", 5 ounce, flat</td><td>215.00</td></tr>
<tr><td>13 ▶</td><td>Tumbler, 4½", 9 ounce, flat</td><td>75.00</td></tr>
<tr><td>8 ▶</td><td>Tumbler, 5", 10½ ounce, footed</td><td>90.00</td></tr>
<tr><td>1 ▶</td><td>Vase, 7", frosted $90.00</td><td>795.00</td></tr>
</table>

** Price is for absolute mint condition

OLD ENGLISH, "THREADING," Indiana Glass Company, Late 1920s

Colors: green, amber, pink, crystal, crystal with flashed colors, and forest green

After photographing Old English last year, we took it to a show wondering if there would be anyone there collecting it. We sold about 90% of what is shown here, and wished we'd had more. One buyer left the covered pitcher as he already had that. Not long afterward, a lady fell in love with it and bought it for display in her home. She was decorating, using colored Depression glass pitchers along the top of her cabinets in her kitchen.

Old English is not a plentiful pattern, but its prices have remained constant. However, there are not enormous amounts of collectors pursuing it — or are there? Sets of green can be gathered slowly, but not all pieces were made in pink. Lamentably, even luncheon sets cannot be accumulated in any color, as there are no cups, saucers, or plates available.

All pieces in our listing were made in green. A few pieces have never been found in amber. Amber Old English is a deep color more suggestive of Cambridge or New Martinsville products which many collectors find more appealing. Most of the amber Old English pieces we have owned over the years have found passionate buyers, but green is less complicated to purchase and sell. Note the unusual amber piece above with its ringed finger hold. We borrowed it to photograph.

Crystal Old English pitchers and tumblers are often found with artistic Deco decorations; unadorned crystal pieces are rarely seen. While researching our Hazel-Atlas book, we discovered that the crystal egg cup (pictured) is a Hazel-Atlas cataloged item, and not Old English as it has been accepted for years.

There are two styles of sherbets. One is cone shaped and the other is straight sided. Both large and small berry bowls and the flat candy dish have supplies inadequate to meet demand. Sugar and candy jar lids have the same cloverleaf-shaped knob as the pitcher. The flat candy lid is similar in size to the pitcher lid; but that pitcher lid is notched along the bottom rim to allow for pouring. If pouring, you need to hold the lid as it only rests atop the pitcher. That flat candy is commonly found in a metal holder.

The fan vase pictured is the only piece we have ever seen in dark green.

		Pink, Green, Amber
8 ▸	Bowl, 4", flat	20.00
14 ▸	Bowl, 9", footed fruit	30.00
18 ▸	Bowl, 9½", flat	33.00
10 ▸	Candlesticks, 4", pair	45.00
15 ▸	Candy dish and cover, flat	65.00
3 ▸	Candy jar with lid	65.00
2 ▸	Compote, 3½", ruffled top	30.00
19 ▸	Compote, 3½" tall, 6⅜" across, 2-handle	20.00
	Compote, 3½" tall, 7" across	25.00
6 ▸	Compote, 3½", cheese for plate	18.00
20 ▸	Creamer	20.00
12 ▸	Egg cup (Hazel-Atlas), crystal only	6.00
16 ▸	Fruit stand, 11", footed	40.00
11 ▸	Goblet, 5¾", 8 ounce	35.00
	*Pitcher	95.00
5 ▸	**Pitcher and cover	155.00
7 ▸	Plate, indent for compote	18.00
23 ▸	Plate w/fingerhold	25.00
4 ▸	Sandwich server, center handle	50.00
1 ▸	Sherbet, 2 styles	18.00
22 ▸	Sugar	17.50
21 ▸	Sugar cover	40.00
	Tumbler, 4½", footed	22.00
9 ▸	Tumbler, 5½", footed	35.00
13 ▸	Vase, 5⅜", fan type, 7" wide	75.00
17 ▸	Vase, 8¼", footed, 4¼" wide	65.00
	Vase, 12", footed	85.00

*Pink $165.00   **Pink $295.00

OLIVE, Line #134, Imperial Glass Company, Late 1930s
Colors: red, light blue, emerald, pink

Imperial's Olive Line #134 is a minor pattern whose major magnetism is it is often mistaken for another Imperial pattern — Old English Line #166. It makes one wonder why the same company made lines so similar. Were they thinking of blending patterns and designs long before it was fashionable? Now, if you can keep Paden City's Popeye and Olive pattern out of the mix, you'll be fine.

Think of round olives when mentally imaging this line and that ought to help. Olive also has circles near the bottom of the pieces along with ribbed feet. Old English Line #166 has elongated indentations reaching upward from its base with olive type balls. The plates in Old English, however, do have a kind of ribbed flower center design. You will notice that the plates in Olive Line #134 have plain centers. Actually, the two patterns are well matched and should you care to collect both as one pattern, few will notice and you can gain tumblers from Old English that you will not have with Olive. Olive has handled mugs which one collector informed us she "used all the time."

You see the sought colors of blue and red pictured here. Although the pale blue looks crystal in our photo, it really is not. One collector recently told us she'd really like a rose bowl, but was having trouble finding one.

		Emerald, Pink	Blue, Red				Emerald, Pink	Blue, Red
	Bowl, 6½", flared, footed	14.00	20.00			Compote, 6½"	12.50	22.50
5 ▸	Bowl, 7", rose (cupped)	20.00	30.00	6 ▸	Creamer	10.00	15.00
	Bowl, 7", shallow	15.00	22.00	7 ▸	Cup	8.00	10.00
2 ▸	Bowl, 9", fruit, pedestal foot	20.00	35.00		Mayonnaise	15.00	18.00
	Bowl, 9", bun or fruit tray	20.00	35.00		Plate, 6"	3.00	5.00
	Bowl, 9", shallow	25.00	35.00		Plate, 8"	6.00	8.00
	Bowl, 10¼", salad	30.00	45.00	4 ▸	Plate, 12"	15.00	25.00
3 ▸	Candle, 2½"	12.00	20.00	8 ▸	Saucer	2.00	3.00
	Candy jar w/lid	30.00	40.00	1 ▸	Sugar	10.00	15.00
	Compote, 6"	11.00	20.00				

"ORCHID," Paden City Glass Company, Early 1930s
Colors: yellow, cobalt blue, crystal, green, amber, pink, red, and black

There are at least three different "Orchid" arrays found on Paden City blanks. Collectors used to buy any of these varieties because so little "Orchid" was found. However, with more interest paid to Paden City patterns due to recent books being published, a single stemmed version has been relegated as a pattern unto itself.

All Paden City patterns were more limited in production than those of some other glass companies. Orchid growers once accounted for major interest in these patterns and the Internet has helped unveil many pieces. Instead of a few dozen buying at shows, there are now hundreds viewing items. It's very popular in today's market.

Originally, it was believed that "Orchid" etched pieces were only made on Paden City's #412 Line, the square, Crow's Foot blank. However, "Orchid" has been located on the #890 rounded Crow's Foot blank, the #401 Mrs. B, and several vase blanks as well. "Orchid" may well be possible on any Paden City blank. The pattern displays better on the transparent pastel colors, but they do not seem to be as popular with the buying public. However, a savvy collector latched onto all our pastel pieces as soon as he spotted them, asking us if we knew how rare they were. A few pieces of "Orchid" are being found on black, but red and cobalt blue are the preferred colors.

9

9

		All other colors	Red, Black, Cobalt Blue
	Bowl, 4⅞", square	30.00	50.00
2 ▶	Bowl, 8½", 2-handle	70.00	150.00
3 ▶	Bowl, 8¾", square	70.00	135.00
	Bowl, 10", footed, square	95.00	195.00
	Bowl, 11", square	85.00	195.00
	Cake stand, square, 2" high	65.00	130.00
10 ▶	Candlesticks, 5¾", pair	125.00	210.00
	Candy with lid, 6½", square, 3-part	90.00	165.00
4 ▶	Candy with lid, cloverleaf, 3-part	85.00	165.00
	Comport, 3¼" tall, 6¼" wide	20.00	50.00
14 ▶	Comport, 4¾" tall, 7⅜" wide	60.00	90.00
	Comport, 6⅝" tall, 7" wide	55.00	110.00
	Comport, 8" high		100.00
6 ▶	Creamer	40.00	75.00
	Ice bucket, 6"	90.00	195.00
	Mayonnaise, 3-piece	65.00	145.00
12 ▶	Plate, 8½", square		125.00
11 ▶	Rose bowl, footed	75.00	150.00
7 ▶	Sandwich server, center handle	75.00	125.00
5 ▶	Sugar	40.00	75.00
8 ▶	Vase, 8"	100.00	250.00
9 ▶	Vase, 10", several styles	120.00	275.00

OVIDE, "NEW CENTURY," Hazel-Atlas Glass Company, 1930 – 1935

Colors: green, black, white Platonite trimmed with fired-on colors in 1950s

Hazel-Atlas used a gaggle of different patterns on this popular Platonite, including one of "flying geese" and the rarely found, but highly desired "Art Deco." New collectors have written over and over to ask what the "Art Deco" design looked like; so, here it is along with those "flying geese." Sellers are often calling other Ovide patterns "Art Deco," but there is only one that truly is. Another popular one, considering the quantity found today, is the black floral design with red and yellow edge trim. That set included a dinnerware line as well as kitchenware items (stacking sets and mixing bowls) which interests collectors of that genre.

Ovide is one pattern available today that can be started economically and collected in colors or designs that please you. Much of what is seen is from the late 40s and early 50s with colorful varieties. You can find those lines in our *Collectible Glassware from the 40s, 50s, 60s...* book. You can buy a multicolored and vibrant useable set as reasonably as buying new dishes to use. Wouldn't you rather own something antique (50 years for glass) than something that decreases in value as you lug it out of the store?

We admit that finding an individual decoration may prove to be a laborious task, but less so today with the Internet creating such possibilities.

Very little black, transparent green, or plain yellow Ovide are ever displayed at shows, but there are a few collectors asking for it. A luncheon set should be possible; but it would be simpler to put together an Ovide set of black or yellow Cloverleaf (on Ovide mould shape) which Depression glass dealers are apt to bring to shows while leaving unadorned Ovide home.

Our new *Hazel-Atlas Glass Identification and Value Guide* book has 11 pages devoted to colors and decorations known on Ovide.

		Black	Green	Decorated White	Art Deco			Black	Green	Decorated White	Art Deco
7 ▸	Bowl, 4¾", berry	4.00		6.00		9 ▸	Plate, 8", luncheon	4.00	3.00	9.00	75.00
8 ▸	Bowl, 5½", cereal			10.00			Plate, 9", dinner			15.00	
	Bowl, 8", large berry			22.50		11 ▸	Platter, 11"			18.00	
	Candy dish & cover	40.00	16.00	35.00		6 ▸	Salt and pepper, pair	25.00	20.00	24.00	
	Cocktail, footed, fruit	4.00	3.00			4 ▸	Saucer	2.50	2.00	3.00	25.00
2 ▸	Creamer	5.00	4.00	12.00	125.00	12 ▸	Sherbet	5.00	2.00	9.00	100.00
3 ▸	Cup	5.00	3.00	10.00	125.00	1 ▸	Sugar, open	5.00	4.00	12.00	125.00
	Egg cup			18.00		5 ▸	Tumbler			15.00	125.00
	Plate, 6", sherbet	4.00	2.00	4.00							

OYSTER AND PEARL, Anchor Hocking Glass Corporation, 1938 – 1940

Colors: pink, crystal, Royal Ruby, Vitrock, and Vitrock with fired-on pink, blue, and green

Royal Ruby Oyster and Pearl is pictured under the Royal Ruby pattern shown on page 203, but prices are also listed here. Pink Oyster and Pearl has consistently been used as complementary pieces for other Depression glass patterns. The 10½" deep bowl with the 13½" sandwich plate, used as an underliner, make a great salad set. The pink relish dish and candlesticks also sell consistently given that they are modestly priced in comparison to other patterns. Though not as true as it once was, Oyster and Pearl prices are as a rule, cheaper than most patterns in this book.

Notice the large crystal Oyster and Pearl ruffled bowl pictured on the right, an unusual piece of Oyster and Pearl to appear. Admittedly, we would have preferred pink, Royal Ruby, or even a fired-

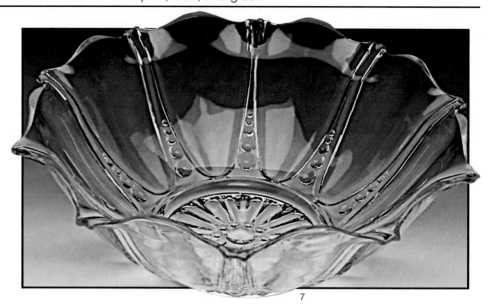

7

on Vitrock. Optimistically, colored varieties may be there for discovery. It was a rather dreary day of searching antique malls in Ohio when Cathy glimpsed this bowl. She understood that crystal was not common, but had no notion that the ruffled top was the thrilling part. You don't have to know everything in order to recognize something rare or special.

There is no divided bowl in Oyster and Pearl; it was (and is) listed as a relish. That relish dish measures 11½" when the handles are added in. We stress that because of letters and e-mails we constantly receive saying someone's dish is 11½" and all we list is a 10½" relish. All measurements in this book are specified without handles unless otherwise mentioned. Glass companies seldom measured the handles or included them in their measurements.

Pink fired over Vitrock was called Dusty Rose; the fired green was called Springtime Green by Hocking. Most collectors love these shades; but we've met a few who spurn them. Many dealers do not stock these colors as they are bulky and take up space needed for other more desired wares. The non-colored Vitrock is irregularly seen, and is not as mesmerizing. Some pieces have been located with fired blue, but this is very scarce.

We have seen a few crystal pieces decorated, and most of them were trimmed in red as pictured on the large plate on page 163. They sell faster than undecorated crystal. The lipped, 5½" bowl is often referred to as heart shaped. It might serve as a gravy or sauce boat although most people use them for candy dishes. The same bowl is found without the spout in Royal Ruby. A spout-less bowl has not been seen in any other color. Dusty Rose and Springtime Green always have a spout when you can find them.

The story of a "lamp" made from candleholders sounded interesting until we saw two candles glued together at their bases to form a ball. Evidently, someone had more leisure time than we do.

		Crystal, Pink	Royal Ruby	White and Fired-On Green or Pink
3 ▸	Bowl, 5¼", heart-shaped, 1-handled	14.00		8.00
	Bowl, 5½", 1-handled		20.00	
6 ▸	Bowl, 6½", deep-handled	18.00	22.00	
1 ▸	Bowl, 10½", deep fruit	25.00	50.00	20.00
7 ▸	Bowl, 10½", ruffled edge	75.00		
2 ▸	Candle holder, 3½", pair	25.00	40.00	18.00
5 ▸	Plate, 13½", sandwich	20.00	40.00	
4 ▸	Relish dish, 10½", oblong, divided	20.00		

"PARROT," SYLVAN, Federal Glass Company, 1931 – 1932
Colors: green, amber; some crystal and blue

8

"Parrot" is a Depression glass pattern that has numerous hard to find pieces. It has a trail of brisk price accelerations, then periods of stability and then prices will take off again. Less enthusiastic collectors have prices slowed to a standstill for now. We have watched these price cycles for years in most patterns, but for once "Parrot" has slipped rather ascended.

Originally, a hoard of 37 pitchers was found in the basement of an old hardware store in central Ohio in the early 1970s. Several of those original ones bit the dust shortly thereafter. One cracked from a dealer dusting it out and bumping a diamond ring in a thin spot. The entire pitcher is thin; but where the pattern is moulded, it is threadlike. Today, there are still more than 30 in existence. They disappeared from the market at any price a few years ago. At first, several of these sold for $35.00, but shortly jumped to $200.00. Prices for the few sold recently have reached a ballpark figure of $3,000.00. A few consumers were willing to pay that price and did. We heard of one being offered in the $4,000 range, but buyers for one piece of glassware in that range are scarce.

"Parrot" has two types of hot plates (or possibly cold plates) as described under Madrid or Georgian. One is moulded like the pointed edged Madrid; the other, round is moulded like the one in Georgian. One of the round ones has emerged in amber, but has never been on the market to determine a price.

Speaking of amber, the butter dish, creamer, and sugar lid are all more difficult to find than those in green; and even fewer mint butter dish tops or sugar lids have surfaced. Non-mint ones are available. (Damaged glassware should not bring mint prices.) We bought an amber butter at an auction of rare glass in Ohio a couple of years ago. In tracing its history, we found it was the same one we had sold in the late 1970s. It's a very small world in rarely found pieces of Depression glass. Strangely enough, we paid less than we sold it for originally. Some Depression glass is so rare that there are few collectors searching for it today. Back then, there were a multitude of collectors buying only butter dishes as well as amber "Parrot" collectors. Fierce competition drove up prices; but today, the expensive butters are not as collected as an item. That leaves only amber "Parrot" collectors looking for a butter dish and there are fewer of them around at present.

Butter bottoms have an indented ridge or well for the top. The jam dish is the same size as the butter bottom, but without that ridge. The jam dish has never been found in green, but is available in amber.

"Parrot" tumblers are moulded on Madrid-like shapes except for the heavy-footed tumbler, whose protruding edges are easily damaged. The supply of those heavy, footed tumblers (in both colors), green water tumblers, and thin, flat iced teas in amber has now overtaken demand. Mint ones are not easily found, but there are plenty of damaged ones available if you are willing to settle. Seemingly, the thin, moulded, footed tumbler did not receive the "Parrot" design satisfactorily, and the heavier version was made. The thin, 10 ounce, footed tumbler has only been found in amber and the parrot is often not vividly displayed on the glass. Prices for tumblers have remained stable during the last few "Parrot" price increases as there is a limit to what collectors will pay for one glass. We have seen them priced higher than our listings, but not selling at those prices.

Yes, we know the shaker pictured is cracked as has been pointed out by several readers. It's our way to give glassware with little value a purpose. You still get to see size, shape, and color, and a collector gets to enjoy a good piece. Actually, several dealers now offer us their damaged, hard-to-find pieces, at reasonable prices so we can photograph them for our books. Several craftsmen we've talked with use damaged and broken Depression glass in jewelry, ceramics, glass window art, and the like. After a wreck, we furnished quite a number of boxes of broken glass to a lady creating artful items. You can see examples of her work on the fly sheets of this book. There's great appreciation for this glassware and some find a way to enhance that which used to be thrown away. It's improved recycling.

		Green	Amber			Green	Amber
7 ▸	Bowl, 5", berry	28.00	20.00	10 ▸	Plate, 10½", round, grill	30.00	
	Bowl, 7", soup	50.00	35.00	18 ▸	Plate, 10½", square, grill		30.00
	Bowl, 8", large berry	75.00	75.00		Plate, 10¼", square (crystal only)	26.00	
12 ▸	Bowl, 10", oval vegetable	60.00	65.00	6 ▸	Platter, 11¼", oblong	50.00	70.00
8 ▸	Butter dish and cover	415.00	1,500.00	15 ▸	Salt and pepper, pair	265.00	
	Butter dish bottom	40.00	200.00	14 ▸	Saucer	12.00	15.00
	Butter dish top	375.00	1,300.00	19 ▸	*Sherbet, footed cone	20.00	20.00
16 ▸	Creamer, footed	45.00	75.00		Sherbet, 4¼" high	1,500.00	
13 ▸	Cup	35.00	35.00	1 ▸	Sugar	35.00	50.00
	Hot plate, 5", pointed	895.00	995.00	2 ▸	Sugar cover	175.00	550.00
	Hot plate, 5", round	995.00		3 ▸	Tumbler, 4¼", 10 ounce	175.00	120.00
17 ▸	Jam dish, 7"		35.00	20 ▸	Tumbler, 5½", 12 ounce	195.00	155.00
	Pitcher, 8½", 80 ounce	3,000.00		9 ▸	Tumbler, 5¾", footed, heavy	175.00	155.00
5 ▸	Plate, 5¾", sherbet	24.00	14.00		Tumbler, 5½", 10 oz., ftd (Madrid mould)		175.00
11 ▸	Plate, 7½", salad	30.00					
4 ▸	Plate, 9", dinner	45.00	45.00		* Blue $225.00		

164

"PARTY LINE," "SODA FOUNTAIN," Line #191, 191½, #192, Paden City Glass Company, Late 1920s – 1951; Canton Glass Company, 1950s

Colors: amber, blue, crystal, green, pink (Cheriglo), red, some turquoise green

We first included "Party Line" in our book as a result of numerous collectors requesting it be listed. Paden City promoted it as being "the most complete tableware line in America." Actual dinnerware items are not very available even though it was manufactured as late as the 1950s. An early author of Paden City glass, Jerry Barnett, stated that factory workers called this pattern "Soda Fountain," definitely an apt name considering the abundance of those type items found even now. Didn't a majority of towns in America have at least one soda shop which needed these wares?

Green is the color most often collected. Pink and amber "Party Line" are the colors we see. Amber can be purchased rather inexpensively presently. A few pieces are found with cuttings or decorations.

"Party Line" is rarely seen in light blue, so we were thrilled to find that crushed fruit jar pictured on the right. A set of blue mixing bowls were pictured in one of our earlier *Kitchen Glassware of the Depression Glass Years* books.

	*All colors			*All colors			*All colors
	Banana split, 8½", oval	22.00	9 ▸	Creamer, 7 oz.	8.00		Shaker, pair	35.00
12 ▸	Bottle, 22 oz., wine w/stopper	40.00		Cup, 6 oz.	6.00		Shaker, sugar	155.00
	Bottle, 48 oz., water, no stopper	50.00		Custard, 6 oz.	8.00	11 ▸	Sherbet, 3½ or 4½ oz., footed	10.00
	Bowl, 4½", nappy	8.00		Ice tub & pail	60.00		Sherbet, 6 oz., high foot	12.50
	Bowl, 6½", berry	10.00		Ice tub, 6½", w/tab handle	50.00		Stem, 9 oz.	15.00
	Bowl, 7", mixing	18.00	1 ▸	‡Jar w/lid, high, crushed fruit	75.00	8 ▸	Sugar, 7 oz.	8.00
	Bowl, 8", mixing	22.00		Marmalade, w/cover, 12 oz.	35.00		Sugar w/id, 10 oz., hotel	20.00
	Bowl, 9", berry	22.00	6 ▸	Mayo, 6", footed	25.00		Sundae, 4 or 6 oz., tulip	15.00
	Bowl, 9", low foot comport, flare	25.00		Parfait, 5 oz. (2 styles)	14.00	5 ▸	Sundae, 9 oz., crimped	20.00
	Bowl, 9", mixing	28.00		Pitcher, 30 oz., jug, w/cover	70.00		Syrup, 8 oz.	55.00
	Bowl, 10½", high foot, flare	35.00		Pitcher, 32 oz., grape juice w/lid	100.00		Syrup w/glass cover, 12 oz.	80.00
	Bowl, 11", low foot comport	35.00		Pitcher, 36 oz., measure w/5½" reamer	125.00	10 ▸	Tumbler, 1½ oz., footed, cordial	16.00
	Bowl, 11", vegetable, flare	35.00		Pitcher, 70 oz., jug w or w/optic, w/lid	135.00	3 ▸	Tumbler, 2½ or 3½ oz., ftd, cocktail	10.00
	Butter box, w/cover, round flat lid	60.00		Plate 6"	5.00	7 ▸	Tumbler, 3 oz., wine	10.00
2 ▸	Cake stand, low foot	30.00		Plate, 8"	8.00		Tumbler, 4½ oz., juice	8.00
	Candy, footed w/cover	35.00		Plate, 10½", cracker, w/covered cheese	65.00		Tumbler, 5 oz., cola	12.00
	Cigarette holder w/cover, footed	45.00		Saucer, 5¾"	2.00		Tumbler, 6 oz., 3 styles	12.00
	Cocktail shaker, 18 oz., w/lid	85.00		Server, 10", center handle	35.00		Tumbler, 7 oz., 2 styles	12.00
	Cologne, 1½ oz.	60.00					Tumbler, 8 oz., 3 styles	14.00
							Tumbler, 9 oz., barrel	12.00
						4 ▸	Tumbler, 10 oz., 3 styles	12.00
							Tumbler, 12 oz., blown	15.00
							Tumbler, 12 oz., 4 styles	14.00
							Tumbler, 14 oz., 3 styles	14.00
							Vase, 6", fan	35.00
							Vase, 7", fan	40.00
							Vase, 7", crimped	50.00

*Double the price for red or blue and 50% for crystal.
‡ Blue 150.00

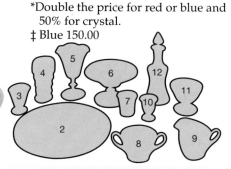

PATRICIAN, "SPOKE," Federal Glass Company, 1933 – 1937
Colors: pink, green, crystal, and amber ("Golden Glo")

Patrician was the first Depression pattern we recognized in central Kentucky when we first started looking for glass. Amber was well circulated in our area. We had stacks of the 10½" Patrician plates in a cabinet under the oven, though Grannie Bear did not remember how she acquired them. Now, we suspect they were in flour as she was always baking something. We learned those plates were premiums with 20-pound sacks of flour and promoted as cake plates. Exhibits of these plates sat on the counter near the cash register, and when you paid for your flour, you were handed one of these as an additional reward. Everyone baked and 20-pound bags of flour were bought regularly; so these plates stacked up. When we started buying Depression glass almost 40 years ago, this plate was, and still is, known as a dinner plate, not a cake.

Amber Madrid was the other plentiful pattern in the area, so it looked like only amber hues were around to be purchased. That assessment changed upon deeper study; but buying those patterns hoping to make a profit selling them was not a great idea at first. Everyone else in our area had the same two amber patterns at flea markets, and the only way you could sell, was to beat their prices which was hard to do when prices were 50¢ to $1.00 with an occasional $2.00 thrown in.

Patrician has never been reproduced; so that makes it a safe pattern for beginners and it's available. Sets of green or pink Patrician can probably be gathered with determination, but at a greater price than for amber.

The jam dish is a butter bottom without the ridge for the top to rest against just like in "Parrot" and Sharon patterns. Federal was alone at this time in including a jam dish in their dinnerware lines. Patrician's jam measures 6¾" wide and stands 1¼" deep, the same measurement as the butter bottom; however, Patrician cereal bowls are sometimes offered as jam dishes. Cereals are 6" in diameter and 1¾" deep. Prices for these two items are close today; therefore, that price is not as significant as it once was when jams were considered hard to find; just be cognizant of which is which. Prices used to double for jam dishes, but collectors seek only one jam dish and varying amounts of cereals which have now attained the price range of the jam. This is another version of pricing concepts changing over time. There are more cereal bowls found, but collectors need more; so demand has pushed the price upward.

Green Patrician is offered more often than either pink or crystal. Even so, green dinner plates are scarce. Completing a set of crystal is a problem since not all crystal pieces were made.

Amber pitchers allegedly were manufactured in two styles. One has a moulded handle. In crystal and green, the applied handled pitcher is the norm, but an amber applied handled pitcher may exist!

Mint condition Patrician sugar lids, footed tumblers, and cookie and butter bottoms are harder to obtain than other pieces. The heavy cookie and butter tops have survived better than the thinner bottoms. All bowls have a tendency to have inner rim roughness. Check them carefully when buying.

		Amber, Crystal	Pink	Green
6 ▶	Bowl, 4¾", cream soup	14.00	20.00	20.00
11 ▶	Bowl, 5", berry	11.00	10.00	10.00
8 ▶	Bowl, 6", cereal	20.00	22.00	26.00
2 ▶	Bowl, 8½", large berry	38.00	30.00	38.00
	Bowl, 10", oval vegetable	30.00	26.00	30.00
	Butter dish and cover	80.00	195.00	125.00
	Butter dish bottom	55.00	155.00	70.00
	Butter dish top	25.00	40.00	55.00
	Cookie jar and cover	85.00		675.00
	Creamer, footed	9.00	10.00	12.00
9 ▶	Cup	7.00	12.00	12.00
	Jam dish	25.00	30.00	40.00
13 ▶	Pitcher, 8", 75 oz., moulded handle	135.00	125.00	165.00
	Pitcher, 8¼", 75 oz., applied handle	*110.00	150.00	175.00

		Amber, Crystal	Pink	Green
1 ▶	Plate, 6", sherbet	7.00	7.00	8.00
4 ▶	Plate, 7½", salad	11.00	14.00	14.00
	Plate, 9", luncheon	10.00	17.00	16.00
3 ▶	Plate, 10½", dinner	8.00	40.00	40.00
	Plate, 10½", grill	12.00	15.00	20.00
	Platter, 11½", oval	25.00	25.00	30.00
5 ▶	Salt and pepper, pair	50.00	120.00	80.00
10 ▶	Saucer	7.00	10.00	9.50
12 ▶	Sherbet	10.00	17.00	14.00
	Sugar	7.00	9.00	15.00
	Sugar cover	50.00	70.00	85.00
7 ▶	Tumbler, 4", 5 oz.	26.00	30.00	30.00
14 ▶	Tumbler, 4¼", 9 oz.	24.00	24.00	26.00
8 ▶	Tumbler, 5½", 14 oz.	35.00	40.00	50.00
	Tumbler, 5¼", 8 oz., footed	50.00		65.00

* Crystal only

"PATRICK," Lancaster Glass Company, Early 1930s
Colors: yellow and pink

"Patrick" caught the eye of many collectors about the same time and prices soared for a while. Today, yellow luncheon sets and a few luncheon pieces of pink are still being found, but there are fewer collectors wanting them. Everyone who prized those items now has them. With few buyers, prices are decreasing. We've noticed few bids for Patrick items on Internet auctions with starting prices often half of what pieces once were selling. "Patrick" was a limited production before anyone ever considered the concept to sell wares for more money.

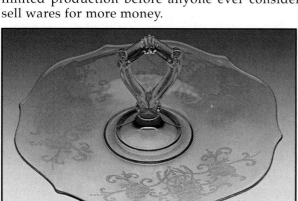

A "Patrick" mayonnaise has been found on two different plates. The raised circle one is the intended plate. The other is simply the salad plate. This difference holds true for Jubilee also. The other piece pictured came from a home in Lancaster, Ohio. The top of the candle has been ground perfectly flat so that the 11" console could be easily attached with glue. How many of these exist, we have no idea; but it was an interesting concept. We priced it by adding the prices of the candle and bowl together and it sold extremely fast the first day we put it out for sale.

It is not "Patrick" unless the "Patrick" etching is found on the piece. "Patrick" serving pieces are rare. There are serving pieces found in other patterns on the same blanks used for "Patrick" and Jubilee. However, "Patrick" mould etchings and Jubilee cuttings are higher priced due to demand and collectibility of those particular patterns.

		Pink	Yellow				Pink	Yellow
15 ▸	Bowl, 9", handled fruit	135.00	100.00	11 ▸	Mayonnaise, 3-piece		175.00	125.00
12 ▸	Bowl, 11", console	120.00	110.00	1 ▸	Plate, 7", sherbet		12.00	8.00
13 ▸	Candlesticks, pair	150.00	130.00		Plate, 7½", salad		16.00	12.00
	Candy dish, 3-footed	195.00	195.00	9 ▸	Plate, 8", luncheon		22.00	15.00
	Cheese & cracker set	110.00	95.00	8 ▸	Saucer		10.00	9.00
6 ▸	Creamer	30.00	25.00	10 ▸	Sherbet, 4¾"		50.00	40.00
7 ▸	Cup	30.00	25.00	5 ▸	Sugar		30.00	25.00
2 ▸	Goblet, 4", cocktail	75.00	75.00	4 ▸	Tray, 11", 2-handled		65.00	50.00
	Goblet, 4¾", 6 ounce, juice	60.00	50.00	14 ▸	Tray, 11", center-handled		95.00	75.00
3 ▸	Goblet, 6", 10 ounce, water	60.00	55.00					

"PEACOCK REVERSE," DELILAH BIRD, "PHEASANT," Line #411, #412 & #991,

Paden City Glass Company, 1930s
Colors: cobalt blue, red, amber, yellow, green, pink, black, and crystal

The "Peacock Reverse" or Delilah bird etch is similar to that of "Peacock and Wild Rose" only the peacock's head is swiveled backwards to look over his shoulder. Paden City's Line #412 ("Crow's Foot"), Line #991 ("Penny Line"), and Line #411 (Mrs. "B" — square shapes with the corners cut off) are the predominant lines on which "Peacock Reverse" was etched. Add to those an octagonal #701 Triumph plate, and almost any other Paden City mould blank may turn up with this etching. When you spot a piece of Paden City by its shape from a distance, you are always wondering what etch it will hold, if any.

The #701 eight-sided "Peacock Reverse" plate is the only pink piece we have owned. Ruby seems to be the color most encountered. We have turned up two colored sugars, but have yet to uncover a creamer in almost 25 years of searching. Few collectors of cups and saucers have "Peacock Reverse" caged. As with "Cupid," cups and saucers may be the toughest pieces in each pattern. A lipped, footed comport on the "Crow's Foot" blank has been called a gravy by collectors. You see this red comport without an etching, but finding it decorated is an accomplishment.

There are several styles of candy dishes. Patterns are only on the lids, as was standard procedure for Paden City candies. Bases are easier to find; and like other dealers, we have several sitting around looking for lids. It has been our experience that prices for "Peacock Reverse" are not established as much by color as other patterns. Pieces are so seldom presented that collectors will welcome any piece in any color, including crystal.

You could plausibly find this etch on almost any piece in our listings under "Crow's Foot" (squared) or "Orchid." The granddaughter of a former Paden City worker told us that workers at the plant referred to these bird patterns as "pheasants." Careful examination of the bird etches shows we may well be stalking the wrong bird.

		All colors			**All colors**
10 ▸	Bowl, 4⅞", square	40.00		Creamer, 2¾", flat	100.00
	Bowl, 6"	40.00	6 ▸	Cup	100.00
4 ▸	Bowl, 8¾", square	110.00		Plate, 5¾", sherbet	20.00
9 ▸	Bowl, 8¾", square with handles	135.00	10 ▸	Plate, 8½", luncheon	50.00
	Bowl, 11¾", console	125.00		Plate, 10⅜", 2-handled	90.00
2 ▸	Candlesticks, 5¾", square base, pair	150.00	7 ▸	Saucer	30.00
3 ▸	Candy dish, 6½", square	150.00	5 ▸	Sherbet, 4⅝" tall, 3⅜" diameter	60.00
13 ▸	Candy dish, round	175.00		Server, center-handled	65.00
	Comport, 3¼" high, 6¼" wide	75.00	1 ▸	Sugar, 2¾", flat	100.00
	Comport, 4¼" high, 7⅜" wide	85.00	8 ▸	Tumbler, 4", 10 ounce, flat	100.00
11 ▸	Comport, footed, 2 spouts	125.00	12 ▸	Vase, 10"	250.00

"PEACOCK & WILD ROSE," "NORA BIRD," "PHEASANT LINE," Line #300,

Paden City Glass Company, 1929 – 1930s
Colors: pink, green, amber, cobalt blue, black, light blue, crystal, and red

As reported in an earlier edition, while working at a photography session where this pattern was being outlined with chalk to make it show in the photograph, Cathy noticed that "Nora Bird" etching was a condensed (or sectioned off) version of the larger "Peacock and Wild Rose" etching. Our discovery has been acknowledged by most Paden City collectors, but some died-in-the-wool old-timers are not willing to accept that fact. If you examine a tall vase, you will see the small bird at the bottom of the design that appears on pieces of what was formerly known as a separate pattern, "Nora Bird." The bird on each piece can be found in flight or getting ready to take flight. Obviously, the entire larger pattern would not fit on smaller pieces; so, a condensed portion was used. That explains why creamers, sugars, and luncheon pieces had never been found in "Peacock and Wild Rose." These pieces from Line #300 are actually the same etching. Abundant quantities of additional pieces in "Peacock and Wild Rose" can now be combined with cups, saucers, creamers, sugars, and luncheon plates of "Nora Bird" to give a complete pattern. Cups and saucers are rarely seen, but are, at least, possible now.

The #300 line candy dish lid fits both the flat, three-part and the footed 5¼" candy dish. The bases to the candy dishes are not etched. An octagonal flat candy pictured in an earlier book was from the #701 Triumph line. The rectangular green tray pictured was listed as a #210 Line refreshment tray and is sometimes found with a sugar and creamer. Light blue has been discovered in the form of a rolled edge console bowl.

There are two styles of creamers and sugars, pointed handles and rounded handles. Both types are also found with the "Cupid" etch. There is an individual (smaller) sugar and creamer with rounded handles, but these are rarely seen.

		All colors			All colors
	Bowl, 8½", flat	110.00		Mayonnaise liner	20.00
	Bowl, 8½", fruit, oval, footed	135.00		Pitcher, 5" high	395.00
	Bowl, 8¾", footed	135.00		Pitcher, 8½", 64 ounce	495.00
	Bowl, 9½", center-handled	135.00		Plate, 8"	20.00
	Bowl, 9½", footed	145.00		Plate, 12", 2-handled	80.00
19 ▶	Bowl, 10", 2-handled	100.00		Relish, 3-part	110.00
	Bowl, 10½", center-handled	100.00	9 ▶	Saucer	15.00
15 ▶	Bowl, 10½", footed	165.00		Sugar, 4½", round handle	55.00
	Bowl, 10½", fruit	150.00	6 ▶	Sugar, 5", pointed handle	55.00
20 ▶	Bowl, 11", console	150.00		Tray, 10¾", center handled	65.00
	Bowl, 11¾", amber, octagon	100.00	11 ▶	Tray 10⅞", oval, footed	125.00
	Bowl, 14", console	160.00		Tray, rectangular, handled	150.00
10 ▶	Cake stand, 2" high	110.00		Tumbler, 2¼", 3 ounce	65.00
1 ▶	Candlestick, 5" wide, pair	110.00		Tumbler, 3"	75.00
4 ▶	Candlesticks, octagonal tops, pair	225.00	16 ▶	Tumbler, 4"	95.00
11 ▶	Candy dish w/cover, 6½", 3-part	175.00	21 ▶	Tumbler, 4¾", footed	110.00
	Candy dish w/cover, 7"	210.00	18 ▶	Tumbler, 5¼", 10 ounce	110.00
13 ▶	Candy with lid, footed, 5¼" high	175.00		Vase, 8¼", elliptical	295.00
	Cheese and cracker set	140.00	14 ▶	Vase, 10", two styles	195.00
	Comport, 3¼" tall, 6¼" wide	100.00		Vase, 12"	270.00
17 ▶	Comport, 6⅜" tall, 8" wide	110.00			
3 ▶	Creamer, 4½", round handle	55.00			
7 ▶	Creamer, 5", pointed handle	55.00			
8 ▶	Cup	60.00			
2 ▶	Ice bucket, 6"	195.00			
5 ▶	Ice tub, 4¾"	185.00			
	Ice tub, 6"	195.00			
	Mayonnaise	80.00			

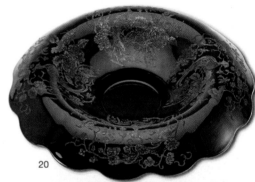

20

"PEBBLED RIM," Line #707, L. E. Smith Glass Company, 1930s
Colors: amber, green, pink

"Pebbled Rim" is a simple L. E. Smith pattern that was marketed as a 40-piece dinner set. Some collectors treasure patterns that are not as "busy"; they find them soothing to their senses. Plainer patterns are also often less inexpensive when compared to well known more ornate wares.

The large, ruffled edge vegetable, deep salad bowl, and platter appear to be the hardest pieces to pinpoint, and any green is more arduous to find than pink.

We have noticed two large sets of pink "Pebbled Rim" trying to be sold in antique malls in Texas and Pennsylvania. Trying is the operative word as one set for eight and the other for around 12, missing a piece or two, have been "available" for several years now. We know because we check each time we're in the area. Both are being marketed as an entire set rather than individual pieces, which eliminates most collectors who are usually looking for specific pieces. Therefore, collectors who would buy parts or pieces aren't interested in a larger initial outlay for an entire set. In addition, both sets have a premium price on them because they are large sets. Sets do not bring a premium, and usually are offered at a discount in order to sell them. On top of that, there is not a great demand for "Pebbled Rim" — so these sellers are totally ignoring their market.

"Pebbled Rim" blends well with other patterns. In fact, we deem that may account for the scarcity of some serving pieces. People are using them with other sets.

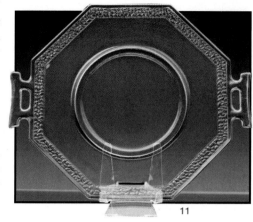

11

		All colors			All colors
	Bowl, 9½", oval	26.00		Plate, 9", dinner	8.00
	Bowl, berry	7.00	9 ▸	Plate, 9", grill	8.00
10 ▸	Bowl, ruffled edge vegetable, deep	26.00	11 ▸	Plate, 9", two-handle	15.00
5 ▸	Bowl, ruffled edge vegetable, shallow	25.00	8 ▸	Platter, oval	18.00
	Candleholder	15.00	2 ▸	Saucer	1.50
3 ▸	Creamer	10.00	4 ▸	Sugar	10.00
1 ▸	Cup (two styles)	6.00			
6 ▸	Plate, 6", bread/butter	2.00			
7 ▸	Plate, 7", salad	3.00			

"PENNY LINE," Line #991, Paden City Glass Company, c. 1930

Colors: amber, crystal, green, Mulberry, pink (Cheriglo), primrose (light yellow), Royal blue, ruby

"Penny Line" is Paden City's Line #991 which is often mistaken for Paden City's "Party Line" #191. They are a different shape, but the name gets switched around in people's minds. Our picture here comes via a dealer friend who found a red set and called to ask if we would like a photo sent to the photography studio in Paducah. We should point out that the shakers pictured belong to Party Line #191. Obviously, the previous owner of this had blended this beautiful red ware.

"Penny Line's" circular, stacked rings appearance was a definite creation of the Deco era and is prized as such. The Deco age in which this pattern had its beginning was all about form, lines, and shapes. Notice the unusual handles on the sugar which reiterate the rippled bands.

Low foot goblets used only one wafer and high foot stems had two. The mayo was cataloged with a liner plate, which we believe was the 6" dessert plate, also used as a sherbet liner. Since we have never come across a mayo with its liner to be certain, that is our guess. The candle is often set upside down and used as a candy comport. It is a dual purpose item commonly found in more elegant patterns.

We are having a difficult time selling cobalt low footed goblets at our listed price even though we have seen them for six times more in a Paden City publication.

14

		*All colors				*All colors
5 ▸	Bowl, 9", hdld.	30.00			Plate, 10", hdld.	26.00
	Bowl, finger	14.00	12 ▸		Saucer	2.00
	Candle	22.00	8 ▸		Server, 10½", center handle	30.00
6 ▸	Creamer	10.00	10 ▸		Shaker, pair	35.00
11 ▸	Cup	10.00	14 ▸		Sherbet, low foot	7.00
	Decanter, 22 ounce w/stopper	45.00			Stem, 1¼ ounce, cordial	18.00
	Goblet, low foot, grapefruit	15.00			Stem, 3½ ounce, cocktail	10.00
	Goblet, low foot, 9 ounce	14.00			Stem, 3 ounce, wine	12.00
	Goblet, high foot	16.00			Stem, 6 ounce, cocktail	10.00
	Pitcher	55.00	9 ▸		Stem, 9 ounce, water	15.00
	Plate, 6"	3.00	2 ▸		Sugar	10.00
4 ▸	Plate, 8", salad	8.00	3 ▸		Tray, rectangular, 2 handled, sugar/cream	25.00
			1 ▸		Tumbler, 2½ ounce, wine	10.00
					Tumbler, 5 ounce, juice	8.00
			13 ▸		Tumbler, 9 ounce, table	10.00
			7 ▸		Tumbler, 12 ounce, tea	12.00

* Add 50% for royal blue or red

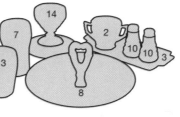

173

PETALWARE, MacBeth-Evans Glass Company, 1930 – 1950

Colors: Monax, Ivrene, pink, crystal, cobalt, and fired-on red, blue, green, and yellow

Pink Petalware has mesmerized various collectors. This delicate pink is still less pricey than most other pink patterns in Depression glass and can be found. The three tumblers to the right, which another author called "Shirley," have been found packed in boxed sets of Petalware.

Petalware Mountain Flowers (top page 175) decoration remains in demand for its multicolored floral display on Monax (MacBeth-Evans's name for their white glass). Original boxed sets of sherbets divulged the Mountain Flowers name.

Crystal Federal Star pitchers and decorated tumblers are shown on the opposite page which were decorated to match the Mountain Flowers design. Pitchers are found satinized or plain as are the tumblers. Most of these tumblers are turning up in northwestern Ohio. Note the crystal sherbet; we have not found a satinized one as yet. We had to buy six juice tumblers with the plain pitcher and even had to promise to sell it that way after photography; so we did.

An original boxed set pictured on page 176 shows straight-sided tumblers painted with matching pastel bands and packed with Ivrene (the opaque, beige color) "Pastel Bands" sets. Pastel decorated Ivrene is the design now being pursued as avidly as Mountain Flowers. We are continually asked for serving pieces at shows. Considering the small amount of it available, demand is beginning to increase prices.

Even if the tumblers in the box are not the Petalware pattern, they were decorated to go with it. These tumblers are found in several sizes, all currently selling in the $7.00 to $10.00 range. We can only guarantee the boxed ones on the right are accurate, but as long as the colored bands correspond with the dinnerware, that is suitable to most collectors. There is no name on the box for what we call "Pastel Bands." A dealer friend insists we point out that the banded ring colors line up in a different way on the Monax and Ivrene. The Ivrene shows blue, green, and pink from center to rim; while the blue and green order is reversed on the Monax.

Collectors are spellbound with an assortment of Petalware decorations. This becomes evident when those items are put out for sale and are quickly grabbed from the table shortly after the show opens.

Florette is the third most collected design. It is the pointed petal, red flower decoration without the red edge trim. Since we now own a 1949 company magazine showing a woman painting this Florette design on stacks of plates, that particular design should belong in our *Collectible Glassware of the 40s, 50s, 60s...* book.

		Crystal	Pink	Cremax, Monax, Plain	Cremax, Lomax, Florette, Fired-on Decorations	Red Trim Floral
	Bowl, 4½", cream soup	4.50	15.00	11.00	20.00	
2 ▸	Bowl, 5¾", cereal	4.00	14.00	9.00	20.00	38.00
	Bowl, 7", soup			55.00	100.00	
12 ▸	*Bowl, 9", large berry	8.50	18.00	18.00	30.00	110.00
13 ▸	Cup	3.00	6.00	5.00	8.00	22.00
7 ▸	**Creamer, footed	3.00	9.00	7.00	10.00	30.00
	Lamp shade (many sizes) $8.00 – 15.00					
	Mustard with metal cover in cobalt blue only, $10.00					
5 ▸	Pitcher, (Mountain Flowers) juice (crystal or frosted)					300.00
	Pitcher, 80 ounce (crystal decorated bands)	35.00				
1 ▸	Plate, 6", sherbet	2.00	4.00	3.00	4.00	16.00
9 ▸	Plate, 8", salad	2.00	6.00	5.00	8.00	20.00
11 ▸	Plate, 9", dinner	4.00	15.00	12.00	18.00	30.00
	Plate, 11", salver	4.50	15.00	12.00	18.00	
10 ▸	Plate, 12", salver		16.00	15.00	18.00	32.00
	Platter, 13", oval	8.50	22.00	16.00	25.00	
14 ▸	Saucer	1.50	2.00	2.00	3.50	6.00
	Saucer, cream soup liner			15.00		
	Sherbet, 4", low footed			30.00		
8 ▸	**Sherbet, 4½", low footed	3.50	10.00	8.00	18.00	35.00
6 ▸	**Sugar, footed	3.00	9.00	7.00	10.00	30.00
17 ▸	Tidbit servers or Lazy Susans, several styles $12.00 to 17.50					
4 ▸	Tumbler, 3⅝", 6 ounce					50.00
3 ▸	Tumbler, 4⅝", 12 ounce					55.00

‡Tumblers (crystal decorated pastel bands or fruit decorations) $10.00 – 15.00

* Also in cobalt at $65.00   ** Also in cobalt at $35.00   ‡ Several sizes

Petalware

Ivrene

Found with sets of decorated fruit plates.

176

PILLAR OPTIC, "LOGS," "LOG CABIN," Anchor Hocking Glass Company, 1937 – 1942

Colors: crystal, green, pink, Royal Ruby; amber and iridescent, possible Federal Glass Co.

Hocking's Pillar Optic has been noticed by kitchenware collectors for quite a while. It was pictured in our *Kitchen Glassware of the Depression Years* of the early 1980s. The pretzel jar is often found with mugs and a pitcher which was initially promoted as a pretzel set. The introduction was after Prohibition so those mugs were probably not for root beer. Most collectors call that 130-ounce jar a cookie, but it was promoted as a pretzel jar. The top is hard to find, particularly undamaged. These jars are occasionally found satinized and with hand-painted flowers. Crystal ones are rarely found without the satinization.

The 60-ounce pitcher came in three colors. Two styles of 80-ounce ones are pictured on the right. The panels of Pillar Optic are evenly spaced (note the pitcher with ice lip) and not like Old Cafe's alternating large panel with two smaller ones. It is only the ice lip style that is similar to Old Cafe. We received a letter not long after adding this pattern to the book stating that we had interfered with several sales of pink Old Cafe pitchers with our new listing. Pillar Optic pitchers are collectible, just not as expensive as Old Cafe ones to collectors of that pattern.

Royal Ruby Pillar Optic items are continuing to be unearthed as you can see by the photo. The cup, saucer, creamer, and sugar are extremely rare in red. We recently found out there was a two-handled sandwich plate found at an estate sale in Florida. Originally there were over 50 pieces. Evidently, a retiree from the north brought it with them. Up until that time, we had only seen one other grouping of Royal Ruby and that was displayed at a Depression glass show years ago.

Amber and iridescent flat tumblers are being discovered, but Federal Glass Company is known to have manufactured similar patterned tumblers and in all likelihood these came from them rather than Anchor Hocking. Glass companies always kept up with what the competition was selling and were fast to introduce anything that "caught on."

There are two styles of cups; a rounded cup found in green and pink and a flatter Royal Ruby or pink one, evocative of Hocking's Colonial styled cups. We finally found a green saucer, but no pink one yet. We have not seen flat green cups or rounded pink ones. The pink sugar and creamer we own came out of the attic of a former Hocking employee who also had a set of Royal Ruby Miss America.

Crystal Pillar Optic tumblers have been a fundamental part of Anchor Hocking's restaurant line for years. In fact, in one of their later catalogs, it is shown under the heading "Old Reliable." Some restaurants still use that Pillar Optic style tumbler and pitcher today.

		Crystal	Amber, Green, Pink	Royal Ruby
18 ▸	Bowl, oval vegetable			165.00
21 ▸	Bowl, 9", two-handle		65.00	165.00
19 ▸	Creamer, footed		65.00	100.00
2 ▸	Cup, 2 styles	7.00	12.00	75.00
	Mug, 12 oz.	10.00	35.00	
12 ▸	Pitcher, w/o lip, 60 oz.	10.00	30.00	
9 ▸	Pitcher, w/lip, 80 oz.	15.00	35.00	
11 ▸	Pitcher, w/o lip, 80 oz.	20.00	40.00	
17 ▸	Plate, 6", sherbet	2.00	6.00	25.00
7 ▸	Plate, 8", luncheon	5.00	12.00	30.00
	Plate, 12", 2 hdld.			150.00
16 ▸	Platter, 11", oval			165.00
4 ▸	Pretzel jar, 130 oz.	85.00	150.00	

		Crystal	Amber, Green, Pink	Royal Ruby
1 ▸	Saucer w/indent	2.00	4.00	25.00
13 ▸	Sherbet, 2 styles		12.00	30.00
20 ▸	Sugar, footed		65.00	100.00
14 ▸	Tumbler, 1½ oz., whiskey	5.00	8.00	
5 ▸	Tumbler, 3¼", 3 oz., footed	8.00	12.00	30.00
	Tumbler, 4", 5 oz., juice, ftd.	8.00	14.00	40.00
10 ▸	Tumbler, 5 oz., juice		12.00	
	Tumbler, 5¼", 10 oz., ftd.	10.00	15.00	50.00
8 ▸	Tumbler, 7 oz., old fashioned	10.00	25.00	
15 ▸	Tumbler, 9 oz., water	2.50	12.00	
6 ▸	Tumbler, 11 oz., ftd., cone	12.00	15.00	
3 ▸	Tumbler, 13 oz., tea	4.00	22.00	

PRIMO, "PANELED ASTER," U.S. Glass Company, Early 1930s
Colors: green and yellow

The Primo pattern seems to grow with each passing edition of our book as new pieces continue to be unearthed. A grill plate with a raised cup rim made its presence known in green, but there are no reports of this piece in yellow, as yet. The regular grill plate is complicated enough to find, but the cup ring one heretofore was nearly invisible.

Primo was advertised in 1932 as a 14-piece bridge set (with plates, cups, saucers, and sugar and creamer), a 16-piece luncheonette (with grill plates, tumblers, cups, and saucers), an 18-piece occasional set (with plates, tumblers, sugar, creamer, cups, and saucers), a 19-piece hostess set (add a tray), or a 7-piece berry set.

That two-handled hostess tray finally showed up in green, so those 19-piece settings may not have been as widespread as other groupings. The 11" three-footed console bowl (listed as large berry in old ads) created a furor among Primo collectors when it first appeared in an earlier book. No one seemed too thrilled about the 6¼" sherbet plate not previously known. We were tickled enough for everybody when we first glimpsed them in a Louisiana antique mall. We wanted only the sherbet plates, but had to buy the sherbets to get them. Finding new pieces for patterns is now our "pleasure." We can truly attest to there still being some surprises left after 36 years of doing this.

All bowls, dinner, grill, or cake plates will take exploration. Though we have revealed several new items in yellow and green, we have yet to find a green berry bowl to picture.

Exasperation in finding Primo is only one problem. Often items are found with extreme mould irregularity and inner rim damage. We have bought more Primo along the Gulf Coast than any other place we have searched, so it seems likely it may have been a premium item for something in that area.

Primo's tumbler exactly fits the coaster/ashtray, but no Primo design is found on them. These coasters have been found in boxed sets with Primo tumblers that were advertised as "Bridge Service Sets." It seems that U.S. Glass used these as a common item with other patterns as well. The coasters are also found in pink and black.

		Yellow, Green				Yellow, Green
3 ▸	Bowl, 4½"	25.00			Plate, 10", dinner	30.00
1 ▸	Bowl, 7¾"	40.00	10 ▸	Plate, 10", grill	15.00
5 ▸	Bowl, 11", 3-footed	75.00		Plate, 10", grill w/indent	25.00
4 ▸	Cake plate, 10", 3-footed	40.00	7 ▸	Saucer	3.00
9 ▸	Coaster/ashtray	8.00	2 ▸	Sherbet	12.00
	Creamer	12.00		Sugar	12.00
6 ▸	Cup	10.00		Tray, 2-handle hostess	50.00
11 ▸	Plate, 6¼"	15.00	8 ▸	Tumbler, 5¾", 9 ounce	20.00
	Plate, 7½"	9.00			

PRINCESS, Hocking Glass Company, 1931 – 1935
Colors: green, Topaz yellow, apricot yellow, pink, and light blue

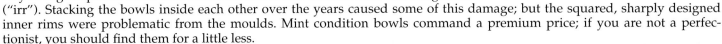

Gathering Princess continues, albeit at a slightly lower price, which benefits collectors, but is socking dealers in the pocketbook who purchased inventory at higher prices. Note that most Princess bowls exhibit inner rim roughness ("irr"). Stacking the bowls inside each other over the years caused some of this damage; but the squared, sharply designed inner rims were problematic from the moulds. Mint condition bowls command a premium price; if you are not a perfectionist, you should find them for a little less.

Princess footed iced tea tumblers are hard to acquire in all colors. Collectors of green Princess have to search long and hard for the undivided relish and the square-footed pitcher with tumblers to match. Some dealers call the undivided Princess relish a soup bowl. To us, it seems too shallow for a soup bowl; but if you can find one for sale, it will make a divot in your cash supply. Followers of pink Princess also have problems purchasing square-foot pitchers, matching tumblers, coasters, and ashtrays. The hardest to find yellow pieces include the butter dish, juice pitcher, undivided relish, 10¼" handled sandwich plate, coasters, and ashtrays. That handled sandwich is just like the handled grill plate without the dividers. We have only found two of these in all our years of searching for glass and they were labeled Patrician.

In Topaz, the official color name listed by Hocking, there is an obvious color variation. Topaz is a bright, attractive shade of yellow. However, some yellow produced looks more amber than yellow and has been branded "apricot" by collectors. Most desire the Topaz, which makes the darker, amber shade taxing to sell. No one tries to blend these as they are so mismatched it appears Hocking meant to produce two separate colors.

For some reason (possible distribution through premiums) yellow Princess sherbets, cereal bowls, and berry bowls flourish in the Detroit area. On the other hand, all but one of the known yellow Princess juice pitchers have been found in northern and central Kentucky. Cups, saucers, footed water tumblers, and dinner and grill plates are available in yellow. Sets containing these items were widely distributed and that promotion evidently worked well. You can still find basic items.

A few blue Princess pieces are found once in a while. The cookie jar, cup, saucer, and dinner plate find a ready market. We show a cup and saucer below. There is circumstantial evidence that blue Princess was shipped to Mexico, and most of what is found has been in the Southwest. There was once even a mistaken reproduction report circulated about blue dinner plates, but they turned out to be the real thing.

The grill plate without handles and dinner plate were changed to read 9½" in our listing instead of the 9" listed in Hocking catalogs. However, it turns out that there are 9" plates as well. Prices are comparable, but you need to specify whether you want 9" or 9½" if ordering dinner plates through the mail or from an Internet source. Be sure to measure across and not diagonally. Yes, that has happened.

On a bothersome level, reproductions in cobalt blue, green, pink, and amber (candy dishes and cookie jars) have been reported. Thankfully, the colors are not close to those originally made. Cobalt and amber were never made originally. The green will not glow under ultraviolet (black) light and the pink has an orange hue. We haven't wasted money to buy one to compare the actual design since the colors are so off.

Both styles of Princess cups are shown above with the green one being unusual.

		Green	Pink	Topaz, Apricot
	Ashtray, 4½"	70.00	80.00	110.00
13 ▸	Bowl, 4½", berry	30.00	30.00	50.00
1 ▸	Bowl, 5", cereal or oatmeal	35.00	36.00	38.00
	Bowl, 9", octagonal, salad	42.00	52.00	175.00
5 ▸	Bowl, 9½", hat-shaped	50.00	50.00	150.00
19 ▸	Bowl, 10", oval vegetable	25.00	25.00	60.00
3 ▸	Butter dish and cover	75.00	110.00	800.00
	Butter dish bottom	25.00	30.00	200.00
	Butter dish top	50.00	80.00	600.00
	Cake stand, 10"	30.00	32.00	
9 ▸	*Candy dish and cover	50.00	70.00	
	Coaster	45.00	75.00	120.00
22 ▸	**Cookie jar and cover	55.00	65.00	
4 ▸	Creamer, oval	20.00	18.00	18.00
11 ▸	‡ Cup	9.00	9.00	7.00
	Pitcher 6", 37 ounce	60.00	70.00	995.00
	Pitcher, 7⅜", 24 ounce, ftd.	525.00	475.00	
	Pitcher, 8", 60 ounce	55.00	60.00	100.00
12 ▸	‡‡ Plate, 5½", sherbet	7.00	7.00	2.00
6 ▸	Plate, 8", salad	14.00	16.00	12.00
	§ Plate, 9" or 9½", dinner	22.00	20.00	12.00

		Green	Pink	Topaz, Apricot
	**Plate, 9½", grill	20.00	20.00	8.00
	Plate, 10¼", handled sandwich	25.00	30.00	195.00
15 ▸	Plate, 10½", grill, closed handles	8.00	10.00	5.00
10 ▸	Platter, 12", closed handles	30.00	30.00	60.00
20 ▸	Relish, 7½", divided, 4 part	28.00	30.00	100.00
2 ▸	Relish, 7½", plain	200.00	200.00	265.00
8 ▸	Salt and pepper, 4½", pair	50.00	48.00	60.00
	Spice shakers, 5½", pair	30.00		
12 ▸	Saucer (same as sherbet plate)	7.00	7.00	2.00
14 ▸	Sherbet, footed	15.00	15.00	22.00
7 ▸	Sugar	10.00	15.00	8.50
21 ▸	Sugar cover	30.00	30.00	17.50
17 ▸	Tumbler, 3", 5 ounce, juice	33.00	38.00	32.50
	Tumbler, 4", 9 ounce, water	25.00	32.00	25.00
	Tumbler, 5¼", 13 oz., iced tea	45.00	45.00	30.00
	Tumbler, 4¾", 9 oz., sq. ftd	60.00	60.00	
16 ▸	Tumbler, 5¼", 10 ounce, ftd.	30.00	30.00	17.00
18 ▸	Tumbler, 6½", 12½ oz., ftd.	120.00	110.00	150.00
23 ▸	Vase, 8"	40.00	55.00	

* Beware reproductions in cobalt blue and amber
** Blue $995.00
‡ Blue $125.00
‡‡ Blue $60.00
§ Blue $200.00

QUEEN MARY (PRISMATIC LINE), "VERTICAL RIBBED,"

Anchor Hocking Glass Company, 1936 – 1949
Colors: pink, crystal, and some Royal Ruby

Queen Mary is one of the patterns that is attracting few new collectors since the pink dinner plates and footed tumblers are costly and rarely found. Even though crystal is inexpensive and accessible and has that same linear Deco look of the pink, it does not magnetize admirers like that of the pink. Nothing is as exasperating as trying to find pink Queen Mary dinner plates and footed tumblers. You should be warned that prices for those same items in crystal did exhibit upward trends until demand was overcome with supplies being uncovered. A crystal set can still be completed at manageable prices including dinner plates and footed tumblers. If you can't attend a show, search the Internet — but pay attention to postage and handling charges.

Even some pink Queen Mary prices have shrunk because new collectors are not desperate to own every piece of a set as were collectors in the past. Pink dinners and footed tumblers will sell — at the right price.

The 6" cereal bowl has the same mould shape as the butter bottom but is smaller in diameter. What we call butter dishes were promoted as "preserve dishes" in Hocking's 30s catalogs. There are two different cups. The smaller requires a saucer with cup ring. The larger cup uses the combination saucer/ sherbet plate so characteristic of Hocking's patterns. The pink smaller cup and saucer have surpassed the larger in price. Some dealers are classifying the 5½" tab-handled bowl as a lug or cream soup. The price on that bowl has gone up due to that portrayal that is not in catalog listings.

The frosted crystal butter dish with metal band looks somewhat like a crown. These were made about the time of the English Coronation in the mid-1930s. We have seen these priced as high as $150.00 in an Art Deco shop and as low as $25.00 elsewhere.

A checkered appearing, cross-lined vase (shaped like Old Cafe with a 400-line number) is pictured along with Queen Mary items in early Hocking catalogs. You can buy that as a crystal accessory piece if you wish.

		Pink	Crystal
	Ashtray, 2" x 3¾", oval	5.00	4.00
	*Ashtray, 3¼", round		3.00
	Ashtray, 4¼", square (#422)		4.00
	Bowl, 4", one-handle or none	5.00	3.50
	Bowl, 4½", berry	7.00	4.00
	Bowl, 5", berry, flared	11.00	5.50
1 ▶	Bowl, 5½", two handle, lug soup	18.00	7.50
	Bowl, 6", cereal	12.00	6.00
3 ▶	Bowl, 6", 3-footed	12.00	
	Bowl, deep, 7½" (#477)	35.00	14.00
	Bowl, 8¾", large berry (#478)	25.00	15.00
	Butter dish or preserve and cover (#498)	135.00	25.00
	Butter dish bottom (#498)	20.00	5.00
	Butter dish top (#498)	115.00	20.00
	Candy dish and cover, 7¼" (#490)	65.00	20.00
	**Candlesticks, 4½", double branch, pair		20.00
4 ▶	Celery or pickle dish, 5" x 10" (#467)	50.00	15.00
	Cigarette jar, 2" x 3", oval	7.50	5.50
	Coaster, 3½"	9.00	5.00
	Coaster/ashtray, 3¼", round (#419)	6.00	5.00
	Comport, 5¾"	25.00	15.00
16 ▶	Creamer, footed	60.00	25.00

		Pink	Crystal
13 ▶	Creamer, 5½", oval (#471)	12.00	6.00
	Cup, large	7.00	5.00
	Cup, small	6.00	8.00
8 ▶	Mayonnaise, 5" x 2¾" h, 6" plate	30.00	16.00
	Plate, 6⅝"	5.00	4.00
5 ▶	Plate, 8¾", salad (#438)		5.50
6 ▶	Plate, 9¾", dinner (#426)	50.00	25.00
	Plate, 12", sandwich (#450)	20.00	14.00
	Plate, 14", serving tray	22.00	12.00
	Relish tray, cloverleaf		15.00
	Relish tray, 12", 3-part	18.00	9.00
18 ▶	Relish tray, 14", 5-part	20.00	12.00
	Salt and pepper, 2½", pair (#486)		18.00
	Saucer/cup ring	5.00	2.50
2 ▶	Sherbet, footed or flat	9.00	5.00
12 ▶	Sugar, footed	60.00	25.00
15 ▶	Sugar, 6", oval (#470)	12.00	6.00
	Tumbler, 3½", 5 ounce, juice	13.00	4.00
	Tumbler, 4", 9 ounce, water	15.00	6.00
	Tumbler, 5", 10 ounce, footed	60.00	30.00
	Vase, 6½" (#441)		12.00

* Royal Ruby $5.00; Forest Green $3.00   ** Royal Ruby $150.00

RADIANCE, New Martinsville Glass Company, 1936 – 1939
Colors: red, cobalt and ice blue, amber, crystal, pink, and emerald green

20

Red Radiance and both ice and cobalt blue colors are easier found than any besides amber. They are also the most wanted colors, and do not usually come at a bargain price. The most bothersome pieces to track down in those colors include the butter dish, handled decanter, and pitcher. Vases have been made into lamps in several styles using both plain and ruffled tops. We doubt these were all factory made, but it's possible.

Radiance punch, decanter, and condiment sets never emerge in quantities to suit demand. Punch sets are challenging to find, and the punch ladle is virtually unattainable. The ladle was created by pulling hot glass and attaching that long handle to a punch cup. If not damaged through application, collectors and dealers have added to their dearth trying to transport them to shows. The handle detaches from the cup very easily. One dealer has learned that — twice. He has helped raise the price of red punch ladles all by himself. Observe the Canary yellow (Vaseline) punch cup which is the only known piece in that color, thus far.

A 4" tall cake stand has been found in both red (pictured) and crystal. Watch for other colors.

You can find crystal punch bowls because Viking made them after they bought out New Martinsville in the mid 1940s. These are being found on 14" plates in emerald green (pictured previously) or black. These are found rather frequently — unlike their older counterparts and are difficult to sell unless priced reasonably. These punch bowls flair outward rather than inward, like the older "bowling ball" design. Viking's ladle is plain, so it is not as desirable as the earlier ladle.

Several collectors are pleading that Radiance is too fine a glassware to be included in this book. They are probably right. However, Radiance was designated as Depression glass long before our "Elegant" term for better glassware was coined in 1980 for the *Elegant Glassware of the Depression Era* book.

While shopping on Florida's east coast, we witnessed a pair of vases with decorations of gold and blue with flowers. Vases may be found in an array of colors and you can see several in our *Treasures of Very Rare Glassware* book.

Cobalt blue is striking, but few pieces surface in that color. When they do, they are often used to accompany the ice blue color or as showpieces on their own.

Pink Radiance (creamer, sugar, tray, cup, saucer, vase, shakers) are seen once in a while, but there is so little available today, there is little desire to own them. Price crystal about 50% of amber; both colors we find difficult to sell. Crystal pieces that "item" collectors seek, sell well, if priced inexpensively. They are sometimes decorated with platinum or gold.

		Ice & Cobalt Blue, Red	Amber			Ice & Cobalt Blue, Red	Amber
	Bowl, 5", nut, 2-handle	22.00	12.00	14 ▸	Creamer	15.00	9.00
5 ▸	Bowl, 6", bonbon	33.00	17.50		Cruet, individual	75.00	40.00
	Bowl, 6", bonbon, footed	35.00	20.00	18 ▸	Cup, footed	15.00	10.00
	Bowl, 6", bonbon w/cover	115.00	55.00	6 ▸	Cup, punch	15.00	7.00
	Bowl, 7", relish, 2-part	35.00	20.00	8 ▸	Decanter w/stopper, handle	225.00	125.00
	Bowl, 7", pickle	35.00	20.00	9 ▸	Goblet, 1 ounce, cordial	33.00	23.00
16 ▸	Bowl, 8", relish, 4-part	40.00	35.00		Honey jar, w/lid	125.00	75.00
13 ▸	Bowl, 8½", celery	35.00			Ladle for punch bowl	150.00	100.00
	*Bowl, 9", punch	225.00	125.00		Lamp, 12"	125.00	65.00
	Bowl, 10", celery	45.00	22.00	12 ▸	Mayonnaise, 3-piece, set	95.00	50.00
	Bowl, 10", crimped	45.00	30.00		Pitcher, 64 ounce	325.00	175.00
	Bowl, 10", flared	40.00	25.00	15 ▸	Plate, 8", luncheon	20.00	10.00
10 ▸	Bowl, 12", crimped	60.00	35.00	2 ▸	Plate, 9½", dinner	30.00	
	Bowl, 12", flared	65.00	32.00		Plate, 11½"	35.00	
1 ▸	Butter dish	395.00	195.00		**Plate, 14", punch bowl liner	85.00	45.00
20 ▸	Cake stand, 4" high	125.00			Salt & pepper, pair	75.00	40.00
	Candlestick, 6", ruffled, pair	150.00	70.00	17 ▸	Saucer	6.00	4.00
	Candlestick, 8", pair	225.00	95.00	7 ▸	Sugar	15.00	9.00
	Candlestick, 2-lite, pair	150.00	70.00	11 ▸	Tray, oval	45.00	25.00
19 ▸	Candy, flat, w/lid, 4 part	100.00	50.00	3 ▸	Tumbler, 9 ounce	30.00	16.00
	Cheese/cracker (11" plate) set	130.00	30.00	4 ▸	Vase, 10", flared or crimped	110.00	75.00
	Comport, 5"	30.00	18.00		Vase, 12", flared or crimped	175.00	
	Comport, 6"	30.00	22.00				
	Condiment set, 4-piece w/tray	295.00	165.00		* Emerald green $125.00 ** Emerald green $25.00		

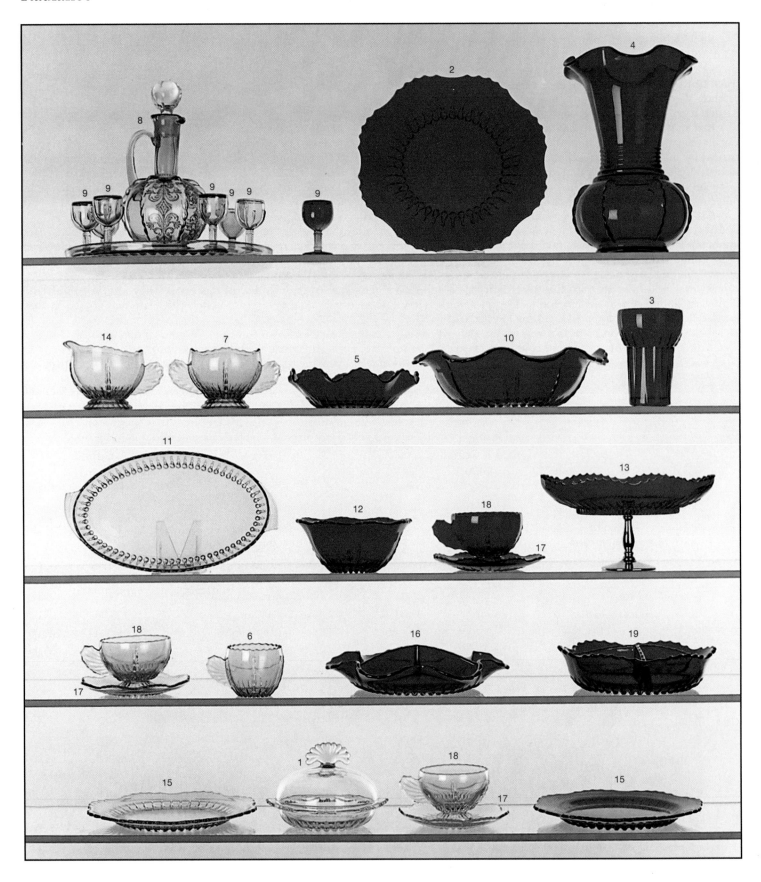

RAINDROPS, "OPTIC DESIGN," Federal Glass Company, 1929 – 1933

Colors: green and crystal

We have been saying that the Raindrops pattern has rounded bumps and not elongated ones since 1972 and yet we find pieces misidentified all the time in flea markets and antique malls. Elongated bumps belong to another pattern commonly referred to as "Thumbprint." Almost all Raindrops pieces are embossed on the bottom with Federal's trademark F inside a shield. We want to underscore that that mark is not a Fire-King mark as is being misrepresented over the Internet and in many antique malls we patronize. During the three years we were working on *Florences' Ovenware from the 1920s to the Present*, we bought large amounts of Federal glass to be included. At least 20 – 25% of Federal bought was mislabeled Fire-King. Sellers knew Fire-King was valuable; so seeing an F on the bottom was good enough for them to label it wrong. The bad news is that we left quite a few items we could have used in the book; but, being Federal, and not Fire-King, they were priced too expensively to buy. Over the years we have left hundreds of misidentified pieces of glass mistakenly priced too high because it was guessed to be something more expensive. Collectors are savvy and informed. They won't buy Federal as more expensive Fire-King because you say it's so. Leave the company label information blank or buy a good book or two.

Raindrops makes a great small luncheon or bridge set and will stay within the budget of most collectors — if you can find enough. Raindrops will blend well with many other green sets; so, give that a try if you want extra pieces. It even has a few complementary pieces that other smaller sets do not. You can find three sizes of bowls in Raindrops. The 7½" bowl will be the one you will probably find last. That bowl has always been scarce. It is now the second most expensive piece of this pattern having by-passed the sugar lid which is showing up more and more on Internet auctions. The shaker remains the item that rarely appears. One Raindrops shaker is all we have owned. There is a slim possibility of your finding one; but never say never.

There are two styles of cups. One is flat bottomed and the other is slightly footed. The flat-bottomed is 2⁵⁄₁₆" high and the footed is 2¹¹⁄₁₆" (reported by an enthusiastic Raindrops collector). We only have the footed variety.

Prices have slipped some even with the shorter supply being found. Prices for crystal tumblers run from 50% to 60% less than for green.

		Green			Green			Green
4 ▸	Bowl, 4½", fruit	7.00		Salt and pepper, pair	395.00	9 ▸	Tumbler, 2⅛", 2 ounce	5.00
15 ▸	Bowl, 6", cereal	12.00	2 ▸	Saucer	1.00	11 ▸	Tumbler, 3⅞", 5 ounce	6.50
6 ▸	Bowl, 7½", berry	50.00	3 ▸	Sherbet	8.00	7 ▸	Tumbler, 4⅛", 9½ ounce	9.00
1 ▸	Cup	8.00	13 ▸	Sugar	7.50		Tumbler, 5", 10 ounce	9.00
14 ▸	Creamer	7.50	12 ▸	Sugar cover	30.00		Tumbler, 5⅜", 14 ounce	14.00
5 ▸	Plate, 6", sherbet	2.00		Tumbler, 3", 4 ounce	5.00	10 ▸	Whiskey, 1⅞", 1 ounce	7.00
8 ▸	Plate, 8", luncheon	5.00						

185

REEDED, WHIRLSPOOL, "SPUN," Line #701, Imperial Glass Company, c. 1936 – 1960s

Colors: black, crystal, cobalt, dark green, amber, tangerine, Midas gold, turquoise, pink, milk, mustard

Reeded is the name given this pattern by Imperial, but it has been called "Spun" by collectors for many years. In the mid 1930s it was broadly publicized in beverage sets which must have sold well due to the quantity of pitchers and tumblers available today. A relatively uncommon vanity set (powder and perfume) was integrated amid its dinnerware items. The perfume has a spade shaped stopper. Additional items (vases and decanters) were added to the line in the 1960s and we have included a catalog page from this later time. We were persuaded to incorporate Reeded in our book as a result of Imperial's shutting down, making their wares more desirable and because of intense collector scrutiny. For a while, dealers couldn't keep any supply of Reeded on hand.

Candles were made from a small ivy ball vase fitted with a crystal glass candle insert (see the cobalt one pictured here). It is the insert that is difficult to find and valued as much as the vase. You might find these in crystal vases reasonably priced; so buy them for the inserts. Along with the 6" ball, candles were marketed as a console set in the 1950s.

The jar below is called Whirlspool and is found with a glass lid as pictured or with triangular metal knobs. Glass lids are favored, but the metal knobbed variety is accepted by collectors.

Gold trimmed items were referred to as Midas when introduced in the 50s.

	*All colors
Ashtray, 2¼", cupped	10.00
Bottle, 3 oz., bitters	40.00
Bowl, 4½", fruit	20.00
Bowl, 7", nappy, straight side	33.00
Bowl, 8", nappy	33.00
Bowl, 10", deep salad	45.00
7 ▸ Candle, 2½", ball w/crystal glass insert	45.00
Candy box, footed w/cone lid	50.00
Cigarette holder, wider mouth, 2½" ball	20.00
Cocktail shaker, 36 oz., w or w/o handles	75.00
Creamer, footed	25.00
1 ▸ Cup	20.00

	*All colors
Ice tub	60.00
Jar, Whirlspool, 4", tall, w/lid or w/metal knob	50.00
Jar, Whirlspool, 5", tall, w/lid or w/metal knob	60.00
8 ▸ Jar, Whirlspool, 6", tall, w/lid or w/metal knob	70.00
Jar, Whirlspool, 7", tall, w/lid or w/metal knob	80.00
Muddler, 4½"	10.00
Perfume w/triangle stop	50.00
Pitcher, 80 oz., ice lip	65.00
Plate, 8", salad, belled rim	20.00

		*All colors				*All colors
	Plate, 13½", cupped edge	30.00			Tumbler, 12 oz., tea, bulb top	14.00
	Plate, 14", server, flat	32.50			Vase, 2½", ball	20.00
	Powder jar w/lid	50.00			Vase, 3½", ivy ball, footed	35.00
2 ▶	Saucer	8.00			Vase, ivy ball, 6½", footed	55.00
3 ▶	Sherbet	17.50			Vase, 4", ball	17.50
	Sugar, footed	25.00			Vase, 5", bud	35.00
	Syrup, ball w/chrome spout & handle	50.00			Vase, 5", bulbous, tall neck rose	45.00
	Tumbler, 2 oz., shot	18.00			Vase, 5", rose	40.00
	Tumbler, 3½ oz., cocktail	25.00		6 ▶	Vase, 6", ball, rose	45.00
	Tumbler, 5 oz., juice, straight	10.00			Vase, 6", bud	40.00
	Tumbler, 7 oz., old fashioned	12.00			Vase, 6", slender	40.00
	Tumbler, 9 oz.	12.00			Vase, 8½"	40.00
4 ▶	Tumbler, 12 oz., tea, straight side	13.00			Vase, 9"	50.00

*Add 50% for red or blue; deduct 50% for crystal

"Turquoise" 701C—48 oz. Shaker "Mustard" "Bead Green" "Mustard" 385—6¾" Horseshoe Ash Tray "Flask Brown" "Bead Green"

IMPERIAL GLASS CORPORATION.
BELLAIRE, OHIO

"MIDAS"

701/4/Dec 9"   701/1/Dec 5"   701/Dec   701/2/Dec   703/Dec

"RIBBON," Hazel-Atlas Glass Company, Early 1930s

Colors: green; some black, crystal, and pink

"Ribbon" is a Hazel-Atlas pattern that is also moulded on Ovide shapes as was Cloverleaf. "Ribbon" has clean lines and shapes, which manage to portray elegance and movement at the same time and is representative of the era in which it was inaugurated.

We seldom see "Ribbon" for sale at glass shows except for sugars, creamers, and candy dishes. These items have come to symbolize "Ribbon" to new collectors, but there is more to be had. Then again, some dealers have begun to "jump" the prices asked for these items and we see more sitting than leaving with buyers. A candy dish makes a great first piece of a collection due to its practicality for the owner. New collectors love to buy a usable piece as a display item and candies fit that niche quite well.

"Ribbon" bowls are amongst the most unrevealed in all of Depression glass. They are in shorter supply than those of its sister pattern, Cloverleaf; but, thankfully prices for Ribbon have not caught up with those, yet. We had a letter from a long-time collector explaining that we were wrong in listing the cereal because it did not exist in Ribbon. (He had an older book. We told him it was pictured now.) He wanted to buy the bowl and not the book. He was told that if he bought the book, he could look at the bowl anytime he wanted. This is the only one we have been able to buy since we started writing, but surely others are waiting to be found.

"Ribbon" is another of the patterns not uncovered in the west according to dealers who travel those areas. In our trips to California and Seattle, we only see it in booths of dealers from the east. We find more in Ohio and Pennsylvania than any place.

The panel design on pieces that flare at the top expands, as shown by the sugar and creamer in the picture. The normally found "Ribbon" design has evenly spaced small panels. This natural flared expansion is especially noticeable on a belled rim vegetable bowl found in both black and green coloring. We received a letter wondering if that flared bowl was the "Ribbon" pattern because it looked so different. This flared version has been accepted as "Ribbon" for as long as we have been in the business. The 8" bowl with straight sides is pictured here shaped like the berry and cereal and is most certainly true "Ribbon" bowl.

We have never been convinced that shakers exist in green although some found are similar and sold as "Ribbon." Our expectations are that real ones would be Ovide shaped like Cloverleaf with rings near the foot.

		Green	Black				Green	Black
1 ▸	Bowl, 4", berry	35.00			7 ▸	Plate, 6¼", sherbet	4.00	
2 ▸	Bowl, 5", cereal	45.00				Plate, 8", luncheon	7.00	14.00
	Bowl, 8", large berry, flared	35.00	40.00			*Salt and pepper, pair	30.00	45.00
4 ▸	Bowl, 8", straight side	85.00				Saucer	2.00	
3 ▸	Candy dish and cover	55.00			9 ▸	Sherbet, footed	10.00	
6 ▸	Creamer, footed	12.00			5 ▸	Sugar, footed	12.00	
10 ▸	Cup	5.00			8 ▸	Tumbler, 6", 10 ounce	32.00	

* Pink $35.00

RING, "BANDED RINGS," Line #300, Hocking Glass Company, 1927 – 1933

Colors: crystal, crystal w/bands of pink, red, blue, orange, yellow, black, silver, etc.; green, pink, "Mayfair" blue, and Royal Ruby

To be Ring, molded rings have to be in the design — not just applied colored bands on the glass. We are continually receiving e-mails about non listed items. Green "Ring-like" pieces are showing up in the form of goblets and tumblers. These are not old Hocking Ring and will not glow under ultra-violet light as the older green does. (Green glows due to uranium oxide used in the formula for making it. It is not Vaseline which is yellow in color.) The questionable pieces are marked MSE for Martha Stewart Everyday.

Crystal with colored bands interests more collectors than the ever-abundant, unadorned crystal which makes great useable serving ware that is inexpensive. Crystal with platinum (silver) bands is the next favored form of Ring.

There is a predominant colored Ring arrangement of black, yellow, red, and orange in that order, but other assorted arrangements exist. The foot of Ring stems and tumblers are found plain or with a block/grid design like are also found in Mayfair and Princess.

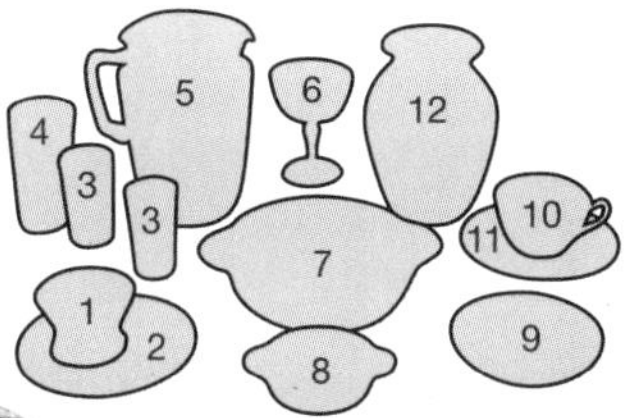

A subscription to Country *Gentleman* in the 1930s gave you a premium of a green Ring berry bowl set consisting of an 8" berry and six 5" berry bowls. Green Ring berry bowls have not been plentiful over the years; so that enticement might have worked better for a woman's magazine than it did a man's.

A Wisconsin collector indicated that pink was a dairy premium in her area. The tumblers were packed with cottage cheese. Pink sets remain plentiful and hard to market in that dairy country according to her.

Royal Ruby and "Mayfair" blue pieces of Ring are occasionally found. Ring moulds had to be brought out of retirement to make those items because production for Ring supposedly ended in 1933 and Royal Ruby was not made until 1938.

		Crystal	Green, Dec.
8 ▸	Bowl, 5", berry, tab handles	4.00	8.00
	Bowl, 7", soup	20.00	35.00
9 ▸	Bowl, 5¼", divided	10.00	35.00
7 ▸	Bowl, 8", large berry, tab handles	7.00	14.00
	Butter tub or ice tub	20.00	35.00
	Cocktail shaker	20.00	30.00
10 ▸	**Cup	6.00	9.00
	Creamer, footed	6.00	10.00
	Decanter and stopper	25.00	40.00
	Goblet, 7¼", 9 ounce	14.00	20.00
	Goblet, 3¾", 3½ ounce, cocktail	12.00	18.00
	Goblet, 4½", 3½ ounce, wine	13.00	20.00
	Ice bucket	20.00	35.00
	Pitcher, 8", 60 ounce	17.50	30.00
5 ▸	*Pitcher, 8½", 80 ounce	22.00	40.00
13 ▸	Pitcher, 9¼", 84 ounce		60.00
	Plate, 6¼", sherbet	2.00	2.50
2 ▸	Plate, 6½", off-center ring	6.00	8.00
	‡Plate, 8", luncheon	4.00	15.00

		Crystal	Green, Dec.
	Plate, 11¼", sandwich	7.00	14.00
	‡‡Salt and pepper, pair, 3"	25.00	55.00
	Sandwich server, center handle	20.00	27.50
11 ▸	Saucer	1.50	2.00
1 ▸	Sherbet, low (for 6½" plate)	8.00	12.00
6 ▸	Sherbet, 4¾", footed	6.50	11.00
	Sugar, footed	6.00	10.00
	Tumbler, 3", 4 ounce	4.00	12.00
3 ▸	Tumbler, 3½", 5 ounce	5.00	12.00
	Tumbler, 4", 8 ounce, old fashioned	12.00	18.00
	Tumbler, 4¼", 9 ounce	4.50	15.00
4 ▸	Tumbler, 4¾", 10 ounce	7.50	13.00
	*Tumbler, 5⅛", 12 ounce	8.00	10.00
	Tumbler, 3½" footed, juice	6.00	10.00
	Tumbler, 5½" footed, water	6.00	18.00
	Tumbler, 6½" footed, iced tea	10.00	22.00
12 ▸	Vase, 8"	15.00	35.00
	Whiskey, 2", 1½ ounce	7.00	15.00

*Also found in pink. Priced as green. **Red $65.00, Blue $45.00 ‡ Red $17.50 ‡‡ Green $55.00

ROCK CRYSTAL, "EARLY AMERICAN ROCK CRYSTAL," McKee Glass Company, 1915 – 1940s and 1920s – 1930s in colors

Colors: four shades of green, aquamarine, Canary yellow, amber, pink and frosted pink, red slag, dark red, red, amberina red, crystal, frosted crystal, crystal with goofus decoration, crystal with gold decoration, amethyst, milk glass, blue frosted or "Jap" blue, and cobalt blue

---

Rock Crystal pieces are not being collected just for themselves any more. Collectors of other patterns are using the variety of pieces found as supplementary items. Vases, cruets, candlesticks, and an abundance of serving pieces are some of the favored items. Serving pieces display extremely well; enjoy using them.

Rock Crystal had the longest manufacturing run of any pattern in this book. It was first produced around 1915 in crystal and marketed as one of their Prescut lines. Prescut was McKee's trademarked name for moulded patterns near the end of the cut glass production era. Early Rock Crystal pieces will be embossed Prescut, inside the piece. All major glass companies designed moulded wares to simulate cut glass when automation became possible and skilled cut workers left the glass shops for the war.

Allegedly, hand-cut wares made for a king's table centuries ago inspired this McKee design. Crystal was made until the early 1940s, so that quarter of a century run makes crystal more available than other colors. Some items were only made for a short time and are not easily found.

Color production ran from the 1920s until the late 1930s. Some Rock Crystal designed pieces had mostly only occurred in earlier pattern or Elegant glass productions rather than Depression glass ones. These include salt dips, syrups, cruets, and egg cups.

Catalogs depicting every piece have never been found and it is likely none exist. As new catalogs were made available, old ones were trashed — usually burned. Colored glassware production years are well documented, but unanticipated pieces still show up. A red syrup pitcher was discovered years ago, but syrup pitchers were supposedly not made during the time red was produced. Evidently an older syrup pitcher mould was revived and used during the red production. Often older moulds were pulled out to experiment with a color being run at that time; according to older glassmakers, as many as 50 pieces would be run to see if the mould was usable. Those short or experimental runs give us some of the rarest and most desirable Depression glassware today.

We bought a large collection of red Rock Crystal from a former McKee employee in the late 1970s. He had eight or nine flat candy bottoms in this lot, which, he explained, were soup bowls. We assume that may have been a method to get rid of excess stock.

A problem with McKee's red is its range of hues. Yellow shows through the red mixture and is called amberina by collectors. Some red is so dark it almost looks black. When we collected red, we tried to match all our pieces to the same medium hue. We did not buy amberina or the red that looked black, so we missed out on some rarer pieces that were only being found in those colors.

Wide assortments of pieces are available; you just need to decide what items you want. Instead of buying every tumbler and stem made, you can select a couple of styles you favor. Even collectors with limited budgets can start a small crystal or amber set. Red will be more of a problem.

We found out the hard way that there are two different sizes of punch bowls. The base for the larger bowl has an opening 5" across, and stands 6¹⁄₁₆" tall. This base fits a punch bowl that is 4³⁄₁₆" across the bottom. The other style base has only a 4³⁄₁₆" opening, but is also 6¹⁄₁₆" tall. This base only fits the bowl that is 3½" across the bottom.

Egg plates are often found with gold trim; they were probably a promotional item in central Florida. We notice quite a few Lazy Susans here each year consisting of a revolving metal stand with a Rock Crystal relish for a top.

		Crystal	All other colors	Red
	*Bonbon, 7½", s.e.	22.00	30.00	50.00
	Bowl, 4", s.e.	12.00	20.00	30.00
24 ▸	Bowl, 4½", s.e.	15.00	20.00	30.00
	**Bowl, 5", finger bowl with 7" plate, p.e.	30.00	38.00	55.00
36 ▸	Bowl, 5½", s.e.	22.00	20.00	40.00
	Bowl, 7", pickle or spoon tray	30.00	35.00	65.00
	Bowl, 7", salad, s.e.	22.00	35.00	65.00
	Bowl, 8", salad, s.e.	25.00	35.00	75.00
	Bowl, 8½", center handle			195.00
23 ▸	Bowl, 9", salad, s.e.	35.00	40.00	110.00
34 ▸	Bowl, 10½", salad, s.e.	25.00	40.00	100.00
	Bowl, 11½", 2-part relish	35.00	40.00	80.00
8 ▸	Bowl, 12", oblong celery or relish	28.00	40.00	75.00
	‡Bowl, 12½", footed center bowl	75.00	110.00	250.00
	Bowl, 12½", 5-part relish	35.00	50.00	
	Bowl, 13", roll tray	30.00	50.00	90.00
	Bowl, 14", 6-part relish	50.00	55.00	
	Butter dish and cover	295.00		
	Butter dish bottom	160.00		
	Butter dish top	135.00		
35 ▸	‡‡Candelabra, 2-lite, pair	25.00	98.00	250.00
25 ▸	Candelabra, 3-lite, pair	30.00	150.00	350.00
	Candlestick, flat, stemmed, pair	35.00	50.00	135.00

Rock Crystal

		Crystal	All other colors	Red
	Candlestick, 5½", low, pair	35.00	50.00	165.00
	Candlestick, 8", tall, pair	75.00	110.00	395.00
3 ▶	Candy and cover, footed, 9¼"	65.00	90.00	295.00
26 ▶	Candy and cover, round	75.00	75.00	225.00
31 ▶	Cake stand, 11", 2¾" high, footed	30.00	35.00	110.00
	Cheese stand, 2¾" and cracker plate, 10¾"	50.00	75.00	125.00
27 ▶	Comport, 7", s.e.	40.00	45.00	80.00
	Comport, 7", p.e.	25.00	28.00	
	Creamer, flat, s.e.	37.50		
	Creamer, 9 oz., footed	15.00	28.00	60.00
	Cruet and stopper, 6 oz., oil	95.00		
11 ▶	Cup, 7 oz.	12.00	22.00	60.00
	Egg plate	35.00		
18 ▶	Goblet, 7½ oz., 8 oz., low footed	17.00	27.50	50.00
17 ▶	Goblet, 11 oz., low footed, iced tea	17.00	30.00	60.00
9 ▶	Ice dish (3 styles)	30.00		
	Jelly, 5", footed, s.e.	25.00	27.50	42.00
	Lamp, electric	295.00	395.00	695.00
7 ▶	Parfait, 3½ oz., low footed	20.00	30.00	60.00
	Pitcher, quart, s.e.	165.00	200.00	
15 ▶	Pitcher, ½ gallon, 7½" high	100.00	100.00	
	Pitcher, 9", large covered	175.00	295.00	895.00
	Pitcher, fancy tankard	195.00	695.00	995.00
5 ▶	Plate, 6", bread and butter, s.e.	6.00	9.50	16.00
14 ▶	Plate, 7½", p.e. & s.e.	8.00	10.00	18.00
30 ▶	Plate, 8½", p.e. & s.e.	12.00	12.50	26.00
29 ▶	Plate, 9", s.e.	15.00	20.00	45.00
28 ▶	Plate, 10½", s.e.	25.00	30.00	65.00
13 ▶	Plate, 10½", dinner, s.e. (large center design)	40.00	60.00	150.00
	Plate, 11½", s.e.	18.00	25.00	60.00
	Punch bowl and stand, 14" (2 styles)	595.00		
	Punch bowl stand only (2 styles)	250.00		
	Salt and pepper (2 styles), pair	70.00	100.00	
	Salt dip	60.00		
	Sandwich server, center-handle	30.00	40.00	110.00
12 ▶	Saucer	6.00	8.50	14.00
19 ▶	Sherbet or egg, 3½ oz., footed	10.00	28.00	40.00
	Sherbet, 6 oz.	10.00	20.00	30.00
	Spooner	45.00		
21 ▶	Stemware, 1 oz., footed, cordial	15.00	35.00	40.00
	Stemware, 2 oz., wine	16.00	28.00	36.00
6 ▶	Stemware, 3 oz., wine	14.00	33.00	40.00
	Stemware, 3½ oz., footed, cocktail	12.00	21.00	35.00
2 ▶	Stemware, 6 oz., footed, champagne	12.00	20.00	30.00
	Stemware, 7 oz.	12.00	25.00	40.00
22 ▶	Stemware, 8 oz., large footed goblet	12.00	20.00	50.00
	Sundae, 6 oz., low footed	10.00	18.00	30.00
	Sugar, 10 oz., open	12.00	20.00	40.00

		Crystal	All other colors	Red
	Sugar lid	33.00	50.00	110.00
1 ▶	Syrup with lid	225.00		895.00
	Tray, 5⅜" x 7⅜", ⅞" high	50.00		
	Tumbler, 2½ oz., whiskey	16.00	25.00	40.00
20 ▶	Tumbler, 5 oz., juice	14.00	22.00	45.00
	Tumbler, 8 oz., old fashioned	18.00	26.00	55.00
16 ▶	Tumbler, 9 oz., concave or straight	20.00	24.00	45.00
10 ▶	Tumbler, 12 oz., concave or straight	25.00	30.00	60.00
4 ▶	Vase, 6", cupped	80.00		
	Vase, cornucopia	100.00	150.00	275.00
32 ▶	Vase, 11", footed	75.00	125.00	195.00

* s.e. McKee designation for scalloped edge   ** p.e. McKee designation for plain edge
‡ Red Slag $350.00; Cobalt $325.00   ‡‡ Cobalt $325.00

"ROMANESQUE," L. E. Smith Glass Company, early 1930s

Colors: black, amber, crystal, pink, yellow, and green

"Romanesque" continues to attract a few collectors through its interesting bejeweled design and shapes. It is a smaller pattern; but more admirers are becoming aware of it through Internet listings and auctions. There were always a few avid collectors, but they were sparsely scattered across the country. We'd sell a piece here and there as we set up at shows. In the last few years, we rarely leave a show with a piece of "Romanesque" remaining. The fan vase used to go incognito as "Romanesque." We were able to buy them reasonably and sell them as fast as we displayed them as long as we placed them with other pieces that pointed out that they were "Romanesque." We should mention that we've recently encountered several collectors of only fan vases. They were looking for some rare and expensive Elegant ones, but several bought our "Romanesque" ones. Unfortunately for dealers, the Internet has exposed an abundance of these vases in green and amber causing the price to drop. That's great for collectors unless they bought them in the $65.00 range and can now add them to their collection for around $20.00. Of course buying another one or two will "average out the costs" as one admirer said.

"Romanesque" seems to be widespread in both green and amber. We concentrated on buying amber which was often found inexpensively. Up to now, we have found plates, candles, ruffled sherbets, two-handled plates, and the bowl part of the console. The yellow being found is a bright, canary yellow that is known as "vaseline" to some collectors. We have only seen bowls and cake stands in black.

Pink "Romanesque" seems to be the seldom seen color. There were some wild prices bandied about on the footed console in that particular color; but that, too, has settled to more reasonable levels.

Flat console bowls have a separate base, usually black, but sometimes amber. The black pattern is on the bottom so it has to be displayed upside down as in our photo to ascertain it is "Romanesque." The plain, octagonal detached base has to be aligned accurately with the bottom of the bowl for it to sit flat. These are still shaky if a little weight is added to one side of the bowl and not the other. A number of companies made bowls during this era, which resided on matched or different colored stands. Usually these type bowls held a glass frog in the center for standing floral arrangements. You may find the bowl separate from the base these days, making it appear something like a turned edge plate. These were originally designed as console sets, having candles at each side, to be used as centerpieces. The stands elevated the bowls for visual appeal. For a while, there was a flurry of activity regarding the stands for bowls.

Snack trays were sold with a sherbet to hold fruit or dessert. An original ad called these a luncheon set. Most company's luncheon sets included plates, cups, and saucers.

	*All colors			*All colors			*All colors
8 ▸ Bowl, 10", footed, 4¼" high	70.00	1 ▸ Plate, 8", octagonal	13.00	9 ▸ Tray, snack	14.00
Bowl, 10½"	40.00	Plate, 8", round	10.00	Sherbet, plain top	10.00
Cake plate, 11½" x 2¾"	40.00	4 ▸ Plate, 10", octagonal	25.00	Sherbet, scalloped top	12.00
3 ▸ Candlestick, 2½", pair	30.00	Plate, 10", octagonal, 3-part	25.00	Vase, 7½", fan	50.00
7 ▸ Plate, 5½", octagonal	7.00	6 ▸ Plate, 10", octagonal, 2-hndl	30.00		
5 ▸ Plate, 7", octagonal	10.00	Powder jar	50.00	* Black or canary add 30%	

194

ROSE CAMEO, Belmont Tumbler Company, 1931

Color: green

Hazel-Atlas supposedly made Rose Cameo, but research revealed the Belmont Tumbler Company had patented it. Talking to some long-time collectors from West Virginia led to some interesting speculation. It seems that several "diggers" at the old Hazel-Atlas factory site found shards of Rose Cameo there. (Did you know some glass collectors engage in archaeological digs for glass?) They felt that although the patent was held by Belmont, it was made at Hazel-Atlas. One even stated that no records existed that showed Belmont ever made any glassware except tumblers. Who now knows, but it is interesting food for thought.

Actually, as we learn more about how the companies lent out their moulds and/or contracted glass runs with other firms, anything is possible. Rather than lose a contract, a company could make some agreement with another who was running the requested color rather than change over vats to run it themselves. A bonded person transferred the valuable moulds between the plants. We talked with a man whose job was just that. He made an average of three runs per week between glass factories. That may be why there are patterns showing up on the mould shapes of another company such as Hazel-Atlas's Florentine turning up on Jeannette's Floral mould.

There are only seven known pieces of Rose Cameo. All three Rose Cameo bowls are difficult to find; but the smaller berry turns up more often than the others. Most collectors are not finding the straight-sided 6" bowl at any price. Rose Cameo is not confusing new collectors as it once did. Cameo, with its dancing girl, and this cameo-encircled rose were often misidentified in the past when we were all learning. A well educated collecting public rarely makes those mistakes today.

There are two styles of tumblers; one flares and one does not. Tumblers abound on Internet auctions; but bowls do not.

3 ▸	Bowl, 4½", berry		15.00
1 ▸	Bowl, 5", cereal		20.00
5 ▸	Bowl, 6", straight sides		30.00
4 ▸	Plate, 7", salad		12.00
6 ▸	Sherbet		12.00
2 ▸	Tumbler, 5", footed (2 styles)		15.00

ROSE POINT BAND, "WATER LILY," "CLEMATIS," Indiana Glass Company, c. 1915

Color: crystal

Rose Point Band's production initially began around 1913, but it was being produced during the Depression era as well due to its long run. We have included it basically because it's appealing and can be found existing alongside Depression wares on flea market and antique mall shelves. Some believe this is much older Pattern glass rather than Depression era. It actually entered the world toward the end of the Pattern glass era and did not exit until our Depression glass years.

Rose Point Band was promoted to dealers as a "sure repeater and money maker" and was their "peerless common sense assortment" of eight dozen pieces. You received a half dozen of sixteen different items. Those did not incorporate the plate, sauce bowl, and small-footed sugar and creamer. The plate and footed sugar shown in our picture were not even included in our Indiana catalog listing; so, there may be other surviving items also. When it was first dispersed, a wholesaler could buy 240 pounds of it for $13.20 and command a net profit of $5.78. Most items were priced from 10¢ to 15¢, though the pitcher was 25¢. These pieces were not as reasonably priced as were some patterns, but it evidently sold well. You can still find this in today's market.

5 ▸	Bowl, sauce, 3 ftd.	8.00
	Bowl, 7½", deep berry	15.00
	Bowl, 7½", footed salad	15.00
	Bowl, 8½", footed fruit	22.50
	Bowl, 9½", footed, fancy	27.50
	Bowl, 10", crimped berry	30.00
	Bowl, 10", orange (flared, straight rim)	30.00
1 ▸	Butter w/cover	40.00
	Compote (footed jelly)	18.00
2 ▸	Compote w/cover, 7½"	28.00
	Creamer, ftd.	12.50

4 ▸	Creamer, flat	12.50
	Cruet (vinegar)	50.00
3 ▸	Goblet, wine	15.00
	Pitcher, ½ gal.	58.00
8 ▸	Plate, 8"	9.00
	Plate, 11¾", ped. foot	30.00
	Spoon (cupped tumbler for spoons)	25.00
3 ▸	Sugar, ftd.	12.50
7 ▸	Sugar w/cover	20.00
	Tray, 8½", footed (flat compote)	22.00
	Vase (celery)	35.00

ROSEMARY, "DUTCH ROSE," Federal Glass Company, 1935 – 1937

Colors: amber, green, pink; some iridized

Rosemary is a charming pattern particularly in green or pink, but unfortunately, most often found in amber. Rosemary's amber is prevalent in Florida, and we rarely see a piece or two — usually a large grouping. We had never heard anybody say they regretted choosing to collect Rosemary except for one frustrated collector searching for pink tumblers and cream soups which remain fairly invisible today. Rosemary's pattern was a redesign of Federal's delightful Mayfair pattern because of Hocking's earlier patent of the Mayfair name. The story of Rosemary's having been redesigned from Federal's Mayfair pattern can be read on page 127.

An amber set can be put together without much difficulty as there are only a few limited items, namely the cereal bowl and tumblers. Other than that, the supply is more than adequate for the market. If you like amber, this would be one set we can recommend as a possibility to gather. One consideration is that you rarely see a chipped piece of Rosemary. You might see it worn and scratched from use, but not chipped. The heavier edges held up over the years.

Pink or green cream soups, cereals, or tumblers are the pieces driving collectors' searches. Pink Rosemary grill plates, oval bowls, and platters can be added to the short supply list. Even searching the Internet, rarely are pink items listed or auctioned. We understand it is exasperating to try to collect a color or pattern that does not seem to appear at any price. If you saw the sad letters we get relating how Depression glass was given away, sold for next to nothing, or plain trashed in their relative's estate, there should be quite a bit more available to the market. In their defense, this colored glass traditionally had little value to people — and perhaps the "throw away generation" started before the current one.

New collectors should know that grill plates are the three-part divided plates usually associated with diners or grills (restaurants) of that time. Food was kept from running together by those raised partitions (normally three). These still work well for people, like Cathy, who do not like their food to run together.

The sugar has no handles and is often misidentified as a sherbet. There is no sherbet.

		Amber	Green	Pink			Amber	Green	Pink
9 ▸	Bowl, 5", berry	3.00	9.00	14.00	5 ▸ Plate, dinner		6.00	15.00	20.00
	Bowl, 5", cream soup	10.00	33.00	48.00	2 ▸ Plate, grill		8.00	20.00	30.00
11 ▸	Bowl, 6", cereal	16.00	35.00	45.00	4 ▸ Platter, 12", oval		12.00	27.00	40.00
10 ▸	Bowl, 10", oval vegetable	12.00	30.00	45.00	8 ▸ Saucer		2.00	5.00	6.00
	Creamer, footed	6.00	12.50	25.00	1 ▸ Sugar, footed		6.00	12.50	25.00
7 ▸	Cup	4.00	9.50	12.00	3 ▸ Tumbler, 4¼", 9 ounce		20.00	35.00	65.00
6 ▸	Plate, 6¾", salad	5.00	8.50	12.00					

197

ROULETTE, "MANY WINDOWS," Hocking Glass Company, 1935 – 1938
Colors: green, pink, and crystal

Roulette is the authenticated name of the pattern which collectors previously referred to as "Many Windows." Those notches around the glass are supposed to remind you of the indentations on a roulette wheel. Was the designer a gambler — or just gambling the design would sell?

Cups, saucers, sherbets, and luncheon plates can only be acquired in green. The 12" sandwich plate and fruit bowls are not so easily unearthed. Most elusive are juice tumblers and the old fashioned. We have not found a green juice in several years. Whiskeys used to sell very well to the shot-glass collecting group that is making its presence known in collecting spheres, but those prices have taken a hit recently. Crystal and pink whiskeys are available with some searching, but green ones are a different story. Crystal tumbler and pitcher sets are more limited in supply; however, there is less demand for the few that have surfaced. Some crystal beverage sets are decorated with colored stripes. In fact, this striped effect gives them an Art Deco appearance that pleases the Deco crowd.

Hocking marketed Roulette as a "winning" pattern. That gamble paid off better than the roulette wheel normally does since so many pitchers, especially pink, are found now. Roulette has six assorted tumblers which were used for promotion with pitchers as beverage sets. Pitchers were packaged with various sizes of tumblers and presented to retailers as advertising baits to lure customers to their stores. Once there for the "bargain" (usually a pitcher and six tumblers for around $1.00), it was up to the shop owner to convince the customer he needed more of his wares. These promotions evidently worked and seemed to be the norm of the time. Pink pitchers and tumblers are easier to find than green ones, but pink Roulette was not made in additional pieces. There are five sizes of pink flat tumblers; but we have never heard of a pink-footed tumbler. Evidently, the green footed tea was used with more of the promotions than other tumblers. Once fairly hard-to-find, they have been removed from that endangered species list due to so many appearing in Internet auctions.

Green Roulette dinnerware was also peddled in these promotions. Sometimes a full luncheon set of 14 or 19 pieces was the bait. It possibly was never retailed as a pattern by itself.

		Crystal	Pink, Green			Crystal	Pink, Green
10 ▸	Bowl, 9", fruit	9.50	25.00		Sherbet	3.50	7.00
1 ▸	Cup	4.00	8.00		Tumbler, 3¼", 5 ounce, juice	7.00	25.00
11 ▸	Pitcher, 8", 65 ounce	32.00	45.00	3 ▸	Tumbler, 3¼", 7½ oz., old fashioned	25.00	45.00
	Plate, 6", sherbet	3.50	5.00	4 ▸	Tumbler, 4⅛", 9 ounce, water	13.00	20.00
6 ▸	Plate, 8½", luncheon	4.00	7.00	5 ▸	Tumbler, 5⅛", 12 ounce, iced tea	16.00	32.00
8 ▸	Plate, 12", sandwich	11.00	16.00		Tumbler, 5½", 10 ounce, footed	14.00	35.00
2 ▸	Saucer	1.50	3.50	9 ▸	Whiskey, 2½", 1½ ounce	14.00	15.00

"ROUND ROBIN," Economy Glass Co., Probably early 1930s
Colors: green, iridescent, and crystal

"Round Robin's" green sherbets and berry bowls are few and far between. We have never found a green berry bowl to photograph. Green saucers seem to be harder to find than cups. A "Round Robin" cup is footed, a style not plentiful in Depression glass. We wonder if the cups may have been advertised without saucers as a stand alone custard. That could explain the foot and lack of green saucers being seen today. Sherbets and berry bowls are plentiful in iridescent, but where are the cups and saucers in this color?

The Domino tray is the expensive, unanticipated piece in this very small pattern. Hocking's Cameo is the only other Depression glass pattern which tendered a sugar cube tray. That tray's name came from the sugar brand that furnished cubes of sugar — Domino®. The indentation in the center of the tray is for a cream pitcher with sugar cubes placed around it. Consequently, having this piece in this small pattern is out of the ordinary. If they were more bountiful, we'd conjecture that they were from a premium contract with the sugar company; but alas, they apparently were not. This tray has only been found in green "Round Robin," and few have ever been displayed at shows. When shown, they have been captured for collections of sugar related items or by a collector of "Round Robin" who is ecstatic to find one.

Some crystal "Round Robin" is found today. Crystal was sprayed and baked to accomplish the iridized look. Obviously, not all the crystal was sprayed, since we find it occasionally.

		Green	Iridescent
1 ▸	Bowl, 4", berry	8.00	7.00
	Bowl, 6¾", 2½", high		15.00
8 ▸	Cup, footed	6.00	7.00
3 ▸	Creamer, footed	11.00	8.00
7 ▸	Domino tray	150.00	
6 ▸	Plate, 6", sherbet	3.50	2.50
5 ▸	Plate, 8", luncheon	7.00	4.00
	Plate, 12", sandwich	12.00	10.00
9 ▸	Saucer	1.00	1.00
4 ▸	Sherbet	10.00	10.00
2 ▸	Sugar	11.00	8.00

ROXANA, Hazel-Atlas Glass Company, 1932

Colors: Golden Topaz, crystal, and some white

Roxana has seven known pieces that are pictured below. We said that in a previous book and a reader wrote to say she had found three more, so now there were ten. We should have said there are seven "different" pieces known; as ex-school teachers we should have been more specific in our writing.

This small pattern was evidently created strictly as promotional ware for a product; thus its shortage of pieces. All are small enough to be placed inside a product, so if that product were nationally distributed there would be more found. We know it was offered in a regional oats promotion. In Star brand oats you received one piece of "Golden Topaz" table glassware in every package. This "Golden Topaz" is what we now call yellow and Roxana was the pattern. We have displayed an ad promoting this offer in previous books. It can now be found in our new *Hazel-Atlas Glass Identification and Value Guide* book. That ad may show why the deep 4½" bowl and the 5½" plates are so hard to find. They were not packed as a premium in those oats. Maybe they were included with some other product. It is improbable such a minute pattern with only small items would have been offered for retail sale. Roxana was produced for only one year by Hazel-Atlas, lending credence to its having been made for promotional products.

Only the 4½" deep bowl has been found in Platonite; if you find any other item in Platonite, please let us know.

		Yellow	White
6 ▸	Bowl, 4½" x 2⅜"	15.00	15.00
4 ▸	Bowl, 5", berry	16.00	
1 ▸	Bowl, 6", cereal	18.00	
2 ▸	Plate, 5½"	9.00	
5 ▸	Plate, 6", sherbet	9.00	
3 ▸	Sherbet, footed	10.00	
7 ▸	Tumbler, 4¼", 9 ounce	22.00	

ROYAL LACE, Hazel-Atlas Glass Company, 1934 – 1941
Colors: cobalt blue, crystal, green, pink; some amethyst (See Reproduction Section.)

Royal Lace collectors have always shown partiality for cobalt blue; but over the years, additional green is finding its way into the market. New collectors noticed its accessibility and lesser price and many are embracing that as their color of choice. Green is found in unheard of amounts in England. Many of these pieces are coming home via Internet selling. English container shipments of furniture used to have glassware added to fill the empty spaces. Today, there are shippers specializing in gathering American glassware and other "smalls" to send back rather than large pieces of furniture. We know of one antique mall owner who receives English shipments regularly and often offers patterns of Depression glass more economically than we can buy it here. Royal Lace, both green and pink, is one pattern he often has for sale.

An abundance of green basic "tea" sets are in England, i.e. cups, saucers, creamers, and sugars. For some reason sugar lids did not seem to appear with the sugar bowls; so, they are still rarely seen. Since the English use sugar cubes, a lid was not necessary for them. The straight-sided pitcher must have been the prevalent style in England as we bought a half dozen or more from a dealer there. It took a while (three years) to sell that many of one form of pitcher. Our contact never found any other style and only water tumblers to go with them. Shakers with original Hazel-Atlas labels declaring "Made in America" were on several sets we purchased. We had never seen that label before — and not since. We speculate that Hazel-Atlas named this pattern purposely for this "royal" market. Almost no blue is found in England, but cobalt was not made until 1938 and may have been too late to ship there due to the early stages of the war.

Royal Lace in cobalt blue remains dear to our hearts because of box loads of it we took and sold at the first Depression glass show we attended in Springfield, Missouri, in 1971. Selling it to dealers and authors alike vastly improved our paltry teaching salaries. Meeting the established authors, Weatherman and Stout, and dealers who would buy glass from us for years made it definitely a worthwhile experience. Weatherman said that the cobalt color for the Royal Lace pattern was something of a stroke of luck according to a factory employee. A cereal contractor cancelled his order for more Shirley Temple cobalt glassware causing Hazel-Atlas to scramble to find something else to use the vats of cobalt glass. Royal Lace was already running so in order to use up tanks of cobalt blue that were on hand, cobalt Royal Lace was born.

There are five different pitchers found in Royal Lace: 48 ounce, straight side; 64 ounce, 8", no ice lip; 68 ounce, 8", w/ice lip; 86 ounce, 8", no ice lip; and 96 ounce, 8½", w/ice lip. The 10-ounce difference in the last two listed is caused by the spout on the pitcher without lip dipping below the top edge of the pitcher. This causes the liquid to run out before you get to the top. All spouted pitchers will vary in ounce capacity (up to 10 ounces) depending upon how the spout tilts or dips. Always measure ounce capacities until no more liquid can be added without running out. The 68-ounce pitcher with ice lip and the 86 ounce without lip may not exist in cobalt blue. A crystal 68 ounce pitcher recently sold for a mind-numbing price to someone who had searched for it for years.

Some cobalt Royal Lace collectors only purchase water tumblers and the straight-sided pitcher for their collections. That style of pitcher with water tumblers is more plentiful and, therefore, more inexpensively priced than any other pitcher or tumbler size. We should point out that "inexpensive" in cobalt Royal Lace may be considered expensive in other patterns.

Be aware that the cookie jar, juice, and water tumblers have been reproduced in a very dark cobalt blue which is quite dull looking in comparison to the older color. These are also out now in pink and green. These new pieces have lots of air bubbles and imperfections in the glass and are easily spotted. Cobalt juice tumbler reproductions are easily distinguished due to color and mould design; however the older juices are now selling for half or less — if they sell at all. After some record breaking prices on Internet auctions, prices are settling down once again to those of years ago.

A rolled-edge console bowl and candlesticks were found in amethyst Royal Lace but are now in separate collections. The only other amethyst pieces known are the sherbets in metal holders and the cookie jar bottom used for toddy sets.

Royal Lace once could be mail ordered from the Sears catalog.

Royal Lace

		Crystal	Pink	Green	Blue
10 ▸	Bowl, 4¾", cream soup	17.50	28.00	32.00	38.00
2 ▸	Bowl, 5", berry	18.00	40.00	50.00	70.00
12 ▸	Bowl, 10", round berry	20.00	28.00	30.00	85.00
	Bowl, 10", 3-legged, straight edge	35.00	65.00	75.00	90.00
	*Bowl, 10", 3-legged, rolled edge	395.00	135.00	145.00	750.00
17 ▸	Bowl, 10", 3-legged, ruffled edge	32.00	75.00	110.00	850.00
3 ▸	Bowl, 11", oval vegetable	28.00	40.00	45.00	70.00
	Butter dish and cover	60.00	225.00	275.00	625.00
	Butter dish bottom	40.00	140.00	180.00	450.00
	Butter dish top	20.00	55.00	95.00	175.00
22 ▸	Candlestick, straight edge, pair	40.00	75.00	95.00	165.00
	**Candlestick, rolled edge, pair	60.00	105.00	150.00	550.00
11 ▸	Candlestick, ruffled edge, pair	50.00	150.00	195.00	575.00
6 ▸	Cookie jar and cover	35.00	65.00	100.00	250.00
21 ▸	Creamer, footed	15.00	16.00	24.00	35.00
19 ▸	Cup	9.00	21.00	20.00	29.00
	Nut bowl	650.00	500.00	500.00	1,695.00
7 ▸	Pitcher, 48 ounce, straight sides	40.00	100.00	135.00	145.00

		Crystal	Pink	Green	Blue
	Pitcher, 64 oz., 8", w/o lip	45.00	90.00	120.00	325.00
	Pitcher, 8", 68 oz., w/lip	350.00	115.00	225.00	
23 ▸	Pitcher, 8", 86 oz., w/o lip		135.00	175.00	
	Pitcher, 8½", 96 oz., w/lip	65.00	150.00	160.00	495.00
	Plate, 6", sherbet	8.00	10.00	12.00	15.00
16 ▸	Plate, 8½", luncheon	8.00	25.00	16.00	30.00
14 ▸	Plate, 9⅞", dinner	15.00	24.00	30.00	44.00
13 ▸	Plate, 9⅞", grill	11.00	25.00	28.00	38.00
18 ▸	Platter, 13", oval	24.00	42.00	42.00	65.00
9 ▸	Salt and pepper, pair	42.00	60.00	140.00	275.00
20 ▸	Saucer	5.00	7.00	10.00	11.00
24 ▸	Sherbet, footed	17.00	20.00	25.00	60.00
1 ▸	‡Sherbet in metal holder	6.00			35.00
5 ▸	Sugar	8.00	15.00	18.00	32.00
4 ▸	Sugar lid	16.00	35.00	55.00	175.00
	Tumbler, 3½", 5 ounce	15.00	33.00	40.00	50.00
8 ▸	Tumbler, 4⅛", 9 ounce	12.00	18.00	28.00	38.00
15 ▸	Tumbler, 4⅞", 10 ounce	60.00	85.00	100.00	150.00
	Tumbler, 5⅜", 12 ounce	55.00	95.00	75.00	110.00
	‡‡Toddy or cider set includes cookie jar, metal lid, metal tray, 8 roly-poly cups, and ladle				295.00

* Amethyst $900.00   ** Amethyst $900.00   ‡ Amethyst $40.00   ‡‡ Amethyst $195.00

ROYAL RUBY, Anchor Hocking Glass Company, 1938 – 1940
Color: Ruby red

Anchor Hocking's Royal Ruby (red) color was patented in 1938 and used their existing moulds of patterns they already had in production. Later on new moulds were designed, but first they needed to ascertain if the color would suit the buyers of their glassware. A diminutive amount of Royal Ruby has been found in Anchor Hocking lines of Colonial, Ring, Manhattan, Queen Mary, Pillar Optic, and Miss America. These Royal Ruby pieces are generally considered rare in these highly collected patterns; and most are of extraordinary quality for Anchor Hocking, having ground bottoms, which are usually not found on their normal mass-produced glassware.

This book categorizes and prices only pieces of Royal Ruby produced before 1940. Royal Ruby pieces made after 1940 are now in *Collectible Glassware from the 40s, 50s, 60s....* Remember, only Anchor Hocking's red can officially be designated Royal Ruby even though many dealers and collectors mistakenly use that term for any red glassware.

Oyster and Pearl, Old Café, Manhattan, Sandwich, and Coronation were among the collectible patterns used in those earliest Royal Ruby productions. There were other numbered lines and designs produced that were never given pattern names. None of those items are priced in the listing below.

We wonder if the name of the color was inspired by our country's fascination with the English coronation of Edward VIII in 1936 and his subsequent renouncing of that royal crown. After all, other American glass companies were so inspired.

	Bonbon, 6½"		8.50		Cup (Old Cafe)	10.00
	Bowl, 3¾", berry (Old Cafe)		9.00	3 ▸	Cup (Ring)	20.00
	Bowl, 4½", handled (Coronation)		8.00		Cup, round	6.00
10 ▸	Bowl, 4⅞", smooth (Sandwich)		12.50	7 ▸	Goblet, ball stem	12.00
	Bowl, 5¼", scalloped (Sandwich)		20.00		Jewel box, 4¼", crystal w/Ruby cover	12.50
9 ▸	Bowl, 5½", 1-handled (Oyster & Pearl)		20.00	8 ▸	Lamp (Old Cafe)	150.00
12 ▸	Bowl, 5½", cereal (Old Cafe)		30.00		Marmalade, 5⅛", crystal w/Ruby cover	7.50
15 ▸	Bowl, 6½", deep-handled (Oyster & Pearl)		22.00		Plate, 9⅛", dinner, round	11.00
	Bowl, 6½", handled (Coronation)		18.00	4 ▸	Plate, 13½", sandwich (Oyster & Pearl)	50.00
	Bowl, 6½", scalloped (Sandwich)		27.50		Puff box, 4⅝", crystal w/Ruby cover	9.00
	Bowl, 8", handled (Coronation)		18.00	5 ▸	Relish tray insert (Manhattan)	4.00
18 ▸	Bowl, 8¼", scalloped (Sandwich)		50.00		Saucer, round	2.50
17 ▸	Bowl, 10½", deep fruit (Oyster & Pearl)		50.00	1 ▸	Sherbet, low footed (Old Cafe)	12.00
	Candle holder, 3½", pair (Oyster & Pearl)		55.00	14 ▸	Sugar, footed	7.50
2 ▸	Candle holder, 4½", pair (Queen Mary)		150.00		Sugar, lid	11.00
16 ▸	Candy dish, 8" mint, low (Old Cafe)		16.00		Tray, 6" x 4½"	12.50
	Candy jar, 5½", crystal w/Ruby cov. (Old Cafe)		25.00	6 ▸	Tumbler, 3", juice (Old Cafe)	20.00
11 ▸	Cigarette box/card holder, 6⅛" x 4", crystal w/Ruby top		50.00		Tumbler, 4", water (Old Cafe)	30.00
13 ▸	Creamer, footed		9.00		Vase, 7¼" (Old Cafe)	55.00
	Cup (Coronation)		6.00		Vase, 9", two styles	17.50

"S" PATTERN, "STIPPLED ROSE BAND," MacBeth-Evans Glass Company, 1930 – 1933

Colors: crystal; crystal w/trims of silver, blue, green, amber; pink; some amber, green, fired-on red; ruby, Monax, and light yellow

"S" Pattern is pretty and was eagerly gathered when Depression glass first became "a happening" in the early '70s. There was real enthusiasm toward it because it came in an assortment of colors and trims, with a couple of styles of pitchers and a 13" cake plate like the much-beloved Dogwood one. A spring vacation trip to Ohio in 1972 brought a sighting of six or seven red "S" Pattern luncheon plates like those of American Sweetheart, but which had never been documented in "S" Pattern. Those sold extremely fast for $70.00 each and people were eager for more. A dozen more could have been sold without any trouble. Since then, we had only seen one other that was priced for $100.00 about 10 years ago. Then two years ago, we came across a group of five and have been unable to sell them for $30.00 each, some 35 years later. The interest in rarely seen red "S" Pattern has waned since no other red pieces were found to go with these luncheon plates. They should sell as "decorative display items" if nothing else.

Times change, as do collectors' interests. Early on, color and unusual pieces were electrifying in the market; but today, collectors shy from big prices for odd colors and unusual pieces unless they are in a major, highly desired pattern. Even then, prices are no longer those of days gone by.

Today, we notice this delicate little pattern, which had a short production run, being disregarded at markets. We found a setting for eight with a platinum band in a mall last summer. It was reasonably priced and after photographing one of each piece for this book, we priced it and put it out for sale. Everything left except one luncheon plate. It sold because it was inexpensive, displays beautifully, and is striking as a table setting. But mostly, it was priced cheaply. Beginning collectors have to start some place and many show dealers have forgotten that and are still pricing in the stratospheres known 10 years ago.

Amber-, blue-, and green-banded crystal was produced. These are more popular with collectors than plain crystal items, but are harder to find.

Amber "S" Pattern often appears more yellow than amber. The color is almost as varied as that of Hocking's Princess. A dinner plate does exist in amber "S" Pattern and the amber pitcher in this pattern is rare, but there is little demand for it now. No crystal (nor crystal with trim) dinner plates have been spotted.

Pink or green pitcher and tumbler sets appear occasionally. The only pink or green tumblers found in "S" Pattern have an applied, silk-screened "S" Pattern design on the glass like those of Dogwood. Years ago, there were a number of pitcher collectors per se; rare pitchers sold fast in the $200.00 – 500.00 range. Now, those same pitchers are establishing four-figure prices, but, alas, not those of "S" Pattern which find little interest. We once were privileged to view a vast pitcher collection in custom lighted cases as walls of a den. Talk about a spectacular and awesome surrounding.

Finding a pink tumbler that has a moulded blossom design will indicate a Dogwood moulded tumbler and not "S" Pattern. However, crystal tumblers are found with moulded "S" Pattern designs.

		Crystal	Yellow, Amber, Crystal w/Trim			Crystal	Yellow, Amber, Crystal w/Trim
7 ▶	*Bowl, 5½", cereal	5.00	9.00	5 ▶	Plate, grill	6.50	9.00
	Bowl, 8½", large berry	15.00	20.00		Plate, 11¾", heavy cake	60.00	75.00
9 ▶	*Creamer, thick or thin	6.00	7.00		‡Plate, 13", heavy cake	75.00	95.00
10 ▶	*Cup, thick or thin	3.50	5.00	11 ▶	Saucer	2.00	2.50
	Pitcher, 80 ounce (like Dogwood), green or pink $550.00	60.00	160.00	2 ▶	Sherbet, low footed	4.50	7.00
				8 ▶	*Sugar, thick and thin	6.00	6.50
	Pitcher, 80 ounce (like American Sweetheart)	95.00		3 ▶	Tumbler, 3½", 5 ounce	5.00	8.00
					Tumbler, 4", 9 ounce, green or pink $50.00	9.00	10.00
6 ▶	Plate, 6", sherbet, Monax 8.00	2.50	3.00	1 ▶	Tumbler, 4¾, 10 ounce	10.00	12.00
4 ▶	**Plate, 8¼", luncheon	7.00	7.00		Tumbler, 5", 12 ounce	12.00	16.00
	Plate, 9¼", dinner		10.00				

* Fired-on red items will run approximately twice price of amber   ** Red $40.00; Monax $10.00   ‡ Amber $77.50

SANDWICH, Indiana Glass Company, 1920s – 1980s

Colors: crystal late 1920s – today; teal blue 1950s – 1980s; milk white mid-1950s; amber late 1920s – 1980s; red 1933, 1970s; Smokey Blue 1976 – 1977; pink, green 1920s – early 1930s

Now that Indiana Glass has closed, perhaps there will be collectors for their later made Tiara Sandwich lines. There are speculators out there who certainly hope so. At a large glassware auction in Cincinnati last fall, a huge Tiara Sandwich collection of over 1,000 amber pieces averaged around $2.00 each. Many items sold for 25¢ and 50¢ and some lots brought even less. The highest price we heard was $25.00 for a canister set and that was a dealer hoping to sell it for more.

Ever since green Indiana Sandwich was selected by the editorial staff at Collector Books for the cover of our *Pocket Guide to Depression Glass, 12th Edition*, we have been inundated with calls and letters from people who think they have old Indiana Sandwich and are willing to sell it. If you have any piece that is not priced under the Pink/Green column below, you actually have Tiara's 1980s version called Chantilly. You can test your green with an ultraviolet (black) light against old which will glow vividly under that light. Understand, this is not a general test for age of glass. There is glass made yesterday which will fluoresce under black light. It is a test for old green Sandwich vs. new Tiara Chantilly pattern. Indiana also made a lighter pink in recent years.

Realize that the majority of amber found today is from the Tiara issues and is not Depression-era glass. Early amber Sandwich was very light in color. There is no easy way to distinguish old crystal from new as most of the newly made was from Indiana's original moulds.

Only six items in red Sandwich can be dated from 1933, i.e., cups, saucers, luncheon plates, water goblets, creamers, and sugars. Tiara's Sandwich is more amberina than red; today, there is little pricing difference for red unless you have some marked 1933 Chicago World's Fair, which will command considerably more as guaranteed old and as a World's Fair collectible.

		Amber, Crystal	Teal Blue	Red	Pink, Green
4 ▸	Ashtrays (club, spade, heart, diamond shapes, each)	2.50			
	Basket, 10" high	30.00			
	Bowl, 4¼", berry	3.50			
	Bowl, 6"	4.00			
7 ▸	Bowl, 6", hexagonal	4.00	12.00		
12 ▸	Bowl, 8½"	11.00			
11 ▸	Bowl, 9", console	16.00			40.00
	Bowl, 11½", console	18.50			50.00
	Butter dish and cover, domed	22.00	*155.00		
	Butter dish bottom	6.00	42.50		
	Butter dish top	16.00	112.50		
10 ▸	Candlesticks, 3½", pair	14.00			45.00
	Candlesticks 7", pair	25.00			
	Creamer	9.00		45.00	
9 ▸	Celery, 10½"	16.00			
6 ▸	Creamer and sugar on diamond shaped tray	15.00	30.00		
	Cruet, 6½ oz., and stopper	26.00	135.00		175.00
1 ▸	Cup		3.50	8.50	27.50
	Decanter and stopper	25.00		80.00	150.00
2 ▸	Goblet, 9 oz.	13.00		45.00	

		Amber, Crystal	Teal Blue	Red	Pink, Green
8 ▸	Mayonnaise, footed, 3 pc.	18.00			40.00
	Pitcher, 68 oz.	20.00		130.00	
	Plate, 6", sherbet	2.00	7.00		
	Plate, 7", bread and butter	3.00			
	Plate, 8", oval, indent for cup	4.00			15.00
3 ▸	Plate, 8⅜", luncheon	4.00		20.00	
	Plate, 10½", dinner	7.00			20.00
	Plate, 13", sandwich	12.00	24.00	35.00	25.00
	Puff box	16.00			
	Salt and pepper, pair	15.00			
	Sandwich server, center	16.00		45.00	35.00
	Saucer	2.00	4.50	7.50	
	Sherbet, 3¼"	5.50	14.00		
	Sugar, large	9.00		45.00	
	Sugar lid for large size	12.00			
	Tumbler, 3 oz., footed, cocktail	6.00			
	Tumbler, 8 oz., footed, water	9.00			
	Tumbler, 12 oz., footed, iced tea	10.00			
	Wine, 3", 4 oz.	6.00		12.50	25.00

*Beware recent vintage sell $22.00

SHARON, "CABBAGE ROSE," Federal Glass Company, 1935 – 1939
Colors: pink, green, amber; some crystal (See Reproduction Section.)

Sharon was one of the most widely distributed patterns in Depression glass and if you don't believe it, go to an Internet auction and search for it under glass. There have been over 700 auctions in the last three weeks or an average of around three dozen a day. With all that available, prices have plunged for amber and have tumbled quite a bit for pink and green. Facts are facts, no matter how you say it; there is an oversupply of Sharon on the market now. Basic dinnerware including cups, saucers, creamers, sugars, sherbets, and dinner or sherbet plates have taken the hardest hit; do realize you can find these at bargain prices now; it's time to stock up.

New collectors were apprehensive about starting this extremely popular pink pattern a few years ago due to some reproductions flooding markets. However, once everyone learned how to recognize them (see the reproduction section), demand for this durable, 70-year-old pattern flourished once again. Then the latest economic uncertainties hit and collecting has slowed and prices simply followed. This, too, shall pass.

In the last few books, we pictured an old advertising page where coupons from some product could be redeemed for an assortment of items of Federal's "Golden Glow" (amber) glassware. In that ad was a plain pitcher (without design) in the shape of Sharon made by Federal; that is not Sharon. As with all patterns in this book, if the pattern is not on the piece, it is only moulded like the item and not the pattern itself. We understand some of these have been presented as Sharon.

Green Sharon pitchers and tumblers in all sizes are difficult to find, but few are looking for them; so price can likely be negotiated if you see them. You will find thick or thin flat iced teas and waters. The thick tumblers are easier to find in green; and the price reflects that. At that first Depression show in 1971, a collector paid $20.00 for a green Sharon pitcher and everyone thought he had lost a few marbles on his way there. A few years later, he was thought a very smart man. Things changed. Amber and pink heavy iced teas are more rarely seen than the waters. Those differences do not mean as much today as they once did, as most collectors are happy to find any tumbler.

Footed amber tumblers in Sharon are rare and amber pitchers with ice lips are twice as difficult to locate as pink. However fewer collectors for amber translate into fewer dollars being supported by the market. Demand drives prices.

Cathy's grandmother told her she remembered the drummer who came around selling Sharon put a plate on the floor upside down and stood on it to show how sturdy this ware was. Someone tried that feat and it didn't work for him as it shattered. Wonder if anyone else tried that? Don't!

The price for a pink Sharon cheese dish has entered four figures, and that fact alone stopped many potential owners. The top for the cheese and butter dish is the same piece. The bottoms are different. The butter bottom is a 1½" deep bowl with a sloping, indented ledge while the cheese bottom is a flat salad plate with a raised band of glass on its surface within which the lid rests. Obviously, the bottom piece is the rare part of this cheese.

Amber cheese dishes were made; but none has ever surfaced in green except as a reproduction. A collector told me he'd found an old ad showing these were a special promotion item run for some cheese products. It would appear no one much wanted the product, else more of these dishes would have been produced and we wouldn't have such a scarcity of them, today. The jam dish is like the butter bottom except it has no indentation for the top. It differs from the 1⅞" deep soup bowl by standing only 1½" tall. There are no green soup bowls, only jam dishes. It's the pink jam dish that is rarely found.

206

		Amber	Pink	Green
20 ▸	Bowl, 5", berry	7.00	11.00	16.00
18 ▸	Bowl, 5", cream soup	20.00	38.00	50.00
4 ▸	Bowl, 6", cereal	16.00	20.00	30.00
	Bowl, 7¾", flat soup, 1⅞" deep	45.00	45.00	
17 ▸	Bowl, 8½", large berry	5.00	28.00	35.00
2 ▸	Bowl, 9½", oval vegetable	16.00	24.00	33.00
11 ▸	Bowl, 10½", fruit	20.00	34.00	40.00
16 ▸	Butter dish and cover	35.00	40.00	75.00
	Butter dish bottom	15.00	22.00	40.00
	Butter dish top	20.00	20.00	35.00
7 ▸	*Cake plate, 11½", footed	25.00	40.00	65.00
5 ▸	Candy jar and cover	40.00	45.00	160.00
	Cheese dish and cover	195.00	1,750.00	
12 ▸	Creamer, footed	10.00	15.00	18.00
1 ▸	Cup	6.00	10.00	18.00
6 ▸	Jam dish, 7½"	30.00	250.00	60.00

		Amber	Pink	Green
6 ▸	Pitcher, 80 oz., w/ice lip	135.00	195.00	450.00
13 ▸	Pitcher, 80 oz., w/o ice lip	140.00	185.00	475.00
9 ▸	Plate, 6", bread and butter	3.00	6.00	7.00
10 ▸	**Plate, 7½", salad	12.00	18.00	22.00
8 ▸	Plate, 9½", dinner	10.00	15.00	22.00
3 ▸	Platter, 12½", oval	16.00	24.00	28.00
11 ▸	Salt and pepper, pair	30.00	40.00	60.00
	Saucer	4.00	6.00	10.00
5 ▸	Sherbet, footed	9.00	13.00	35.00
15 ▸	Sugar	8.00	12.00	16.00
14 ▸	Sugar lid	22.00	32.00	40.00
25 ▸	Tumbler, 4⅛", 9 oz., thick	24.00	35.00	75.00
21 ▸	Tumbler, 4⅛", 9 oz., thin	24.00	35.00	80.00
24 ▸	Tumbler, 5¼", 12 oz., thin	50.00	40.00	100.00
	Tumbler, 5¼", 12 oz., thick	60.00	90.00	100.00
22 ▸	‡Tumbler, 6½", 15 oz., footed	60.00	45.00	

*Crystal $10.00   **Crystal $50.00   ‡ Crystal $20.00

"SHIPS" or "SAILBOAT" also known as "SPORTSMAN SERIES,"

Hazel-Atlas Glass Company, Late 1930s

Colors: cobalt blue w/white, yellow, and red decoration, crystal w/blue

Mint condition Moderntone cobalt blue decorated with white "Ships" is becoming a thing of the past. You can find it out there for sale, but the ships are faded, badly worn, discolored, or almost missing. Wish we had a nickel for every time we have heard, "It is mint, except…" or "It is just like the one in the book, except…!" There are no exceptions to mint condition — it is as simple as it either is or is not. Some collectors are picky and will not settle for less than mint. Admittedly, they don't get to buy as much that way and they may pay higher prices, but they are happier to find mint pieces. When the "Ships" pattern is partially missing, it would be easier to sell if the whole ship had sunk, and you only had a cobalt blue Moderntone piece left.

Prices have held for hard-to-find mint pieces, but tumblers and pitcher supplies are greater than demand. "Ships" decorated sherbet plates are harder to find than dinner plates, but both have evaporated into early collections. There is no Moderntone cup with a "Ships" decoration that fits the saucer, which does have a "Ships" motif. The cup is just a common Moderntone cup. A design on the bottom of the cup would have interfered with seeing the ship on the saucer.

The shadowy "Ships" shot glass is the smallest (2¼", two ounce) tumbler, not the heavy bottomed tumbler that holds four ounces and is 3¼" tall. We still receive an occasional letter from someone who purchased this four-ounce tumbler under the notion it was a shot glass. We have been preaching this is not a shot glass for at least 20 years. The four-ounce heavy bottomed tumbler was sold as a liquor tumbler with the cocktail shaker, but never as the shot. No shot glass ever holds more than two ounces according to some of my drinking friends. There is a large price difference between the authentic, two ounce shot and the four-ounce tumbler. The price for that four-ounce tumbler is finally going down, perhaps due to its lack of sales as the supposed shot glass.

At least one yellow (mustard) "Ships" old-fashioned tumbler has surfaced. We enjoyed finding the decorations that have the red boats with white sails on blue. So far, only pitchers and three sizes of tumblers have been forthcoming with this patriotic red, white, and blue combination.

We should mention that no red glass pitcher has ever been found to go with the red glass, cylinder shaped "ships" tumblers ($8.00 – 10.00) often found in the markets.

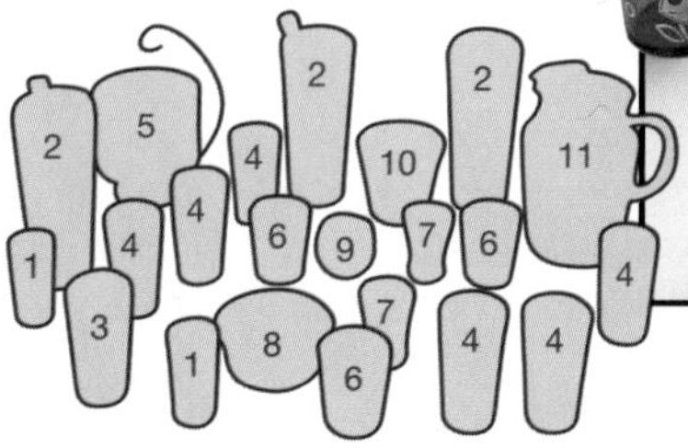

			Blue, White				Blue, White
8 ▸	Bowl, 6", white rings		20.00		Tumbler, 2 oz., 2¼", shot glass		200.00
18 ▸	Cup (Plain), Moderntone		10.00		Tumbler, 3½", whiskey		25.00
	Cocktail mixer w/stirrer		35.00	7 ▸	Tumbler, 4 oz., 3¼", heavy bottom		25.00
2 ▸	Cocktail shaker		40.00	1 ▸	Tumbler, 5 oz., 3¾", juice		16.00
5 ▸	Ice bowl		40.00	9 ▸	Tumbler, 6 ounce, roly poly		14.00
10 ▸	Ice tub		35.00	6 ▸	Tumbler, 8 oz., 3⅜", old fashioned		20.00
	Pitcher w/o lip, 82 ounce		65.00	14 ▸	Tumbler, 9 oz., 3¾", straight, hi-ball		16.00
11 ▸	Pitcher w/lip, 86 ounce		70.00	20 ▸	Tumbler, 9 oz., 4⅝", water		13.00
13 ▸	Plate, 5⅞", sherbet		30.00	4 ▸	Tumbler, 10½ oz., 4⅞", iced tea		16.00
15 ▸	Plate, 8", salad		30.00	3 ▸	Tumbler, 12 oz., iced tea		28.00
16 ▸	Plate, 9", dinner		40.00		Tumbler, 15 oz.		45.00
	Saucer		20.00				

"Go-with" accessories

"Go-with" accessories

SIERRA, "PINWHEEL," Jeannette Glass Company, 1931 – 1933
Colors: green, pink, and some Ultra Marine and Delphite

Jeannette's Sierra is aptly named as the word of Spanish origin means saw or sawtooth. This pleasing 1930s Jeannette glassware had been called "Pinwheel" by old-time collectors. Those pointed edges are quickly noticed, but also easily broken or chipped. Collectors are enamored by it though it is now all but fading from the market in both colors. Pink and green pitchers, tumblers, and oval vegetable bowls are safely tucked into collections and few are being offered for sale. We looked at an oval vegetable bowl in a mall, recently, only to notice one of the points was missing. However, it was priced as if it were all there. It will be difficult to get a collector to pay mint price when it is definitely not. If you are going to pay over $100.00 for an item, we suspect you'll inspect it thoroughly. Why price something with an obvious flaw as if it were perfect? If pieces were much used, one or more of those points is usually chipped or nicked. Many times these chips are underneath the point, so look there also.

Always examine any pink Sierra butter dishes to check for the Adam/Sierra combination lid. That is how our first one was discovered. Be sure to read about this elusive and pricey butter under Adam.

Incorrect cups are often placed on Sierra saucers. Any pink cup of nondescript origin can be found atop the saucers. Note that original cups have the design on the cup without the serrated rim. You would have a superlative dribble cup if the rim were sawtoothed. Cups, pitchers, and tumblers all have smooth, not serrated, edges. Therefore, they do not chip as easily, but that does not make the pitcher and tumblers any easier to find.

Mint sugar bowls are harder to acquire than lids because of the points on the bowl. Years ago, lids were priced higher than the bowls, but times have changed. There have been at least four Sierra Ultra Marine cups found, but no saucer has been reported. Were these a sample run made at Jeannette when they made Ultra Marine Doric and Pansy or Swirl?

		Pink	Green			Pink	Green
11 ▸	Bowl, 5½", cereal	14.00	15.00	3 ▸	Platter, 11", oval	35.00	65.00
13 ▸	Bowl, 8½", large berry	32.00	35.00		Salt and pepper, pair	38.00	38.00
12 ▸	Bowl, 9¼", oval vegetable	100.00	125.00	2 ▸	Saucer	8.00	9.00
10 ▸	Butter dish and cover	75.00	80.00	7 ▸	Serving tray, 10¼", 2 handles	22.00	20.00
6 ▸	Creamer	20.00	25.00	8 ▸	Sugar	25.00	30.00
1 ▸	Cup	14.00	14.00	9 ▸	Sugar cover	20.00	20.00
5 ▸	Pitcher, 6½", 32 ounce	125.00	150.00	4 ▸	Tumbler, 4½", 9 ounce, footed	65.00	90.00
14 ▸	Plate, 9", dinner	20.00	25.00				

SPIRAL, Hocking Glass Company, 1928 – 1930
Colors: green, crystal, and pink and fired-on red

Hocking's Spiral is one of the abundant spiraling patterns from the Depression era which had their origins in older, pattern glass lines. Almost every company made some sort of a spiraling design from elegant to klutzy styles. A few pieces of Hocking Spiral have turned up in crystal. At this stage of collecting, we are removing pink from our color list even though it's mentioned in an old catalog. We have asked for 10 years to "show us a piece" and no one has. Do not confuse the new pink swirling pattern marked "made in France" as Spiral or any other Depression glass. It is *newly* made, and not close to Depression glass as it is so often branded by sellers. First of all, to be Depression glass as we know it, it has to be *made in North America*.

A genuine obstacle lies in identification of Hocking's Spiral among the others produced during this period. First, observe the shape. Most pieces of Hocking's Spiral, the ice tub, platter, cake plate, creamer, and sugar, are shaped like their popular Cameo and Block Optic counterparts. The seldom seen platter has closed or tab handles, as do many oval platters made by Hocking. There is a 5¾" vase shaped like Cameo's footed one. It can be found iridized with a green foot (pictured) or as part of Hocking's Rainbow line. We have found a Spiral one in Tangerine; so watch for other possible colors. Rainbow's being opaque colored, makes you have to look inside it to see the spirals.

A Spiral luncheon set can be put together quite inexpensively when compared to other Depression patterns. Spiral is not a pattern often offered for sale at glass shows; you may have to ask the dealer for it; but it abounds on the Internet. However, at a show, you will probably buy it more economically from someone who actually knows what the pattern really is.

The Hocking Spiral center-handled server has a solid handle while its confusing Imperial Glass Company counterpart, Twisted Optic (Line #313), has an open handle. The Spiral pitcher shown has the rope top treatment like those found in Cameo and Block Optic. There is also a 7⅝", 54-ounce bulbous based one (like shown in Block Optic) available with the Spiral pattern.

There are two styles of sugars and creamers found in Spiral, one a flat utilitarian style, like the Block Optic flat style; and one is footed with a fancier handle, like Cameo. Generally speaking, Hocking's Spiral swirls go to the left or clockwise while Imperial's Twisted Optic spirals go to the right or counterclockwise. (Westmoreland's #1710 Spiral line and Duncan's Spiral Flutes have hand-polished bottoms on flat pieces, something not found on Hocking's machine-made Spiral.) Those items most confused with Hocking Spiral all have different shapes from the Hocking line.

You might find a footed cake plate with an embossed ad for White Lily flour around the edge which tickles those looking for advertising items. There are several Depression items that have embossed product names, but not many. In other glass collecting fraternities, advertising pieces are expensive — but usually not in Depression glass.

		Green
	Bowl, 4¾", berry	6.00
	Bowl, 7", mixing	12.00
	Bowl, 8", large berry	12.00
	Cake plate	18.00
1 ▸	Creamer, flat or footed	10.00
13 ▸	Cup	6.00
9 ▸	Ice or butter tub	20.00
11 ▸	Pitcher, 7⅝", 54 ounce, bulbous	40.00
	Pitcher, 7⅝", 58 ounce	35.00
7 ▸	Plate, 6", sherbet	2.00
8 ▸	Plate, 8", luncheon	3.50

		Green
4 ▸	Platter, 12"	35.00
5 ▸	Preserve and cover	28.00
	Salt and pepper, pair	35.00
12 ▸	Sandwich server, center handle	22.00
14 ▸	Saucer	2.00
3 ▸	Sherbet	5.00
2 ▸	Sugar, flat or footed	10.00
	Tumbler, 3", 5 ounce, juice	4.50
	Tumbler, 5", 9 ounce, water	10.00
10 ▸	Tumbler, 5⅞", footed	18.00
6 ▸	Vase, 5¾", footed	75.00

SPRINGTIME, Monongah Glass Company, c. 1927
Color: crystal w/24-karat gold band decoration

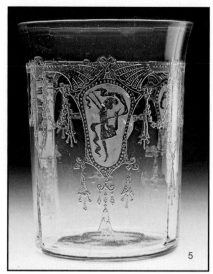

Monongah, who publicized themselves as "pioneers in the manufacture of the automatic machine pressed tumbler," was bought by Hocking; and their Springtime apparently was the inspiration for Hocking's extremely admired Cameo pattern. Springtime etching was applied by hand. The Cameo pattern was transformed to an automatic mould process by Hocking and a Depression glass star was born.

Springtime was only made in crystal, and most often with a 24-karat gold band trim. Eighty years later, that gold trim is generally missing from pieces you notice. Gold is particularly vulnerable to modern dishwater treatment. Lemon enhanced soaps will remove the gold or make it disappear a little at a time.

Springtime mould blanks have an optic rib effect, often found in older wares, but it is very faint. You find Springtime only occasionally; so we would suggest that you buy whatever crosses your path if you wish to collect this lovely older design. Usually, the price is inexpensive since it often goes unrecognized. However, since including Springtime in our book, recognition has increased and there may not be as many bargains as in the past. If you do find some bargains, when you see an expensive piece, the prices will average out in the long run.

	Bowl, finger	40.00		Stem, 5½ oz., parfait	35.00
	Creamer	35.00		Stem, 5½ oz., high sherbet	15.00
	Decanter, 26 oz., w/cut facet stop	125.00		Stem, 5½ oz., low sherbet	15.00
	Pitcher, 30 oz., juice w/lid	100.00	3 ▸	Stem, 9 oz., goblet	22.00
	Pitcher, 50 oz., water, straight rim	135.00		Stem, 6" confection stand (compote)	26.00
	Pitcher, 50 oz., tea w/lid	195.00		Sugar, open	35.00
	Pitcher, 60 oz., water, slope rim	165.00	7 ▸	Tumbler, 2½ oz., whiskey	65.00
	Plate, 6½"	6.00	6 ▸	Tumbler, 5 oz., juice	35.00
4 ▸	Plate, 8½", luncheon	16.00		Tumbler, 7 oz., ginger ale	35.00
1 ▸	Stem, ¾ oz., brandy cordial	100.00		Tumbler, 8 oz., water	30.00
	Stem, 1½ oz., ftd., almond	30.00	5 ▸	Tumbler, 9 oz., water	30.00
2 ▸	Stem, 2½ oz., wine	25.00		Tumbler, 10 oz., tea	35.00
	Stem, 2½ oz., cocktail	25.00		Tumbler, 13 oz., hdld. ice tea	70.00
	Stem, 4 oz., claret	35.00		Tumbler, 13 oz., tea	50.00

* Deduct 10% – 20% for missing gold trim

SQUARE, "HAZEN," Line #760 et al., Imperial Glass Company, c. 1930s

Colors: crystal, green, pink, ruby, cobalt

Imperial's Square pattern was issued as Line #760 in their catalogs, but has been called "Hazen," a name designated by an earlier author who named patterns. It is an attractive small line which was presented in luncheon sets having 15, 21, or 27 pieces. Imperial also used it as a blank for some of their etchings. We found a partial red set, consisting of 19 pieces, in an antique mall. The owner had no idea what it was, but priced it as if it were gold. When we first saw the price, we left it; but Cathy went back and bought it for the book while I was out of town. The unusual style handles and rich, ruby coloring are truly captivating in Square.

It is often not feasible to purchase red, cobalt blue, black, or older canary glass from sellers who have no clue what they have. Color is routinely highly priced, and frequently inflated because the sellers think that their glass might be rare because they heard red and blue are "good." Instead of researching or finding out, they price it high and hope for a prospect to come along less informed than they. Sometimes it works, but often their nondescript glass sits and gathers dust and they then complain to anyone who will listen that their wares are not selling.

As an example, we looked at a piece of emerald green Cambridge at a flea market searching for a price sticker. The owner informed us that it was an old piece of "vaseline" and he only wanted $125.00 (for that $20.00 item on a very good day). I told him it was Cambridge emerald green and was told again it was rare old "vaseline." No form of green is "vaseline" even if it does glow under an ultraviolet light. "Vaseline" was a term used by collectors for vibrant yellow colored glassware. Today this is emphasized by showing "vaseline" glowing under an ultraviolet light. Some green colors will also glow due to uranium oxide content of the glass formula, but that does not make it "vaseline" yellow. Our experience has shown that you cannot explain anything to oblivious sellers who already know more than you do. Just watch for their mistakes in pricing; they will make some.

We are finding red Square, but are having difficulty picking up other colors. The only green item we have noticed is the green cup pictured for which we have been unable to obtain a saucer. We did see a cobalt blue creamer and sugar priced for $125.00 for the pair, but left them in Pennsylvania for someone who valued them more than we.

		Crystal, Pink, Green	Ruby, Cobalt			Crystal, Pink, Green	Ruby, Cobalt
	Bowl, 4½", nappy	12.00	20.00	4 ▸	Plate, 8", salad	12.00	18.00
	Bowl, 7", square, soup/salad	18.00	25.00	3 ▸	Saucer	4.00	8.00
5 ▸	Creamer, footed	28.00	28.00	1 ▸	Server, 10½", center handled	35.00	50.00
2 ▸	Cup	15.00	25.00		Shaker, square, foot, pair	40.00	70.00
	Plate, 6", dessert	6.00	9.00	6 ▸	Sugar, footed	25.00	28.00

STARLIGHT, Hazel-Atlas Glass Company, 1938 – 1940

Colors: crystal, pink; some white, cobalt

Starlight is not lighting up the night for collectors as it once did. Even though it is another inexpensively priced pattern, the hurdle lies in gaining it. Starlight has never been accumulated by large numbers of collectors, but the ones who have tried have reported that shortages of sherbets and cereals are alleviated now using Internet auctions; but finding either the 11½" or 12" large bowls and 13" liner/serving plate are still proving to be quite a task.

A large salad bowl, with an added metal base and rim, make up a small punch or cider set. This set is similar to the Royal Lace toddy set, having a bowl in a metal holder with an extending flat rim being big enough to hold a dozen cups. A metal ladle with a red knob lies in the bowl to complete it. This was not a production of Hazel-Atlas, but of some other company who bought the glass and added their own paraphernalia to it. Companies buying wares for enhancement was a standard practice at this time, and Hazel-Atlas provided a number of patterns that are found with metal accoutrements today.

Pink and cobalt blue bowls make nice companion pieces with crystal, but only bowls are available in those colors.

The 5½" cereal is tab handled, as are all Starlight bowls, and measures 6" including the handles. Measurements in this book do not normally include handles, unless specified.

Shakers are the most familiar items in Starlight. We see them regularly in Florida and finally found out why there are so many here after discovering an original boxed set sold as a souvenir. The tops were specifically calculated to keep the salt "moisture proof." Labeled Airko (for the top) shakers with these tops are often found in southern areas where the humid air caused shaker holes to clog. One of these moisture-proof shakers is pictured here with an original label. They must have worked as they obviously sold well here.

		Crystal, White	Pink				Crystal, White	Pink
10 ▶	Bowl, 5½", cereal, closed handles	8.00	12.00	1 ▶	Plate, 9", dinner		8.00	
12 ▶	*Bowl, 8½", closed handles	12.00	20.00	4 ▶	Plate, 13", sandwich		15.00	18.00
13 ▶	Bowl, 11½", salad	25.00		6 ▶	Relish dish		12.00	
	Bowl, 12", 2¾" deep	35.00		3 ▶	Salt and pepper, pair		25.00	
11 ▶	Creamer, oval	6.00		9 ▶	Saucer		2.00	
8 ▶	Cup	5.00		2 ▶	Sherbet		15.00	
5 ▶	Plate, 6", bread and butter	2.00		7 ▶	Sugar, oval		6.00	
	Plate, 8½", luncheon	5.00			* Cobalt $30.00			

STRAWBERRY, U.S. Glass Company, Early 1930s

Colors: pink, green, crystal; some iridized

Collectible Depression glass patterns that U.S. Glass made are often reminiscent of earlier pattern glassware designs of the late 1890s and early 1900s. We realize that even more after just releasing our new book *American Pattern Glass Table Sets* book. To some degree, the Strawberry pattern itself, is a reversion to pattern glass. New styles and newly designed glassmaking equipment were emerging that left the heavier, bulkier, roughly moulded glass behind. Even pieces that are acknowledged as mint may have extra glass burrs on seams where it came out of the mould. However, Strawberry and its sister pattern, Cherryberry, are noticed by today's collectors despite those earlier shortcomings. This shows a certain ageless, continuity of appreciation, which is nice to see. Strawberry, particularly, is regularly requested at every show we do.

Crystal and iridescent pitchers are rarely on the market today as old-time collectors have held onto the meager supply. It was not necessarily Strawberry collectors who plucked them, but pitcher and carnival collectors. Treasured iridescent Strawberry pitchers and tumblers are more highly regarded by carnival collectors than Depression glass admirers. By that, we mean they will "shell out" more for them. However, a problem persists which makes carnival collectors leave pitchers sitting. If the iridescent color fades anyplace or goes toward crystal, they will not consider buying it. The pitcher or tumbler has to have full, vivid color to be considered by them at all. This intolerance carries over somewhat with Depression glass collectors who also want strong color. Crystal is priced with iridescent because it is, definitely, rare. Only two or three crystal pitchers have ever been seen and those probably exist because they were fugitives from being sprayed as iridescent.

Green Strawberry requires a bit more attention than pink because matching green color tints seems to be a troubling issue to some. Some green tends to lean toward a blue-green and mismatches what is usually found. If you are in a color correctness mode, be aware of that small problem. Both Strawberry colors can be collected as a set; however, there are no cups, saucers, or dinner-sized plates.

Strawberry sugar covers and the 6¼", 2" deep bowl are hard to find. Some older sellers erroneously label the sugar with no lid and no handles as a spooner which was a common piece sold that way in earlier times; however, by the Depression era, spooners were rarely used. Of course selling a sugar with no lid is difficult; so marketing it as a spooner to the unsuspecting might move it faster.

Strawberry has a plain butter dish bottom that is analogous to other U.S. Glass patterns. Some of those other U.S. Glass pattern butters have been robbed of their bottoms over the years to use with Strawberry tops. Strawberry butter dishes have been sought since day one. In fact, in the "pioneering" days of Depression glass collecting, there was a strong nucleus of butter dish collectors. That hobby would be truly expensive today. Many of the rarer butters are already in collections and seldom appear on the market at any price.

		Crystal, Iridescent	Pink, Green			Crystal, Iridescent	Pink, Green
4 ▶	Bowl, 4", berry	6.00	11.00	14 ▶	Olive dish, 5", one-handle	9.00	22.00
	Bowl, 6¼", 2" deep	65.00	165.00	5 ▶	Pickle dish, 8¼", oval	9.00	20.00
12 ▶	Bowl, 6½", deep salad	15.00	25.00	11 ▶	Pitcher, 7¾"	160.00	210.00
13 ▶	Bowl, 9", oval	30.00	30.00	9 ▶	Plate, 6", sherbet	4.00	10.00
	Butter dish and cover	115.00	145.00	15 ▶	Plate, 7½", salad	10.00	15.00
3 ▶	Butter dish bottom	60.00	80.00		Sherbet	7.00	10.00
2 ▶	Butter dish top	55.00	65.00	6 ▶	Sugar, small, open	12.00	22.00
7 ▶	Comport, 5¾"	18.00	35.00	8 ▶	Sugar, large	20.00	45.00
18 ▶	Creamer, small	12.00	22.00	1 ▶	Sugar cover	40.00	75.00
10 ▶	Creamer, 4⅝", large	22.50	40.00	17 ▶	Tumbler, 3⅝", 8 ounce	20.00	35.00

"SUNBURST," "HERRINGBONE," Jeannette Glass Company, Late 1930s
Color: crystal

"Sunburst" may not ring a bell as yet, but we bet you recognize the Iris shapes and have probably noticed the omnipresent candlesticks while out scouring for other patterns. Outside of those easily spotted candles, you will have some difficulty rounding up a sizeable set. Sherbets, dinner plates, and tumblers are the hardest to corral. The tumbler is similar in style to the flat Iris one with a flared top. Not only that, but a juice tumbler has also been found. As we write this, we do not know if the editorial staff at Collector Books can "clean up" my poor attempt of showing both tumblers side by side. They were brought in to a show in Florida for us to photograph. Having a camera does not mean much, if you are not proficient in its use. Our camera was new and I was recovering from surgery a month before and having trouble remembering where I was, let alone getting a great photo. If the photo is useable, thank miracle workers and if not, realize not only are water tumblers hard to find, but you need to look for a juice as well.

Wouldn't one of these stylish berry bowls or the divided relish have been great additions to the Iris pattern? As with Iris, those straight sided inner rims are easily nicked and need to be checked just as carefully as those of the Iris pattern; and to protect rims, especially on plates and bowls, they should be stacked with paper plates between each one. Additionally, large clear areas on plates will highlight any excessive wear and scratches, so check that out when buying plates.

Collectors would probably not have noticed "Sunburst" had it not been for the popular sister pattern, Iris. Several collectors told us they started buying "Sunburst" after Iris attained those lofty prices that it fetches today. They liked the Iris shapes; so this gave them a less expensive pattern to collect.

When we first put this pattern out for sale, we absolutely delighted a lady who remembered it as her mother's "good" Sunday dishes.

10 ▸	Bowl, 4¾", berry	7.00		8 ▸	Plate, 11¾", sandwich	20.00
9 ▸	Bowl, 8½", berry	16.00		5 ▸	Relish, 2-part	12.00
14 ▸	Bowl, 10¾"	20.00		12 ▸	Saucer	2.00
3 ▸	Candlesticks, double, pair	20.00		7 ▸	Sherbet	14.00
1 ▸	Creamer, footed	8.00		2 ▸	Sugar	8.00
11 ▸	Cup	6.00			Tray, small, oval	10.00
	Plate, 5½"	6.00			Tumbler, 4", 9 ounce, flat	32.00
6 ▸	Plate, 9¼", dinner	15.00				

SUNFLOWER, Jeannette Glass Company, 1930s

Colors: pink, green, some Delphite; some opaque colors and Ultra Marine

Undoubtedly, Sunflower is a familiar pattern of Depression glass even for noncollectors. Everyone is familiar with sunflowers and the widespread cake plate may be the most ubiquitous piece of Depression glass found today. Cake plates were packed in or given away with 20-pound bags of flour, which sold in huge quantities in the 1930s because home baking was the norm then. With a 50-pound bag, you were lucky enough to receive two. Sometimes, displays of the give-away items were near the cash register and you were handed one when you made your purchase. However, we've been advised these Sunflower cake plates were packaged in the sacks themselves. You not only got the flour sack from which you made everything from tea towels to curtains, but you also got a cake plate on which to display your baking skills. How many cake plates can one use? Many were stored away or passed down through the family. We once heard of a cache found in an old barn behind a well-known restaurant that contained over 500 — both pink and green. Considering that, who knows how many more are lurking out there to be placed on the market. An example of what we mean is illustrated by a popular Internet auction we just searched and found a mixture of 78 pink and green cake plates listed. That is only auctions listing Jeannette's cake plate. Who can imagine how many are listed with no idea of who made them or what pattern it is — or how many are out there unlisted?

There is still some puzzlement over the cake plate and the rarely found Sunflower trivet. Think 7 inches. The 7" trivet has an edge that is slightly upturned and it is 3" smaller than the omnipresent 10" cake plate. The 7" trivet remains the most elusive piece of Sunflower and we are showing it for your viewing pleasure once again. Collector demand for the rare trivet keeps prices steady. That heavy, round green piece is a paperweight found in a former Jeannette employee's home.

Green Sunflower pieces are found less often than pink as evidenced by our photo; accordingly, prices for green are a little more than for pink.

Sunflower saucers are in shorter supply than cups. Perhaps cups were a premium, or cups were offered for longer than the saucers?

The Ultra Marine ashtray pictured is the only piece we have found in that color. Opaque colors show up sporadically, usually creamers and sugars. Only a creamer, plate, 6" tab-handled bowl, cup, and saucer have been documented in Delphite blue. They have all been pictured in previous books.

		Pink	Green			Pink	Green
2 ▸	*Ashtray, 5", center design only	9.00	11.00	8 ▸ Plate, 9", dinner		18.00	22.00
5 ▸	Cake plate, 10", 3 legs	15.00	15.00	7 ▸ Saucer		8.00	10.00
4 ▸	**Creamer, opaque $85.00	25.00	25.00	3 ▸ Sugar, opaque $85.00		25.00	25.00
6 ▸	Cup, opaque $75.00	18.00	20.00	9 ▸ Tumbler, 4¾", 8 ounce, footed		35.00	35.00
1 ▸	Paperweight		150.00	11 ▸ Trivet, 7", 3 legs, turned up edge		395.00	395.00
10 ▸	Plate, 8", luncheon, green only		35.00	* Found in Ultra Marine $30.00	** Delphite $95.00		

SUNSHINE, Lines #731 – #737, Lancaster Glass Company, c. 1932
Colors: pink, green w/crystal

Sunshine is one of the few patterns where serving bowls and plates far outnumber anything else. That works as many collectors of pink seem to buy this to supplement other sets short on serving pieces. Green Sunshine doesn't work as well that way, since the green is rather an unusual hue that does not match other patterns.

Sunshine occurs both satinized and nonsatinized as you can see from our photo. In our first attempt at picturing it, we only showed nonsatinized ware even though we had bought some satinized pieces. This time we are showing both, but are not seeing nonsatinized in the market. Finding glass seems to run in woeful cycles for some reason. As a dealer on a buying trip, if you have a huge inventory of a pattern, that is the one you will see so reasonably priced that you are forced to buy more. If you have needs for a customer to fill, you won't see one piece for every 1,000 miles of travel. If you go to a show or flea market in the car, you won't have enough room to haul all you find back. Take the van and both items you discover rattle around in the back.

Sunshine was another of those small lines sold as an assortment of pieces. There appears to have been a series of hexagonal blanks used. You could buy up to a 36-piece assortment of Sunshine; so there should be more of it available than seems to be showing up. We have never heard of any dinner plates, though they may have been made judging from the other luncheon type pieces we do know were available. Notice the use of plates being turned into bowls, a practice often employed to get as many items as possible from a single mould.

You will seldom find a piece of this line inexpensively priced, not because the dealer has any notion what it is, just because it "looks like better glass." Most of the larger pieces pictured here were at least $40.00 when we found them for sale.

		Pink, Green			Pink, Green
1 ▸	Bowl, 6", 2-handled, hex edge	25.00		Creamer, round, footed	22.00
2 ▸	Bowl, 8", 2-handled, hex edge	45.00	9 ▸	Mayonnaise, 5½", 2-handled, hex edge	35.00
	Bowl, 9", 2-handled, hex edge	55.00	5 ▸	Mayonnaise, liner, 7¼", 2-handled, hex edge	15.00
8 ▸	Bowl, 10½ x 8", oval, 2 raised sides, 2-handled, hex edge	60.00	3 ▸	Plate, 10½", 2-handled, hex edge	30.00
			4 ▸	Plate, 14", serving, hex edge	40.00
6 ▸	Bowl, 12", flat rim, hex edge	50.00		Server, 10", center handled sandwich, hex edge	40.00
	Candle, single, hex foot	30.00	7 ▸	Sugar, round, footed	22.00
				Tray, 10", roll edge, bun tray, hex edge	50.00

Notice our new format to portray these. Our problem was that we could not come up with every type of the earlier styles we pictured in previous books.

We often hear interesting comments when our display of Swanky Swigs is noticed at shows. "Why, I remember those. We used them when I was growing up!" or "Look, Mommy, those are like I use at Granny's house!"

Internet auctions have seriously messed up the definition of Swanky Swigs which were so deemed by Kraft in advertisements for their glass contained products. A 1935 ad told of cheese in seven delicious flavors in reusable "Swanky Swig" glasses. Now Internet auctions call any decorated small or large glass a Swanky Swig. It is a problem for which we see no solution forthcoming. Only the Kraft containers usually made by Hazel-Atlas should be so labeled.

See *Collectible Glassware from the 40s, 50s, 60s...* for later made Swanky Swigs and a sample of their various metal lids, which have become collectible themselves.

Band No.1, 3⅜": blue, 3.50 – 5.00; red & black (not shown), 2.00 – 3.00; red & blue (not shown), 3.00 – 4.00. Band No. 2: red & black, 3⅜", 3.00 – 4.00; red & black, 4¾" (not shown), 4.00 – 5.00. Band No. 3, 3⅜": red & blue, 3.00 – 4.00.

Circle & Dot: green, 3½", 4.00 – 5.00; black, 3½", 5.00 – 6.00; blue, 3½", 5.00 – 6.00; red, 4¾", 8.00 – 10.00; red, 3½", 4.00 – 5.00; blue, 4¾" (not shown), 8.00 – 10.00; green, 3½" (not shown), 4.00 – 5.00. Dot (not shown): black, 4¾", 7.00 – 9.00; blue, 3½", 5.00 – 6.00.

Star: black, 3½", 3.00 – 4.00; blue, 3½", 3.00 – 4.00; blue, 4¾", 7.00 – 8.00; green, 3½", 3.00 – 4.00; red, 3½", 3.00 – 4.00; cobalt w/white stars, 4¾" (not shown), 18.00 – 20.00.

Centennials: Texas, cobalt, 4¾", 30.00 – 35.00; Texas, blue (not shown), black, or green, 3½", 30.00 – 35.00; West Virginia, cobalt (not shown), 4¾", 22.00 – 25.00.

Checkerboard: red, blue, or green, 3½", 25.00 – 30.00.

Sailboat: red or blue, 3½", 10.00 – 12.00; green or light green, 3½", 12.00 – 15.00; blue, 4½" (not shown), 12.00 – 15.00; red or green, 4½" (not shown), 12.00 – 15.00.

Tulip No. 1: blue, 3½", 3.00 – 4.00; blue, 3½", w/label, 20.00 – 22.00; blue, 4½", 15.00 – 20.00; black, 3½", w/label, 20.00 – 22.00; 3½", 3.00 – 4.00.

Tulip No. 1: light green, 3½", 3.00 – 4.00; 3½", w/label, 20.00 – 22.00; 4½", 15.00 – 20.00; 3½", 3.00 – 4.00.

Tulip No. 1: red, 3½", 3.00 – 4.00; red, 4½", 15.00 – 20.00; yellow, 3½", 3.00 – 4.00.

Tulip No. 2: red, blue, green, or black, 3½", 30.00 – 35.00.

Tulip No. 3: yellow, red, 3¾", 3.00 – 4.00; 3¼", 15.00 – 20.00; 4½", 15.00 – 20.00.

Tulip No. 3: dark blue, light blue, 3¼", 15.00 – 20.00; 3¾", 2.50 – 3.50; 4½", 15.00 – 20.00.

SWIRL, "PETAL SWIRL," Jeannette Glass
Company, 1937 – 1938
Colors: Ultra Marine, pink, Delphite; some amber and ice blue

Collecting Swirl has been waning with each passing year. Several factors can be attributing to that, and at first we felt that the supply had dried up. However, in looking at Internet auctions, there seems to be more than ample supply and therein may lie the problem. More is turning up than is being needed. You can find some bargains if you take the time to look. Be sure to take postage and handling into consideration as a seeming bargain can turn into an overpayment easily.

Swirl is found with two different borders on most bowls and plates — ruffled or plain. Ultra Marine can be found with both, but pink is routinely found with plain rims. You need to specify what style you want if ordering by mail or off the Internet, though there should be little difference in price.

A footed Swirl Ultra Marine pitcher (pictured in previous editions) is unavailable at this time. So far, we know of only three that have turned up since the first one was found in 1974; and all of those are residing in collections. None have been offered in pink. Some collectors of Jeannette Swirl integrate this pattern with Jeannette's "Jennyware" kitchenware line that does have a flat, 36-ounce pink pitcher in it. If you find mixing bowls, measuring cups, or reamers, then you have crossed into the kitchenware line and out of Swirl dinnerware. See *Kitchen Glassware of the Depression Years* for complete "Jennyware" listings and pricing.

Swirl candy and butter dish bottoms are more numerous than tops. Bear that in mind before you buy only a bottom unless it is very reasonably priced. That dearth of tops holds true for 90% of the butter and candy dishes in Depression glass. Unless you have the ability to remember color hues, it might be beneficial to take your half piece with you when trying to match this Ultra Marine color. Swirl has some green-tinged pieces as well as the normally found color. This discoloration problem occurs with any Jeannette patterns made in Ultra Marine. Candy dishes and butter dishes have both dropped in price. There are fewer collectors of candy jars or butters per se, than in the past; so supplies are way ahead of demand.

Pink candleholders are not regarded as rare even though they were accidentally omitted from the listings in some earlier editions. Prices were "up there" until we listed them; but they are back in line now.

Pink coasters are regularly found inside a small rubber tire and used for ashtrays. Such tire advertisements have become desirable. More demand exists for those with a tire manufacturer's name on the glass insert, but a glass insert in an embossed named miniature tire is also desirable. Many of these tires dried up or came apart over the years leaving only the glass inserts as reminders, particularly here in Florida. Rubber and Florida's heat do not co-exist well. You should see what it does for elastic in clothing.

Swirl was produced in several experimental colors, but most of these are found as bowls. However, a smaller set can be compiled in Delphite blue as shown below; it would only have basic pieces and a serving dish or two.

Swirl

		Pink	Ultra Marine	Delphite
1 ▸	Bowl, 4⅞" & 5¼", berry	8.00	16.00	12.00
2 ▸	Bowl, 9", salad	24.00	25.00	25.00
	Bowl, 9", salad, rimmed	25.00	20.00	
15 ▸	Bowl, 10", footed, closed handles	35.00	25.00	
	Bowl, 10½", footed, console	20.00	25.00	
	Butter dish	150.00	300.00	
	Butter dish bottom	25.00	40.00	
	Butter dish top	125.00	260.00	
11 ▸	Candle holders, double branch, pair	60.00	35.00	
	Candle holders, single branch, pair			100.00
13 ▸	Candy dish, open, 3 legs	12.00	16.00	
	Candy dish with cover	110.00	150.00	
	Coaster, 1" x 3¼"	12.00	20.00	
7 ▸	Creamer, footed	8.00	10.00	12.00
4 ▸	Cup	10.00	12.00	10.00
	Pitcher, 48 ounce, footed		2,000.00	

		Pink	Ultra Marine	Delphite
17 ▸	Plate, 6½", sherbet	5.00	5.00	5.00
10 ▸	Plate, 7¼"	10.00	12.00	
	Plate, 8", salad	10.00	12.00	8.00
9 ▸	Plate, 9¼", dinner	15.00	16.00	10.00
4 ▸	Plate, 10½"			25.00
16 ▸	Plate, 12½", sandwich	20.00	28.00	
3 ▸	Platter, 12", oval			35.00
14 ▸	Salt and pepper, pair		40.00	
18 ▸	Saucer	3.00	4.00	4.00
	Sherbet, low footed	10.00	15.00	
	Soup, tab handle (lug)	40.00	50.00	
6 ▸	Sugar, footed	8.00	10.00	12.00
5 ▸	Tray, 10½", 2-handle			27.50
	Tumbler, 4", 9 ounce	20.00	35.00	
	Tumbler, 4⅝", 9 ounce	15.00		
	Tumbler, 5⅛", 13 ounce	50.00	110.00	
19 ▸	Tumbler, 9 ounce, footed	20.00	40.00	
	Vase, 6½" footed, ruffled	26.00		
12 ▸	Vase, 8½" footed, two styles		27.50	

TEA ROOM, Indiana Glass Company, 1926 – 1931

Colors: pink, green, amber, and some crystal

24 11 24

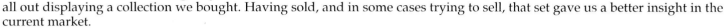

Our pictures of Tea Room received quite a few comments from readers; so we are glad you noticed we went all out displaying a collection we bought. Having sold, and in some cases trying to sell, that set gave us a better insight in the current market.

We mentioned previously that the Internet was expanding finds of Tea Room from New Zealand and Australia. Measurements from there have been a problem as the reported a 9½" amber ruffled vase shrunk an inch in shipping. Once it reached the States, it only was 8½" tall. Several smaller 6½" amber Tea Room ruffled vases have been unearthed "down under." A green tumbler shipped back home exhibited a slightly different hue from those normally found here. We have known for 25 years that rare pieces in some patterns were only rare in the States. This may have to do with their being used as ballast materials in ships. With the Internet, more discoveries are being found to the extent it is difficult to for us to keep up.

As the name insinuates, the very Deco styled Tea Room pattern was marketed for use in the tea rooms and ice cream parlors of that day. It is the raison d'être for so many soda fountain items occurring that are not seen in other patterns. Two styles of banana splits are found with flat ones more costly than footed. In the past you, could find flat banana splits modestly priced because they went unrecognized; now that rarely happens in this world of educated collectors.

Tea Room suffered damage from past use and sometimes, mysterious flaws appear from mishandling by consumers. Most customers known to treat this glass with respect, but there are a cadre of "lid lifters" and "clinkers" who have no idea how fragile our glass is or simply don't care. Finding mint condition pieces of Tea Room is no easy task. Check the underneath sides of flat pieces, which are inclined to chip and flake on all the unprotected ridges. Mint means no damage at all. It is perfectly fine to buy or use flawed pieces; just don't expect to pay mint prices for them. Prices below are for mint items. A good starting point for a minor damaged piece is 50% and down from there depending upon the damage.

We're sure that pieces pulled from moulds were marred at that moment. It was an inherent flaw in the design and manufacturing process. We've told you before about examining original boxed Tea Room where over 25% was not in mint condition when closely examined.

Green Tea Room is wanted more than pink; and some people search for crystal. Crystal pieces are fetching prices listed for pink except for the commonly found 9½" ruffled vase (which is hard to sell) and the very pricey, rarely found pitcher.

		Green	Pink
36 ▸	Bowl, finger	60.00	55.00
35 ▸	Bowl, 7½", banana split, flat	155.00	180.00
38 ▸	Bowl, 7½", banana split, footed	90.00	100.00
18 ▸	Bowl, 8¼", celery	30.00	32.00
33 ▸	Bowl, 8¾", deep salad	90.00	100.00
11 ▸	Bowl, 9½", oval vegetable	50.00	45.00
24 ▸	Candlestick, low, pair	60.00	50.00
	Creamer, 3¼"	22.00	20.00
8 ▸	Creamer, 4½", footed, amber $125.00	22.00	18.00
21 ▸	Creamer, rectangular	25.00	25.00
1 ▸	Creamer, 4"	20.00	20.00
32 ▸	*Cup	50.00	40.00
25 ▸	Goblet, 9 ounce	60.00	55.00
10 ▸	Ice bucket	75.00	75.00
29 ▸	Lamp, 9", electric	155.00	140.00
	Marmalade, notched lid	210.00	195.00
5 ▸	Mustard, w/plain or notched lid	210.00	175.00
	Parfait	150.00	150.00
20 ▸	**Pitcher, 64 ounce, amber $695.00	185.00	150.00
30 ▸	Plate, 6½", sherbet	22.00	22.00
37 ▸	Plate, 8¼", luncheon	28.00	28.00
14 ▸	Plate, 10½", 2-handle	55.00	50.00
34 ▸	Relish, divided	22.00	26.00
15 ▸	Salt and pepper, pair	70.00	70.00
31 ▸	*Saucer	15.00	15.00
19 ▸	Sherbet, low, footed	25.00	20.00
27 ▸	Sherbet, low, flared edge	25.00	20.00
13 ▸	Sherbet, tall, footed, 4½"	45.00	40.00
	Sugar w/lid, 3"	150.00	150.00
2 ▸	Sugar, 4"	20.00	20.00
7 ▸	Sugar, 4½", footed, amber $125.00	22.00	18.00
22 ▸	Sugar, rectangular	22.00	18.00
	Sugar, flat with cover	225.00	200.00
4 ▸	Sundae, footed, ruffled top	115.00	145.00
28 ▸	Tray, center-handle, 10"	160.00	100.00
3 ▸	Tray, handled, sugar/creamer	30.00	30.00
23 ▸	Tray, rectangular sugar & creamer	65.00	40.00
16 ▸	Tumbler, 8 ounce, 4³⁄₁₆", flat	150.00	140.00
	Tumbler, 6 ounce, footed	35.00	30.00
9 ▸	Tumbler, 8 ounce, 5¼", high, footed, amber $125.00	30.00	30.00
26 ▸	Tumbler, 11 ounce, footed	40.00	40.00
17 ▸	Tumbler, 12 ounce, footed	45.00	45.00
12 ▸	‡ Vase, 6½", ruffled edge	75.00	65.00
39 ▸	‡ ‡ Vase, 9½", ruffled edge	100.00	
6 ▸	Vase, 11", ruffled edge	250.00	250.00
	Vase, 11", straight	150.00	155.00

*Prices for absolutely mint pieces **Crystal $695.00 ‡ Amber $350.00 ‡ ‡ Crystal $16.00

THISTLE, MacBeth-Evans, 1929 – 1930
Colors: pink, green; some yellow and crystal

Thistle pattern has been a thorn in the side of every photographer we have had in 35 years of trying to capture it on film or now, digitally. Several times it looked great in photos but did not print as well as it had looked in the shots. We have had seven or eight photographers trying to keep the thistles showing and sometimes they did, but more often they did not. Photography lights cause Thistle to do a fading act, something all too recurring for Thistle collectors. Our photographer seems to have captured it, but you will never know how many angles glass was turned or twisted nor how many Polaroid test shots were made before both the delicate color and the pattern were finally acquired.

When you come across a thick butter dish, pitcher, tumbler, celery, spooner, creamer, sugar, or other heavy moulded pink or green pieces with impressed Thistle designs, they are probably newly made. Mosser Glass Company in Cambridge, Ohio, is making these pieces in various colors. They are not a part of this pattern, but are designs based on a much older Cambridge pattern glass. Should you encounter the older Cambridge ware, it will probably be embossed with the words "near cut" in its center. If you do have a piece of Thistle not in the photograph, then you probably do not have a piece of Depression glass Thistle made by MacBeth-Evans. All seven pieces known in the pattern are shown here. Thistle designs were all too common at this time and in other glass company productions.

Green Thistle is even less available than pink except for the large fruit bowl that is practically an illusion in pink. We owned the one pictured here for over 32 years. Our arms have been twisted many times over the years to sell it, and that day finally came and the couple who bought it will probably keep it another 30 years.

Thistle pieces have the same mould shapes as thin Dogwood; however, no Thistle creamer or sugar has ever been found. The Thistle grill plate has the pattern only on the edge. Those plain centers scratched easily; beware of that should you locate a grill plate. Frankly, they are so scarce now, if you find one with a distinguishable pattern, be thankful and buy it.

		Pink	Green
7 ▸	Bowl, 5½", cereal	30.00	24.00
4 ▸	Bowl, 10¼", large fruit	595.00	395.00
1 ▸	Cup, thin	25.00	25.00
5 ▸	Plate, 8", luncheon	15.00	15.00
3 ▸	Plate, 10¼", grill	30.00	35.00
6 ▸	Plate, 13", heavy cake	150.00	145.00
2 ▸	Saucer	9.00	10.00

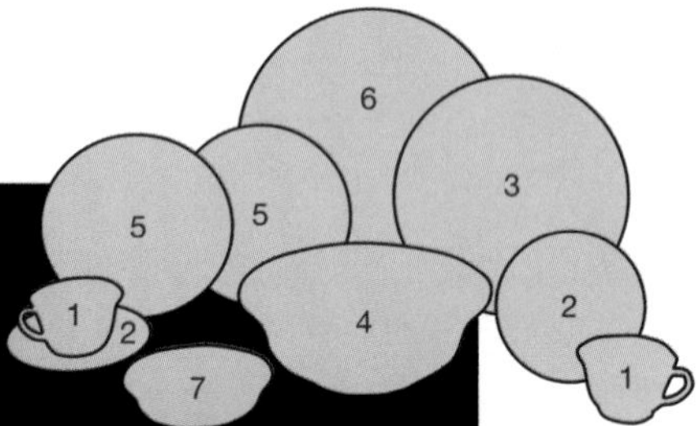

"TOP NOTCH," "SUNBURST," New Martinsville, c. 1930s

Colors: amethyst, red, green, cobalt, amber

In the south, "Sunburst" is the name used for this pattern; but since we already have Jeannette's Sunburst, we'll use the designation of northeast dealers' "Top Notch." Others also call it "Top Prize." Most of the pieces we have found have been in the northeast. Cathy asked a Florida dealer where her identifying label came from on her green set, and she said she "found it in some old magazine a couple of years ago" though she couldn't pinpoint which one. No matter what it's being called, it is a wonderful design and comes in rich jewel colors. We had letters from people who thought they had pieces in amethyst and amber and we are awaiting confirmation on both.

We know the items pictured are from a luncheon set, but whether there are additional pieces available is a mystery. We have, however, run into another green set in Florida having the same items shown here. Finding glassware patterns in Florida does not help much in source problem-solving, since no one knows where it was before being relocated here. A lot of excellent collectible glass was brought here by retirees and much of that is now reaching the market.

We purchased the red cup and saucer in Kentucky and have seen another set in blue that was not for sale. It was nice to know it existed.

		All colors
5 ▶	Cup	18.00
2 ▶	Creamer	25.00
6 ▶	Plate, luncheon	18.00
3 ▶	Plate, serving tray	35.00
4 ▶	Saucer	7.00
1 ▶	Sugar	25.00

TULIP, Dell Glass Company, Late 1930s – Late 1940s
Color: amethyst, turquoise (blue), crystal, green

Showing the amethyst Tulip decanter exposed others. No one knew what to look for since the bottom was flowerless. The decanter bottom has an optic in the glass with only the stopper displaying tulips in the design. After illustrating it in the previous book, we were still able to find a blue decanter sans stopper for $6.00 in an antique mall. If you don't buy books to keep informed, you'll likely leave a few bargains for those of us who search for them.

We started gathering Tulip almost 20 years ago when we ran across nine green sugar/cream soup bowls for $10.00. We did not know whether there were collectors or not, but we soon found out. Those sugars are regularly found in groups of four or more without creamers, making us surmise they may have been sold as cream soups. Another inkling toward that conjecture is seeing a dozen sugars for every creamer.

Today, price escalation has been held in check and a few items are selling for less than previously. Crystal is priced with the green since you will not see much of it. Crystal may be the rarest "color."

The scalloped rims have a penchant to damage and most of it occurs under the rim edge. Be sure to turn the piece over and check each of the pointed scallops from the opposite side. Many times a scallop or two will be almost absent and not show from the top. Some of this type roughness may have occurred in removal from the mould, but that is only speculation.

Two varieties of candleholders are found. One style is made from an ivy bowl (not a sherbet as the piece was formerly believed to be). That ivy bowl is pictured in the 1946 Montgomery Ward catalog with ivy growing in it. We have pictured that ad in past books. For clarification, the violin vase pictured here and in that ad is not officially considered to be part of the pattern, although the neck of the violin is rather like the neck on the decanter. Many collectors buy these to add to their Tulip display. Also, that violin vase can be found in all Tulip colors.

The juice tumbler (shown as a cigarette holder in an ad in previous books) is 2¾" tall and holds three ounces; the whiskey is only 1¾" and holds one ounce. Prices are similar, but shot glass collectors decrease the larger supply buying the latter. That ad for Tulip showed no stippling on some pieces. Early in buying Tulip, we ignored pieces without stippling. That changed after conversations with a collector who told us both are acceptable to Tulip collectors.

		Amethyst, Blue	Crystal, Green			Amethyst, Blue	Crystal, Green
15 ▸	Bowl, oval, oblong, 13¼"	90.00	85.00	12 ▸	Ice tub, 4⅞" wide, 3" deep	55.00	50.00
13 ▸	Candleholder, 3¾" (ivy bowl)	35.00	28.00	10 ▸	Plate, 6"	8.00	7.00
16 ▸	Candleholder, 5¼" base, 3" tall	50.00	40.00	14 ▸	Plate, 7¼"	12.00	12.00
9 ▸	Candy w/lid, footed (6" w/o lid)	225.00	185.00	6 ▸	Plate, 10"	30.00	28.00
2 ▸	Creamer	14.00	18.00	5 ▸	Saucer	6.00	5.00
4 ▸	Cup	16.00	12.00	1 ▸	Sherbet, 3¾", flat (ivy bowl)	20.00	18.00
8 ▸	Decanter stopper	25.00	25.00	3 ▸	Sugar	12.00	15.00
17 ▸	Decanter w/stopper	495.00		11 ▸	Tumbler, 2¾", juice	30.00	20.00
				7 ▸	Tumbler, whiskey	35.00	25.00

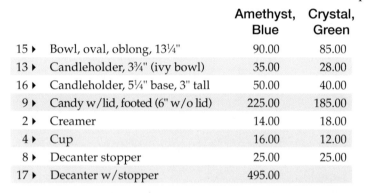

TWISTED OPTIC, Line #313, Imperial Glass Company, 1927 – 1930 and onward
Colors: pink, green, amber; some blue and Canary yellow, ruby and iridized crystal

Imperial's Twisted Optic is one of many twisting or spiraling patterns made by glass companies during this era (see Hocking's Spiral previously presented in this book and read about a new non-Depression spiral pattern on page 217).

The Canary yellow color photographed here is often identified as "vaseline." The term "Vaseline" is used by collectors for vibrant yellow colored glassware. The fluorescence of this color is not done true justice by a photo, but we tried. We were able to buy one of each different piece from a dealer selling his collection, just to illustrate Canary color. Seeing all the items he had accumulated besides these was breathtaking. Yes, it flew off our tables when we put it out for sale after photographing it.

Of course, there are more pieces of Twisted Optic than we show. Space limitations are forcing us to eliminate a page or two on some patterns, but you can refer to previous editions to see larger quantities of Twisted Optic including additional items in Canary. We should mention that old catalog pages show a three-piece sandwich set, using the rolled edge mayonnaise bowl and spoon at the center of a 14" plate. Also, the 10" handled tray was called a lunch tray, rather than a center-handled server.

		Blue, Canary Yellow	All other colors			Blue, Canary Yellow	All other colors
	Basket, 10", tall	100.00	60.00		Plate, 7", salad	8.00	4.00
	Bowl, console, scroll tab hdld., oval, ftd.	60.00	50.00		Plate, 7½" x 9", oval with indent	12.00	5.00
					Plate, 8", luncheon	8.00	7.00
	Bowl, 4¾", fruit	22.00	15.00		Plate, 9½", cracker	30.00	18.00
	Bowl, 5", cereal	14.00	9.00		Plate, 10", sandwich	30.00	9.00
	Bowl, 7", crimped	28.00	20.00		Plate, 12"	30.00	15.00
	Bowl, 7", salad	22.00	15.00		Plate, 14", buffet	40.00	25.00
	Bowl, 9"	32.00	15.00		Platter, oval	35.00	25.00
	Bowl, 9¼", salad	35.00	25.00		Powder jar w/lid	90.00	45.00
	Bowl 10", salad	40.00	30.00		Preserve (same as candy w/slotted lid)		30.00
	Bowl, 10½", console	40.00	25.00				
	Bowl, 11½", 4¼" tall	50.00	30.00	7 ▶	Sandwich server, open center handle, 2 styles	40.00	20.00
	Candlesticks, 3", pair (3 styles)	50.00	50.00				
	Candlesticks, 8½", pair	80.00	55.00		Sandwich server, two-handle	20.00	12.00
2 ▶	Candy jar w/cover, flat	80.00	50.00	9 ▶	Saucer	5.00	2.00
	Candy jar w/cover, flat, flange edge	100.00	55.00		Server, center handle, bowl shape	42.00	20.00
	Candy jar w/cover, ftd., flange edge	100.00	55.00	4 ▶	Sherbet	14.00	6.00
3 ▶	Candy jar w/cover, ftd., short, fat	110.00	60.00		Sugar	18.00	10.00
	Candy jar w/cover, footed, tall	125.00	60.00		Tumbler, 4½", 9 ounce		6.00
	Compote, cheese	20.00	12.00		Tumbler, 5¼", 12 ounce		8.00
	Creamer	18.00	10.00	6 ▶	Vase, 7¼", 2-handle, rolled edge	75.00	45.00
8 ▶	Cup	15.00	7.00		Vase, 7¼", flat rim	65.00	40.00
	Mayonnaise	50.00	30.00		Vase, 8", 2-handle, fan	95.00	50.00
	Pitcher, 64 ounce		45.00	1 ▶	Vase, 8", 2-handle, straight edge	95.00	45.00
5 ▶	Plate, 6", sherbet	5.00	3.00		Vase, 8½", 2-handle, bulbous neck	11.00	65.00

"U.S. SCROLL," "STAR FLOWER," "PINWHEEL," United States Glass Company, c. 1925

Colors: black, green, pink

The entwined U.S.G. (United States Glass) symbol is customarily found on most pieces of this smaller octagonal pattern. We came across a few black items to display, but notice they have to be shown from the bottom or back to see the scroll design that is prominent on each transparent piece.

Pink was cataloged, but we have been unable to come up with a piece of "Scroll" illustrating it. Do you have one? We commonly see "Scroll" in small groups rather than a piece at a time. Regrettably, damaged pieces are the norm which may be indicative of excessive use and the angular profile which invite bumps. You will see green most often but need to be familiar with its shape to spot any black. This should answer those many letters we receive each year asking what we know about this pattern.

A recent e-mail from Canada told us that a green 10", three-footed cake plate was found there. You can see one pictured on the right.

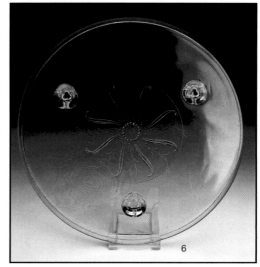

		Black	Green, Pink
6 ▸	Cake plate, 10", 3-footed		30.00
5 ▸	Creamer	12.00	9.00
2 ▸	Cup	8.00	7.00
	Plate, 7½"	8.00	5.00
4 ▸	Plate, 8½"	12.00	10.00
3 ▸	Saucer	3.00	2.00
1 ▸	Sugar	12.00	9.00

"U.S. SWIRL," U.S. Glass Company, Late 1920s

Colors: green, some pink, iridescent, and crystal

"U.S. Swirl" is another of the many swirling or spiraling patterns; but it is more readily recognized due to its mould shapes and pieces similar to the popular Aunt Polly and Strawberry patterns made by U.S. Glass. The 24-pointed star found on the bottom of most pieces is another obvious characteristic. Most other swirled or spiral patterns have plain bottoms. Pink, iridescent, and crystal items are encountered once in a while in "U.S. Swirl," but green is the predominant color.

We have only found one pink shaker, a butter dish, and a couple of tumblers in all the years we have been hunting. Very little pink was dispersed, conceivably only a few special items. In the listings, we have separated the colors based on demand for green outweighing that of pink, but apparently not all items exist in pink. If more pink were available, it would surely bypass green prices due to rarity. Since it is so rarely seen, there are few searching for it; so the demand factor does not yet influence price.

Occasionally, we witness crystal sherbets, but have not seen other crystal pieces. The 5⅜" tall, rarely found comport was labeled a large sherbet when we bought it; and it could be used that way. Comports were ordinarily used as an open candy; but some, today, favor them for martini or margarita glasses. (That's why Hocking's Manhattan comport supplies have dried up. Collectors are buying six or more for drink use instead of one for candy.)

"U.S. Swirl" iridescent butter dishes appear once in a while, as do sherbets. In early days of collecting, those butters would have been snapped up by collectors of those. Today, with fewer butter dish collectors, they are harder to sell. The eight-ounce tumbler listing 3⅝" conforms to the only known size of Aunt Polly and Cherryberry/Strawberry tumblers; but the 12-ounce tumbler, pictured, has only been found in this pattern.

"U.S. Swirl" has the plain butter bottom that is compatible with other patterns made by U.S. Glass. The green butter dish in this pattern is the one that many Strawberry or Cherryberry collectors have purchased over the years to borrow the base for their butter lids. This plundering has reduced the number of butters in "U.S. Swirl." Had there ever been iridescent butter dishes found in Cherryberry/ Strawberry patterns, the iridescent "U.S. Swirl" butters might have disappeared entirely with the crossover butter bottom usage.

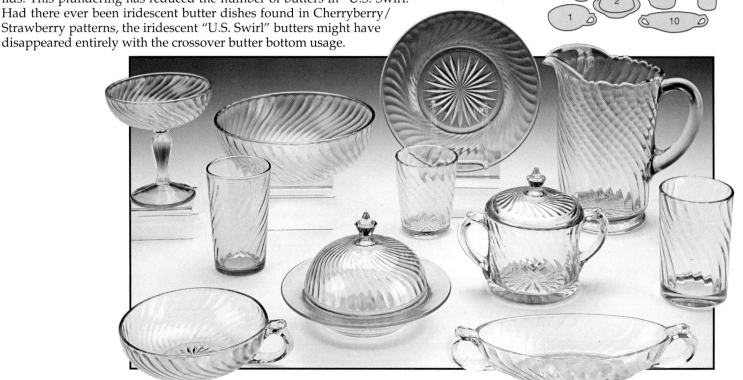

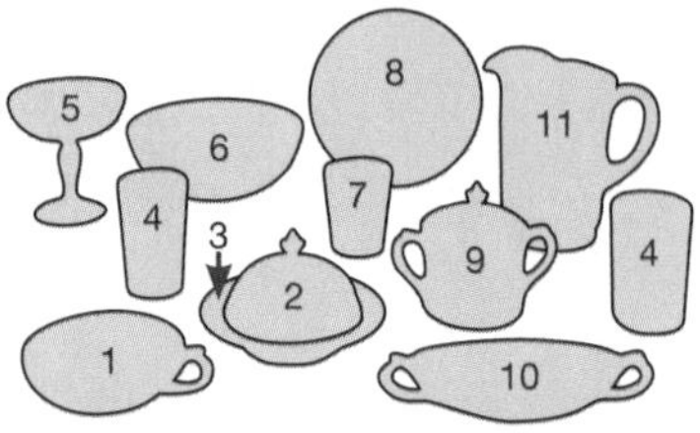

		Green	Pink				Green	Pink
	Bowl, 4⅜", berry	5.50	6.50		Creamer		25.00	25.00
1 ▶	Bowl, 5½", 1-handle	9.50	10.50	10 ▶	Pickle dish, 8¼", oval		30.00	30.00
6 ▶	Bowl, 7⅞", large berry	15.00	16.00	11 ▶	Pitcher, 8", 48 ounce		75.00	75.00
	Bowl, 8¼", oval (2¾" deep)	50.00	45.00		Plate, 6⅛", sherbet		2.50	2.50
	Bowl, 8⅜", oval (1¾" deep)	60.00	55.00	8 ▶	Plate, 7⅞", salad		5.50	6.50
	Butter and cover	110.00	110.00		Salt and pepper, pair		75.00	75.00
3 ▶	Butter bottom	80.00	80.00		Sherbet, 3¼"		4.50	5.00
2 ▶	Butter top	30.00	30.00	9 ▶	Sugar w/lid		50.00	50.00
	Candy, footed, 2-handled	35.00	30.00	7 ▶	Tumbler, 3⅝", 8 ounce		10.00	10.00
	Candy w/cover, 2-handled	27.50	35.00	4 ▶	Tumbler, 4¾", 12 ounce		15.00	16.00
5 ▶	Comport	35.00	30.00		Vase, 6½"		30.00	25.00

"VICTORY," Diamond Glass-Ware Company, 1928 – 1931

Colors: amber, pink, green; some cobalt blue and black

"Victory" was one of the last of Diamond's patterns produced before the factory was reduced to ashes in 1931. Fortunately, it was around for the 1929 cobalt blue introduction. We visited some newly opened antique malls in central Kentucky last year and came upon some inexpensively priced cobalt blue "Victory." Sadly, most of it was chipped and scratched, but we were able to salvage eight or nine pieces including a dinner plate which is rarely found in this day. Years ago, "Victory" was being seen all over the northeast and especially in Maine. There must have been a promotional push or "Victory" premiums packed in a product in that area.

"Victory" is a pattern where colors are often combined by collectors. Notice how well the amber and black complement each other. It is often used for fall or Halloween table displays at shows. One new collector told us that photo combination in a previous book prompted her quest for "Victory." Since she lived in New England, she had a better chance of completing her selection than elsewhere. We have purchased almost all the "Victory" pictured here from the northeast part of the country.

Intermingling colors is certainly catching on among collectors. It gives you more than just one color to pursue, and aids in completing your tableware needs. Many times, you will observe your pattern for sale only to have it be a wrong color. This is disheartening and does not happen as often if you search for several colors.

The black with gold trim displays better in the photo than the gold-trimmed amber. As with most black glass of this era, the pattern is on the reverse; you have to flip it over to see the piece is "Victory" unless you can recognize it from the indented edges. Collectors of black glass are more apt to own black "Victory" than Depression glass people. Those collectors often bring "Victory" to shows for identification since they have no clue it's an actual named pattern.

Several enhancements are found on "Victory" besides the 22K gold trim. There are floral decorations and even a Deco looking black design on pink and green. We have glimpsed more floral decorated console sets (bowl and candlesticks) than anything.

"Victory" sets can be assembled in pink, green, or amber with some searching, particularly if you live in New England which might make it a little easier. Cobalt blue or black will take more hunting and some good fortune; but prices are more reasonable today than a few years ago and the Internet opens more possibilities than ever.

Oval gravy boats with platters are the expensive pieces to own in all colors. An amber, a green, and three cobalt blue ones have found us over the years. The "Victory" goblet, candlestick, cereal, soup, and oval vegetable bowls will keep you looking long and hard no matter what color you desire.

233

"Victory"

		Black, Amber, Pink, Green	Blue			Black, Amber, Pink, Green	Blue
	Bonbon, 7"	11.00	20.00		Goblet, 5", 7 ounce	25.00	75.00
8 ▶	Bowl, 5", 2 handled	15.00		10 ▶	Gravy boat and platter	210.00	300.00
9 ▶	Bowl, 6½", cereal	12.00	40.00		Mayonnaise set: 3½" tall, 5½" across, 8½" indented plate, w/ladle	40.00	90.00
	Bowl, 8½", flat soup	20.00	60.00				
12 ▶	Bowl, 9", oval vegetable	35.00	100.00				
	Bowl, 11", rolled edge	30.00	50.00		Plate, 6", bread and butter	4.00	12.00
	Bowl, 12", console	35.00	65.00	5 ▶	Plate, 7", salad	5.00	15.00
11 ▶	Bowl, 12½", flat edge	30.00	70.00		Plate, 8", luncheon	6.00	25.00
	Candlesticks, 3", pair	32.00	120.00		Plate, 9", dinner	16.00	50.00
	Cheese & cracker set, 12" indented plate & compote	40.00			Platter, 12"	28.00	95.00
7 ▶					Sandwich server, center handle	35.00	65.00
6 ▶	Comport, 6" tall, 6¾" diameter	15.00		2 ▶	Saucer	3.00	8.00
3 ▶	Creamer	12.00	40.00		Sherbet, footed	12.00	22.00
1 ▶	Cup	10.00	25.00	4 ▶	Sugar	12.00	40.00

Hocking's spontaneous hurdle into the milk glass market resulted in their pattern Vitrock. It was a mid-1930s milk white color similar to Hazel-Atlas's Platonite. There are a variety of items found in this very robust line, and a few collectors have embraced this "Flower Rim" Vitrock dinnerware to gather.

Vitrock's main claim to fame is its kitchenware line of reamers, measuring cups, and mixing bowls. Of late, shakers and range sets have been the most desired Vitrock items. It was advertised as ware that "will not craze or check," a major detriment of many pottery lines of the time and consequently, an excellent selling point.

You can see additional Vitrock items in our book *Kitchen Glassware of the Depression Years*. Some collectors are blending patterns that cross fields. Vitrock is a prime example of a color/pattern that fits into both kitchen and dinnerware arenas. Hazel-Atlas did the same with their Platonite wares. It made business sense to sell supporting items that matched your everyday dishes. At the time, Vitrock competed with Hazel-Atlas's Platonite; and looking back at supplies available now, Platonite won.

Today, the "Flower Rim" decorated platters, soup plates, and cream soups are pieces that are nearly impossible to find; but so few are trying, they do not fetch prices close to what rarely found items usually do. White glassware apparently is one color you either love or hate, and lovers are losing out.

We finally found a regular Vitrock flat soup with label. These are exceptional since we have bought a dozen or more decorated with Lake Como before spotting this one. Also turning out harder to find than they should be are the 9½" vegetable bowls which may still be in use by families. Several admirers have indicated that fired-on Vitrock is even less available and that makes sense as we only have two pieces.

		White				White
9 ▶	Bowl, 4", berry	3.00	4 ▶	Plate, 7¼", salad		3.00
1 ▶	Bowl, 5½", cream soup	12.00	2 ▶	Plate, 8¾", luncheon		4.00
12 ▶	Bowl, 6", fruit	5.00	11 ▶	Plate, 9", soup		20.00
	Bowl, 7½", cereal	8.00	3 ▶	Plate, 10", dinner		8.00
10 ▶	Bowl, 9½", vegetable	12.00		Platter, 11½"		18.00
5 ▶	Creamer, oval	6.00	8 ▶	Saucer		1.00
7 ▶	Cup	5.00	6 ▶	Sugar		6.00

WATERFORD, "WAFFLE," Hocking Glass Company, 1938 – 1944
Colors: crystal, pink; some yellow, Vitrock; forest green 1950s

Crystal Waterford sells well due to its availability, pricing, and attractiveness. Inexpensive is the key word to pricing anymore. We bought a set of over 300 pieces of crystal a few years ago. We were buying other patterns and the seller wanted to get rid of it, so we bought it, too. Waterford is impressive when displayed as a table setting. Over half of it sold almost immediately, and most of it left our inventory within six months.

Regrettably, pink is rarely spotted any more outside of major glass shows. Only a few of the commonly found items are making Internet appearances which is a little help. Those searching for pink would be ecstatic about pink cereal bowls, a pitcher, or a butter dish populating their table setting. Of these three pieces, the cereal is the most elusive. It has always been perplexing to find, and worse, challenging to find mint. The inside rim is unavoidably damaged from stacking and use. One customer said she had looked for over five years for one cereal and would be happy finding it — even glued together if that is what it took. A little roughness is expected; do not let that keep you from owning a hard-to-find piece. Because of the scalloped rim design, Waterford chips or flakes more easily on the inside than do other patterns.

Scarce crystal pieces include cereal bowls, pitchers, and water goblets. There is a rarely seen 7¾" bowl standing 2" high that turns up occasionally, but is missing from most collections. Those crystal shakers pictured were used by many restaurants through the 1960s and into the 1970s. We have been in a few southern diners in our travels that still use them which is why they are commonly seen today. There are two styles of crystal sherbets. One has a scalloped top and base. It is not commonly found; but it is not as accepted as the regular, plain edged one.

Advertising ashtrays, such as "Post Cereals," are selling for $15.00 to $20.00 depending upon the significance of the advertising on the piece. A promotional one for Anchor Hocking itself will fetch more.

A few pieces of Vitrock Waterford and some Dusty Rose and Springtime Green decorated ashtrays turn up once in a while, and sell near crystal prices unless they have the label identifying the color on them. Those with labels are in demand and sell around $15.00 Examples of those rose and green colors can be seen in the Oyster and Pearl pattern (page 163).

Large Forest Green Waterford 13¾" plates were made in the 1950s promotion of Forest Green; these are usually found in the $20.00 range, but are presently not fast sellers. The large green plate was used as the E 2900/100 seven-piece relish base with five Ivory sections sitting around them similar to those relish tray inserts found in Manhattan. Some crystal Waterford has also been found trimmed in red. There is not enough of the red trim to collect a set unless you are fortunate to find it all at once.

Items listed below with Miss America shape (noted in parentheses) are Waterford patterned pieces with the same mould shapes as Miss America, having three rings above the pattern. Examples of these can be found in the seventh edition of this book and our *Treasures of Very Rare Depression Glass* book.

Those yellow and amber goblets shown above are compliments of Anchor Hocking's photographer from items stored in their morgue. I have never seen yellow ones for sale, but amber ones used to sell for around $25.00 when they were found. With few collectors buying odd colors today, they rarely fetch $10.00 now.

There is a footed cup that is often listed for sale as a Waterford punch cup. These cups, and the larger lamps that are often mislabeled as Waterford, are only similar to Hocking's Waterford. There is a round, softball-sized cologne bottle with a tiny neck and mitered diamonds that belongs to Duncan and Miller's Miter line, as well.

Waterford has a flattened (not rounded) diamond shape on each section of the design. There is also a large pink pitcher with an indented, circular design in each diamond, which is not Waterford. This pitcher was made by Hocking, but has more of a bull's-eye look. These pink pitchers with circular indents usually sell for $40.00 and crystal for $20.00; do not pay Waterford prices for one.

		Crystal	Pink				Crystal	Pink
21 ▶	*Ashtray, 4"	7.50				Plate, 6", sherbet	3.00	6.00
1 ▶	Bowl, 4¾", berry	7.00	16.00	11 ▶	Plate, 7⅛", salad	5.00	13.00
13 ▶	Bowl, 5½", cereal	18.00	35.00	12 ▶	Plate, 9⅝", dinner	10.00	24.00
4 ▶	Bowl, 8¼", large berry	12.00	20.00	6 ▶	Plate, 10¼", handled cake	10.00	14.00
16 ▶	Butter dish and cover	25.00	195.00	5 ▶	Plate, 13¾", sandwich	12.00	35.00
	Butter dish bottom	7.00	20.00		Relish, 13¾", 5-part	20.00	
	Butter dish top	18.00	175.00	17 ▶	Salt and pepper, 2 types	8.00	
18 ▶	Coaster, 4"	3.00		8 ▶	Saucer	3.00	5.00
3 ▶	Creamer, oval	5.00	12.00	9 ▶	Sherbet, footed	5.00	18.00
	Creamer (Miss America shape)		45.00	23 ▶	Sherbet, footed, scalloped top	6.00	
7 ▶	Cup	6.50	15.00	2 ▶	Sugar	5.00	10.00
	Cup (Miss America shape)		50.00	22 ▶	Sugar cover, oval	10.00	25.00
19 ▶	Goblets, 5¼", 5⅝"	17.00			Sugar (Miss America shape)		45.00
	Goblet, 5½" (Miss America shape)	40.00	135.00		Tumbler, 3½", 5 oz. juice (Miss America shape)		125.00
	Lamp, 4", spherical base	26.00					
20 ▶	Pitcher, 24 ounce, tilted, juice	24.00		10 ▶	Tumbler, 4⅞", 10 ounce, footed	12.00	18.00
14 ▶	Pitcher, 80 ounce, tilted, ice lip	42.00	160.00				

* With ads $15.00 – 40.00 depending on item popularity

White Band with contrasting red stripes "produces a pleasing effect" according to Hocking's 1935 catalog. We are showing you a portion of that catalog rather than the glass this time. It shows all the goblets and tumblers with identification and terminology better than we can. First are the "shell" tumblers in 6, 10, and 12 ounces. These are straight sided, flat tumblers sometimes referred to by other companies as cylinder tumblers. This is the only time we can find that shell designation in any Hocking pattern. It is usually reserved for restaurant plain tumbler listings. The term saucer champagne we found unusual for Hocking since most other patterns such as Cameo and Mayfair call these high sherbets, a practice begun during Prohibition.

White Band is available, particularly in central Ohio, but you need to find pieces that were not heavily used. It's easy to spot them when still showing both the wide White Band and the red stripes. While searching for this for photography, we saw hundreds of pieces unacceptable for putting on display. White Band is an ideal name as the red stripes disappear with use and that white band is all that is left. You will not want to use this in the dishwasher unless you wish to own unadorned ware.

Note the martini mixer is normally called a cocktail shaker by collectors. There is a quart cocktail shaker in this pattern, but the martini mixer is only a pint, or half the cocktail size. We couldn't put our hands on a #780 pitcher; it is large, holds 80 ounces, is without an ice lip, and has optic panels should you spot one. Luncheon items including plates, cups, and saucers are not easy to find in mint condition. Evidently, these were well used and the decoration did not hold up well to years of use. Goblets in excellent condition seem more available than tumblers.

Cocktail shaker, 32 oz.	25.00
Cup	8.00
Decanter, w/ground stopper, 32 oz.	32.00
Goblet, 3 oz., cocktail	9.00
Goblet, 3 oz., wine	10.00
Goblet, 7 oz., saucer champagne	8.00
Goblet, 9½ oz., water	12.00
Ice bowl, 5⅞"	27.50
Martini mixer, flat lid, 16 oz.	20.00
Pitcher, 80 oz.	35.00
Plate, 6", sherbet	3.00
Plate, 8", salad	8.00
Saucer, 6"	2.00
Sherbet, 5 oz.	7.00
Tumbler, 1½ oz., whiskey	15.00
Tumbler, 3½ oz., ftd., cocktail	6.00
Tumbler, 6 oz., shell	7.00
Tumbler, 7½ oz., old fashioned	9.00
Tumbler, 9 oz., table	8.00
Tumbler, 10 oz., ftd., tumbler	12.00
Tumbler, 10 oz., shell	9.00
Tumbler, 12 oz., shell	10.00
Tumbler, 13 oz., ftd., iced tea	15.00

ATTRACTIVELY STRIPED GLASSWARE

COLORFUL, DECORATED CRYSTAL-WARE

There have been many stripe decorations applied to Crystal Glassware, but none more effective than our Decoration 97, illustrated above. The wide White Band with the contrasting red stripes produces a particularly pleasing effect. In ordering remember that the Tumblers and Stemware are multiple sellers and are seldom sold in less than sets of six. You'll need far more of these than you will of the pieces which are sold singly. Instruct your salespeople to recommend the purchase of Luncheon Plates, Cups, Saucers, Sherbets and Footed Tumblers for an attractive Luncheon Service.

REF.	ITEM NO.	DESCRIPTION	SIZE	DOZ. CTN.	WT. CTN.	REF.	ITEM NO.	DESCRIPTION	SIZE	DOZ. CTN.	WT. CTN.
A	182	Footed Cocktail, Dec 97	3½ oz.	4	12 lb	E	142	Goblet, Dec 97	9½ oz.	4	29 lb
	181	Footed Tumbler, Dec 97	10 oz.	4	30 lb		34	Saucer Champagne, Dec 97	7 oz.	4	23 lb
	188	Footed Iced Tea, Dec 97	13 oz.	4	32 lb		32	Cocktail, Dec 97	3 oz.	4	11 lb
B	507	Whiskey, Dec 97	1½ oz.	6	16 lb		30	Wine, Dec 97	3 oz.	4	13 lb
	665	Old Fashioned Dec 97	7½ oz.	6	41 lb	F	33	Sherbet, Dec 97	5 oz.	4	18 lb
	101	Table Tumbler, Dec 97	9 oz.	12	44 lb		729	Sherbet Plate, Dec 97	6"	4	22 lb
	3511	Shell, Dec 97	6 oz.	12	34 lb	G	172	Ice Bowl, Dec 97	5⅞"	1	23 lb
	3514	Shell, Dec 97	10 oz.	12	47 lb	H	702	Decanter w/ G. S., Dec 97	32 oz.	1	26 lb
	3515	Shell, Dec 97	12 oz.	6	27 lb	J	749	Cocktail Shaker C. T., Dec 97	32 oz.	1	18 lb
C	179	Cup, Dec 97	4"	4	20 lb	K	40	Salad Plate, Dec 97	8"	4	40 lb
	29	Saucer, Dec 97	6"	4	22 lb	L	780	Pitcher, Dec 97	80 oz.	1	38 lb
D	170	Martini Mixer, Dec 97	16 oz.	1	16 lb						

WINDSOR, "WINDSOR DIAMOND," Jeannette Glass Company, 1936 – 1946

Colors: pink, green, crystal; some Delphite, amberina red, and ice blue

Since Windsor crystal has items never found in pink or green, a larger variety is possible. Crystal fits the criteria of inexpensively priced and findable. The one-handled candlestick, 10½" pointed edge tray, three-part platter, and three sizes of footed tumblers are only available in crystal, but there are others if you look at our price list. When prices are dropping, less costly items do not descend as much as expensive ones do.

There are numerous collectors for colored Windsor, but fewer hunt crystal at present. Due to wartime shortages, color was discontinued about 1940 in many glass factories, but crystal pieces were cataloged at Jeannette as late as 1946. Revamped moulds for the Windsor butter, creamer, and sugar were later passed on to the well-known Holiday pattern when that was launched in 1947. This redesign instigated two styles of sugars and lids. One is shaped like Holiday and has no ledge for the lid to rest upon; the other sugar has a ledge for the lid. The pink sugar and lid shaped like Holiday are rare and expensive when found. Luckily, that is not so in crystal.

Green Windsor tumblers are hard to grab today. The water tumbler, commonly found in pink, is scarce. Mould roughness is found on seams of tumblers; and Windsor tumblers have a proclivity to chip on any of those protruding sides. The diamond pattern pokes outward, making the sides an easy target for chips and flakes. Check these vigilantly before you buy. There are color variations in green; be mindful of that.

Square relish trays can be found with or without tabbed (closed) handles. Trays without handles commonly appear in crystal, but pink trays without handles are seldom found. Two styles of sandwich plates were produced. The normally found one is 10½" and has open handles. A recently discovered crystal one is 10" and has closed handles.

The large pink 13⅜" chop plate is often seen in old ads as an underliner tray for a beverage set consisting of a pitcher and six water tumblers. This set may have been an excellent premium item since so many pitchers and water tumblers are discovered today. Those plates are also beginning to appear bountiful. Prices for pink tumblers and the 11¾" x 7" boat-shaped bowl have receded due to the quantities available outpacing demand. Green tumblers do not experience this profusion and prices are holding for now. The lack of collectors buying green juice and ice tea tumblers to go with their sets has stabilized those prices. Water tumblers suffice for glasses and they are doing without the other sizes. The 8" pointed edge rim bowl is rarely seen in pink, but is being found in crystal and even crystal with red trim. Pointed edge bowls are rarely found undamaged. Those points are targets for any mishandling. In the 1970s, there were newly made comports in crystal with sprayed colors that have a beaded top edge. The older comport did not have beads and could serve as a punch bowl stand fitting inside the rimmed base of the large bowl.

Unusual Windsor colors and items can be found pictured in our *Treasures of Very Rare Depression Glass* book.

Windsor

		Crystal	Pink	Green
	*Ashtray, 5¾"	13.50	25.00	55.00
18 ▶	Bowl, 4¾", berry	4.00	12.00	12.00
36 ▶	Bowl, 5", pointed edge	5.00	30.00	
	Bowl, 5", cream soup	5.00	35.00	30.00
3 ▶	Bowls, 5⅛", 5⅜", cereal	8.50	25.00	30.00
25 ▶	Bowl, 7⅛", three legs	9.00	25.00	
15 ▶	Bowl, 8", pointed edge	18.00	60.00	
35 ▶	Bowl, 8½", large berry	10.00	22.00	22.00
26 ▶	Bowl, 9", 2-handle	10.00	22.00	22.00
21 ▶	Bowl, 9½", oval vegetable	8.00	22.00	28.00
	Bowl, 10½", salad	15.00		
13 ▶	Bowl, 10½", pointed edge	30.00	150.00	
31 ▶	Bowl, 12½", fruit console	28.00	125.00	
9 ▶	Bowl, 7" x 11¾", boat shape	15.00	15.00	30.00
1 ▶	Butter dish (two styles)	22.00	35.00	90.00
33 ▶	Cake plate, 10¾", footed	8.50	25.00	28.00
	Candleholder, one handle	15.00		
19 ▶	Candlesticks, 3", pair	25.00	110.00	
	Candy jar and cover	20.00		
24 ▶	Coaster, 3¼"	5.00	12.00	18.00
36 ▶	Comport	10.00		
16 ▶	**Creamer	5.00	12.00	16.00
4 ▶	Creamer (shaped as Holiday)	7.50		
8 ▶	**Cup	5.00	8.00	12.50
	Pitcher, 4½", 16 ounce	20.00	175.00	
34 ▶	‡Pitcher, 6¾", 52 ounce	15.00	25.00	50.00
	Plate, 6", sherbet	2.00	4.00	7.00
6 ▶	Plate, 7", salad	4.50	16.00	20.00
	**Plate, 9", dinner	8.00	15.00	22.00

		Crystal	Pink	Green
	Plate, 10", sandwich, closed handle		22.00	
	Plate, 10½", pointed edge	8.00		
30 ▶	Plate, 10¼", sandwich, open handles	6.00	14.00	16.00
32 ▶	Plate, 13⅝", chop	15.00	25.00	33.00
22 ▶	Platter, 11½", oval	12.00	18.00	25.00
2 ▶	‡‡Powder jar	14.00	60.00	
	Relish platter, 11½", divided	15.00	250.00	
10 ▶	Salt and pepper, pair	16.00	24.00	40.00
23 ▶	Saucer, ice blue $15.00	2.00	2.00	5.00
	Sherbet, footed	3.00	12.00	15.00
5 ▶	Sugar & cover	12.00	30.00	33.00
	Sugar & cover (like Holiday)	15.00	135.00	
7 ▶	Tray, 4", square, w/handle	4.00	8.00	10.00
	Tray, 4", square, w/o handle	10.00	50.00	
	Tray, 4⅛" x 9", w/handle	4.00	10.00	16.00
17 ▶	Tray, 4⅛" x 9", w/o handle	12.00	60.00	
14 ▶	Tray, 8½" x 9¾", 3-part	20.00	90.00	
	Tray, 8½" x 9¾", w/handle	6.50	24.00	35.00
	Tray, 8½" x 9¾", w/o handle	15.00	110.00	
27 ▶	Tumbler, 3¼", 5 ounce	10.00	18.00	30.00
28 ▶	**Tumbler, 4", 9 ounce, red 55.00	6.00	14.00	24.00
29 ▶	Tumbler, 5", 12 ounce	10.00	18.00	45.00
	Tumbler, 4⅝", 11 ounce	9.00		
11 ▶	Tumbler, 4", footed	8.00		
	Tumbler, 5", footed, 11 ounce	11.00		
	Tumbler, 7¼", footed	15.00		

* Delphite $45.00 ** Blue $65.00 ‡ Red $450.00
‡‡ Yellow $175.00; Blue $185.00

"WOOLWORTH," "STIPPLED GRAPE," "OREGON GRAPE,"

Westmoreland Glass Company, c. 1930s
Colors: crystal, green, pink

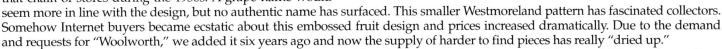

We used to love to see Windsor pop up on our computer screen as it was the last pattern to rewrite in the book. One of the dealers whose favorite pattern it was, used to tell everyone that we skimped on writing everything we knew about Windsor because we were in a hurry to finish the book. Well, here it is years later, and Windsor has been done and we are still writing.

This grape pattern made by Westmoreland has been hailed as "Woolworth" because it was mainly promoted in that chain of stores during the 1930s. A grape name would seem more in line with the design, but no authentic name has surfaced. This smaller Westmoreland pattern has fascinated collectors. Somehow Internet buyers became ecstatic about this embossed fruit design and prices increased dramatically. Due to the demand and requests for "Woolworth," we added it six years ago and now the supply of harder to find pieces has really "dried up."

The creamer and sugar are seen regularly, but plates and bowls are inconsistently seen. "Woolworth" is another pattern where plates were formed into bowls by turning up the sides, so measurements vary. Our measurements are taken from the pieces pictured. We discovered up to ½" discrepancy on similar bowls due to the amount of flaring and ruffling on each one. This ruffling and widening out were done by hand with a tool while the glass was still hot. A heavy-handed worker might push down harder making a bowl shallower than one made by a light-handed worker. We have never spotted a smooth edged bowl, so evidently it was only scalloped edge plates that were used. Green plates and bowls appear less often than pink.

Crystal prices are beginning to descend from their lofty perch as more and more is being discovered; and now, supply has outlasted the demand. Most collectors we have talked to buy all colors and not just one. That is definitely "rainbow" collecting, a different concept just starting in collecting most other patterns. One collector said he bought every piece he could find in the Atlanta area, and proved it by picking all our "Stippled Grapes" displayed.

		Crystal	Green, Pink				Crystal	Green, Pink
2 ▸	Basket, 5½", hdld.	18.00	30.00		Bowl, 7⅝", round, 1⅞" shallow nappy	18.00	25.00
	Bowl, 5½", hdld.	16.00	20.00	11 ▸	Bowl, 7⅞", 1½", shallow nappy	18.00	25.00
1 ▸	Bowl, 5⅞", square nappy	20.00	30.00	4 ▸	Creamer	12.00	18.00
10 ▸	Bowl, 6⅜", round, 2¼" deep nappy	15.00	20.00	6 ▸	Plate, 8½", scalloped rim	16.00	22.00
8 ▸	Bowl, 6¾", round, 2¼" deep nappy	15.00	20.00	5 ▸	Plate, 8⅝", plain rim	18.00	24.00
3 ▸	Bowl, 7⅜", round, 2" shallow nappy	18.00	25.00	7 ▸	Sugar	12.00	18.00
9 ▸	Bowl, 7½", 1¾", shallow nappy	18.00	20.00				

REPRODUCTIONS

NEW "ADAM," Privately produced out of Korea through St. Louis importing Company only the Adam Butler dish has been reproduced.

The reproduction Adam butter dish is finally off the wholesale market as far as I can determine. Identification of the reproduction is easy. Do not use any of the following information for any piece of Adam save the butter dish.
Top: Notice the veins in the leaves.
New: Large leaf veins do not join or touch in center of leaf.
Old: Large leaf veins all touch or join the center vein.

A further note about the original Adam butter dish: the veins of all the leaves at the center of the design are very clear cut and precisely moulded; in the new, these center leaf veins are very indistinct and almost invisible in one leaf of the center design.
Bottom: Place butter dish bottom upside down for observation. Square it, flat side, to your body.

New: Four arrowhead-like points line up in northwest, northeast, southeast, and southwest directions of compass. These points head in the wrong directions from old. There are very bad mould lines and a very glossy light pink color on the butter dishes we examined

Old: Four arrowhead-like points line up in north, east, south, and west directions of compass.

NEW "AVOCADO," Indiana Glass Company Tiara Exclusives Line, 1974 – 1980s
Colors: pink, green, and fifteen additional colors never made originally

In 1979, a green Avocado pitcher was reproduced. It was darker than the original green and was a limited hostess gift item. Yellow pieces are all recently made. Yellow was never made originally.

The old pink color Indiana made was a delicate, attractive pink. The first reproduced pink pitcher appeared in 1973. The newer, tends to be more orange than the original color. The other colors shown pose little threat since none of those colors were made originally.

We understand that Tiara sales counselors told potential customers that their newly made glass was collectible because it was made from old moulds. We do not share this view. We feel it's like saying that since you were married in your grandmother's wedding dress, you will have the same happy marriage for the 57 years she did. All you can truly say is that you were married in her dress. We think all you can say about the new Avocado is that it was made from the old moulds. Time, scarcity, and people's whims determine collectibility as far as we're able to determine it. It has taken nearly 50 years or more for people to turn to collecting Depression glass — and that's done, in part, because of what we call the "nostalgia factor" — everyone remembers it; they had some in their home at one time or another; it has universal appeal. Who is to say what will be collectible in the next 50 years? If we knew, we could all get rich. Now, that Tiara is out of business, perhaps some of their wares will become collectible. Unhappily, there are many collectors who were taken in by some of this glass being represented as old, and most of them have long enough memories to avoid it during their generation.

If you like Tiara products then of course buy them; but don't do so depending upon their being collectible. You have an equal chance, we feel, of going to Las Vegas and depending upon getting rich at the blackjack table.

NEW "CAMEO"
Colors: green, pink, cobalt blue (shakers); yellow, green, and pink (children s dishes)

We hope you can still see how very weak the pattern is on this reproduction shaker. It was originally made by Mosser Glass Company in Ohio, but is now being made overseas. In addition, you can see how much glass remains in the bottom of the shaker; and, of course, the new tops all make this easy to spot at the market. These were to be bought wholesale at around $6.00 but did not sell well. An importer made shakers in pink, cobalt blue, and a terrible green color. These, too, are weakly patterned. They were never originally made in the blue, but beware of pink.

Children's dishes in Cameo (called "Jennifer" by the manufacturer) pose no problem to collectors since they were never made originally. These, also made by Mosser, are scale models of the larger size. This type of production we have no quarrel with since they are not made to dupe anyone.

There are over 50 of these smaller pieces; thus, if you have a piece of glass that looks like a miniature (child's) version of a larger piece of Cameo, then you probably have a newly manufactured item.

REPRODUCTIONS

NEW "CHERRY BLOSSOM"
Colors: pink, green, blue, Delphite, cobalt, red, and iridized colors

Use information provided only for the piece described. Do not apply the information on the tumbler for the pitcher, etc. Realize that with various importers now reproducing glass, there are more modifications than we can possibly scrutinize for you. Know your dealer and hope he knows what he is doing.

Due to all the altered reproductions of the same pieces over and over, please understand this is only a guide as to what you should look for when buying. We've now seen some reproductions of those reproductions. All the items pictured on the next page are easy to spot as reproductions once you know what to look for with the possible exception of the 13" divided platter pictured in the center. It's too heavy, weighing 2¾ pounds, and has a thick ⅜" of glass in the bottom; but the design isn't too bad. The edges of the leaves aren't smooth; but neither are they serrated like old leaves.

There are many differences between old and new scalloped bottom, AOP Cherry pitchers. The easiest way to tell the difference is to turn the pitcher over. The branch crossing the bottom of my old Cherry pitchers looks like a branch. It's knobby and gnarled and has several leaves and cherry stems directly attached to it. One variation of the new pitcher just has a bald strip of glass cutting the bottom of the pitcher in half. Further, the old Cherry pitchers have a plain glass background for the cherries and leaves in the bottom of the pitcher. In the new pitchers, there's a rough, filled in, straw-like background. You see no plain glass.

As for the new tumblers, look at the ring dividing the patterned portion of the glass from the plain glass lip. The old tumblers have three indented rings dividing the pattern from the plain glass rim. The new has only one. Again, the pattern at the bottom of the new tumblers is brief and practically nonexistent in the center curve of the glass bottom. The pattern, when there is one, mostly hugs the center of the foot.

two-handled tray — old: 1⅞ lb.; ³⁄₁₆" glass in bottom; leaves and cherries east/west from north/south handles (some older trays were rotated so this is not always true); leaves have real spine and serrated edges; cherry stems end in triangle of glass. **new**: 2⅛ lb.; ¼" glass in bottom; leaves and cherries north/south with the handles; canal type leaves (but uneven edges; cherry stem ends before canal shaped line).

cake plate — new: color too light pink; leaves have too many parallel veins that give them a feathery look; arches at plate edge don't line up with lines on inside of the rim to which the feet are attached.

8½" bowl — new: crude leaves with smooth edges; veins in parallel lines.

cereal bowl — new: wrong shape, looks like 8½" bowl, small 2" center. **old**: large center; 2½" inside ring; nearly 3½" if you count the outer rim before the sides turn up.

dinner plate — new: smooth-edged leaves, fish spine type center leaf portion; weighs one pound plus; feels thicker at edge with mould offset lines clearly visible. **old**: center leaves look like real leaves with spines, veins, and serrated edges; weighs ¾ pound; clean edges; no mould offset (a slight step effect at the edge).

cup — new: area in bottom left free of design; canal centered leaves; smooth, thick top to cup handle (old has triangle grasp point).

saucer — new: offset mould line edge; canal leaf center.

The Cherry child's cup (with a slightly lopsided handle) having the cherries hanging upside-down when the cup was held in the right hand appeared in 1973. After we reported this error, it was quickly corrected by re-inverting the inverted mould. These later cups were thus improved in design but slightly off color. The saucers tended to have slightly off center designs, too. Next came the child's butter dish that was never made by Jeannette. It was essentially the child's cup without a handle turned upside-down over the saucer and having a little glob of glass added as a knob for lifting purposes.

Pictured are some of the colors of butter dishes made so far. Shaker reproductions were introduced in 1977 and some were dated '77 on the bottom. Shortly afterward, the non-dated variety appeared. How can you tell new shakers from old — should you get the one in a million chance to do so?

First, look at the tops. New tops could indicate new shakers. Next, notice the protruding edges beneath the tops. In the new they are squared off juts rather than the nicely rounded scallops on the old. The design on the newer shakers is often weak in spots. Finally, notice how far up inside the shakers the solid glass (next to the foot) remains. The newer shakers have almost twice as much glass in that area. They appear to be ¼ full of glass before you ever add the salt.

In 1989, a new distributor began making reproduction glass in the Far East. He made shakers in cobalt blue, pink, and a hideous green, that is no problem to spot. These shakers are similar in quality to those made before. However, the present pink color is good; yet the quality and design of each batch could vary greatly. Realize that only two original pairs of pink Cherry shakers have ever been found and those were discovered before any reproductions were made in 1977.

Butter dishes are naturally more deceptive in pink and green since those were the only original colors. The major flaw in the new butter is that there is one band encircling the bottom edge of the butter top; there are two bands very close together along the skirt of the old top.

REPRODUCTIONS

NEW "FLORAL," Importing company out of Georgia

Reproduction Floral shakers can now be found in pink, red, cobalt blue, and a dark green color. Cobalt blue, red, and the dark green Floral shakers are of little concern since they were never made in those colors originally. The green is darker than the original green, but not as deep as forest green. The pink shakers are not only a very good pink, but they are also a very good copy. There are many minor variations in design and leaf detail to someone who knows glassware well; but the easy way to tell the Floral reproductions is to take off the top and look at the threads where the lid screws onto the shaker. On the old, there is a pair of parallel threads on each side or a least a pair on one side, which end right before the mold seams down each side. The new Floral has one continuous line thread that starts at one side and continues around the shaker until it ends above the beginning line on the other side. There is approximately one inch of overlapped thread making two lines for that inch; but the whole thread is one continuous line and not two separate ones as on the old. No other Floral reproductions have been made as of May 2007.

NEW "FLORENTINE NO. 1," Importing company out of Georgia

Although a picture of a reproduction shaker is not shown, we would like you to know it exists.
Florentine No. 1 shakers have been reproduced in pink, red, and cobalt blue. There may be other colors to follow. No red or cobalt blue Florentine No. 1 shakers have ever been found, so those colors are no problem. We have only examined one reproduction shaker, and it is difficult to know if all shakers will be as badly molded as this is. There is little or no design on the bottom. We compared the pink shaker to several old pairs. The old shakers have a major open flower on each side. There is a top circle on this blossom with three smaller circles down each side. The seven circles form the outside of the blossom. The new blossom looks more like a strawberry with no circles forming the outside of the blossom. This repro blossom looks like a poor drawing. Do not use the Floral thread test for the Florentine No. 1 shakers, however. It won't work for Florentine although the same importing company out of Georgia makes these.

NEW "FLORENTINE NO. 2," Importing company out of Georgia

A reproduced footed Florentine No. 2 pitcher and footed juice tumbler appeared in 1996. First to surface was a cobalt blue set that alerted knowledgeable collectors that something was strange. Next, sets of red, dark green, and two shades of pink began to be seen at the local flea markets. All these colors were dead giveaways since the footed Florentine No. 2 pitcher was never made in any of those shades.

The new pitchers are approximately ¼" shorter than the original and have a flatter foot as opposed to the domed foot of the old. The mold line on the lip of the newer pitcher extends ½" below the lip while only ⅜" below on the original. All of the measurements could vary over time with the reproductions and may even vary on the older ones. The easiest way to tell the old from the new, besides color, is by the handles. The new handles are ⅞" wide, but the older ones were only ¾" wide. That ⅛" seems even bigger than that when you set them side by side as shown at right.

The juice tumbler differences are not as apparent; but there are two. The old juice stands 4" tall and the diameter of the base is 2⅛". The reproduction is only 3¹⁵⁄₁₆" tall and 2" in base diameter.

NEW "IRIS," Importing company

New Iris cocktails appeared in August 2004. The easiest way to tell the new ones is to look inside from the top. The new ones have what looks like a dot, looking down into it (see right photo). The old ones do not have a dot.

New Iris iced tea tumblers have two distinct differences. First, turn these upside down and feel the rays on the foot. New rays are very sharp and will almost cut your finger if you press on them hard. Old tumbler rays are rounded and feel smooth in comparison. The paneled design on the new tumbler gets very weak in several places as you rotate it in your hand. Old tumbler paneled designs stay bold around the entire tumbler.

New dinner plates have two characteristics. The extreme edge of the pattern on the new dinners is pointed outward (upside down V). Old dinner plate designs usually end looking like a stack of the letter V, though optical illusions sometimes distort that a bit. In addition, the inside rim of the new dinner slopes inward toward the center of the plate, whereas original inside rims are almost perpendicular and steeper sided against the center portion of the plate.

New flat tumblers do not have herringbone in the bottom pattern design. There are other differences, especially the crystal, clear color of the new ones; however, missing the herringbone is the easiest to observe.

In the fall of 2000, several large lots of Iris coasters appeared on an Internet auction site. All of these coasters had origins in Ohio and were like the tumblers and dinner plates in one major respect. The crystal color was too good. If you take any old piece of Iris and place it on a white background, it will have a gray or yellow tint to it. If you place the new dinner plates or iced tea tumblers on white, they have no tinted hue of any sort. The coasters and cocktails are the same — no tint. The other sure-fire way to tell these newer coasters is to look from the side across the coaster edge. New ones look half-full of glass or slightly over. The older ones are only a quarter-full of glass. You can keep up with current reproductions through a website where I have posted pictures. Go to www.glassshow.com and then the Reading Room. Click on Reproductions for the latest information available.

Iris 6½", footed ice tea tumblers (new on left).

New flat tumblers (left) do not have herringbone in the pattern. There are many other minor differences, but that is the easiest to observe.

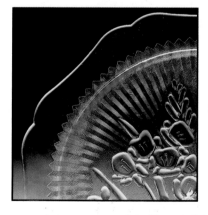
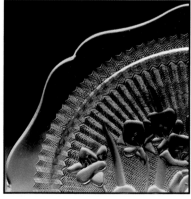

Iris dinner plate (new on left).

Iris coasters (new on right).

REPRODUCTIONS

NEW "MADRID" CALLED "RECOLLECTION," Recently being made

We hope you have already read about Recollection Madrid on page 122. Indiana Glass made Madrid in teal after making it in blue, pink, and crystal. This light teal color was never made originally, so there is no problem of it being confused with old. The teal was sold through all kinds of outlets ranging from better department stores to discount catalogs. In the past couple of years, we have received several ads stating that this is genuine Depression glass made from old moulds. None of this is made from old glass moulds unless you consider 1976 old. Most of the pieces are from moulds never made originally.

The light blue was a big seller for Indiana according to reports we are receiving around the country. It is a brighter, more fluorescent looking blue than the soft, original color. More and more of it is turning up in antique malls. Buy it if you like it; just don't pay antique prices for it.

Look at the picture below. Only the cup, saucer, and oval vegetable were ever made in old Madrid. The new grill plate has one division splitting the plate in half, but the old had three sections. A goblet or vase was never made. The vase is sold with a candle making it a hurricane lamp. The heavy tumbler was placed on top of a candlestick to make this a vase/hurricane lamp. That candlestick gets a workout. It was attached to a plate to make a pedestal cake stand and to a butter dish to make a preserve stand. That's a clever idea, actually. You would not believe the mail spawned by those last two, newly manufactured pieces.

The new shakers are short and heavy. The latest item we have seen is a heavy 11-ounce flat tumbler being sold in a set of four or six called "On the Rocks." The biggest giveaway to this newer pink glass is the pale, washed out color.

The only concerns in new pink Madrid pieces are the cups, saucers, and oval vegetable bowl. These three pieces were made in pink in the 1930s. None of the others shown were ever made in the 1930s in pink; so realize that when you see the butter dish, dinner plate, soup bowl, or sugar and creamer. These are new items. Once you have learned what this washed-out pink looks like by seeing these items for sale, the color will be a clue when you see other pieces.

The least difficult piece for new collectors to tell new from old is the candlestick. The new ones all have three raised ridges inside to hold the candle more firmly. Old ones do not have any inside ridges. You may even find new candlesticks in black.

NEW "MAYFAIR," Importing company

Colors: pink, green, blue, cobalt (shot glasses), 1977; pink, green, amethyst, cobalt blue, red (cookie jars), 1982; cobalt blue, pink, amethyst, red, and green (odd shade), shakers 1988; green, cobalt, pink, juice pitchers, 1993

Only the pink shot glass need cause any concern for collectors because that glass was not made in any other color originally. At first glance, the color of the newer shots is often too light pink or too orange. Dead giveaway is the stem of the flower design, however. In the old that stem branched to form an "A" shape at the bottom; in the new, you have a single stem. Further, in the new design, the leaf is hollow with the veins moulded in. In the old, the leaf is moulded in and the veining is left hollow. In the center of the flower on the old, dots (anther) cluster entirely to one side and are rather distinct. Nothing like that occurs in the new design. Do not use this information for any piece except shot glass.

As for the cookie jars, at cursory glance the base of the cookie has a very indistinct design. It will feel smooth to the touch, because it's so faint. In the old cookie jars, there's a distinct pattern that feels like raised embossing to the touch. Next, turn the bottom upside-down. The new bottom is perfectly smooth. The old bottom contains a 1¾" mould circle rim that is raised enough to catch your fingernail in it. There are other distinctions as well; but that is the quickest and easiest way to tell old from new.

In the Mayfair cookie lid, the new design (parallel to the straight side of the lid) at the edge curves gracefully toward the center "V" shape (rather like bird wings in flight); in the old, that edge is a flat straight line going into the "V" (like airplane wings sticking straight out from the side of the plane as you face it head on).

The green color of the cookie, as you can see from the picture, is not the pretty, yellow/green color of true green Mayfair. It also doesn't glow under black light as the old green does; so, that is a simple test for green.

NEW "MAYFAIR"

The corner ridges on the old Mayfair shaker rise half way to the top and then smooth out. The new shaker corner ridges rise to the top and are quite pronounced. The measurement differences are listed below, but the diameter of the opening is the critical and easiest way to tell old from new. New lids will not fit old shakers as they are too small.

	OLD	NEW
Diameter of opening	¾"	⅝"
Diameter of lid	⅞"	¾"
Height	4¹⁄₁₆"	4"

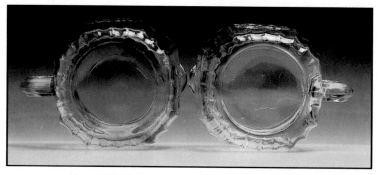

OLD   NEW

Mayfair juice pitchers were reproduced in 1993. The old pitchers have a distinct mould circle on the bottom that is missing on the newly made ones. Note the oddly applied handles on the reproductions make them easily spotted. The blue pitcher is the old one in the photos.

OLD   NEW

NEW "MISS AMERICA"

Colors: crystal, green, pink, ice blue, red amberina, cobalt blue

Miss America reproduction creamers and sugars are smaller than the originals; Miss America was not made in cobalt, but other colors have followed. These creamer and sugars are poorly made. There are many bubbles in the glass of the ones we have seen.

The reproduction butter dish in the Miss America design is probably the best of the newer products; yet there are three differences to be found between the original butter top and the newly made ones. The obvious thing is how the top knob sticks up away from the butter caused by a longer than usual stem at the knob.

Pick up the top of the new dish and feel up inside it. If the butter top knob is filled with glass so that it is convex (curved outward), the dish is new; the old inside knob area is concave (curved inward).

Finally, from the underside, look through the top toward the knob. In the original butter dish, you would see a perfectly formed multi-sided star; in the newer version, you see distorted rays with no visible points.

Miss America shakers have been made in green, pink, cobalt blue, and crystal. The latest copies of shakers are becoming more difficult to distinguish from the old. The measurements given below for shakers do not hold true for all the latest reproductions. It is impossible to know which generation of shaker reproductions that you will encounter, so you have to be careful on these.

New shakers most likely will have new tops; but since some old shakers have been given new tops, that isn't conclusive at all. Unscrew the lid. Old shakers have a very neatly formed ridge of glass on which to screw the lid. It overlaps a little and has rounded off ends. Old shakers stand 3⅜" tall without the lid. Most new ones stand 3¼" tall. Old shakers have almost a forefinger's depth inside (female finger) or a fraction short of 2½". Most new shakers have an inside depth of 2", about the second digit bend of a female's finger. (I'm doing finger depths since most of you will carry those with you to the flea market, rather than a tape measure.) In men, the old shaker's depth covers my knuckle; the new shaker leaves my knuckle exposed. Most new shakers simply have more glass on the inside of the shaker — something you can spot from 12 feet away. The hobs are more rounded on the newer shaker, particularly near the stem and seams; in the old shaker, these areas remained pointedly sharp.

New Miss America tumblers have ½" of glass in the bottom, have a smooth edge on the bottom of the glass with no mould rim, and show only two distinct mould marks on the sides of the glass. Old tumblers have only ¼" of glass in the bottom, have a distinct mould line rimming the bottom of the tumbler, and have four distinct mould marks up the sides of the tumbler.

New Miss America pitchers (without ice lip only) are all perfectly smooth rimmed at the top edge above the handle. All old pitchers that I have seen have a hump in the top rim of the glass above the handle area, rather like a camel's hump. The very bottom diamonds next to the foot in the new pitchers squash into elongated diamonds. In the old pitchers, these get noticeably smaller, but they retain their diamond shape. As of May 2007, these are the only pieces of Miss America that have been reproduced.

REPRODUCTIONS

NEW "ROYAL LACE," Importing company
Color: Cobalt blue

The first thing you notice about the reproduced pieces of Royal Lace is the harsh, extra dark, vivid cobalt blue color or the orange cast to the pink. It is not the soft cobalt blue originally made by Hazel-Atlas. So far, only the cookie jar, juice, and water tumblers have been made as of May 2007.

The original cookie jar lid has a mould seam that bisects (cuts in half) the center of the pattern on one side, and runs across the knob and bisects the pattern on the opposite side. There is no mould line at all on the reproduction.

There are a multitude of bubbles and imperfections on the bottom of the new cookie jar that I am examining. The bottom is poorly moulded and the pattern is extremely weak. Original bottoms are plentiful anyway; learn to distinguish the top and it will save you money.

As for tumblers, the first reproduction tumblers had plain bottoms without the four-pointed design. The new juice tumbler has a bottom design, but it is as large as the one on the water tumbler and covers the entire bottom of the glass. Originally, this design was very small and did not encompass the whole bottom, as does this reproduction. Additionally, there are design flaws on both size tumblers that stand out. The four ribs between each of the four designs on the side of the repro tumblers protrude far enough to catch your fingernail. The original tumblers have a very smooth, flowing design that you can only feel.

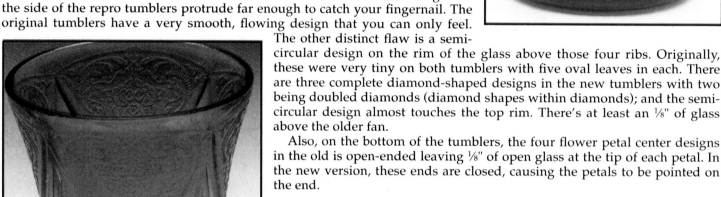

The other distinct flaw is a semi-circular design on the rim of the glass above those four ribs. Originally, these were very tiny on both tumblers with five oval leaves in each. There are three complete diamond-shaped designs in the new tumblers with two being doubled diamonds (diamond shapes within diamonds); and the semi-circular design almost touches the top rim. There's at least an ⅛" of glass above the older fan.

Also, on the bottom of the tumblers, the four flower petal center designs in the old is open-ended leaving ⅛" of open glass at the tip of each petal. In the new version, these ends are closed, causing the petals to be pointed on the end.

NEW "SHARON," Privately Produced 1976
Colors: blue, dark green, light green, pink, cobalt blue, opalescent blue, red, burnt umber

A blue Sharon butter turned up in 1976 and turned our phone line to liquid fire. The color was Mayfair blue — a fluke and dead giveaway as far as real Sharon is concerned. The original mastermind of reproductions did not know his patterns very well and mixed up Mayfair and Sharon. (He admitted that when we talked to him.)

When Sharon butters are found in colors similar to the old pink and green, you can immediately tell that the new version has more glass in the top where it changes from pattern to clear glass. It is a thick, defined ring of glass as opposed to a thin, barely defined ring of glass in the old. The knob of the new dish tends to stick up more. In the old butter dish, there is barely room to fit your finger to grasp the knob. The new butter dish has a sharply defined ridge of glass in the bottom around which the top sits. The old butter has such a slight rim that the top easily scoots off the bottom.

In 1977 a cheese dish appeared having the same top as the butter and having all the flaws inherent in that top which were discussed in detail above. However, the bottom of this dish was wrong. It was about half way between a flat plate and a butter dish bottom — bowl shaped; and it was very thick, giving it an awkward appearance. The real cheese bottom was a salad plate (not bowl) with a rim of glass for holding the top inside that rim. These round bottomed cheese dishes are but a parody of the old and are easily spotted.

Some of the latest reproductions in Sharon are a too-light-pink creamer and sugar with lid. They are pictured with the "Made in Taiwan" label. These retail for around $15.00 for the pair and are easy to spot as reproductions. we'll just mention the most obvious differences. Turn the creamer so you are looking directly at the spout. In the old creamer, the mould line runs dead center of that spout; in the new, the mould line runs decidedly to the left of center spout.

On the sugar, the leaves and roses are "off" but not enough to describe it to new collectors. Therefore, look at the center design, both sides, at the stars located at the very bottom of the motif. A thin leaf stem should run directly from that center star upward on both sides. In this new sugar, the stem only runs from one; it stops way short of the star on one side; or look inside the sugar bowl at where the handle attaches to the bottom of the bowl; in the new bowl, this attachment looks like a perfect circle; in the old, its an upside down "v"-shaped teardrop.

As for the sugar lid, the knob of the new lid is perfectly smooth as you grasp its edges. The old knob has a mould seam running mid circumference (equator). You could tell these two lids apart blindfolded.

While there is a slight difference between the height, mouth-opening diameter, and inside depth of the old Sharon shakers and those newly produced, we will not attempt to upset you with those sixteenths and thirty-seconds of an inch of difference. It is safe to say that in physical appearance, they are very close. However, when documenting design on the shaker, they are miles apart.

The old shakers have true appearing roses. The flowers really look like roses. On the new shakers, the roses appear as poorly drawn circles with wobbly concentric rings. The leaves are not as clearly defined on the new shakers as the old are. However, forgetting all that, in the old shakers, the first design you see below the lid is a rose bud. It is angled like a rocket shooting off into outer space with three leaves at the base of the bud (where the rocket fuel would burn out). In the new shakers, this bud has become four paddles of a windmill. It is the difference between this ❀ and this ✖.

New Sharon candy dishes have been made in pink, green, cobalt blue, red, and opaque blue that goes to opalescent. These candy jars are among the easiest items to discern old from new. Pick up the lid and look from the bottom side. On the old there is a 2" circle ring platform below the knob; on the new, that ring of glass below the knob is only ½". This shows from the top also but it is difficult to measure with the knob in the center. There are other major differences, but this one will not be easily corrected. The bottoms are also simple to distinguish. The base diameter of the old bottom is 3¼" and the new is only 3". On the example we have, quality of the new is rough, poorly shaped and moulded; but we do not know if that will hold true for all reproductions of the candy. We hope so.

OTHER TITLES FROM THE FLORENCES

FLORENCES' OVENWARE
FROM THE 1920S TO THE PRESENT
Item #6641 • ISBN: 978-1-57432-449-7 • 8½ x 11 • 208 Pgs. HB • $24.95

NEWEST EDITION

COLLECTIBLE GLASSWARE FROM THE 40S, 50S & 60S, NINTH EDITION
Item # • ISBN: 978-1- • 8½ x 11 • 256 Pgs. • HB • $19.95

NEWEST RELEASE

AMERICAN PATTERN GLASS TABLE SETS
Item #7362• ISBN: 978-1-57432-546-1 • 8½ x 11 • 192 Pgs. • HB • $24.95

ELEGANT GLASSWARE, OF THE DEPRESSION ERA, TWELFTH EDITION
Item #7029 • ISBN: 978-1-57432-514-0 • 8½ x 11 • 256 Pgs. • HB • $24.95

KITCHEN GLASSWARE OF THE DEPRESSION YEARS, SIXTH EDITION
Item #5827 • ISBN: 978-1-57432-220-0 • 8½ x 11 • 272 Pgs. • HB • $24.95

POCKET GUIDE TO DEPRESSION GLASS & MORE, FIFTEENTH EDITION
Item #7027 • ISBN: 978-1-57432-512-6 • 5¹₂ x 8½ • 224 Pgs • PB • $12.95

FLORENCES' GLASSWARE
PATTERN IDENTIFICATION GUIDES
Vol. I • Item #5042 • ISBN: 978-1-57432-045-9
8½ x 11 • 176 Pgs. • PB • $18.95
Vol. II • Item #5615 • ISBN: 978-1-57432-177-7
8½ x 11 • 208 Pgs. • PB • $19.95
Vol. III • Item #6142 • ISBN: 978-1-57432-315-3
8½ x 11 • 272 Pgs. • PB • $19.95
Vol. IV • Item #6643 • ISBN: 978-1-57432-451-8
8½ x 11 • 208 Pgs. • PB • $19.95

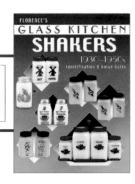

GLASS CANDLESTICKS OF THE DEPRESSION ERA
Vol. 1 • Item #5354 • ISBN: 978-1-57432-136-4 • 8½ x 11 • 176 Pgs. • HB • $24.95
Vol. 2 • Item #6934 • ISBN: 978-1-57432-495-2 • 8½ x 11 • 224 Pgs. • HB • $24.95

ANCHOR HOCKING'S FIRE-KING & MORE,
THIRD EDITION
Item #6930 • ISBN: 978-1-57432-491-4 • 8½ x 11 • 224 Pgs. • HB • $24.95

FLORENCES' GLASS
KITCHEN SHAKERS, 1930 – 1950S
Item #6462 • ISBN: 978-1-57432-389-4 • 8½ x 11 • 160 Pgs • PB • $19.95

UPDATED PRICES

FLORENCES' BIG BOOK OF
SALT & PEPPER SHAKERS
Item #5918 • ISBN: 978-1-57432-257-6 • 8½ x 11 • 272 Pgs. • PB • $24.95

THE HAZEL-ATLAS GLASS
IDENTIFICATION AND VALUE GUIDE
Item #6562 • ISBN: 978-1-57432-420-4 • 8½ x 11 • 224 Pgs. • HB • $24.95

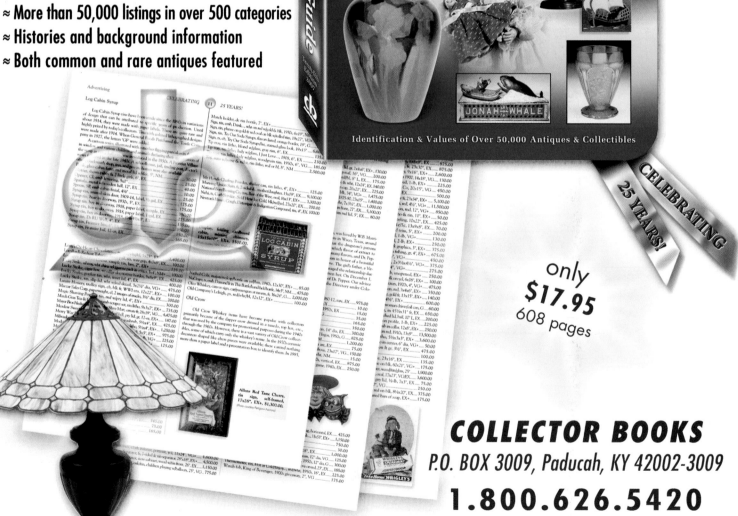